The JPS LIBRARY of
JEWISH CLASSICS

THE TREATISE TA'ANIT

THE TREATISE

TA'ANIT

OF THE

BABYLONIAN TALMUD

CRITICALLY EDITED AND PROVIDED WITH
A TRANSLATION, INTRODUCTION, AND NOTES

BY

HENRY MALTER

PHILADELPHIA
THE JEWISH PUBLICATION SOCIETY OF AMERICA

מסכת

תענית

מן

תלמוד בבלי

הוגהה על פי כתבי יד שונים והוצאות עתיקות ונעתקה
לשפת אנגלית

על ידי

צבי מלטער

פילאדלפיא
החברה היהודית להוצאת ספרים אשר באמריקא

LIBRARY OF CONGRESS CATALOG CARD NO. 67–19134
ISBN 0–8276–0108–5
PRINTED IN THE UNITED STATES OF AMERICA

THE TREATISE TA'ANIT

CONTENTS

ix

INTRODUCTION

An INTRODUCTION to a single tractate of the Talmud should properly be preceded by a characterization of the Talmud as a whole. For from whatever point of view one wishes to approach his particular subject, he finds it inextricably tangled up with a number of larger problems which deal with the entire talmudic literature. And yet I must beg to be absolved from such a task. I am quite sure that a renewed effort in this direction would bring no new results, while, on the other hand, it would encumber the special task of the editor. The introductions to the Talmud already in existence and the numerous general essays on the Talmud and the various characterizations thereof in Hebrew and in modern languages cover the field as well as the nature of the subject makes it possible.* What is needed today is a critical edition

* Introductions: Herman L. Strack, *Einleitung in Talmud und Midraš*, 5th ed., Munich, 1921; M. Mielziner, *Introduction to the Talmud*, 2nd ed., New York, 1908. Essays: Emanuel Deutsch, *The Talmud*, special series Jewish Publ. Soc. of America, No. 3, Philadelphia, 1893; Arsène Darmesteter, *The Talmud*, translated from the French by Henrietta Szold, Philadelphia, 1897; S. Schechter, in Hastings' Dict. Bible, extra volume, 1912, pp. 57–66;

of the talmudic text based on a minute collation
of all the existing manuscripts and early editions
of the Talmud itself, as well as of the Mishnah,
Tosefta, the numerous halakic and haggadic
Midrashim, the Yerushalmi, and the so-called
Minor Tractates; and, what is of equal importance, on a careful examination of the extracts,
quotations, and critical data accumulated in the
vast post-talmudic rabbinical literature from
the time of the Geonim onward, for which, too,
manuscripts should, as far as possible, be compared. The text so prepared should be adequate-
ly translated and elucidated for the benefit of
a wider circle of readers, who are not in a
position to study the original.

Strange as it may seem to the uninitiated
reader, despite the unequalled career of the
Talmud through many climes and ages, no
attempt has ever been made to publish even one
single page of it according to the method here
described. Prior to the discovery of printing,
talmudists of various periods often suggested, or
actually made, changes on the margin or in the
text of their copies, either on the basis of internal
evidence or of a comparison with some other

idem., *Studies in Judaism*, 3rd Series, Philadelphia, 1924,
pp. 143–237 (see ibidem p. 291); W. Bacher, J. E. XII,
pp. 1–27, where a more detailed Bibliography is given.

manuscript copy, the readings of which seemed preferable. Instances of this kind are well known to every student of the Talmud from the commentary of Rashi and many other works, and need not be further discussed. Often enough such suggestions and even explanatory glosses were subsequently embodied in the text, of which they now form a constituent part, and are no longer recognizable as changes or additions. In later periods men of great talmudic learning and critical acumen, like Solomon Luria (1510-73), Samuel Edels (1555-1631), and others incorporated in their larger works on the Talmud thousands of textual corrections, which, especially those of Luria, were subsequently embodied by unscrupulous printers in the text of the Talmud. Other talmudists of fame, like Joel Saerkes (1561–1640), Isaiah (Pick) Berlin (1719–99), Elijah Gaon of Wilna (1720–97), to mention only those best known, wrote special works under the title הגהות, i. e., critical notes and corrections to the Talmud. These and similar "Annotations" of still later authors (e. g., Z. H. Ch., S. Straschun) are printed in various editions of the Talmud either on the margin or at the end of the tractates and, so far as I know, have not influenced the text proper. Some of the authors, like Saerkes and the Gaon of Wilna, drew upon manuscripts that are no longer in existence, and the enormous material accumulated in their notes must be carefully sifted and examined in preparing a critical apparatus for the talmudic text. It goes without saying that the writings of modern authors dealing with textual criticism of the Talmud, many of which are scattered in Hebrew and German periodicals, are likewise to be utilized for the purpose.

Of the greatest importance, and in a way epoch-making in the field of textual criticism, is the voluminous work דקדוקי סופרים (*Variae lectiones*, Munich-Przemysl, 1867–1897), in sixteen volumes, by Raphael Nathan Rabbinovicz. Here for the first time in the history of the Talmud the received text was minutely compared, first with the famous Munich manuscript, and then with other available manuscripts and rare editions of Mishnah and Talmud, all the variants being systematically recorded. In the extensive notes on the manuscript material, showing the author's amazing familiarity with the entire range of the traditional literature, he endeavors in each case to indicate the significance and acceptability of the given variants as against the less warranted ones, thus laying the ground for a scientific critical edition of the Talmud. Unfortunately, only about two-thirds of the

Talmud were thus covered, the author's learned career having been prematurely closed by death (in 1888) at the age of 43 years.

The foregoing is a brief survey of the material to be used for a critical edition of the Talmud. An edition of the entire Talmud that would take into account this enormous material, scattered as it is in hundreds of manuscripts and printed volumes, could only be undertaken by an organized body of experienced scholars, who would have to be equipped not only with the necessary talmudic learning but also with a thorough knowledge of Hebrew and Aramaic grammar and a keen linguistic sense, which in the last instance is the safest guide through the labyrinths of conflicting and confusing readings. The prospects for such an organization are not bright at present, but this fact should not deter one from making a beginning in that direction. Others may then follow on the same line. So far, nearly all the work in the field of Jewish literature has been undertaken and carried out by individuals, and often it has been work of surprising dimensions.

The present edition and translation of a talmudic tractate is the first attempt on the lines above described. The selection of the tractate Ta'anit for this purpose was made by the late Professor Schechter, obviously because of its great value as a source for Jewish history, liturgy, folklore, and other matters of interest. I mention only the minute descriptions of the institution of public fasts on occasions of national calamities, and of the congregational services connected therewith (pp. 20 ff.); the discussion of Nicanor Day and Trajan Day with reference to the Scroll of Fasts (pp. 260 f.); the detailed information given about the origin of the so-called *Mishmarot* and *Ma' amadot*, *i. e.*, the divisions of Priests, Levites and lay Israelites (see notes 224–230), whose services at the Temple in Jerusalem and in the Palestinian country-towns were the foundation for the development of the synagogue and the synagogal services of today; the interesting account of the origin of the wood-offerings (pp. 401, 430 ff.), which, to my knowledge, occurs nowhere else in talmudic literature; the historical and legendary data relating to the destruction of the first and second Temples (pp. 402, 432, 440, 442) and to the customs and manners of wooing and betrothals in ancient Israel (pp. 404, 474 f.). There is, furthermore, no other treatise in the Talmud that contains such a collection of beautiful legends about the lives and doings of pious Israelites of the past, as we find in this treatise (pp. 272–320,

334–382). Despite the peculiar Oriental form of these legends—they remind one of the Arabian Nights—no one can fail to recognize the moral lessons they intend to convey, and to admire the goodness and genuineness, the simplicity and nobility of the characters they portray. Medieval authors have properly named this section of the treatise the "Chapter of the Pious" (פרקא דחסידי). Even the few halakic portions of this treatise happen to be mostly free from that subtle and perplexing reasoning which is characteristic of the Halakah. It thus seems that the choice of this tractate for publication in the Series of Jewish Classics was well made and requires no further justification.

It now remains to give some account of the manuscripts used, and the method employed in the preparation of the text. As all the details and technicalities are treated in the Hebrew introduction to the *editio maior* (referred to hereafter as *E. M.*), containing text and critical apparatus, I can limit myself here to a few general statements:

I have used *all* the manuscripts of Ta'anit, complete and fragmentary, the existence of which, in European and American libraries or private collections, has so far become known. The following is a descriptive list of the total of twenty-one manuscripts, arranged in the alphabetical order of the Hebrew *sigla* used to designate them in the critical apparatus:

A. *Complete Manuscripts*

‫א‬ (=‫אוכספורד‬). Codex Oxford, No. 366 (Neubauer, *Catalogue of Hebrew Manuscripts in the Bodleian Library*), small square Oriental characters in a very beautiful hand and presenting a most correct text, though not altogether free from insertions and omissions: folio, two columns to each. A full description of the manuscript is given by Rabbinovicz, *op. cit.*, Introduction to vol. IV, p. 6; according to him it dates from the eleventh or twelfth century; comp. *ibidem*, I, 78f.

‫ב‬ Codex Munich, No. 140, 141 (Steinschneider, *Die hebraeischen Handschriften der k. Hof-und Staatsbibliothek in München*), which I had photographed while in Munich in the summer of 1921; parchment; folio; large square beautiful characters; of French or German origin, and dating, according to Rabbinovicz, I, 37, from the twelfth century. Steinschneider, however, puts it down (with a query) to the beginning of the fifteenth century. It is relatively the most correct manuscript of our treatise. The margins show glosses and corrections from a later hand. Through

Rabbinovicz this manuscript has become known
as כ״י ב (*i. e.*, the *second* Ms., as distinguished
from the other Munich manuscript, listed below
under מ, which was the basis of his work).
To avoid confusion I have retained the same
designation.

ל (=לונדון). Codex British Museum, London (G. Margoliouth, *Catalogue of the Hebrew
and Samaritan Manuscripts in the British Museum*,
II, London, 1905, p. 53, No. 400, 8), measuring
about 11×9 inches, 35–37 lines to the page;
Spanish square characters, poor hand, often
blurred and hard to read; twelfth or thirteenth
century (so Margoliouth, *op. cit.*; Rabbinovicz,
IV, 7, puts it about ק״נ—1390); defective at
the end, the last words being אפילו משש שעות
ולמטה (fol. 30a, line 15, of the editions, not 29b,
as Rabbinovicz, *l. c.*, has it; fol. 29b of my photograph is so blurred, however, that only a few
words here and there are legible). On the whole
it is the least correct of the complete manuscripts,
though occasionally offering preferable variants.

מ (=מינכן). Codex Munich, No. 95, the
famous manuscript and the only one that contains the entire Babylonian Talmud, barring a
few pages in tractate Pesaḥim. It was published
in enlarged facsimile by the late Professor
Strack, Leiden, 1912; see the detailed description

by Rabbinovicz, I, 27–35; Steinschneider, *l. c.*,
No. 95. The manuscript is dated 1343 and
was written in Germany. As regards correctness it is by far inferior to either א or ב, but superior to ל.

ג (= נוירק). A manuscript from the collection of Elkan N. Adler of London, recently
acquired by the Jewish Theological Seminary
of America in New York (*No. 84*). The volume,
bound, counts 142 leaves, containing, in the
manner of the well-known haggadic collections
הגדות התלמוד (13th or 14th century; anonymous)
and עין יעקב, all the Haggadah of the tractates
Ta'anit (fol. 1–47a), Megillah (47a–82a), and
Ḥagigah (82b–95b, 97a–98b), and a mixture of
extracts from various other tractates (fol.
96, 99a–124, 134–142) and from Geonic Responsa
(124b–134a). The text, measuring 5×3½ inches
and counting 19 lines to the page, is written in a
clear oriental hand, square characters with a
slight turn to cursive. At the beginning of
Ḥagigah (fol. 82) and more explicitly on fol.
124a the scribe, evidently a Persian Jew and,
judging from his Hebrew style and occasional
vocalization, a man of deficient knowledge,
gives his name as "Elijah b. Obadiah b. Elijah
b. Obadiah b. Abraham b. Judah b. Menasseh,"
and the date of the 25th of Iyyar of the year

1796, *era Contractuum*, that is, 1485 of the common era. He adds that the number of the
tractates (המסכתות שבזה הנוסחה) is six, namely,
כפורים, יום טוב, סוכה (commonly known as *Yoma*),
and the three mentioned above. Our manuscript thus represents the second half of the
original volume. Between fols. 1 and 2 a leaf
(perhaps two leaves) is missing (the haggadic
portions of fol. 3a–4b of the editions); likewise
one leaf after fol. 2 and one after fol. 3 (ed. fols.
5b and 7a, respectively). Some leaves are also
missing in the tractates Megillah and Ḥagigah.

Among the extracts referred to above there
are again several from Ta'anit, altogether 16
pages, belonging to various parts of the tractate:
Fol. 96b = editions fol. 21a (part of the story
of Nahum with the heading מעשה); 100a–101a =
edd. 19b–20a (the story of Naḳdimon); 113b =
edd. 10a (יובשני to ת"ר ארץ מצרים); 113b–116b = edd.
10b (למפוחא דמלי זיקא to 12a (ת"ר הרי שהיה מתענה);
116b = edd. 14b (אר"א אין אדם חשוב רשאי to the
end of the chapter); 116b–117a = edd. 16a
(ת"ר (אל בשמים to אחינו לא שק); 117a = edd. 17a
(תלתין הוי to מלך); 117a (last line); 117b = edd.
17b (וד"ס צריכין חזוק to תניא ימים הללו); 117b = edd.
18b (דיופלי מרומי to תניא ניקנור); 140a = edd. 27b
(וי אבדה נפש to במה אדע כי אירשנה); 140b = edd. 30a–
30b (שאינו מתאבל אינו רואה בשמחתה to ת"ר כל מצות);

xxi

141a–141b = edd. 23b–24a (אינקיטו כרעי דסוסיהו to
(גבאי צדקה טשו).

The text of these extracts is an exact copy
of the corresponding passages found in the complete collection spoken of before, without any
addition whatever, and although the script
looks somewhat different and less regular than
that of the three tractates (and the number of
lines to the page is 22 and 23 instead of 19),
the whole seems to have been written by the
same scribe, who was professionally preparing
copies of the same books at different times, which
explains the seeming difference in writing.
I have therefore refrained from recording in
the apparatus the readings of the extracts,
except in a few instances, where the two texts,
owing to a scribal error, do not tally, or where the
corroboration of a reading by the extracts seemed
significant.   The text of the extracts is designated by נא.

פ (= פנצי).   A Mishnah codex of the Jewish
Theological Seminary, New York, containing
the entire order Mo‘ed written by "Benjamin
b. Isaac b. Benjamin b. Solomon b. Judah b.
Benjamin Finci b. Menahem b. Judah b. Menahem ממשפחת ר"ם"; vellum, Italian square characters, finished Friday, the second of Iyyar, 1361.

B. *Fragments* (mostly from the Genizah)

1. Genizah fragment, two leaves (four pages), 17–18 lines to the page, old Oriental script verging toward cursive. Leaf a=editions fol. 4b, line 21 (א״ל ר״ז לר׳ אסי) to 5a, line 5 (יום הכפורים); leaf b=edd. fol. 6a, line 9 (בשבעה עשר בעשרים) to 6b, line 2 (משתרד*).

2. Genizah fragment, two leaves (four pages), 10–12 lines to the page, Oriental rabbinical script. Leaf a=edd. fol. 7b, line 17 from below (אל תיקרי ישונה) to *ibidem*, bottom (אם ראית תלמיד); leaf b=edd. fol. 9b, line 19 (ומאי פורחות; the preceding אר״י סימן למטר פורחות is placed there after the sentence of R. Papa; see *E. M.*, notes *ad locum*) to *ibidem*, line 31 (למטר שמים).

3. Genizah fragment, six pages, 15 lines to the page, square Oriental script (bound in a separate fascicle with leaves from tractate Ketubōt; the leaves from Taʿanit are misplaced, last leaf belonging to the beginning of the fragment). The text corresponds to edd. fol. 27b, line 17 (ואיל משולש ותור וגוזל] אמר לפניו) to fol. 28a, line 1 (רווחא), followed by the Mishnah, fol. 26a (פרשה גדולה to כבוד השבת), and Gemara, fol. 28a, lines 3–13 (כקורין את שמע to גמ׳ איבעיא להו), then the same Mishnah, continued (כל יום to

* The words here and in what follows are given as they are in the respective manuscripts.

כבן עזאי; much mutilated) and followed by Gemara, fol. 28a, lines 14–15 (גמ' מה הפרש), and again
the Mishnah (from ולוים וכל מי to זמן עצי כהנים,
but mostly torn off).

4. Genizah fragment, two leaves (four pages),
16–17 lines to the page, script very much like
that of No. 2, perhaps the same hand. Leaf
a = edd. fol. 30a, line 5 from below (של בית רבן
בטלין) to 30b, line 21 (ר' יהודה מחייב); leaf *b* = edd.
fol. 31a, line 14 (ובת כהן גדול) to the end of the
tractate.

All these fragments came from Mr. Elkan
N. Adler, who was kind enough to lend them
to the Dropsie College for my use, and are now
in the Jewish Theological Seminary in New York.
They are designated by the letter ה (letters ג and
ד having been used for other designations).

5. Mishnah, fragmentary manuscript, of the
Jewish Theological Seminary of New York, originally in the collection of the late Mayer Sulz-
berger (found by E. Deinard in Ḡubbar, near
Damascus), mostly vocalized, vellum, eleventh
century; contains, among other tractates, the
first chapter of the Mishnah of Ta'anit (badly
damaged on the lower outer margin) and the
greater part of the second, breaking off with the
words אצל חכמים אמרו = edd. fol. 15b, line 9. It is
designated by ז (= זולצברגר).

6. Göttingen, Universitäts-Bibliothek, *codex
hebr*. 13: thirteen pages in small folio-size, very
large beautiful square characters; beginning of
the 13th century (discovered by Theodor
Nöldeke; comp. Lagarde, *Semitica*, I, 69f.,
Göttingen, 1878). It extends from fol. 25a,
line 13 of the editions (דנישקליה מינך) to 30a,
line 13 (מותר ותרויהו לקולא), where one folio
is misssing, and from 31a, line 4 (שלא הסריחו) to
the end of the tractate. I obtained a photograph of this valuable fragment through the
kind efforts of Professor I. Elbogen of Berlin and
especially of Dr. Behrend, Rabbi of Göttingen,
to both of whom I wish to record my gratitude.
This manuscript is designated by ט.

7. Munich, codex hebr. 119 (XIII—. Four
folio-pages, in two columns each, 39 lines to
the column; parchment, square characters similar to those shown in Neubauer's Facsimiles
of Hebrew Manuscripts, table XXII, hence
probably written in Greece towards the end of
the thirteenth century (discovered by Prof.
I. I. Kahan). It is interesting to note that in this
manuscript, as in the one listed below, No. 13,
the order of chapters 2 and 3 of the editions is
reversed. Pages 1–2=edd. fol. 19a, line 13
from below (יולדתך היו מתענין) to fol. 20b,
line 15 (בפני מי שגדול). Of the second and third

columns (*i. e.*, *recto* and *verso*) the margin was cut off lengthwise, taking away about a third of the text. Pages 3–4=edd. fol. 18a, line 10 (יהודה בן שמוע) to the end of the second chapter (fol. 18b), followed, in accordance with the reversed order, by the Mishnah, fol. 26a, line 7 (בשלשה פרקים) to fol. 27a, line 6 (תיקנו מעמדות). Both portions of the fragment are designated by ם (=מינכן).

8. Oxford Genizah fragment, four pages, 12mo, paper; Yemen, square characters (Neubauer II, No. 2861, 34); pp. 1–2=edd. fol. 22b, lines 34–40 (לסנף—כל עיקר), followed by the Mishnah, fol. 19a, lines 22–36 (מתני׳ ועל כל צרה-ישמח); pp. 3–4=edd. fol. 23a, lines 30–43 (=שלעולם עמך ישראל-בשוב י״י את). Designated by ס.

9. Oxford Genizah fragments, six pages, Spanish rabbinical characters; pp. 1–2 (Neubauer, II, No. 2691, 3)=edd. fol. 23a, lines 32–50 (שיהא ריוח בעולם — שמעתתא). I wish to thank Mr. Herbert Loewe of Oxford, who has carefully copied this fragment for me. Pages 3–4 (Neubauer, II, No. 2828, 22; by oversight page 3 has not been listed there)=edd. fol. 26a, Mishnah, lines 3 and 2 from below (באחד בטבת שבו—קרבן עצים), followed by Gemara, fol. 28a, line 25 (גמ׳ תנו רבנן) to 28b, line 4 (לך לא); pages 5–7 (Neubauer, II, No. 2828, 22)=edd. fol.

30b, line 14 from below (יום מחילה וסליחה)
to fol. 31a, line 3 from below (ר' אלעזר). The
six pages should have been listed by Neubauer
under the same number, as, in my opinion, they
are parts of one and the same manuscript. It
is designated by ע.

10. Cambridge University Library, Add. 1009,
four pages in small folio size, measuring 10×6
inches, 28 lines to the page; Spanish rabbinical
characters; pp. 1–2=edd. fol. 24b, line 13 from
below (ליה בחלמא) to fol. 25b, line 5 (ונאמר ארז);
pp. 3–4=edd. fol. 30b, line 4 (אין עושין) to
the end of the tractate. Designated by פ (not
to be confused with פ, which is employed in
the *Notes* to the Mishnah only as the initial
of פנצי; see above under A. Complete Manuscripts).

11. Oxford Genizah fragment (Neubauer, II,
No. 2862, 39), two pages, 28 and 27 lines; cursive
=edd. fol. 29b, last line (חנה חדשה ושבתה) to fol.
30b, line 6 (תניא); designated by צ.

12. Oxford Genizah fragment (Neubauer, II,
No. 2673, 2–3), four pages, folio 10×8 inches,
36 lines to the page; small square characters
with a tendency toward cursive; poor hand and
badly preserved, with numerous corrections
and notes between the lines from a later hand,
equally poor. Pages 1–2=edd. fol. 17a, line

3 from below (יין בזמן ביאה) to fol 19a, line
15 from below (מה אעשה שאתה); pages 3–4
(partly blurred and readings uncertain) = edd.
fol. 22a, line 14 (לגביה אזל בתריה) to 23a, line 12
from below (עד כמה); designated by ק. I am
indebted to Mr. Herbert Loewe, who has taken
great pains in copying and practically editing
fols. 1–2 of this fragment, as the photograph at
my disposal was illegible.

13. Cod. Vatic., No. 487 (see the description
by Rabbinovicz, XI, 20) from a photograph in
the library of the University of Illinois, No. 892,
4, V45, where the number of the codex is mis-
takenly given as 467. In this very old fragment
of twelve pages, which forms part of a thick volume in folio, containing talmudic treatises and
collections from various liturgical works, the
order of chapters 2 and 3 of our treatise is
reversed (see above, No. 7), beginning fol.
24b, line 12 from below, of the editions
(למחר אשכחיה לפוריה), and continuing to the
end of the third chapter (fol. 28a), which is
followed by the entire second chapter (fols.
15a–18b), then by chapter 4 (fol. 26a–26b,
line 8, last words: ובחמישי מותרין מפני). The
fragment is designated by ר (=רומא, Rome).
I wish here to express my thanks to the authorities
of the Library of the University of Illinois,

who lent the volume to the Dropsie College for my use.

14. An exceedingly valuable manuscript from the collection of Mr. Elkan N. Adler of London (No. 1799), now in the Jewish Theological Seminary, New York, parchment, folio, text 7½×5 inches, large, beautiful Spanish characters; dated Rome, Thursday, the 21st of Siwan, 1328 (the date is on fol. 77a and reads: זה סדר תפילת תענית ציבור נעשה ברומא ביום ה' כ"א בסיון שנת פ"ח (כשנסעו שלוחי הקהל ללכת בחצר. The manuscript contains:

A. An anonymous commentary on Ta'anit which is identical with the one wrongly printed in the editions under the name of Rashi (see *E. M.*, Notes). It offers numerous variants to the printed pseudo-Rashi, many of which, though not all, I have recorded under the abbreviation (כתב יד נויורק) = כי"נ. There are also, especially on the first 5 or 6 pages, numerous passages which do not occur in the printed commentary. The copyist, who appears to have been a learned man, interpolated also passages from Tosafot and other sources. I did not investigate the matter in detail, as it did not strictly belong to the present work. The commentary ends on fol. 31b.

B. An anonymous commentary (fols. 32a-

72b) on Taʿanit compiled from the commentaries of R. Hananel, R. Gershom, and ר"א, whom
I have thus far been unable to identify with
certainty (perhaps R. Eljakim, one of the teachers
of Rashi), and from various Geonic sources.
Once (fol. 47a) רבי' יצחק is quoted, no doubt
referring to R. Isaac Alfâsi. On nine occasions
the author inserts comments of his own in the
Arabic language. Very frequently he expresses
his opinion for or against his authorities. At the
time of this writing the commentary is being
published by Dr. B. M. Lewin of Haifa, Palestine, who has recently copied it for this purpose
in the Library of the Jewish Theological Seminary. In *E. M.* Notes this commentary is
quoted as פרוש כתב יד = פכ"י.

As the commentaries of Hananel, Gershom,
and Rashi are among the oldest and most important sources for the establishing of a reliable
text of the Talmud, this manuscript volume
proved of great value for our textual criticism,
all the more so since the texts of these commentaries, as printed in the Wilna editions of the
Talmud, cannot be relied upon, the editors having often changed the readings of the commentaries to tally with those in the received text
of the Talmud.

For the sake of completeness it should be

added that folios 73b–79a of the manuscript contain Geonic Responsa relating, likewise, to Ta'anit (fol. 15a–16b) and two Rituals for the communal services on public fast days. This part, however, did not offer much for our purpose.

15. Oxford, fragments, from the Order of R. Amram Gaon, containing excerpts from Ta'anit (Neubauer, II, 2826, 21); see *E. M.*, Notes to fol. 11b.

16. Fragments of the code of Isaac Alfâsi from the collection of Elkan N. Adler in the Jewish Theological Seminary; see *E. M.*, Notes to the Mishnah, fol. 26a–b.

As manuscript material must further be considered all texts of first editions of Mishnah and Talmud, or of later works containing large portions thereof (such as commentaries, compendia, codes, Haggadah collections, etc.). Of the former I had at my disposal the *editio princeps* of the Mishnah, Naples 1492; the Mishnah of the Jerusalem Talmud edited from a unique manuscript by W. H. Lowe, Cambridge 1883; the Bomberg edition of the Talmud (Venice 1520-23), which, though based on the preceding Soncino edition, has used manuscripts also (Rabbinovicz, מאמר על הדפסת התלמוד, Munich, 1877, appended also to volume VIII of his *Variae lectiones*), and several of the later editions (Constantinople, Basle, Amsterdam, etc.). Parallel passages in the Munich manuscript of other talmudic tractates or in other manuscripts of such tractates, as recorded in the various volumes of Rabbinovicz's work, as also the parallels in L. Goldschmidt's facsimile edition of three tractates of the Order Nezikin (especially in the tractate Baba Batra; see *E. M.*, Notes to fols. 30b, 31a), have likewise been carefully compared.

Of the numerous works of medieval authors, the first editions of which I have compared throughout, I mention here only the הלכות גדולות of Jehudai Gaon (8th century), שאילתות of R. Aḥa of Shabbeḥa (8th century), סדר רב עמרם (Ritual Order of R. Amram Gaon; 9th century), רי"ף, ערוך, ראב"ן, רוקח, כלבו, אור זרוע, תורת האדם, רא"ה, רא"ש, אגדה, ילקוט שמעוני, מנורת המאור, הגדות התלמוד, and עין יעקב (the last four from the Library of the Jewish Theological Seminary; the הגדות התלמוד, a very rare work, has been lent to me through the Dropsie College for a very considerable time by the Library of Congress in Washington, to which thanks are here expressed). A more detailed list of these and many other works of this class, as also a list of the numerous abbreviations used in the critical apparatus, will be given in *E. M.* Here I should only add that when the readings of the commentaries are recorded alongside of those of the various manuscripts, they are also, like the latter, indicated by single letters, ג thus designating the commentary of Gershom, ח that of Hananel, ש that of (pseudo-) Rashi (=שלמה), ת = Tosafot; otherwise they are mostly quoted by the abbreviations commonly in use, namely, ר״ג, ר״ח, רש״י, and תוס׳. The same applies to י for the Jerusalem Mishnah (ed. Cambridge) and to ד (=דפוסים) for the editions of the Talmud.

After most careful sifting and scrutiny of the conflicting data I have been unable to discover any relation between the different manuscripts, and no grouping can, therefore, be attempted. All that can be said in a general way is that of the complete manuscripts those designated by א, ב, and ג are the most correct ones, and their readings are most frequently supported by other sources. The text established in this edition is thus entirely eclectic, the decision having in each case been based on internal and external evidences of various descriptions, as shown in the Hebrew Notes in *E. M.*

A task of special importance was the collection of all the parallel passages to our tractate, scattered in the vast tannaitic, midrashic, and talmudic literature. In the Talmud editions there are marginal references to such parallels, called מסרת התלמוד (compiled by Joshua Boaz of the Family Baruk and printed first in the third Venice edition, 1546–51). This "Masorah," however, gives only the parallels in the Babylonian Talmud. In later editions reference is occasionally made to the Tosefta or some other tannaitic work. But in a critical edition of the Talmud a systematic comparison by the student of the given text with all the parallels, verbal or otherwise, in the entire kindred and contemporaneous literature appears to be indispensable. Under the heading מסרת הש"ס והמדרשים, printed on each page below the text, I tried to supply this want by giving, so far as I know, all references to the early traditional literature, that is, Mishnah, Tosefta, Mekilta of R. Ishmael and of R. Simon b. Yoḥai, Sifra, Sifrē, and Sifre Zuṭa, Midrash Tannaim, the Babylonian and Palestinian Talmuds, Pesiḳta of R. Kahana, Pesiḳta Rabbeti, Abōt of R. Nathan, the Minor Tractates (Soferim, Kallah, Semaḥōt, and Dérek Érez); Midrash Rabbōt, the two Tanḥumas, the Midrashim to the books of Samuel, Psalms, Proverbs, and Esther (Buber), occasionally Pirkē R. Eliezer, Tanna debe Eliyahu Rabba and Zuṭa and the Targumim;

to the exclusion, however, of various collections
of later Midrashim (as Midrash Aggadah, ed.
Buber, Midrash ha-Gadōl, ed. Schechter, etc.),
the parallels of which are discussed in the Hebrew Notes (*E. M.*) together with those found in
other mediaeval works (as Yalḳuṭ, etc.).

The references to the Bible are given on
the lower margin under the traditional heading
תורה אור, but while the editions give only the
chapters of the respective books of the Canon,
I have also added the numbers of the verses in
order to facilitate reference. In the talmudic
text the quotations from the Bible, frequently
faulty, have been corrected in accordance with
the Masoretic text. Thus all the *matres lectionis* common in unvocalized texts have been
eliminated. With the exception of the generally
accepted 'וכו, 'וגו (or כו'), and 'ה (for the tetragram-
maton), all abbreviated phrases current in the
editions (as תנ"ה, ש"מ, קמ"ל, מנה"מ, הקב"ה, ה"ק, א"ר, א"ל,
ת"ש, ת"ר, etc.) have been written out in full. Abbreviations of that kind have often been the
cause of curious mistakes. Here only one instance: P. 93, l. 3: editions and some MSS. have
לכל דבריהן for לכ"ד, which is the abbreviation of
לעשרים וארבע; see *E. M.*, Notes *ad locum*. Otherwise no changes have been made in the appearance of the talmudic text and no punctuation

(except that already in use, like colon and parentheses) has been introduced.

As the pages of this edition do not agree with those of the common editions, the beginning of the pages in the latter are indicated in our text by a vertical line |, and on the margin opposite by the respective number.

A very embarrassing situation presented itself in trying to adopt some uniform system of spelling for the talmudic text, especially in the Aramaic portions, which constitute the bulk of the tractate. In the critical apparatus, which is devoted to the elucidation of general textual questions, matters of orthography could be touched upon only incidentally. To note minutely all the plene and defective writings, as they occur in the numerous manuscripts and early editions, would have been an endless task, and the value of such a Masorah to the one particular tractate seemed, besides, rather problematical. But in giving to the body of the text itself its final form the editor is repeatedly compelled to decide for himself whether, in view of the absence of all vocalization, he should retain the usual vowel letters (א, ו, י) or risk their elimination, a question which, as every grammarian knows, is not always easy to decide. The difficulty is enhanced by the fact that the manuscripts not only disagree among themselves, some, like א, ל, and more so מ, using these letters extravagantly, while others, like ב and partly also ג, employ them only sparingly, but are quite inconsistent within their own limits, so that defective writings are sporadically found also in מ, even in the same words, and, conversely, plene writing often occurs in ב. In matters of geography, as in other matters, no one manuscript could therefore be followed exclusively. Moreover, מ is the only manuscript that covers the entire Talmud; all others, and some of them much more correct, contain only single tractates or fractions, and assuming that the whole Talmud is to be critically edited, as it should be, the editors, in order to produce an orthographically uniform text, would all have to follow that one manuscript, a procedure which for various reasons does not recommend itself. The *matres lectionis*, used so freely by מ, may be a valuable help to the philologian in tracing and fixing the grammatical forms, but, in my opinion, they are even in this respect of subordinate importance. In such matters the philologian derives his main support from Syriac, Mandaic, the Targumim (especially those with superlinear vocalization), and the cognate Aramaic dialects. To further complete his knowledge

he cannot rely on the data of one given manuscript, but must examine all. For the general
student, again, who approaches the Talmud
with a different object in view, and, usually,
without philological training, the vowel letters,
as means of vocalization, are not only entirely
inadequate, but in most cases positively confusing and misleading. There is not a talmudist
in existence who, with the help of these "mothers"
alone, could correctly vocalize one page in the
entire Talmud.

I would, therefore, if I were to follow my in-
clination, have preferred to have all vowel letters
eliminated, except those that represent a radical
element (e. g., מסאני, v. סאן, נורא, רישא, and
similarly in verbal forms) or serve to produce
the lengthening of a syllable, where this is
required as a characteristic of nominal or verbal
forms (גבורתא, מדינתה, יקטלון, קטלין, and the
like). In fact, the chief cause of confusion is
the use of these letters also to indicate the quality
of the short vowels ŭ, ĭ, (ĕ), as in בישרא, חומרא,
איתעבד, the י especially before gemination:
מינך, עיא, איתמר, and the א, in oriental manuscripts, often for ă in the middle of words:
קארו, זעירן, בָּאבִי, as also the almost general
use of ו and י in certain accentuated syllables:

נְוֹב, בְּרִיה (imperative), עָבִיד, נֶעֱבַּיד, מַוַּבִּין and the like. The doubling in most manuscripts of the consonantal ו and י, as in צִיְּדָי, שָׁוֵי, נִפְּוְתָא, זְוֹדִין, תְּרֵנוַיְיהוּ, הֲוֵנְיָן, חֲזְיָיה, בְּעֵינְיְיהוּ, etc., likewise contributes to the general confusion. However, the uncertainties in this field are so many, the vocalization so fluctuating and the orthography accordingly so ambiguous that one does not feel competent enough to risk any radical method of procedure. After long and tiresome comparing and sifting of the orthographic data in the diverse manuscript sources, I came to the realization that in all manuscripts, which in many regards must be considered as the most reliable, the tendency to use defective writing is, despite sporadic inconsistencies, decidedly predominant. With a cautious consideration of the incidental grammatical rules as a controlling factor, I have followed that tendency throughout, leaving the plene writing in those cases only in which it is persistently adhered to in all manuscripts. This procedure, naturally, led to various inconsistencies, and, besides, is based only on observations limited to manuscripts of the present tractate, but it seemed the most conservative and the safest way out of the difficulties described above. At any rate, I do not think that an examination of the text as here fixed will reveal anything contrary to the established rules of talmudic-Aramaic grammar. For the benefit of the expert grammarian I have prepared a classified list of the characteristic plene and defective writings of the manuscripts, which will be appended to *E. M.*

As regards the purely Hebrew portions of the text the matter was much simpler. Here I followed the Masoretic vocalization of the Scriptures, eliminating the *matres lectionis* in all but a few instances. Thus שִׁבֹּלֶת, בְּצֹרֶת, קֹדֶשׁ, עֹמֶר, תכבסת appear for עוֹמֶר, etc.; כִּסּוּי, דִּבּוּר; קֻבָּה, כָּלֶם; קֶטַע נֶדֶם; (adjectives) תְּחִית, פָּפַּת, שְׁנִיָּה, תְּחִלָּה, חֲמִשָּׁה, עֲסָה, מְטָה; (Nif'al forms) נִתָּן, נִצַּל, נִטַּל; שַׁעַר, צַעַר, בְּטֵל, (Pi'el) חֲרֻבָּה, גְּזֵרָה, תְּבָה, שָׁנָה, לֵדָה, (מְטוּפָּל, but מְטֻפָּל); אֵלּוּ, אֵלּוּ; (שְׁאֵלַת שָׁלוֹם but חֲבֵרִים, בְּטֵלִים, so also in the dual forms קַבַּיִם, טְפָחַיִם, זְרָתַיִם, and in the suffixes יָדִי, בָּנִי, etc., for בְּנַיי (a spelling current in rabbinical sources). For the sake of clearness I made an exception in words like יוֹקֶר, רוֹב, חוֹל, זוֹל and also in the verbs קַיָּם, חַיָּב, בַּיָּשׁ, etc., and all their derivatives. Much arbitrariness prevails in the plural endings of masculine nouns and adjectives, as בטלין—בטלים; תלמידין—תלמידים, etc. I left them as they are mostly found in the manuscripts. For היתר, היסח, and the like the manuscripts often exhibit התר, הסח. Here, however, the predominantly plene writing seems to indicate a later phase in the pronunciation of such words, i. e., הֶתֵּר for הֶתֵּר, which is probably the reason also for the occasional spelling of היפקר, היפסד for הפקר, הפסד, etc.

Not much is to be said about the English translation. I have, of course, followed the text closely, as one should in a scientific translation of any ancient technical text. But as literal translation is at times impossible, I have, in order to avoid the writing of too many explanatory notes, in such cases, added a word or more in parentheses, so as to make the passage intelligible. For the biblical verses I used the translation issued by the Jewish Publication Society of America, Philadelphia, 1917. It is customary in Hebrew when quoting the Bible to quote merely the initial words of a verse, although the complete idea which the verse is supposed to convey can only be found in some of the last words. The Hebrew reader is expected, and usually is able, to supplement the rest of the verse from memory. In English this method did not recommend itself, and I have, therefore, sometimes added in [ ] the missing part of the verse or verses. There are two German translations of Ta'anit, based on the received text (D. Straschun, Halle, 1883, and L. Goldschmidt, Berlin, 1899) and an uncritical fragmentary English translation (L. Rodkinson), none of which was of any aid to me. There are also some English translations of the Mishnah* of Ta'anit, the latest by A. W. Greenup, London, 1921, with learned literary notes.

The transliteration of the proper names offered many difficulties, as the etymology and hence the pronunciation are very often doubtful (comp. Lidzbarsky, *Ephemeris*, II, 1–23). So far as possible I tried to ascertain the correct form, in other cases I followed the traditional pronunciation. For particulars see the Index at the end of this volume. For geographical names of places, rivers, etc., the sources are given in the English Notes.

In the Notes to the English translation I have, except on a few occasions, refrained from making references to modern works touching

---

* D. A. de Sola and M. J. Raphall, *Eighteen Treatises from the Mishna*, London, 1843; Joseph Barclay, *The Talmud. A Translation of Eighteen Treatises from the Mishna*, London, 1878.

on the various subjects under consideration, limiting myself throughout to the elucidation of the plain meaning of the text. Such elucidations were particularly necessary in the haggadic portions, where the biblical verses are always given a meaning which is in no way borne out by the standard translations of the Bible, which had to be followed in the English text, so that the application of the respective verses would, without an explanatory note, remain altogether unintelligible. The instances are numerous; see notes 64–67, 106–107, 110–125, 134, 145, 151, 165–6, 325. On this matter, as on some others relating to the haggadic exegesis, the remarks of Rev. A. Cohen, in his recent work, *The Babylonian Talmud: Tractate Berakot*, Cambridge, 1921, pp. XXXII ff., are pertinent.

THE TREATISE TA'ANIT

Mishnah: 1. When should one begin to mention "the Power of rain?"[1] R. Eliezer says, on the first day of the feast of Tabernacles; R. Joshua says, on the last[2] day of that festival. Said R. Joshua: Since rain during the festival is but a sign of divine displeasure,[3] why should one make mention of it (in his prayer)? "Indeed," replied R. Eliezer, "I did not say that one should *pray* for rain but that he should merely mention it with the words, "He causeth the wind to blow and the rain to fall in its season." "If so," said R. Joshua, "one ought to be mentioning it all the time."

2. One should not pray for rain until shortly before the season of rain.[4]

R. Judah says in the name of Ben Bathyra: Of

---

[1] The phrase "Power of rain" is commented upon in the Talmud below. The fact that the reference to rain is inserted in the second benediction, beginning with the words: "Thou art powerful," may account for this phraseology. The benediction is also generally designated as גבורות (power).

[2] Namely, Shemini-'azeret, the concluding festival of Sukkot.

[3] See Mishnah, *Sukkah*, II, 9.

[4] This clause is here in the wrong place, which has caused much confusion among the authorities of the Talmud (see below, fol. 4a) and more so among later commentators

פרק ראשון

מאימתי מזכירין גבורות גשמים רבי אליעזר
אומר מיום טוב הראשון של חג רבי יהושע אומר
מיום טוב האחרון של חג אמר רבי יהושע הואיל
ואין הגשמים אלא סימן קללה בחג למה הוא
5 מזכיר אמר לו רבי אליעזר אף אני לא אמרתי
לשאול אלא להזכיר משיב הרוח ומוריד הגשם
בעונתו אמר לו רבי יהושע אם כן לעולם יהא
מזכיר:

אין שואלין את הגשמים אלא סמוך לגשמים:

10 רבי יהודה אומר משום בן בתירה העובר

---

of the Mishnah. שואלין certainly does not mean mention,
but ask, pray for, and the Mishnah refers to the prayer
for dew and rain (ותן טל ומטר), which is inserted in the
ninth benediction. The sentence should therefore have
been placed *after* the clause beginning "R. Judah says,"
etc., immediately before עד מתי שואלין (until what time,
etc.). Such transposition would do away with all the
difficulties raised by the Talmud and later authors;
see for details the Hebrew notes here and below, fol. 4a;
comp. also below, note 48; Geiger, *Jüd. Zeitschr.*, VII, pp.
263f, 271f.

3

those who go before the ark as readers on the concluding day of the feast of Tabernacles, the last[5] one should make mention of the rain, but the first[6] one should not do so; conversely, on the opening day of Passover the first is to mention the rain, but not the last.

Until what time should the prayer for rain be continued? R. Judah says, until the end of Passover; R. Jose says, until the month of Nisan is passed, as it is said (Joel, 2.23): "And He causeth to come down for you the rain, the former rain and the latter rain, in the first month."[7]

3. On the third of Marḥeshwan one is to begin praying for rain; Rabban Gamaliel says, on the seventh of that month, fifteen days after the feast of Tabernacles, so that even the tardiest Israelite may reach the Euphrates.[8]

4. If the seventeenth of Marḥeshwan has come and there has been no rainfall, distinguished individuals begin to fast.[9] On the nights preceding

---

[5] That is, the one who reads the Musaf prayer, the last in the service.

[6] The one who reads the Shaḥarit or morning prayer.

[7] That is, Nisan. The verse is cited to prove that this whole month is part of the period of rain, and thus also part of the time during which one should pray for rain.

[8] On his way home from the pilgrimage to Jerusalem, which took place on each of the three festivals. Those who lived east of the Euphrates river were exempt from the duty of making the pilgrimage on account of the great distance from Jerusalem.

[9] The number of fasts was limited to three, and their order of succession was Monday, Thursday, and Monday

לפני התבה ביום טוב האחרון של חג האחרון
מזכיר והראשון אינו מזכיר ביום טוב הראשון של
פסח הראשון מזכיר והאחרון אינו מזכיר:

עד מתי שואלין את הגשמים רבי יהודה
5 אומר עד שיעבור הפסח רבי יוסי אומר עד שיצא
ניסן שנאמר ויורד לכם גשם מורה ומלקוש
בראשון:

בשלשה במרחשון שואלין את הגשמים רבן
גמליאל אומר בשבעה בו חמשה עשר יום אחר
10 החג כדי שיגיע האחרון שבישראל לנהר פרת:

הגיע שבעה עשר במרחשון ולא ירדו גשמים
התחילו היחידים מתענין אוכלין ושותין משחשיכה

תורה אור   מסרת הש״ס והמדרשים

6 יואל ב׳ כ״ג.   4 (עד מתי) תענית ד׳: ה׳. ירושלמי
נדרים ח׳ ז׳; תוספתא כאן ריש פ״א
(וע׳ ויק״ר ל״ה י״ב).   8 (בשלשה) תענית ד׳: ו׳ י׳. ב״מ כ״ח. ירוש׳ כאן
א׳ ב׳.   10 (פרת) ע׳ ירוש׳ שביעית י׳ ב׳: ר״ה ג׳ א׳; נדרים ו׳ י״נ (מ׳
א׳); סנה׳ א׳ ב׳ (י״ח ד׳).   11 (הגיע) תענית י׳.

(below, fol. 10a). More than two fasts a week was considered too hard a decree. The same order had to be
observed during all the fasts mentioned below.

the fasts they may eat and drink, and on the fast days proper they may engage in work, may bathe, anoint themselves, wear shoes, and cohabit with their wives.

5. If the first day of the month of Kislew has come and no rain has yet fallen, the court orders three fasts for the community. On the nights preceding the fasts the people may eat and drink, and on the fast days they may engage in work, bathe, anoint themselves, wear shoes, and cohabit with their wives.

6. If these fast days are over and the community's prayer has not been answered, the court orders three more fasts for the community. On the days preceding these fasts one may eat and drink until sunset only, and on the fast days proper, work, bathing, anointing oneself, wearing shoes, and cohabitation are forbidden. The bath-houses must be closed. If these fast days, too, are over and the community has not been answered, the court orders seven additional fasts for the community, making in all thirteen fasts. In what respect are these (seven) fasts more rigorous than the (three) immediately preceding ones? In that on these the alarm must be sounded and the shops must be closed. On the fasts falling on a Monday, the doors of the shops may be slightly opened toward nightfall, while on Thursdays they may be kept open all day for the sake of the approaching Sabbath.[10]

7. If all these fast days are passed and the community has not been answered, all business trans-

[10] That the people may buy their food supply for the Sabbath, Friday being considered too late for the purpose.

ומותרין במלאכה וברחיצה ובסיכה ובנעילת
הסנדל ובתשמיש המטה:

הגיע ראש חדש כסלו ולא ירדו גשמים בית
דין גוזרין שלש תעניות על הצבור אוכלין ושותין
משחשיכה ומותרין במלאכה וברחיצה ובסיכה
ובנעילת הסנדל ובתשמיש המטה:

עברו אלו ולא נענו בית דין גוזרין שלש תעניות
אחרות על הצבור אוכלין ושותין מבעוד יום
ואסורין במלאכה וברחיצה ובסיכה ובנעילת
הסנדל ובתשמיש המטה ונועלין את המרחצאות׃

עברו אלו ולא נענו בית דין גוזרין עוד שבע
שהן שלש עשרה תעניות על הצבור ומה אלו
יתרות על הראשונות שבאלו מתריעין ונועלין את
החנויות בשני מטין עם חשיכה ובחמשי מותרין כל
היום מפני כבוד השבת:

עברו אלו ולא נענו ממעטין במשא ובמתן

מסרת הש״ס והמדרשים

7 (עברו) תענית י״ב: 8 (מבעוד   כ״ט: ירושלמי כאן ב׳ י״ב וד׳ ט׳;
יום) פסחים נ״ד: 15 (כבוד השבת)   יבמות ספ״ו; מו״ק ג׳ א׳.   16 (עברו)
יבמות מ״ג. לקמן י״ב: ט״ו: כ״ו: תענית י״ב: מגלה ה׳:

actions, building, planting, betrothals, **marriages,** and greetings[11] should be limited, as behooves persons excommunicated in the sight of God. Distinguished individuals begin again to fast till the end of Nisan. If there is rainfall after the end of Nisan, it is the sign of a curse,[12] as it is said (I Samuel, 12.17): "Is it not wheat harvest today?" etc.

Gemara: What authority has the Tanna[13] for the requirement of mentioning the rain at all that he inquires at what time it should begin?

The Tanna bases himself on a Mishnah (Berakot, 33a), which teaches: The Power of rain should be mentioned in the prayer for the resurrection of the dead;[14] rain should be prayed for in connection with the prayer for a prosperous year;[15] and the *Habdalah*[16] should be inserted in the prayer for the granting of wisdom. In view

---

[11] Literally: Mutual inquiries after one's well-being, greetings.

[12] Because then begins in Palestine the time for harvesting. The verse from Sam., 12.17 is intended to prove that rain in harvest time is a punishment for evil deeds.

[13] Literally: Where does the Tanna stand, that is, on what ground does he assume that one is obliged to mention the rain in the prayer at all?—Tanna, plural Tannaim, designates an authority mentioned in the Mishnah either by name or anonymously.

[14] The second of the Eighteen benedictions; see above, note 1.

[15] The ninth of the eighteen benedictions; see above, note 4.

[16] The piece אתה חוננתנו, which is inserted in the fourth

בבנין ובנטיעה בארוסין ובנשואין ובשאילת שלום
שבין אדם לחברו כבני אדם הנזופין למקום
היחידים הוזרין ומתענין עד שיצא ניסן יצא ניסן
וירדו גשמים סימן קללה שנאמר הלוא קציר חטים
5 היום וגו':

גמרא: תנא היכא קאי דקתני מאימתי תנא
התם קאי דתנן מזכירין גבורות גשמים בתחיית
המתים ושואלין את הגשמים בברכת השנים
והבדלה בחונן הדעת וקתני מאימתי מזכירין

תורה אור	מסרת הש"ס והמדרשים
4 שמואל א י"ב י"ז.	1 (ובשאילת) מו"ק ט"ו. 3 (יצא
	ניסן) תענית ב': י"ב: 6 (היכא
	קאי) ברכות ב'. 7 (דתנן) ברכות ל"ג.

---

benediction and in which God is praised for having distinguished the Sabbath day from other days, hence the
name *habdalah* = distinction.

of this Mishnah, the Tanna now informs us regarding the *time* at which we should begin to mention the Power of rain.

But why did not the Tanna make the statement there? Why did he leave it for this place?

The proper explanation, then, is that our Mishnah is intended as a continuation of the one in the tractate Rosh ha-Shanah,[17] where it is taught: In the feast of Tabernacles the world is judged as to whether it should have rain. In connection with this teaching he informs us here at what time we should begin to mention the Power of rain.

But why does he not say: "At what time should we begin to mention the rain?" What is the meaning of "Power" of rain?

Said R. Johanan: He uses the term because rain comes down by the power of God, as it is written (Job, 5.9): "Who doeth great things and unsearchable, marvellous things without number." And immediately after: "Who giveth rain upon the earth and sendeth water upon the fields."

How do these verses bear out the idea?[18]

Said Rabbah bar R. Shila: The inference is made from the word *ḥeḳer* (search), used both in the verse just quoted and in a verse referring to the creation of the world; for here (Job, 5.9) Scripture says: "Who doeth great things and unsearchable" (*ḥeḳer*), while there (Is., 40.28) it says: "Hast thou not known? Hast thou not

[17] The Tractate Ta'anit follows in the Babylonian Talmud immediately upon that of Rosh ha-Shanah; see Maimon-

גבורות גשמים ולתנייה התם מאי שנא דשבקיה
עד הכא אלא תנא מראש השנה סליק דתנן
ובחג נדונין על המים ואיידי דתנא ובחג
נדונין על המים תנא נמי מאימתי מזכירין גבורות
גשמים ולתני מאימתי מזכירין את הגשמים מאי ⁵
גבורות גשמים אמר רבי יוחנן מפני שיורדין
בגבורה שנאמר עשה גדלות ואין חקר וכתיב
בתריה הנתן מטר על פני ארץ ושלח מים על
פני חוצות:

מאי משמע אמר רבה בר רב שילא אתיא ¹⁰
חקר חקר מבריתו של עולם כתיב הכא עשה
גדלות ואין חקר וכתיב התם הלוא ידעת אם לא

תורה אור	מסרת הש״ס והמדרשים
7 איוב ה׳ ט׳. 8 איוב ה׳ י׳.	2 (דתנן) ר״ה ט״ז. 11 (חקר)
12 ישעיה מ׳ כ״ח.	לקמן ט׳: ב״ר י״ג ד׳.

---

ides' Introduction to his Commentary on the Mishnah.

[18] The word 'power,' used by the Mishnah, does not occur
in these verses, hence the objection. Rabbah b. R. Shila,
therefore, tries first to establish through the word 'ḥeḳer'
a relation between Job, 5. 9 and Is., 40. 28 (comp. below,
note 163), then relates the latter verse, by its content and
reference to creation, to Ps., 65. 7, in which the word *might*
= power (*geburah*) does occur. The reasoning thus is: A
= B, B = C, hence A = C.

heard that the everlasting God, the Lord, the
Creator of the ends of the earth, fainteth not,
neither is weary? His discernment is past searching (*ḥeḳer*) out." Furthermore, Scripture says
(Ps., 65.7). "Who by Thy strength settest fast
the mountains, Who art girded about with
might."

But whence do we know that it is in the prayer
that one is to mention the rain?

It is found in the following Baraita (Sifre, Deut.
§ 41): "To love the Lord your God and to serve
Him with all your heart and with all your soul"
(Deut., 11.13). Now "service" is prayer. You
say it is prayer, may it not be (sacrificial) service? No, Scripture says: "with all your *heart*";
what service is that of the heart? You must
say that it is prayer; while immediately following, Scripture says: "Then I will give the rain of
your land in its season, the former rain and the
latter rain."[19]

Said R. Johanan: The following three keys
have not been entrusted to the keeping of any
angel:[20]—for a woman in travail, for rain, and for
resurrection. For a woman in travail, it is written
(Gen., 30.22): "And God hearkened to her and
opened her womb"; of rain it is written (Deut.,
28.12): "The Lord will open unto thee His good

[19] The juxtaposition of service of the heart, which is
prayer, and the promise of rain, makes it appear proper
that the latter should be mentioned in the former.

[20] Literally: Agent, messenger (שליח = ἄγγελυς), the
idea is that God Himself attends to these matters, as borne
out by the verses quoted.

שמעת אלהי עולם ה' בורא קצות הארץ לא ייעף
ולא ייגע אין חקר לתבונתו וכתיב מכין הרים
בכחו נאזר בגבורה:

ומנא לן דבתפלה דתניא לאהבה את ה'
5   אלהיכם ולעבדו בכל לבבכם ובכל נפשכם
עבודה זו תפלה אתה אומר תפלה או אינו אלא
עבודה תלמוד לומר בכל לבבכם איזו היא
עבודה שהיא בלב הוי אומר זו תפלה וכתיב
בתריה ונתתי מטר ארצכם בעתו יורה ומלקוש·

10   ואמר רבי יוחנן שלש מפתחות לא נמסרו ביד
שליח ואלו הן של חיה ושל גשמים ושל תחית
המתים של חיה דכתיב וישמע | אליה אלהים   בב'
ויפתח את רחמה של גשמים דכתיב יפתח ה' לך   עב'

תורה אור	מסרת הש"ס והמדרשים
2 תהלים ס"ה ז'. 4 דברים	4 (דתניא) ספרי עקב מ"א; ירושלמי
י"א י"ג. 9 דברים י"א י"ד.	ברכות ד' א'; מדרש שמואל ב' פסוק
12 בראשית ל' כ"ב. 13 דברים	י'; מדרש תנאים צד 35. 10 (מפתחות)
כ"ח י"ב.	סנהדרין קי"ג. פס"ר מ"ב (צד קע"ח
	עיי"ש במאיר עין); ת"י דברים כ"ח

י"ב; תרגום ירושלמי בראשית י' כ"ב; ב"ר פע"נ ד'; ד"ר ז' ו'; מדרש תהלים
ע"ח; מדרש תנאים 35; בית המדרש ח"ו צד 62.

treasure the heaven to give the rain of thy land
in its season" [fol. 2b]; of resurrection it is written
(Ez., 37.13): "And ye shall know that I am the
Lord when I have opened your graves."

In Palestine they mention also the key of sustenance, as it is written (Ps., 145.16): "Thou
openest Thy hand, and satisfiest every living
thing with favour."

Why did R. Johanan omit this key? Because
he thinks rain is the same as sustenance.

*R. Eliezer says, on the first day of the feast of
Tabernacles*, etc.

The question was raised: Did R. Eliezer derive his view from the *lulab*, or from the libation
of water? If he derived it from the lulab, then
just as the lulab comes into use on (the morning
of) the first day of Tabernacles, so also the mentioning of the rain should begin on that day. Or,
perhaps, did he derive it from the libation of
water, and then, just as the latter may take place
on the evening preceding the first day, so the
mentioning of the rain will begin on that evening
[for it has been taught (Temurah, 14a): The
words: "And their meal offering and their drink
offering" (Num., 29.18)[21] should be interpreted
to mean that drink offerings may be brought in

[21] According to the tosafist Jacob Tam (*Menaḥot*, 44b)
reference is here had to Lev., 23.18. Neither of the verses
expresses the idea here suggested, but such interpretations
for the purpose of obtaining new rules or supporting old
ones are a common occurrence in the Talmud. For the
understanding of the passage it is sufficient to know that
by law all animal sacrifices, as well as the accompanying
meal and drink offerings, had to be brought on the altar

את אוצרו הטוב את השמים לתת מטר ארצך
בעתו של תחית המתים דכתיב וידעתם כי אני
ה' בפתחי את קברותיכם:
במערבא אמרי אף מפתח של פרנסה דכתיב
5 פותח את ידך ומשביע לכל חי רצון:
ורבי יוחנן מאי טעמא לא קא חשיב להא
אמר לך גשמים היינו פרנסה:
רבי אליעזר אומר מיום טוב הראשון של חג כו':
איבעיא להו רבי אליעזר מלולב גמר לה
10 או מנסוך המים גמר לה מלולב גמר לה מה לולב
ביום אף הזכרה נמי ביום או דלמא מנסוך המים
גמר לה מה נסוך המים מאורתא אף הזכרה נמי
מאורתא דאמר מר ומנחתם ונסכיהם בלילה

תורה אור		מסרת הש״ס והמדרשים
2 יחזקאל ל״ז י״ג 5 תהלים קמ״ה 4 (פרנסה) פס״ר ל״ג (מאיר עין		

תורה אור: 2 יחזקאל ל״ז י״ג. 5 תהלים קמ״ה. 13 במדבר כ״ט י״ח.

מסרת הש״ס והמדרשים: 4 (פרנסה) פס״ר ל״ג (מאיר עין ט״ז. הערה נ״ו); ב״ר כ׳ ט׳; צ״ז ג׳; מדרש תהלים פ׳, פ״ט, קל״ו. 7 (גשמים) ברכות ל״ג. (ושם היא מימרא דרב יוסף וע׳ פסחים קי״ח.); ירושלמי כאן א׳ א׳ (דף ס״ג ג׳); ברכות ה׳ ב׳ (ט׳ א׳) וע׳ ב״ר פי״ג. 13 (דאמר מר) תמורה י״ד. זבחים ח׳. פ״ד. מנחות מ״ד: נ״ב.

during the day. On the basis of the verse here quoted,
however, a provision was made that under certain circumstances the meal and drink offerings could be brought
on the evening of the same day or at a still later time.   In
case, therefore, R. Eliezer had based his opinion on the
practice of libation, which usually consisted of wine, but

the evening and even at a subsequent time]?[22] Come and listen: R. Abahu said: R. Eliezer derived his view from the lulab exclusively.

Some say that R. Abahu had a tradition for this statement; others maintain that he had a Baraita as his authority. What Baraita? The Baraita reads as follows: At what time should one begin to mention the Power of rain? R. Eliezer says: At the time one begins to wave the lulab; R. Joshua says: At the time when it is discarded. Said R. Eliezer: Inasmuch as the Four Species[23] are used only in order to obtain the favor of God that He may give rain, one must argue that just as these four species cannot exist without water, so the world cannot exist without rain. R. Joshua replied: Is not rain during the feast of Tabernacles but the sign of divine displeasure? Said R. Eliezer, I did not say that one should *pray* for rain, but that one should[24] make mention of it.

during the feast of Tabernacles, also of water, and, as said before, was permissible also in the evening, the mention of the rain would likewise have to begin in the evening, that is, the evening *preceding* the first day (אורתא), although in the matter of libation, particularly that of wine, only the evening *following* the first day could come into consideration; see Tosafot *ad locum* and *ad Menaḥot, l. c.*

[22] The word למחר means here any time subsequent to the sacrificing of the animal; Rashi to *Temurah, l.c.* The quotation of the Baraita in not found in all the texts of the Talmud (see R. Gershom and Rashi) and is therefore put in brackets.

[23] See Lev., 23.40.

[24] I follow the interpretation of Tosafot, fol. 2a, *s. v.*

16

ומנחתם ונסכיהם אפילו למחר תא שמע דאמר רבי

אבהו לא למדה רבי אליעזר אלא מלולב:

איכא דאמרי רבי אבהו גמרא גמיר לה

ואיכא דאמרי מתניתא שמיע ליה מאי היא דתניא

‏5 מאימתי מזכירין גבורות גשמים רבי אליעזר

אומר משעת נטילת לולב רבי יהושע אומר משעת

הנחתו אמר רבי אליעזר הואיל וארבעת מינין

הללו אינן באין אלא לרצות על המים כשם

שארבעת מינין הללו אי אפשר להם בלא מים

‏10 כך אי אפשר לעולם בלא גשמים אמר לו רבי

יהושע והלא גשמים בח אינן אלא סימן קללֹה

אמר לו רבי אליעזר אף אני לא אמרתי לשאול

מסרת הש״ס והמדרשים

7 (הנחתו) לקמן ג׳. ד׳. ירושלמי   ריש פרקין.

For just as one mentions the resurrection of the dead throughout the year, although it is to take place at a particular time only, so one may mention also the rain during the whole year, although it is to fall only at a given time, and hence if one actually desires to mention it throughout the year, he may do so.

Rabbi said: I am of the opinion that when one ceases praying for rain,[25] one should also cease mentioning it. R. Judah b. Bathyra said: One should begin to mention the rain on the second day of Tabernacles. R. 'Aḳiba said: One should begin to mention it on the sixth day of Tabernacles. R. Judah said in the name of R. Joshua: Of those that go before the ark as readers on the concluding day of Tabernacles, the last[26] should mention the rain, but not the first; on the opening day of Passover, the first reader should mention it and the last one should not.

Was not R. Eliezer's argument perfectly correct?

R. Joshua might answer, that it is quite right to mention the resurrection of the dead (during the year), because resurrection would always be in time whenever it came, but is it true of rain that it would be in time whenever it came? Do we not read: If rain falls after Nisan is passed it is a sign of a curse?

R. Judah b. Bathyra said: One should begin to mention the rain on the second day of Tabernacles.

---

[25] That is, on the first day of Passover, when the prayer for *dew* begins. Rabbi disagrees with R. Eliezer, making no distinction between praying for rain and mentioning it.

[26] See above, notes 5–6.

אלא להזכיר וכשם שמזכירין תחית המתים כל
השנה כלה ואינה אלא בזמנה כך מזכירין גבורות
גשמים כל השנה כלה ואינן אלא בזמנן לפיכך
אם בא להזכיר כל השנה כלה מזכיר:

רבי אומר אני משעה שפוסק מלשאול 5
פוסק מלהזכיר רבי יהודה בן בתירה אומר בשני
בחג הוא מזכיר רבי עקיבא אומר בששי בחג הוא
מזכיר רבי יהודה אומר משום רבי יהושע העובר
לפני התבה ביום טוב האחרון של חג האחרון
מזכיר והראשון אינו מזכיר ביום טוב הראשו של 10
פסח הראשון מזכיר והאחרון אינו מזכיר:

שפיר קאמר ליה רבי אליעזר לרבי יהושע
אמר לך רבי יהושע בשלמא תחית המתים
מזכיר דכל אימת דאתיא זמניה הוא אלא גשמים
כל אימת דאתיין זמניהו הוא והתנן יצא ניסן וירדו 15
גשמים סימן קללה הם:

רבי יהודה בן בתירה אומר בשני בחג הוא

מסרת הש"ס והמדרשים

14 (דכל אימת) ירושלמי כאן א' א'   (ס"נ ד').   15 (והתנן) תענית י"ב

What is R. Judah's reason? It is as stated in the following Baraita: R. Judah b. Bathyra says: In prescribing the order of sacrifices for the second day, scripture says (Num., 29.18): "and *their* drink-offerings" (ונסכיהם), in the order for the sixth day (*ib.*, 29.31), the expression is: "and *its* drink-offerings" (ונסכיה), while in the order for the seventh day (*ib.*, 29.33) we read: "After *their* ordinance" (כמשפטם), thus obtaining the letters *mem*, *yod*, *mem*, which put together read *mayim* (מים = water). Here we have a biblical allusion to the institution of water libation.

But why should R. Judah insist on the second day? Because the allusion to water is given first in the order for the second day. Accordingly it is on the second day that we must begin to mention the rain.

R. 'Akiba said: One should begin to mention it on the sixth day of Tabernacles.

What is R. 'Akiba's reason? It is as stated in the following Baraita: In the order of sacrifices of the sixth day the expression used is: "and its drink-offerings" (plural). Scripture, therefore, has reference to two libations, the one being the libation of water and the other that of wine. May not both be of wine? On that point R. 'Akiba agrees with R. Judah b. Bathyra, who says that in the quoted verse water is alluded to. [fol. 3a]. But if he agrees with R. Judah b. Bathyra, let him also have the rain mentioned on the second day! R. 'Akiba holds that the Scriptural allusion to an additional libation is found first in the verse referring to the sixth day.

מזכיר מאי טעמיה דרבי יהודה בן בתירה דתניא

רבי יהודה בן בתירה אומר נאמר בשני ונסכיהם

בששי ונסכיה בשביעי כמשפטם מ"ם יו"ד מ"ם הרי

מים מכאן רמז לנסוך המים מן התורה ומאי שנא

5 בשני דנקט דכי רמיזי מיא בשני הוא דרמיזי

הלכך בשני מדכרינן:

רבי עקיבא אומר בששי הוא מזכיר

מאי טעמיה דרבי עקיבא דתניא נאמר בששי

ונסכיה בשני נסוכין הכתוב מדבר אחד נסוך המים

10 ואחד נסוך היין ואימא תרוייהו דחמרא סבר לה

כרבי יהודה בן בתירה דאמר מיא רמיזי הכא

ג' ע"א | אי סבר לה כרבי יהודה בן בתירה לדכר בשני
10

אמר לך רבי עקיבא נסוך יתירא כי כתיב בששי

הוא דכתיב:

תורה אור	מסרת הש"ס והמדרשים
2 במדבר כ"ט י"ח.	1 (דתניא) שבת ק"ג; ספרי פנחס ק"נ;
	ירושלמי שביעית א' ז'; סוכה ד'

א' (ועיי"ש ד' ו'); ר"ה א' ג' (נ"ז ב'); פסדר"כ ל' (באבער צד קצ"ה).
9 (בשני נסוכין) זבחים קי"י:

A Baraita teaches: R. Nathan says: The verse (Num., 28.7): "In the holy place shalt thou pour out a drink-offering of strong drink unto the Lord," speaks of two libations,[26a] one of water and one of wine.

Is it not possible that both libations are meant to be of wine? In that case the text should read either *hassēk hassēk* or *nések nések*, why *hassēk nések?* This change of expression implies both ideas.[27] But if this be so, on whose authority will you base the Mishnah (*Sukkah*, iv, 1): The water libation was observed during the entire week of the festival? If this Mishnah follows R. Joshua, there was only one[28] day of libation; if it follows R. 'Aḳiba, there were two days; and if R. Judah b. Bathyra, there were six days! The Mishnah certainly follows R. Judah b. Bathyra, who, however, agrees with R. Judah (b. 'Ila'i); for we read (*ib.*, iv, 9): R. Judah (b. 'Ila'i) says: One *log*[29] of water was used daily for libation during eight days; but R. Judah b. Bathy-

---

[26a] The inference of two libations is made from the doubling of the verb form, hassēk nések (הסך נסך).

[27] The Talmud often uses the combination in the Bible of two verbal forms as a basis for new interpretations; see below, notes 145, 315. Here this combination is interpreted to indicate two kinds of libations, of wine and of water.

[28] According to R. Joshua the mention of rain must begin as soon as the *lulab* is put away, that is, at the expiration of the seventh day of Sukkot. Now, if this time is to coincide with the beginning of the libation ceremonies, these ceremonies could not have occupied even "one

תניא רבי נתן אומר בקדש הסך נסך שכר
לה׳ בשני נסוכין הכתוב מדבר אחד נסוך המים
ואחד נסוך היין ואימא תרוייהו דחמרא אם כן
לכתוב קרא או הסך הסך או נסך נסך מאי
5 הסך נסך שמעת מינה תרתי אלא הא דתנן נסוך
המים כל שבעה מני אי רבי יהושע חד יומא
הוא אי רבי עקיבא תרי יומי הוו אי רבי יהודה
בן בתירה שיתא יומי הוו לעולם רבי יהודה
בן בתירה היא וסבר לה כרבי יהודה דתנן
10 רבי יהודה אומר בלוג היה מנסך כל שמונה

תורה אור   מסרת הש״ס והמדרשים

1 במדבר כ״ח ז׳.   1 (תניא) ספרי פנחס קמ״נ וק״נ:
                 ירושלמי סוכה ד׳ ו׳.   5 (דתנן)
סוכה מ״ב: (ע׳ כאן בהערה).   9 (דתנן) סוכה מ״ח:

---

day" (the seventh) of the Sukkot festival. R. Gershom
and Rashi seem to take משעת הנחתו (the time the *lulab*
is put away) as extending over the whole of the seventh day,
which was the day of libation. Others think that "one
day" actually refers to the eighth day (Shemini-'azeret).
Neither of these assumptions is satisfactory, and the
solution lies in the marginal note of the Munich MS.,
which reads, "not even one day" (see the Hebrew notes),
but it is hazardous to change the text on this basis;
comp. Rabbinovicz, *ad locum*, letter ת.

[29] A liquid measure; see Lev., 14.10.

ra excludes the first day and includes the eighth.
Why does he exclude the first day? Is it not because the allusion to water is found in connection
with the second day? If so, the eighth day too
should be excluded, since Scripture speaks of the
seventh only and not of the eighth day! The
only solution, therefore, is that the seven days' libation is based on a tradition; for R. 'Asi said in
the name of R. Johanan, who in turn said it in the
name of R. Neḥunya of the Plain of Bet-Ḥawar-
tan:[30] The laws concerning the ten plants,[31] the
willow-branch,[32] and the water libation are halakas
given to Moses on Sinai.[33]

It was said above: R. Judah says in the name
of R. Joshua. Which R. Joshua is here meant?
Is it R. Joshua (b. Hananiah) who is named above
in our Mishnah? If so, you will meet with the
difficulty that he said: (we begin to mention the
rain) "on the last day of the festival;" or is it the
R. Joshua who is named above in the Baraita?
He said: (we begin to mention rain) "at the time
the lulab is discarded." Moreover, when we

[30] See Neubauer, *La géographie du Talmud*, p. 50;
S. Klein, in the *Festschrift* for Adolf Schwarz (1917),
p. 395: Jech. Hirschenson, שבע חכמות, Lemberg, 1883, pp.
81, 111.

[31] An old law required the cessation of all field work one
month before the beginning of the Sabbatical year, but
to save young trees from decay the same law permitted
their cultivation during that month, provided they were
planted at such distance from one another that *ten* of
them, equally distributed, would cover fifty square cubits.
If they were closer together than the proportion indicated,

מפיק ראשון ומעייל שמיני ומאי שנא ראשון
דלא דכי רמיזי מיא בשני הוא דרמיזי שמיני נמי
שביעי אמר רחמנא ולא שמיני אלא נסוך המים
כל שבעה גמרא גמיר לה דאמר רבי אסי אמר
רבי יוחנן משום רבי נחוניא איש בקעת בית חוורתן
עשר נטיעות ערבה ונסוך המים הלכה למשה
מסיני:

אמר מר רבי יהודה אומר משום רבי יהושע
הי רבי יהושע אילימא רבי יהושע דמתניתין הא
אמר מיום טוב האחרון של חג אלא רבי יהושע
דברייתא האמר משעת הנחתו ותו הא דתנן רבי

מסרת הש"ס והמדרשים

4 (ר' אסי) סוכה ל"ד. מ"ד. שביעית א' ה'; סוכה ד' א'.
מו"ק ג': זבחים ק"י: ירושלמי 9 (הי ר"י) ע' ירושלמי דיש פרקין.

cultivation, it was assumed, would be of no use anyhow
and therefore was not to be allowed, see Mishnah,
Shebi'it, i, 6.

[32] That is, its use in the Temple during the feast of
Tabernacles in connection with the daily processions
around the altar, as described in the Mishnah, *Sukkah*,
iv, 5–6.

[33] Established customs and practices for which no Scriptural basis could be found and whose exact origin was
not known were generally termed, "laws revealed to Moses
(privately) on Mount Sinai."

read in our Mishnah: R. Judah says in the name of Ben Bathyra, of those who go before the ark on the concluding day of the festival, the last should mention the rain, but the first one should not, the question again arises which Ben Bathyra is there referred to? Is it R. *Judah* b. Bathyra? He said (in the Baraita): "We begin to mention the rain on the second day of the festival!" Said R. Naḥman b. Isaac: Both designations, "R. Joshua" and "Ben Bathyra," refer to R. Joshua b. Bathyra, for he was sometimes quoted by the name of his father and sometimes by his own name. What was the reason therefor?—In the first form he was quoted before he had been ordained and in the latter after his ordination.

We read in a Baraita: The Sages did not make it obligatory to mention the dew and the winds in the prayer, but if one wishes to mention them, he may do so. What is the reason? Said R. Ḥanina, because dew and winds are never withheld. Whence do we know that dew is never withheld? It is written (I Kings, 17.1): "And Elijah the Tishbite, who was of the settlers of Gilead, said unto Ahab: 'As the Lord, the God of Israel, liveth, before whom I stand, there shall not be *dew* nor rain these years, but according to my word.'" Further on it is written (*ib.* 18.1): "Go show thyself unto Ahab, and I will send *rain* upon the land," but dew is not mentioned. Now, what is the reason for this omission? Certainly the reason is [fol. 3b] that dew is never withheld. But if dew is never withheld, why did Elijah swear (that there would be no dew)? Elijah meant to say that the dew (though never

יהודה אומר משום בן בתירה העובר לפני התיבה
ביום טוב האחרון של חג האחרון מזכיר והראשון
אינו מזכיר הי בן בתירה אילימא רבי יהודה בן
בתירה הא אמר בשני בחג הוא מזכיר אמר רב
נחמן בר יצחק תהא כרבי יהושע בן בתירה זמנין
דקרי ליה בשמיה דאבוה וזמנין דקרי ליה בשמיה
דידיה ומאי שנא הא מקמי דסמכוה והא לבתר
דסמכוה:

תנא בטל וברוחות לא חייבו חכמים להזכיר
ואם בא להזכיר מזכיר מאי טעמא אמר רבי
חנינא לפי שאינן נעצרין וטל מנלן דלא מיעצר
דכתיב ויאמר אליהו התשבי מתשבי גלעד אל
אחאב חי ה' אלהי ישראל אשר עמדתי לפניו אם
יהיה השנים האלה טל ומטר כי אם לפי דברי
וכתיב לך הראה אל אחאב ואתנה מטר על פני
האדמה ואלו טל לא קאמר ליה מאי טעמא משום
דלא מיעצר וכי מאחר דלא מיעצר אליהו
אשתבועי למה ליה הכי קאמר ליה אפילו טל

תורה אור

12 מ״א י״ז א׳.   15 מ״א י״ח א׳.

סנהדרין מ״א:

מסרת הש״ס והמדרשים

1 (העובר) ירושלמי כאן א׳ ב׳
(ס״ד א׳).   6 (דקרי ליה) ע׳
9 (תנא) ירושלמי ברכות ה׳ ב׳; תענית א׳ א׳ (ס״נ ד׳).
11–16 ירושלמי ברכות שם ותענית שם; סנהדרין י׳ ב׳ (כ״ח ב׳).

ע״ב
נ״ג

withheld) would not be of a fructifying nature.[34] If so, why did he not, subsequently, bring back also the fructifying dew? Because it is not discernible whether or not a dew is of a fructifying nature (which would give Ahab a chance to suspect that the promise was not kept).

Whence do we know that *winds* are not withheld? Scripture says (Zech., 2. 10): "For I have spread you abroad as the four winds of the heaven, saith the Lord." Now what did God mean to say? Did the Holy One, blessed be He, intend to say: I have scattered you to the four *corners* of the world? If so, why *ke-arba'* ("as the four")? He should have said *be-arba'* ("to the four")! The verse therefore means to intimate that just as the world cannot exist without the four winds,[35] so it could not exist without Israel.

Said R. Ḥanina: If, during the summer months,[36] one says in the prayer: "He causes the wind to blow," we do not order him to read the prayer over again correctly, but if he says: "He causes the rain to fall," we order him to read it over again[37]; during the winter months if he fails to say; "He causes the wind to blow," we do not order him to read the prayer over again, but if he fails to say: "He causes the rain to fall," we order him to read the prayer over again. Moreover, even if he says: "He causes the wind to subside and the dew to vanish," we do not order him to read the prayer over again.[38]

[34] Comp. Mishnah, *Sotah*, ix, 12.

[35] We thus learn indirectly that winds cannot be withheld from the world.

דברכה נמי לא אתי ולהדריה לא מינכרא מלתא:
ורוחות מנלן דלא מיעצרי דכתיב כי כארבע
רוחות השמים פרשתי אתכם נאם ה' מאי קאמר
אילימא הכי קאמר להו קודשא בריך הוא לישראל
בדרתינכו בארבע רוחי שמיא האי כארבע
בארבע מיבעי ליה אלא הכי קאמר כשם שאי
אפשר לעולם בלא רוחות כך אי אפשר לעולם
בלא ישראל:

אמר רבי חנינא בימות החמה אמר משיב הרוח
אין מחזירין אותו אמר מוריד הגשם מחזירין אותו
בימות הגשמים לא אמר משיב הרוח אין מחזירין
אותו לא אמר מוריד הגשם מחזירין אותו ולא עוד
אלא אפילו אמר מעביר הרוח ומפריח הטל אין
מחזירין אותו:

מסרת הש״ס והמדרשים		תורה אור
5 (בדרתינכו) ע״ז י״ב'. 10 (מחזירין)		2 זכריה ב' י'.
ירושלמי כאן א' א' (ס״נ ד');		
ברכות ה' ב' (ט' ב').		

---

[36] From the end of Nisan to the feast of Tabernacles.

[37] Because after Nisan is harvest time, when, as was said above, rain is a calamity.

[38] Because wind and rain are never withheld. The reader's insertion is therefore immaterial.

We read in a Baraita: The Sages did not make
it obligatory to mention the clouds and the
winds, but if one wishes to mention them, he
may do so. What is the reason? The reason
is that they are never withheld. Are they not
withheld? Did not R. Joseph transmit the
tannaitic teaching: "The verse (Deut., 11. 17):
'He will shut up the heaven,' indicates the
withholding of clouds and winds; I say 'clouds
and winds,' is it not possible, you may object,
that it indicates only the withholding of rain?
No, for Scripture adds (in the same verse):
'and there shall be no rain,' rain is thus explicitly stated; what then is implied in the preceding 'He will shut up the heaven'? No doubt
the withholding of clouds and winds?" Evidently, then, this (teaching of R. Joseph) contradicts that of the preceding Baraita as regards
both clouds and winds! No, there is no
contradiction as regards clouds, because the
Baraita refers to clouds that appear before the
rain (which are not withheld), while R. Joseph
refers to such as appear after the rain (which are
withheld).[39] Nor is there a contradiction as regards winds, for the one refers to common (mod-
erate) winds (which are not withheld), the other
to uncommon (strong) winds (which are withheld). But are not even strong winds needed
for winnowing? Winnowing can be done with
sieves.[40]

We read in a Baraita: Clouds and winds
rank second to rain (in fructifying value). To

[39] However, for the sake of these alone the Rabbis did
not think it necessary to have it mentioned in the prayer.

30

תנא בעבים וברוחות לא חייבו חכמים להזכיר
ואם בא להזכיר מזכיר מאי טעמא משום דלא
מיעצרי ולא מיעצרי והתני רב יוסף ועצר את
השמים מן העבים ומן הרוחות אתה אומר מן העבים
ומן הרוחות או אינו אלא מן המטר כשהוא אומר
ולא יהיה מטר הרי מטר אמור הא מה אני מקיים
ועצר את השמים מן העבים ומן הרוחות קשיא עבים
אעבים קשיא רוחות ארוחות עבים אעבים לא
קשיא הא בחרפי הא באפלי רוחות ארוחות נמי
לא קשיא הא ברוח מצויה הא ברוח שאינה מצויה
רוח שאינה מצויה נמי הא מיבעיא לבי דרי אפשר
בנפוותא:

תנא עבים ורוחות שניות למטר מאי היא אמר

תורה אור
3 דברים י"א י"ז.

_____

[40] Such winds are therefore not absolutely necessary and
may be withheld.

31

which clouds and winds does this refer? Said
'Ulla, or R. Judah: To those appearing after the
rain. Are we to assume that such winds are
beneficial? Is it not written (Deut. 28. 24):
"The Lord will make the rain of thy land powder
and dust"—which, according to 'Ulla, or according to some, R. Judah, is to be brought about by
winds following after the rain? This is no
contradiction, for in the first place the reference
is to winds that come gently, in the second to
such as come with vehemence (thus stirring up
the dust).

'Ulla, or, according to some, R. Judah, further
said: Winds and clouds and sunshine after rain
are as good as rain. What does this enumeration
exclude? It excludes the glow after sunset and
sunshine between clouds.[41]

Raba said, snow is as beneficial to the mountains as five rainfalls to the level ground, for
it is said (Job, 37. 6): "For He saith to the
snow: Fall thou on the earth; likewise to the
shower of rain, and to the showers of His mighty
rain."[42] Raba further said, snow is beneficial to
the mountains, a vehement rain to the trees, a
gentle rain to the produce of the fields [fol. 4a],
while *urpilla* (a drizzling rain) is helpful even to the
kernel under hard clods. What is (the etymology
of) *'urpilla*? Said R. Mesharshaya, it is a combination of *'ûrû* and *pîlê* (wake up, ye cracks).[43]

[41] These two are of no benefit.

[42] We have in this verse twice the word "rain," once
"shower," and once "showers." The latter, being a
plural, must count at least for two, thus bringing the
number to five. By a homiletical twist Raba interprets

עולא ואיתימא רב יהודה דבתר מטרא למימרא
דמעליותא היא והכתיב יתן ה' את מטר ארצך
אבק ועפר ואמר עולא ואיתימא רב יהודה זיקא
דבתר מטרא לא קשיא הא דאתא ניחא הא דאתא
רזיא ואמר עולא ואיתימא רב יהודה זיקא דבתר
מטרא כמטרא עיבא דבתר מטרא כמטרא שמשא
דבתר מטרא כמטרא למעוטי מאי למעוטי גלוהי
דליליא ושמשא דביני קרחי:

אמר רבא מעלי תלגא לטורי כחמשא מטרי
לארעא שנאמר כי לשלג יאמר הוה ארץ וגשם מטר
וגשם מטרות עזו ואמר רבא תלגא לטורי מטרא
רזיא לאילני מטרא ניחא לפירי עורפילא אפילו
לפרצידא דתותי קלא מהניא מאי עורפילא אמר
רב משרשיא עורו פילי ואמר רבא האי צורבא

תורה אור	מסרת הש״ס והמדרשים
2 דברים כ״ח כ״ד.	10 איוב ל״ז 4 (ניחא רזיא) לקמן י״ט ב'.
	10 (לשלג) ויק״ר ל״ה י״ב.
	ו'.

the verse to mean that when God sends snow on the mountains, it is as good as five rains and showers on flat ground.

[43] 'Urū = עורו, imperative plural of עור, to awake, and
Greek πύλαι = gates, openings, fissures. The idea is that
a drizzling rain penetrates deep into the hardened, *cracked*,
soil and stimulates growth. The etymology is, of course,
not to be taken seriously. עורפילא is evidently the same as
ערפל from ערף, to drip.

Raba further said, a young scholar is like the kernel under a clod which, having once sprouted, grows fast. Raba further said, when a scholar is hot-tempered, it is the Torah that boils within him, as it is said (Jer. 23.29): "Is not My word like as fire and like a hammer that breaketh the rock in pieces? saith the Lord."

R. 'Ashi said: A scholar who is not hard like iron is not a real scholar, as it is said: "And like a hammer that breaketh the rock in pieces." Said R. 'Abba to R. 'Ashi, you derive it from that verse, we derive it from the following (Deut. 8.9): "A land whose stones are iron"; do not read 'ābānēha (its stones), but bōnēha (its builders, i. e., the scholars).[44] Said Rabina: It is nevertheless one's duty to train oneself to be gentle, as it is said (Eccl., 11. 10): "Remove anger from thy heart and put away evil from thy flesh."

R. Samuel b. Nahamani said in the name of R. Jonathan, three men expressed their request in careless language; two of them were answered favorably, but the third was answered unfavorably. They are: Eliezer the servant of Abraham, Saul the son of Kish, and Jephthah the Gileadite. As to Eliezer, Scripture says (Gen., 24. 14): "So let it come to pass that the damsel to whom I shall say, let down thy pitcher," etc. These words include one that is lame or blind. He was answered, however, favorably, in that he happened upon Rebekah. As to Saul, Scripture

[44] Which is to prove that the scholar (builder of minds) must be as hard as iron. The phrase, "read not so (אל תקרי), but so," is very common in the Talmud, serving to bring out some homiletical idea.

34

מרבנן דמי לפרצידא דתותי קלא דכיון דנבט נבט
ואמר רבא האי צורבא מרבנן דרתח אוריתיה
מרתחא ליה שנאמר הלוא כה דברי כאש נאם ה׳
וכפטיש יפצץ סלע אמר רב אשי כל תלמיד חכם
5 שאינו קשה כברזל אינו תלמיד חכם שנאמר וכפטיש
יפצץ סלע אמר ליה רב אבא לרב אשי אתון
מהתם מתניתו לה אנן מהכא מתנינן לה ארץ אשר
אבניה ברזל אל תקרי אבניה אלא בוניה אמר
רבינא אפילו הכי מיבעי ליה לאינש למילף נפשיה
10 ניחותא שנאמר והסר כעס מלבך והעבר רעה
מבשרך:

אמר רבי שמואל בר נחמני אמר רבי יונתן שלשה
שאלו שלא כהוגן לשנים השיבו כהוגן לאחד השיבו
שלא כהוגן ואלו הן אליעזר עבד אברהם ושאול
15 בן קיש ויפתח הגלעדי אליעזר דכתיב והיה הנערה
אשר אמר אליה הטי נא כדך וגו׳ יכול אפילו
חגרת או סומא והשיבוהו כהוגן שנזדמנה לו רבקה

	תורה אור	מסרת הש״ס והמדרשים
3 ירמיה כ״ג כ״ט.	7 דברים	12 (שלשה) בראשית רבה ס׳ ג׳;
ח׳ ט׳.	10 קהלת י״א י׳.	ויקרא רבה ל״ז ד׳; תנחומא
	15 בראשית כ״ד י״ד.	(באבער) בחקותי ז׳.

says (I Sam., 17.25): "And it shall be, that the
man who killeth him, the king will enrich him
with great riches, and will give him his daughter." This might include a slave or a bastard,
but he was answered favorably in that he
happened upon David. As to Jephthah,
Scripture says (Jud., 11.31): "Then it shall be,
that whatsoever cometh forth of the doors of my
house to meet me, when I return in peace from
the children of Ammon, it shall be the Lord's and
I will offer it up for a burnt-offering." This may
mean even something unclean (unfit for a sacrifice), and, indeed, he was answered unfavorably,
in that it was his daughter who came out of the
house. It is with reference to this event that the
prophet said to Israel (Jer., 8.22): "Is there no
balm in Gilead? Is there no physician there?
Why then is not the health of the daughter of my
people recovered?" Hence it is also written
(*ibid.*, 19.5): "Which I commanded not, nor
spoke it, neither came it into My mind." "I
commanded not" refers to the son of Mesha
king of Moab, for it is said (II Kings, 3. 27):
"Then he took his eldest son that should have
reigned in his stead, and offered him for a burnt-
offering upon the wall. And there came great
wrath upon Israel"; "nor spoke it" refers to the
daughter of Jephthah; "neither came it into My
mind" refers to Isaac the son of Abraham.⁴⁵
    R. Berechiah said: The Congregation of Israel

⁴⁵ That is to say, that in none of these three cases was
it the will of God that the person in question should be
sacrificed.

שאול דכתיב והיה האיש אשר יכנו יעשרנו המלך
עשר גדול' ואת בתו יתן לו יכול אפילו עבד או
ממזר והשיבוהו כהוגן שנזדמן לו דוד יפתח דכתיב
והיה היוצא אשר יצא מדלתי ביתי לקראתי בשובי
בשלום מבני עמון והיה לה' והעליתיהו עולה יכול
אפילו דבר טמא והשיבוהו שלא כהוגן נזדמנה לו
בתו והיינו דקאמר להו נביא לישראל הצרי אין
בגלעד אם רפא אין שם כי מדוע לא עלתה ארכת
בת עמי וכתיב אשר לא צויתי ולא דברתי ולא
עלתה על לבי אשר לא צויתי זה בנו של מישע
מלך מואב שנאמר ויקח את בנו הבכור אשר ימלך
תחתיו ויעלהו עלה על החמה ויהי קצף גדול על
ישראל ולא דברתי זו בתו של יפתח ולא עלתה
על לבי זה יצחק בן אברהם:

אמר רבי ברכיה אף כנסת ישראל שאלה שלא

תורה אור	מסרת הש״ס והמדרשים
1 ש״א י״ז כ״ה. 4 שופטים י״א	11 (ויקח) סנהדרין ל״ט ב׳.
ל״א. 7 ירמיה ח׳ כ״ב. 9 שם	13 (יפתח) קהלת רבה י׳ ט״ו;
י״ט ה׳. 11 מ״ב ג׳ כ״ז.	תנחומא שם; אגדת בראשית ל״א;
	תנא דבי אליהו י״א.

likewise presented her request in careless
language, but the Holy One, blessed be He,
answered it favorably. The Congregation of
Israel said to Him: Master of the World!
"Let us know, eagerly strive to know the
Lord, His going forth is sure as the morning; and
He shall come unto us as the rain, as the latter
rain that watereth the earth" (Hos., 6. 3). The
Holy One, blessed be He, however, replied to
her: My daughter! Thou art asking for something which is desirable at times and undesirable
at others;[46] I wish to be unto thee something
that is desirable at all times, as it is said (*ibid.*,
14. 6): "I will be as the dew unto Israel; he shall
blossom as the lily, and cast forth his roots as
Lebanon." The Congregation further asked and
said: Master of the World! "Set me as a seal
upon thy heart, as a seal upon thine arm" (Cant.,
8. 6). The Holy one, blessed be He, replied to
her: My daughter! thou askest for something
that is visible at times and invisible at others;[47]
I shall make of thee something that is visible
at all times, as it is said (Is., 49. 16): "Behold,
I have graven thee upon the palms of My hands;
thy walls are continually before Me."

*One should not pray for rain until shortly
before the season of rain.* The Amoraim understood
that praying for rain and mentioning it are the
same thing. Who then is the author of this state-

---

[46] Rain is not always desirable, dew is.

[47] A seal on the heart or arm is mostly covered by the
garments, not so one on the palm of the hand (finger).

כהוגן והקדוש ברוך הוא השיבה כהוגן אמרה לפניו
רבונו של עולם ונדעה נרדפה לדעת את ה׳ כשחר
נכון מצאו ויבוא כגשם לנו כמלקוש יורה ארץ
אמר לה הקדוש ברוך הוא בתי את שואלת דבר
שפעמים מתבקש ופעמים אינו מתבקש ואני אהיה
לך דבר המתבקש לעולם שנאמר אהיה כטל
לישראל יפרח כשושנה ויך שרשיו כלבנון ועוד
שאלה שלא כהוגן אמרה לפניו רבונו של עולם
שמני כחותם על לבך כחותם על זרועך אמר לה
הקדוש ברוך הוא בתי את שואלת דבר שפעמים
נראה ופעמים אינו נראה ואני נותנך כדבר הנראה
לעולם שנאמר הן על כפים חקותיך חומתיך נגדי
תמיד:

אין שואלין את הגשמים כו׳: סברוה שאלה
והזכרה חדא מלתא היא מאן תנא אמר רבא רבי

ment?[48]   Raba said, its author can only be R.
Joshua, who said (above p. 16) that one is to
mention the rain from the time when "the lulab
is put away." 'Abbayi, however, replied to Raba,
you might just as well say that the author of
that statement is R. Eliezer, for praying for
rain is one thing and mentioning it is another.

Another version: The Amoraim understood
[fol. 4b] that praying and mentioning are two
different things.   Who would then be the author
of the statement?   Raba said it was R. Eliezer,
who said we begin the first day. 'Abbayi, however, replied, you may just as well say the author
is R. Joshua, but praying and mentioning are
one and the same thing.

*R. Judah says in the name of Ben Bathyra, of
those who go before the ark*, etc. A contradiction was
pointed out (by quoting the following Mishnah):
Until what time is one to pray for rain? R. Judah
says, until Passover is over; R. Jose says, until
after Nisan.[49]   Said R. Ḥisda, there is no contradiction, for the one passage of the Mishnah
refers to praying, the other to mentioning; one
may continue to pray until the end of Passover,

---

[48]   The difficulty connected with the clause of the Mishnah
here discussed has been pointed out above, note 4.   If,
as some assumed, שואלין means here the same as מזכירין
(mention), then the provision, "one should not *mention* the
rain until shortly before the rainy season," could only tally
with the view of R. Joshua, who said that we should begin
to mention it after the festival, when the *lulab* has been
discarded, that is shortly before the rainy season; while
according to R. Eliezer it would be a full week earlier.

יהושע היא דאמר משעת הנחתו אמר ליה אביי
אפילו תימא רבי אליעזר שאלה לחוד והזכרה
ד' לחוד ואיכא דאמרי סברוה‖ שאלה לחוד והזכרה
ע"ב
לחוד מאן תנא אמר רבא רבי אליעזר היא דאמר
5 מיום טוב הראשון הוא מזכיר אמר ליה אביי אפילו
תימא רבי יהושע שאלה והזכרה חדא מלתא היא:
רבי יהודה אומר משום בן בתירה העובר לפני
התבה כו': ורמינהי עד מתי שואלין את הגשמים
רבי יהודה אומר עד שיעבור הפסח רבי יוסי אומר
10 עד שיצא ניסן אמר רב חסדא לא קשיא כאן לשאול
כאן להזכיר משאל שאיל ואזיל הזכרה ביום טוב

מסרת הש"ס והמדרשים

1 (הנחתו) תענית ב' ב'; ירושלמי   ה' א'; תוספתא כאן א' א'; ירושלמי
כאן א' א'.   8 (עד מתי) תענית   תענית א' ב'; נדרים ח' ז'.

'Abbayi, however, thinks that the clause in question may
also follow the authority of R. Eliezer, because שואלין can
only mean *pray*, so that while the mention, according
to R. Eliezer, begins on the first day of the festival, the
praying begins later, that is, "shortly before the rainy
season;" comp. Geiger, *Jüd. Zeitschr.*, VII, 271.

[49] The contradiction consists in that R. Judah requires
here the praying for rain to last until after Passover, while
in the Mishnah above he taught that the reader of the
morning prayer on the first day of Passover is to be the
last one to mention the rain.

but the mention of rain must cease on the first
day. Said 'Ulla, what is here said by R. Ḥisda
is "as vinegar to the teeth, and as smoke to the
eyes" (Prov., 10.26), for if one is allowed to
mention the rain even when one is not allowed
to pray for it, is it not logical that one should be
allowed to mention it also at times when one is
allowed to pray for it? 'Ulla therefore suggested
that there existed two different recensions[50] of
R. Judah's statement. R. Joseph said, do you
know what "until Passover is over" means? It
means until the time for the first reader of the
first day of the festival is over.[51] 'Abbayi, however, objected: Is there any opportunity at
all to mention rain in the holiday prayer?[52]
Yes, answered R. Joseph, the Interpreter[53] prays
for rain. Does the Interpreter ever pray for anything which is not needed by the congregation?
'Ulla's answer is, therefore, the best. Rabbah
said, do you know what "until Passover is over"
means? It means until the time for slaughter-

[50] Literally: Two Tannaim differ as to the opinion of
R. Judah.

[51] Disagreeing with 'Ulla, R. Joseph tries to harmonize
the two statements of R. Judah by declaring that "till
Passover is over" means till the morning prayer of the
first day of Passover is over.

[52] The ninth benediction of the daily prayer, in which
the formula of the prayer for rain (ותן טל ומטר) is inserted,
is not recited on holidays. What opportunity, then, has
one to pray for rain on Passover?

[53] The function of the interpreter (תורגמן, turgeman =
dragoman) was to explain to the audience the words of

הראשון פסיק אמר עולא הא דרב חסדא כחמץ
לשנים וכעשן לעינים ומה במקום שאינו שואל מזכיר
במקום שהוא שואל אינו דין שיזכיר אלא אמר
עולא תרי תנאי אליבא דרבי יהודה רב יוסף אמר
מאי עד שיעבור הפסח עד שיעבור זמן שליח צבור
ראשון של יום טוב הראשון של פסח אמר ליה אביי
שאלה ביום טוב מי איכא אמר ליה אין שואל
מתורגמן וכי מתורגמן שואל דבר שאינו צריך לצבור
אלא מחוורתא כדעולא רבה אמר מאי עד שיעבור
הפסח עד שיעבור זמן שחיטת הפסח וכתחלתו

מסרת הש״ס והמדרשים	תורה אור
1 (כחמץ) קדושין מ״ה ב׳.	1 משלי י׳ כ״ו.

---

the lecturing scholar. Here the term cannot possibly have
this meaning. The commentator Ḥananel (11th century)
therefore suggests that in talmudic times there must have
been one who, in times of urgent need, was appointed to
pray for the entire community. He was, as it were, the
interpreter of the people's needs before God (comp. below, fol. 25b). The commentators, Gershom (11th c.) and,
following him, Rashi, think that *turgeman* here means
the same as lecturer and that the one who lectured on the
first day of Passover inserted a special prayer for rain.
Both explanations, however, presuppose that there is
special need for rain on that day of Passover, which is
not plausible. Hence the immediately following objection
of the Talmud: Does the interpreter ever pray, etc.?

ing[54] the Paschal lamb is over, for the discontinuing of the reference to rain must be like the beginning thereof: Just as in the beginning one *mentions* the rain, although one does not *pray* for it, so also at the end of the season one should mention it though not pray for it. 'Abbayi objected: It is quite correct at the beginning of the season to mention the rain without praying for it, because the mention is to serve the purpose of propitiating (God) preparatory to praying, but at the end of the season, what need is there for propitiation (since it is not to be followed by praying)? It is therefore best to accept the answer of 'Ulla.

Said R. 'Asi in the name of R. Johanan, the law is in accordance with R. Judah. Said R. Zera to R. 'Asi: Did R. Johanan really say so? Did we not read (above, p. 2): On the third of Marḥeshwan we begin to pray for rain; R. Gamaliel says on the seventh thereof. Now R. Eleazar, commenting upon the statement, said, the law is in accordance with R. Gamaliel! Said R. 'Asi: Do you pit one authority (R. Eleazar) against another (R. Johanan)?! Moreover, I can say that there is no contradiction between the two, for the one refers to praying and the

---

[54] Which takes place at noon on the eve of Passover (14th of Nisan), on which, being a week-day, the eighteen benedictions are still recited, so that the prayer for rain can be inserted in the ninth benediction of the morning prayer. Here, however, we meet with the difficulty that the eighteen benedictions are recited also in the afternoon prayer of the same day (minḥah). Why then should R.

כן סופו מה תחלתו מזכיר אף על פי שאינו שואל
אף סופו מזכיר אף על פי שאינו שואל אמר ליה
אביי בשלמא תחלתו מזכיר דהזכרה רצוי שאלה
היא אלא סופו מאי רצוי שאלה איכא אלא מחוורתא
כדעולא:

אמר רבי אסי אמר רבי יוחנן הלכה כרבי יהודה
אמר ליה רבי זירא לרבי אסי ומי אמר רבי יוחנן
הכי והתנן בשלשה במרחשון שואלין את הגשמים
רבן גמליאל אומר בשבעה בו ואמר רבי אלעזר
הלכה כרבן גמליאל אמר ליה גברא אגברא קא
רמית ואיבעית אימא לא קשיא כאן לשאול כאן

מסרת הש״ס והמדרשים

6 (ר' יוחנן) ירושלמי תענית א' ריש   תענית י' א'. 10 (גברא) בבא קמא
ה״ב. 8 (והתנן) תענית ו' א', י' א';   מ״ג ב'; סנהדרין ו' א', כ״ה א', ל'
בבא מציעא כ״ח א'. 9 (אלעזר)   ב'; חולין נ״ב ב'.

Judah have pronounced the hour of the slaughtering of the
Paschal lamb, which is at noon, as the limit for the insertion? Rabbah tries to meet this difficulty by saying that
just as before the beginning of the rainy season we mention
the rain for some time before we begin to insert the formal
prayer for rain, so at the end of the season we must continue
to mention the rain for some time after we have stopped
praying for it. We thus continue to mention it after the
slaughtering of the Paschal lamb until the Musaf prayer
of the next day.

other to mentioning. But did not R. Johanan
say, whenever one prays for rain one also
mentions it?[55] This statement refers only to
the time of discontinuation. But was not
reference made to both, R. Johanan saying explicitly, when one begins to mention the rain
he begins to pray for it, and when he stops praying for it he stops mentioning it? Nevertheless there is no difficulty, for in the one statement he has reference to *us* (the Babylonians), in
the other to *them* (the Palestinians). Why
such difference? Is it because we have produce in
the field?[56] (Then there should be no difference,
because) they have pilgrims![57] R. Johanan
speaks of the time after the destruction of the
Temple.[58] Now that we have arrived at this
point we can say that both statements have
reference to *them* (Palestinians), and yet there
will be no contradiction, for the one refers to the
time before, and the other to that after the destruction of the Temple.

What is the proper course for us, who keep
two festival days?[59] Rab says, we should begin to mention the rain in the Musaf prayer
(of the first day), omit the mention in the Afternoon, Evening, and Morning prayers, and take it
up again in the Musaf prayer (of the second day).
Samuel, however, said to the scholars (who re-

[55] Which proves that he makes no distinction between
the two as to the time we are to begin or to stop either one.

[56] In Babylon the produce of the field ripened later than
in Palestine. Rain was therefore not desirable until a
little later in the season, when the produce had been gather-

להזכיר והאמר רבי יוחנן במקום ששואל מזכיר
ההוא להפסקה אתמר והא תרוייהו אתמור דאמר
רבי יוחנן התחיל להזכיר מתחיל לשאול פסק
מלשאול פוסק מלהזכיר אלא לא קשיא הא לן
5 והא להו מאי שנא לדידן דאית לן פירי בדברא
לדידהו נמי הא אית להו עולי רגלים כי קאמר
רבי יוחנן בזמן שאין בית המקדש קיים השתא
דאתית להכי הא והא לדידהו ולא קשיא כאן בזמן
שבית המקדש קיים כאן בזמן שאין בית המקדש
10 קיים ואנן ואנן דאית לן תרי יומי היכי עבדינן אמר רב
מתחיל במוספין ופוסק במנחה ערבית ושחרית
וחוזר ומתחיל במוספין אמר להו שמואל פוקו

1 (במקום) ירוש' תענית א' ב'.	7	ירוש' כאן א' א' (דף ס"ג ד' וע'
(בזמן) ירושלמי שם. 11 (במוספין)	ביפה עינים כאן).

---

ed in, and the mention of the rain was to begin accordingly.

[57] For their sake, too, the mentioning of the rain should
have been postponed (see Mishnah above), as it was in
Babylon for the sake of the produce.

[58] When there were no pilgrimages to Jerusalem.

[59] Should we begin to mention on the first day of the
concluding festival (Shemini-'azeret) or on the second?

ported Rab's view): go and say to 'Abba:[60] "After having declared the day holy, art thou going to declare it again a week-day?"[61] Samuel then decided that one should begin to mention the rain in the Musaf prayer and continue to do so in the Afternoon prayer, but omit it in the Evening and Morning prayer and take it up again in the Musaf prayer [fol. 5a]. Raba says: after having once begun mentioning it, one should not stop. So also said R. Sheshet. Rab, too, reversed his opinion, for R. Hananel said in the name of Rab: Beginning with the New Year's day, one should count twenty-one days, in the same way as one counts ten days from New Year to the Day of Atonement, and then begin mentioning the rain, but once having begun, one should not stop. And this is the law.

And He causeth to come down for you, etc. (Joel, 2.23): Said R. Naḥman to R. Isaac: The former rain does not fall in Nisan, but in Marḥeshwan! For a Baraita reads (Sifrē, Deut., §42): The former rain falls in Marḥeshwan and the latter rain in Nisan! "Thus said R. Johan-

---

[60] 'Abba was the real name of Rab. The latter designation was given him as a sign of honor.

[61] Samuel's objection is that by mentioning the rain in the Musaf prayer of the first day of the concluding festival (Shemini-'azeret), as required by Rab, we, *eo ipso*, mark this day as the real holiday (about which the Jews living far from Jerusalem, where the festival days were proclaimed, were in doubt, making the observance of two days necessary). On the other hand, by omitting the reference to rain in the afternoon prayer

ואמרו ליה לאבא לאחר שעשיתו קדש תעשהו חול
אלא אמר שמואל מתחיל במוספין ובמנחה ופוסק
בערבית ושחרית וחוזר ומתחיל במוספין ן רבא אמר ה'
כיון שהתחיל שוב אינו פוסק וכן אמר רב ששת עא
כיון שהתחיל שוב אינו פוסק ואף רב הדר ביה 5
דאמר רב חננאל אמר רב מונה אדם עשרים ואחד
יום כדרך שמונה עשרה ימים מראש השנה ועד יום
הכפורים ומתחיל וכיון שהתחיל שוב אינו פוסק
והלכתא כיון שהתחיל שוב אינו פוסק:
ויורד לכם גשם וכו': אמר ליה רב נחמן לרבי 10
יצחק יורה בניסן הוא יורה במרחשון הוא דתניא
יורה במרחשון ומלקוש בניסן אמר ליה הכי אמר

מסרת הש"ס והמדרשים

11 (דתניא) ספרי עקב מ"ב;   תענית ו' א'.

(minḥah) of the same day, we again cast a doubt on its
holiness, declaring it, as it were, a weekday. Samuel
therefore requires the reference to be made also in the afternoon prayer. In the evening prayer (maʿarib), the time
which, according to the Jewish calendar, belongs to the next
day, as well as in the following morning prayer, the insertion may be omitted and then taken up again in the Musaf
prayer to be continued until the end of the season.

49

an," replied R. Isaac, "this verse (Joel, 2.23) has proven true (only) in the days of Joel the son of Petuel, for it is written (Joel, 1.4): 'That which the palmerworm hath left hath the locust eaten,' etc. Now there is a tradition that in that year Adar had passed without rainfall, and the first rain did not appear until the first of Nisan. The Prophet then said to the Israelites: Go out and sow! But they replied: Should one who has a Kab[62] of wheat or two Kabs of barley, eat it and live, or sow it and die? The prophet said: Nevertheless go out and sow! They then went out and sowed. Thereupon a miracle happened, that all the grain which was hidden (by mice) in the walls and in crevices (by ants) and in the holes of ants, appeared before their eyes. Again they went out and sowed on the second, third, and fourth (of Nisan); on the fifth there was the second rainfall and on the sixteenth they offered the 'Omer. Thus, produce that used to ripen in six months ripened in eleven days, and the 'Omer which was usually offered from the crop that grew six months was now offered from one that grew in eleven days! With reference to that generation the Psalmist says (Ps., 126. 5–6): 'They that sow in tears shall reap in joy. Though he goeth on his way weeping, bearing forth the seed; he shall come again with joy, bringing his sheaves with him.'"

What does "he goeth on his way weeping"

[62] Κάβος, a measure holding about the third of a peck; comp. II Kings, 6.25; B. Zuckermann, *Das jüdische Maass-system*, Breslau, 1867, p. 37.

רבי יוחנן בימי יואל בן פתואל נתקיים מקרא זה
דכתיב יתר הגזם אכל הארבה וגו' אמרו אותה
שנה יצא אדר ולא ירדו גשמים וירדה להם רביעה
ראשונה באחד בניסן אמר להם נביא לישראל

5 צאו וזרעו אמרו לו מי שיש לו קב חטים או קבים
שעורין יאכלנו ויחיה או יזרענו וימות אמר להם
אף על פי כן צאו וזרעו יצאו וזרעו נעשה להם נס
ונתגלה להם מה שבכתלים ומה שבסדקים ומה
שבחורי נמלים יצאו וזרעו שני ושלישי ורביעי וירדה

10 להם רביעה שניה בחמשה בניסן והקריבו עמר
בששה עשר בניסן נמצאת תבואה הגדלה בששה
חדשים גדלה באחד עשר יום ונמצא עמר הקרב
מתבואה של ששה חדשים קרב מתבואה של אחד
עשר יום ועל אותו הדור הוא אומר הזורעים

15 בדמעה ברנה יקצרו הלוך ילך ובכה נשא משך
הזרע בא יבא ברנה נשא אלמתיו מאי הלוך ילך

תורה אור   מסרת הש ס והמדרשים
2 יואל א' ד'.   14 תהלים קכ"ו   11 (תבואה) ירוש' תענית א' ב';
                                שקלים ו' ב'.   ה'–ו'.

indicate? Said R. Judah, it indicates that
the ox on his way sowing was crying hungrily,
but on his way back he was already eating the
young green from the furrows. What does "he
shall come again with joy, bringing his sheaves
with him" indicate? Said R. Ḥisda or, as some
say, it was taught in a Baraita, it indicates that
in that year the stalk was one span long and the
ear two spans.

R. Naḥman asked R. Isaac, what is the meaning of the verse (II Kings, 8. 1): "For God
hath called for a famine and it shall also come
upon the land seven years?" What did the
people eat during those seven years? "Thus
said R. Johanan," R. Isaac replied, "the first year
they ate what there was in the house, the second
year they ate what was in the field, the third
they ate the meat of clean animals, the fourth
that of unclean animals, the fifth that of abomi-
nations and reptiles, the sixth the flesh of their
sons and daughters, the seventh that of their
own arms, so as to fulfill what is said (Is.,
9. 19): 'They shall eat every man the flesh of
his own arm.'"

R. Naḥman further asked R. Isaac, how do you
explain the verse (Hos., 11. 9): "The Holy One
in the midst of thee, and I will not enter into
the city?"[63] Surely it can not mean, because
the Holy One is in the midst of thee, I shall not
enter into the city?! "Thus said R. Johanan,"

[63] So also the Revised Version. The "New Translation,"
Philadelphia, 1917, translates: I will not come in *fury;*
so also *Tosafot, ad locum.*

ובכה נשא משך הזרע אמר רב יהודה אמר רב
שור כשהיה זורע בהליכה היה בוכה ובחזירתו
אוכל חזיז מן התלם מאי נשא אלמתיו אמר רב
הסדא ואמרי לה במתניתא תנא אותה שנה קנה
5 זרת שבלת זרתים היתה:

אמר ליה רב נחמן לרבי יצחק מאי דכתיב כי
קרא ה' לרעב וגם בא אל הארץ שבע שנים בהנך
שבע שנים מאי אכול אמר ליה הכי אמר רבי יוחנן
שנה ראשונה אכלו מה שבבתים שניה מה שבשדות
10 וכרמים שלישית אכלו בשר בהמה טהורה רביעית
בשר בהמה טמאה חמשית בשר שקצים ורמשים
ששית בשר בניהם ובנותיהם שביעית בשר זרועותיהם
לקיים מה שנאמר איש בשר זרעו יאכלו:

אמר ליה רב נחמן לרבי יצחק מאי דכתיב
15 בקרבך קדוש ולא אבוא בעיר משום דבקרבך
קדוש לא אבוא בעיר אמר ליה הכי אמר רבי יוחנן

מסרת הש"ס והמדרשים	תורה אור
1 (אמר) מדרש תהלים קכ"ב (אך	6 מ"ב ח' א'. 13 ישעיה ט' י"ט.
המזמור ההוא עד מזמור קל"ח	15 הושע י"א ט'.
לקוח מהילקוט ע' באבער שם).	

53

R. Isaac replied, "the Holy One, blessed be He, meant to say: I will not enter into the heavenly Jerusalem until I can enter into the earthly Jerusalem."[64] But is there a heavenly Jerusalem? Yes, for it is written (Ps., 122.3): "Jerusalem, that art builded as a city that is compact together."[65]

R. Naḥman further asked R. Isaac, how do you explain the verse (Jer. 10. 8): "But they are altogether brutish and foolish: the vanities by which they are instructed are but a stock"? "Thus said R. Johanan," replied R. Isaac, "there is one thing that sweeps the wicked into Gehenna,[66] and that is idolatry; for Scripture has here: 'the vanities by which they are instructed are but a stock,' and elsewhere (*ib.*, 10, 15): 'They are vanity, a work of delusion.'"[67]

[64] Jerusalem, it was taught, had its prototype in heaven, and the two cities were situated exactly opposite one another; comp. Jerushalmi, *Berakot*, iv. 5; בית קדשי הקדשים שלמטן מכוון כנגד בית קדש הקדשים שלמעלן. The meaning of the verse thus is that God will not enter the heavenly Jerusalem until Jerusalem on earth is rebuilt. The "Holy One," accordingly, does not refer to God, but to the Holy City of Jerusalem.

[65] According to the commentary of R. Gershom the proof is derived from the word יחדו, together, which indicates two, but Rashi takes it from שחברה לו (compact), and the verse is accordingly to be translated: Jerusalem that art builded like thy companion (counterpart in heaven).

[66] R. Johanan plays on the word יבערו = brutish, which he translates as if it were the *pu'al* of בער, to remove, sweep away. It should be remarked that the Talmud in

אמר הקדוש ברוך הוא לא אבוא בירושלם של
מעלה עד שאבוא בירושלם של מטה ומי איכא
ירושלם למעלה אין דכתיב ירושלם הבנויה
כעיר שחברה לה יחדו:

אמר ליה רב נחמן לרבי יצחק מאי דכתיב
ובאחת יבערו ויכסלו מוסר הבלים עץ הוא אמר
ליה הכי אמר רבי יוחנן אחת היא שמבערת רשעים
לגיהנם ומאי היא עבודה זרה כתיב הכא מוסר
הבלים עץ הוא   וכתיב התם   הבל המה מעשה
תעתעים:

תורה אור	מסרת הש״ס והמדרשים
3 תהלים קכ״ב ג׳. 6 ירמיה י׳ ח׳.	1 (של מעלה) ירושלמי ברכות ד׳
9 ירמיה י׳ ט״ו.	ה׳.

playing upon a word and thus imputing a new meaning to
it, does not care whether or not the rest of the verse can be
explained in accordance with that meaning. Indeed,
in most cases this becomes grammatically or syntactically
impossible. In the case before us, however, the translation
might read: By one thing are they swept into the Gehenna
and proved foolish: by the instruction of idols that are
but a stock.

[67] In Jeremiah 10. 15, the reference of "vanity" to
idolatry is obvious; "vanities" in verse 8 must therefore
be taken in the same sense.

R. Naḥman further asked R. Isaac, how do you explain the verse (*ibid.*, 2.13): "For My people have committed two evils: They have forsaken Me, the fountain of living waters?" Only two did they commit? Did they not commit also twenty-two other evils? Or did He remit twenty-two?[68] "Thus said R. Johanan," replied R. Isaac, "(they committed) one that [fol. 5b] is equal to two, and that is idolatry, for it is written (*ibid.*, 2. 10–11): 'For pass over to the isles of the Kittites, and see; and send unto Kedar, and consider diligently, etc. Hath a nation changed its gods, which yet are no gods? But My people hath changed its glory for that which doth not profit.'" Concerning this it is taught in a Baraita: The Kittites worship water and the Kedarites worship fire, and although they know that water quenches fire,[69] they never changed their gods, "but My people have changed their glory for that which doth not profit."

R. Naḥman further asked R. Isaac, how do you explain the verse (I Sam., 8. 1): "And it came to pass, when Samuel was old"? Did Samuel become old at all? Indeed, Samuel only reached the age of 52, for it is said (Mo'ed Ḳaṭan, 28a) that if one dies at the age of 52,

---

[68] The earliest commentators differ as to the meaning of the number 24. Some of them think that there are 24 sins enumerated in this chapter (Jer. 2). Others find 24 sins mentioned in Ezekiel 22. Still others take it as an allusion to the 24 books of the canon, the Israelites having transgressed all the laws contained therein. The opinion is also quoted that 24 is merely a round number, for which

אמר ליה רב נחמן לרבי יצחק מאי דכתיב כי
שתים רעות עשה עמי תרתי עבוד עשרין ותרתי
לא עבוד או דלמא עשרין ותרתי שביק להו אמר
ליה הכי אמר רבי יוחנן אחת היא׀ששקולה ה'
 ע"ב
5 כשתים ומאי ניהי עבודה זרה דכתיב כי עברו איי
כתיים וראו וקדר שלחו והתבוננו מאד ההימיר גוי
אלהים והמה לא אלהים ועמי המיר כבודו בלא
יועיל תנא כתיים עובדים למים וקדרים עובדים
לאש ואף על פי שיודעין שהמים מכבין את האש
10 לא המירו אלהיהם ועמי המיר כבודו בלא יועיל:
אמר ליה רב נחמן לרבי יצחק מאי דכתיב ויהי
כאשר זקן שמואל ומי קש שמואל כולי האי והא בר
חמשין ותרתין שנין הוה דאמר מר מת בחמשים

תורה אור	מסרת הש"ס והמדרשים
1 ירמיה ב' י"ג. 5 ירמיה ב' י'.	2 (שתים) ירושלמי סוכה ה' ה'
10 ירמיה ב' י"א. 11 ש"א ח' א'.	(ע"ה ג'); שמ"ר מ"ב ח' (וע' ויק"ר
	ל"ג ג' וקה"ר א' י"ג וג' י');
שהש"ר א' פסוק ו' אות ב'. 12 (שמואל) מועד קטן כ"ח א';	
ירושלמי ברכות ד' א'; תענית ד' א'; בכורים ב' א'; שמחות ג' ח';	
מדרש שמואל ב' פסוק ט'.	

there are some analogies in the Talmud; comp. for the whole,
Aruch, ed. Kohut, *s. v.* עסר (עשר).

[69] And vice versa, fire dries up water, the destructibility
of both thus being evident.

he has attained to the age reached by Samuel the Ramathite. "Thus said R. Johanan," replied R. Isaac, "Samuel grew old prematurely, for it is said (*ibid.*, 15. 11): 'It repenteth me that I have set up Saul to be king, for he is turned back from following Me, and hath not performed My commandments. And it grieved Samuel; and he cried unto the Lord all night,' saying: Master of the world! Thou hast declared me equal to both Moses and Aaron, for it is written (Ps., 99. 6): 'Moses and Aaron among His priests, and Samuel among them that call upon His name.' Now just as their work was not destroyed during their life-time,[70] so should my work not be destroyed during my life-time. The Holy One, blessed be He, then said to Himself, what shall I do? Shall I cause Saul to die? Samuel will not let me. Shall I cause Samuel to die? Seeing he is still young, people will speak ill of him.[71] Shall I spare both Saul and Samuel? The time for the kingdom of the house of David has arrived, and the term set for one kingdom must not overlap that of another even by a hair's breadth. Immediately Samuel was overtaken by old age, and hence it is written (I Sam., 22. 6): 'And Saul was sitting in Gibeah, under the tamarisk tree in Ramah.' Now what relation is there

---

[70] Joshua, the pupil of Moses, was, according to the Talmud ('*Erubin* 54b), also a pupil of Aaron and survived both. Samuel therefore prayed that Saul, too, whom he had made his successor, should survive him.

[71] Thinking that he died young in punishment for some

ושתים זו היא מיתתו של שמואל הרמתי אמר
ליה הכי אמר רבי יוחנן זקנה הקפיץ עליו
הקדוש ברוך הוא דכתיב נחמתי כי המלכתי
את שאול למלך כי שב מאחרי ואת דברי לא
5 הקים ויחר לשמואל ויזעק אל ה' כל הלילה
אמר לפניו רבונו של עולם שקלתני כמשה
ואהרן דכתיב משה ואהרן בכהניו ושמואל בקראי
שמו מה משה ואהרן לא בטלו מעשי ידיהם בחייהם
אף אני לא יבטלו מעשי ידי בחיי אמר הקדוש ברוך
10 הוא היכי אעביד לימות שאול לא קא שביק שמואל
לימות שמואל אדזוטר מרני כולי עלמא אבתריה
לא לימות לא שאול ולא שמואל כבר הגיעה מלכות
בית דוד ואין מלכות נוגעת בחברתה אפילו כמלא
נימא מיד הקפיץ עליו זקנה והיינו דכתיב ושאול
15 יושב בגבעה תחת האשל ברמה וכי מה ענין גבעה

תורה אור

3 ש"א ט"ו י"א.   7 תהלים צ"ט ו'.
11 ש"א כ"ב ו'.

מסרת הש"ס והמדרשים

13 (מלכות) ברכות מ"ח ב'; שבת
ל' א'; יומא ל"ח ב'; מועד קטן כ"ח
א'; שהש"ר ג' ה' ה'.   15 (גבעה)
תוספתא סוטה י"א י"ב.

misdeed.   In order to forestall such suspicion, he was made
to look old, his hair becoming prematurely gray.

between Gibeah and Ramah?[72] The idea therefore is that what had enabled Saul to sit (as king)
in Gibeah two and a half years was the prayer of
Samuel the Ramathite." But is the life of one
man set aside (cut short) on account of that of
another?[73] Yes, for R. Samuel b. Naḥamani said
in the name of R. Jonathan: What is the meaning
of the verse (Hos., 6. 5): "Therefore have I
hewed them by the prophets; I have slain them
by the words of My mouth"? It is not said by
the works of their hands[74], but "by the words of
My mouth", which proves that one man may
be set aside on account of another.

R. Naḥman and R. Isaac were dining
together; said R. Naḥman to R. Isaac, tell me
something haggadic, to which the latter replied:
Thus said R. Johanan, one must not converse
while eating, because the windpipe might open
before the gullet and thus endanger one's life.
After they had dined, R. Naḥman said again:
Tell me something haggadic. R. Isaac then
replied: Thus said R. Johanan, our father
Jacob did not die. R. Naḥman thereupon asked,
was it for nought that the embalmers embalmed
and the wailers wailed? R. Isaac replied: Thus
said R. Johanan, I am only interpreting a verse
(Jer., 30. 10):[75] "Fear thou not, O Jacob My

[72] Gibeah is in the land of the tribe of Benjamin, while
Ramah, in the opinion of the Talmud, is in the Mountains
of Ephraim.

[73] As was the life of Samuel on account of David.

[74] That is, by their own sins, but because I have so decreed

אצל רמה אלא לומר לך מי גרם לשאול שישב בגבעה
שתי שנים ומחצה תפלתו של שמואל הרמתי ברמה
ומי מדחי גברא מקמי גברא אין דאמר רבי שמואל
בר נחמני אמר רבי יונתן מאי דכתיב על כן חצבתי
בנביאים הרגתים באמרי פי במעשי ידיהם לא
נאמר אלא באמרי פי אלמא מדחי גברא מקמי
גברא:

רב נחמן ורבי יצחק הוו יתבי בסעודתא אמר
ליה רב נחמן לרבי יצחק לימא לן מר מלתא
דאגדתא אמר ליה הכי אמר רבי יוחנן אין מסיחין
בסעודה שמא יקדים קנה לושט ויבא לידי סכנד
בתר דסעוד אמר ליה הכי אמר רבי יוחנן יעקב
אבינו לא מת אמר ליה וכי בכדי חנטו חנטיא
וספדו ספדיא אמר ליה הכי אמר רבי יוחנן מקרא
אני דורש שנאמר ואתה אל תירא עבדי יעקב נאם

תורה אור   מסרת הש"ס והמדרשים
4 הושע ו' ה'.   15 ירמיה ל' י'.   11 (בסעודה) ירוש' ברכות ו' ו'.

("by the words of My mouth") that the terms of two
kings should not overlap one another.

[75] Which may mean: You need not take it so literally.

servant, saith the Lord; neither be dismayed, O
Israel, for, lo, I will save thee from afar, and thy
seed from the land of their captivity." This verse
compares Jacob to his seed—just as his seed will
then be alive, so will he be alive.

*Dixit R. Isaac: Quicumque dicit Rahab, Rahab,
profluvio genitali statim afficitur. Dixit R. Naḥman: Ego dixi neque tamen afficiebar! "Ego
eum in mente habui," respondit R. Isaac, "qui
eam intus et in cute novit."*[76]

When R. Naḥman and R. Isaac were taking leave
of one another, the former said to the latter,
pray, bless me. R. Isaac replied, let me tell
thee a parable: To what can thy case be compared? To that of a man who was walking in
a desert, suffering fatigue, hunger and thirst, and
then found a tree, whose shade was pleasant
and whose fruit was sweet, while a brook
flowed by it. He rested beneath its shade, ate
from its fruit and drank from its water. When
he was about to leave, he said: O Tree, O Tree!
What blessing shall I bestow upon thee? Shall
I wish thee that thy shade be pleasant?—thy
shade is pleasant; shall I wish thee that thy
fruit be sweet?—thy fruit is sweet; shall I wish
thee that a brooklet may flow by thee?—a brooklet does flow by thee! Therefore I say, may
it be the will of God that all shoots taken from
thee [fol. 6a] be like thee!—So in thy case.
What can I wish thee? Shall I wish thee
learning?—thou hast learning; wealth? thou

[76] It is not at all impossible that Raḥab here, as known
from the Bible, was a general nick-name for every lewd

ה' ואל תחת ישראל כי הנני מושיעך מרחוק ואת
זרעך מארץ שבים מקיש הוא לזרעו מה זרעו בחיים
אף הוא בחיים:

אמר רבי יצחק כל האומר רחב רחב מיד נקרה

5 אמר ליה רב נחמן הא אנא אמינא ולא איכפת לי
אמר ליה כי קאמינא ביודעה ומכירה כי הוו
מיפטרי מהדדי אמר ליה לברכן מר אמר ליה
אמשול לך משל למה הדבר דומה לאדם שהיה
מהלך במדבר והיה עיף ורעב וצמא ומצא אילן

10 שצלו נאה ופרותיו מתוקין ואמת המים עוברת
תחתיו ישב בצלו ואכל מפרותיו ושתה ממימיו
וכשבקש לילך אמר אילן במה אברכך אם אומר
לך שיהא צלך נאה הרי צלך נאה שיהו פרותיך
מתוקין הרי פרותיך מתוקין שתהא אמת המים

15 עוברת תחתיך הרי אמת המים עוברת תחתיך
ע״א אלא יהי רצון שכל נטיעות שינטעו ממך | יהיו
כמותך אף אתה במה אברכך אם בתורה הרי תורה

מסרת הש״ס והמדרשים

4 (רחב) מגלה ט״ו א'.   8 (משל)   במדבר רבה ב' י״ב.

woman, and R. Isaac meant to say that one should not,
in a spirit of levity, so address a woman of the street, as
it may awaken in him salacious thoughts.

hast wealth; children? thou hast children!
Therefore I say, may it be God's will that all
thy offspring be like thee![77]

Our Rabbis have taught (Sifrē, Deut. § 42):
The former rain is called *yoreh* (Deut., 11.14), because it teaches the people to plaster their roofs,
to gather in their fruit, and to make all other
preparations for the winter. Another opinion[78]
is that it is so called because it falls gently, not
vehemently. Still another opinion is: because
it saturates the earth and waters it to its very
depth, as it is said (Ps., 65. 11): "Watering her
ridges abundantly, settling down the furrows
thereof. Thou makest her soft with showers;
Thou blessest the growth thereof." But is it not
possible that it is so called because of its damaging
effect in making the fruit drop (from the trees)
and in washing away the seeds? No, because
Scripture has here also *malḳōsh* (the latter rain),
and just as the latter rain comes as a blessing,
so also the former rain. But may not the latter
rain be called *malḳōsh* because it causes the
houses to fall, breaks the trees, and brings the
crickets? No, because Scripture has in the same
verse also *yoreh* (the former rain), and just as
the former rain comes as a blessing, so also the
latter rain. But whence do you know that
the former rain is a blessing? From the following verse (Joel 2. 23): "Be glad then, ye children

[77] It should be noted that R. Naḥman was chief justice of
Babylonian Jewry and, by his marriage with the daughter
of the Exilarch, became very wealthy and influential; see
J. E., s. v.

[78] All these interpretations are based on artificial con-

אם בעשר הרי עשר אם בבנים הרי בנים אלא
יהי רצון שכל צאצאי מעיך יהיו כמותך:

תנו רבנן יורה שמורה את הבריות להטיח גגותיהן
ולהכניס פרותיהן ולעשות כל צרכיהן דבר אחר

5 יורה שיורד בנחת ואינו יורד בזעף דבר אחר יורה
שמרוה את הארץ ומשקה עד תהום שנאמר תלמיה
רוה נחת גדודיה ברביבים תמוגגנה צמחה תברך
או אינו אומר יורה אלא שמשיר את הפרות ומשטיף
את הזרעים תלמוד לומר מלקוש מה מלקוש

10 לברכה אף יורה לברכה או אינו אומר מלקוש
אלא שמפיל את הבתים ומשבר את האילנות ומעלה
את הסקאי תלמוד לומר יורה מה יורה לברכה
אף מלקוש לברכה ויורה גופיה מנלן דכתיב ובני

מסרת הש״ס והמדרשים   תורה אור

3 (ת״ר) ספרי עקב מ״ב; מדרש   6 תהלים ס״ה י״א. 13 יואל ב׳
תנאים 35 (וע׳ ירושלמי ברכות ט׳   כ״ג.
ב׳ דף י״ג סוף עמוד ג׳).

nections of the word *yoreh* (יורה, the former rain) with
Hebrew roots meaning either to teach (תורה, from ירה)
or to come down, descend (ירד), or to saturate (רוה), or to
throw down (ירה).

of Zion, and rejoice in the Lord your God; for
He giveth you the former rain in just measure."
Why is the latter rain called *malḳōsh?* Said
R. Ḥanilai b. 'Idi in the name of Samuel, be-
cause it crushes the stubbornness of the Israelites.
A Tanna of the school of R. Ishmael reads,
because it fills the grain in its stalks. Another
Baraita reads, because it falls upon both the
ears and the stalks.[79]

Our Rabbis have taught (Sifrē, *ibid.* 42): *Yoreh*
is the rain that falls in Marḥeshwan, and *malḳosh*
is the rain that falls in Nisan. You say *yoreh*
is in Marḥeshwan, is it not the rain that
falls in Kislew? No, Scripture says (Deut.,
11. 14): "In its season, the former rain (*yoreh*),
and the latter rain (*malḳosh*)." Now just as
malḳosh is that one only which falls in its season
(Nisan), so *yoreh* is that one only which falls in
its season (Marḥeshwan).

Another Baraita reads: *Yoreh* is the rain that
falls in Marḥeshwan and *malḳosh* the one that
falls in Nisan; this is the view of R. Meir, but
the other Sages say, *yoreh* is the rain of Kislew.
Who are the other Sages? Said R. Ḥisda, they
are R. Jose,[80] for we read (Tosefta, Ta'anit, ch.
1): When is the time of the fructification-rain-

[79] Here again the word *malkosh* (מלקוש, latter rain) is
artificially explained as מל קשיות (crushing stubbornness,
because when the rain comes late, the Israelites are
brought to prayer and repentance), or ממלא קשין (filling
stalks), or as מלילות (ears) and קשין (stalks).

[80] The plural, "sages," is technical and may apply also
to an individual.

ציון גילו ושמחו בה' אלהיכם כי נתן לכם את
המורה לצדקה:

מאי מלקוש אמר רב חנילאי בר אידי אמר
שמואל שמל קשיותיהן של ישראל דבי רבי ישמעאל
5 תנא שממלא תבואה בקשיה במתניתא תנא שיורד
על המלילות ועל הקשין:

תנו רבנן יורה במרחשון ומלקוש בניסן אתה
אומר יורה במרחשון או אינו אלא בכסלו תלמוד
לומר בעתו יורה ומלקוש מה מלקוש בעתו אף
10 יורה בעתו תניא אידך יורה במרחשון ומלקוש בניסן
דברי רבי מאיר וחכמים אומרים יורה בכסלו מאן
חכמים אמר רב חסדא רבי יוסי היא דתניא מאימתי

תורה אור

9 דברים י"א י"ד.

מסרת הש"ס והמדרשים

7 (ת"ר) ספרי שם.   10 (תניא)
ויק"ר ל"ה י"ב.   11 (מאן) לקמן
כ"ו ב'; ערובין פ"ג א'; יבמות מ"ו א'; ק"ה ב'; כתובות ו' ב', ל"ג ב'; קדושין
ט"ו ב'; גטין כ"ב א', מ"ו ב', ע"ו א'; ב"ק ע"א א'; ב"מ ס"ב ב'; ע"ז ז'
ב'; סנהדרין ס"ו א'; שבועות ל"ו א'; הוריות ג' א', ה' ב'; זבחים מ"ב
א'; מנחות פ"ח ב'; בכורות י"ד ב', י"ז א', ל' א'; חולין ע"ט א'; תמורה
ל' ב', ל"ג ב'; נדה ח' ב', נ"ב ב'.   12 (דתניא) נדרים ס"ג א'; ירוש' תענית
א' ג'; תוספתא תענית א' ג'.

fall? The earlier one on the third of Marḥeshwan, the intermediate on the seventh thereof, and the late on the seventeenth thereof; this is the view of R. Meir; R. Judah says, on the seventh, the seventeenth, and the twenty-third thereof; R. Jose says, on the seventeenth and the twenty-third of Marḥeshwan and on the first of Kislew. In accordance with this R. Jose also said that individuals should not fast for rain before the first of Kislew has come. Said R. Ḥisda, the law follows R. Judah.

'Amemar transmits the statement of R. Ḥisda as referring to the Mishnah (above, p. 2): On the third of Marḥeshwan we begin to pray for rain, R. Gamaliel says, on the seventh of that month. Hereupon R. Ḥisda remarked: The law follows R. Gamaliel.

Whose opinion is represented in the following Baraita (Tos., *ibid.*): R. Simeon b. Gamaliel says, if rain falls seven days without interruption, I consider it either as the combined first and second or as the combined second and third rainfalls? It is the opinion of R. Jose.[81]

It is quite proper to set a date for the first rainfall, because from that date on we are to pray for rain; it is also proper to fix a date for the third rainfall, because from that date on

[81] Because according to the aforementioned opinion of R. Jose only is there a period of seven days (including the days of the rainfall) between *each* rainfall, while according to the views of R. Meir and R. Judah, at least some of the intervals are either shorter or longer.

זמנה של רביעה בכירה בשלשה במרחשון בינונית
בשבעה בו אפילה בשבעה עשר בו דברי רבי
מאיר רבי יהודה אומר בשבעה ובשבעה עשר
ובעשרים ושלשה רבי יוסי אומר בשבעה עשר
5 ובעשרים ושלשה ובראש חדש כסלו וכן היה רבי
יוסי אומר אין היחידים מתענין עד שיגיע ראש
חדש כסלו אמר רב חסדא הלכה כרבי יהודה:

אמימר מתני לה להא שמעתא דרב חסדא אהא
דתנן בשלשה במרחשון שואלין את הגשמים רבן
10 גמליאל אומר בשבעה בו אמר רב חסדא הלכה
כרבן גמליאל:

כמאן אזלא הא דתניא רבן שמעון בן גמליאל
אומר גשמים שירדו שבעה ימים בזה אחר זה ולא
פסקו אתה מונה בהן רביעה ראשונה ושניה ושלישית
15 כמאן כרבי יוסי:

בשלמא רביעה ראשונה   לשאול שלישית

מסרת הש"ס והמדרשים

9 (דתנן) לקמן ד' ב',י' א'; ב"מ   א'); נדרים ח' ו' (מ"א א');
כ"ח א'. 12 (דתניא) ירושלמי כאן   תוספתא כאן א' ד'; שביעית
א' ג' (מ"ד א'); שביעית ט' ז' (ל"ט   ז' י"ח. 16 (לשאול) לקמן י"ט א'.

69

distinguished individuals begin to fast;[82] but
what is the object in fixing a date for the second
rainfall? Said R. Zera: It is of importance for
vows, for we read [fol. 6b] in a Mishnah (Nedarim,
62b): If one sets the rainfall as the time limit to
a vow, he must keep his vow until the appearance
of the *second* rainfall. R. Zebid said: It is of importance with reference to *olives*, for we read
(Peah,8.1): From what time on is everybody free
to take the gleanings,[83] the forgotten sheaves,[84]
and the corners of the field?[85] From the time the
Gropers have gone. Fallen single grapes and small
bunches of grapes[86] may be taken from the time
the poor have searched the place more than once.
Olives[87] may be taken after the second rainfall.

What is meant by "Gropers"? R. Johanan
said, old men walking on staffs; Resh Laḳish
said, the last gleaners.

R. Papa said: The date (for the second rainfall)
is of importance as regards walking through
private property, for we read (Baba Ḳamma, 81a):
One may walk through private property until
the second rainfall.[88] R. Naḥman b. Isaac said:
It is of importance with regard to the removal
of the fruits of the Sabbatical year, for we read
(Shebi'it, 9.7): Until what time are we allowed
to use or destroy[89] the straw and stubble of the

[82] See the Mishnah, above, p. 4.
[83] Lev., 19. 9.
[84] Deut., 24. 19.
[85] Lev., 19. 9.
[86] Lev., 19. 10.
[87] Deut., 24. 20.

להתענות אלא שניה למאי אמר רבי זירא לנדרים

^{ו'} דתנן ׀ הנודר עד הגשמים עד שתרד רביעה שניה
^{ע״ב}

רב זביד אמר לזיתים דתנן מאימתי כל אדם מותרין

בלקט ובשכחה ובפאה משילכו הנמושות בפרט

5 ובעוללות משילכו עניים בכרם ויבאו בזיתים

משתרד רביעה שניה מאי נמושות אמר רבי יוחנן

סבי דאזלי אתיגדא ריש לקיש אמר לקוטי דבתר

לקוטי רב פפא אמר להלך בשבילי הרשות דאמר

מר מהלכים בשבילי הרשות עד שתרד רביעה

10 שניה רב נחמן בר יצחק אמר לבער שביעית דתנן

עד מתי נהנין ושורפין בתבן ובקש של שביעית עד

מסרת הש״ס והמדרשים

2 (הנודר) שביעית פ״ט ט״ז; נדרים	10 (דתנן) שביעית שם. (ושם
ס״ב ב'. 3 (דתנן) פאה פ״ח מ״א;	הגירסא מאימתי ועיי״ש בר״ש
ב״מ כ״א. 9 (מהלכים) ב״ק	ורא״ש וב ,משנה ראשונה' שבמשניות
פ״א א'; ירושלמי ב״ב ה' א'.	הגדולות דפוס ראם).

---

[88] After that time the seed begins to sprout, and walking
upon the field would cause damage.

[89] The destruction of the produce of the Sabbatical
year was forbidden; see the detailed discussions of this
matter in the commentaries on the Mishnah *Shebi'it*, ix, 7.

Sabbatical year? Until the second rainfall, as it is written (Lev., 25. 7): "And for thy cattle and for the beasts that are in thy land, shall all the increase thereof be for food." This means to say that as long as the beasts find food in the field, you may feed your domestic animals from what there is in the house, but when there is nothing left in the field for the beasts,[90] you must also stop feeding the cattle from what is in the house.

Why is the rainfall called *rebi'ah* (fructification)? Said R. 'Abahu, because it fructifies the soil. This agrees with R. Judah, who said that the rain is the husband of the soil, as it is said (Isaiah, 55.10): "For as the rain cometh down and the snow from heaven, and returneth not thither, except it water the earth, and make it bring forth and bud."

R. 'Abahu further said: The first rainfall is satisfactory if there is enough of it to enter the ground to the depth of a handbreadth; the second is satisfactory when the soil is fit to be used for sealing the mouth of a cask. R. Ḥisda said: If there is rainfall enough to make the soil fit to be used for sealing the mouth of a cask, the verse in Deuteronomy (11.17): "He will shut up (the heavens)," etc., has no application. R. Ḥisda further said: If rain fell before the reading of the verse just mentioned in the Shema', the verse in question no longer has application. Said 'Abbayi, this applies to the Shema' read in

---

[90] Which is the case after the second rainfall, when everything left in the field rots and decays.

שתרד רביעה שניה מאי טעמא דכתיב ולבהמתך
ולחיה אשר בארצך תהיה כל תבואתה לאכול כל
זמן שחיה אוכלת מן השדה האכל לבהמתך מן
הבית כלה לחיה מן השדה כלה לבהמתך מן הבית:

מאי לשון רביעה אמר רבי אבהו שרובעת את
הקרקע כדרב יהודה דאמר רב יהודה מטרא
בעלה דארעא שנאמר כי כאשר ירד הגשם והשלג
מן השמים ושמה לא ישוב כי אם הרוה את הארץ
והולידה והצמיחה:

אמר רבי אבהו רביעה ראשונה כדי שתרד
בקרקע טפח שניה כדי לגוף פי חבית אמר רב
חסדא גשמים שירדו כדי לגוף פי חבית אין בהן
משום ועצר ואמר רב חסדא גשמים שירדו קודם
ועצר אין בהן משום ועצר אמר אביי לא אמרן

מסרת הש"ס והמדרשים   תורה אור

1 ויקרא כ"ה ז'.   7 ישעיה נ"ה י'.   2 (כל זמן) ספרא בהר א' א'.
מכדרשב"י 157 ; פסחים נ"ב ב';נדה
נ"א ב'; ירושלמי שביעית ט' ב' (ל"ח ד').   5 (שרובעת) ירושלמי כאן א'
ג' (ס"ד ב'); ברכות ט' ג' (י"ד א'); שביעית ט' ז'; נדרים ח' ו'.
7 (בעלה) ע' פדר"א סוף פ"ה ומדרש תהלים קי"ז סוף סימן א'.
11 (טפח) תוספתא כאן א' ד'; ירושלמי כאן א' ג'; ברכות ט' ב';
ב"ר י"ג י"ג, ט"ז; לקמן כ"ה ב'.

73

the evening, but if rain falls before the reading
of the Shema' in the morning, the verse in question still has application, for R. Samuel, son
of R. Isaac, said (Berakot, 59a): Those morning
clouds have no real value, as it is written (Hos.,
6.4): "Your goodness is as a morning cloud, and
as the dew that early passeth away." Said R.
Papa to 'Abbayi: But do not people say: "If there
is rain at the opening of the doors (in the morning)
—lay down thy bag, O ass-driver, and sleep"?[91]
That is no contradiction, for the proverb refers
to a case when the rain pours down from a heavy
cloud, while R. Samuel refers to a case when
the rain comes from a light cloud.

Said R. Ḥisda: Auspicious is the year whose
Ṭēbēt is a widow (without rain).[92] Some say
this is so because in that case the fields do not
have to lie waste;[93] others say, because the grain
of such a year will not be subject to blast. But
did not R. Ḥisda say: Auspicious is the year
whose Ṭēbēt is slushy (rainy)? This is no contradiction, for in the one case he has in mind
a year in which there was rain previously,[94] in
the other a year in which there was no rain
during the previous months.

R. Ḥisda further said: If rain falls in some
parts of the country but not in others, the verse,

[91] Because it is going to rain all day long, bringing
about plenty.

[92] See above, the saying of R. Judah: Rain is the husband
of the field.

[93] While if Ṭebet is rainy, the people are prevented from
cultivating the soil. תרביצא here is probably the same as

אלא קודם ועצר דאורתא אבל קודם ועצר דצפרא
יש בהן משום ועצר דאמר רב שמואל בר רב יצחק
הני עניני דצפרא לית בהו מששא דכתיב וחסדכם
כענן בקר וכטל משכים הלך אמר ליה רב פפא
לאביי והא אמרי אינשי מטרא במפתח בבי בר ⁵
חמרא מוך שקיך וגני לא קשיא הא דאתא בעיבא
הא דאתא בעננא:

אמר רב חסדא טבא שתא דטבת ארמלתא
איכא דאמרי דלא ביירי תרביצי ואיכא דאמרי
דלא שקיל שודפנא והאמר רב חסדא טבא שתא ¹⁰
דטבת מנוולתא לא קשיא הא דאתא מטרא מעקרא
הא דלא אתא:

ואמר רב חסדא גשמים שירדו על מקצת מדינה

מסרת הש״ס והמדרשים	תורה אור
3 (עניני) ברכות נ״ט א׳.	3 הושע ו׳ ד׳.

תרביעא, *i. e.*, a field watered and fructified by rain, as was
said above by R. Abahu: רביעה שרובעת את הקרקע. For
other interpretations of this passage see the commentaries, especially *Aruch*, *s. v.* תרבץ.

⁹⁴ That is, during the months of Marḥeshwan and
Kislew, for then it is, of course, better that Ṭebet should
be dry.

"He will shut up the heavens," etc., does not apply. But is it not written (Amos, 4.7): "And I also have withholden the rain from you, when there were yet three months to the harvest, and I caused it to rain upon one city, and caused it not to rain upon another city; one piece was rained upon, and the piece whereupon it rained not withered," which verse was interpreted by R. Judah in the name of Rab to the effect that both[95] are meant as a punishment?! This is no contradiction, for the Bible speaks of over-abundant rain,[96] while R. Ḥisda has in mind a rain that comes in normal quantity. R. 'Ashi thereupon remarked, this is indeed the meaning of Scripture, as can be proved from the word *timmatēr*, which means that the piece will be a place deluged by rain. Accept, therefore, this interpretation of the passage.

Said R.'Abahu: When are we to pronounce the blessing over the rain? When the groom goes forth to meet the bride.[97] How does the blessing read? Said R. Judah in the name of Rab: "We thank Thee, O Lord our God, for every drop Thou hast caused to descend for us"; and R. Johanan concluded this prayer thus: "Were our mouth full of song as the sea (is of water) and our tongue as loud as its roaring billows," etc., till "behold, they shall give thanks, blessing, and praise unto Thy name, blessed art

[95] Namely, the rain as well as the withholding of it.

[96] That is, the sections which are selected for rain will get it in such large measure that, like dearth, it will turn out to be a calamity.

ועל מקצת מדינה לא ירדו אין בהן משום ועצר
איני והכתיב וגם אנכי מנעתי מכם את הגשם
בעוד שלשה חדשים לקציר והמטרתי על עיר אחת
ועל עיר אחת לא אמטיר חלקה אחת תמטר וחלקה
אשר לא תמטיר עליה תיבש ואמר רב יהודה אמר
רב שתיהן לקללה לא קשיא הא דאתא טובא הא
דאתא כדמבעי ליה אמר רב אשי דיקא נמי דכתיב
תמטר תהא מקום מטר שמע מינה:

אמר רבי אבהו מאימתי מברכין על הגשמים
משיצא חתן לקראת כלה מאי מברך אמר רב
יהודה מודים אנחנו לך ה' אלהינו על כל טפה
וטפה שהורדת לנו ורבי יוחנן מסיים בה הכי ואלו
פינו מלא שירה כים ולשוננו רנה כהמון גליו כו'
עד הן הם יודו ויברכו וישבחו אֵת שמך ברוך אתה

מסרת הש"ס והמדרשים   תורה אור
3 (והמטרתי) לקמן י"ח ב'; ירושלמי   2 עמוס ד' ז'.
כאן ג' ג' (ס"ו ג'). 6 (שתיהן)
לקמן כ' א'. 9 (מאימתי) ברכות נ"ט ב'. 11 (מודים) ברכות שם;
ירושלמי כאן א' ג'; ברכות ט' ב'; ב"ר י"נ ט"ו; ד"ר ז' ו'; מדרש
תהלים י"ח.

---

[97] Meaning: When the falling rain has already satu-
rated the ground so that it absorbs no more, and the water
which then accumulates on the surface (called figuratively
the bridegroom) rebounds towards each additional drop
of rain (bride).

Thou, O Lord to whom many thanks are due."
"*Many* thanks," and not "all thanks"?! Raba
therefore directed to say, "God to whom thanks
are due." R. Papa said: Let us therefore [fol. 7a]
say both: "Blessed be He to whom many thanks
are due," and "God to whom thanks are due."

Said R.'Abahu: The day of rain is more important than the day of resurrection, for the
day of resurrection is for the righteous only and
not for the wicked, while the day of rain is for
the righteous and for the wicked. This disagrees
with the view of R. Joseph, who said that because the rain is as important as the day of
resurrection it was inserted in the prayer for
resurrection.

R. Judah said: The day of rain is as important
as the day on which the Torah was given to
Israel, as it is said (Deut., 32. 2): "My doctrine
shall drop as the rain." "Doctrine" means the
Torah, as it is said (Prov., 4.2): "For I give you
good doctrine; forsake ye not my teaching."
Raba said: (The day of rain is) more important
than the day on which the Torah was given, for
it is said: "My doctrine shall drop as the rain."
Now, which is usually compared to which? The
more important to the less important, or the
reverse? No doubt, it is the less important that
is compared to the more important.[98]

[98] Thus in the case before us, the doctrine (*Torah*),
which is compared to the rain, is the less important of
the two.

ה' רוב ההודאות רוב ההודאות ולא כל ההודאות
אמר רבא אימא אל ההודאות אמר רב פפא הילכך

ז״
ע״א ונימרינהו לתרוייהו ברוך רוב ההודאות ואל
ההודאות:

5 אמר רבי אבהו גדול יום הגשמים יותר מתחית
המתים דאלו תחית המתים לצדיקים ולא לרשעים
ואלו גשמים בין לצדיקים בין לרשעים ופליגא דרב
יוסף דאמר רב יוסף מתוך שׁשקולה כתחית המתים
קבעוה בתחית המתים:

10 אמר רב יהודה גדול יום הגשמים כיום שׁנתנה
בו תורה לישראל שׁנאמר יערף כמטר לקחי ואין
לקח אלא תורה שׁנאמר כי לקח טוב נתתי לכם
תורתי אל תעזבו רבא אמר יותר מיום שׁנתנה בו
תורה שׁנאמר יערף כמטר לקחי מי נתלה במי קטן

15 נתלה בגדול או גדול בקטן הוי אומר קטן נתלה
בגדול:

תורה אור	מסרת הש״ס והמדרשים

11 דברים ל״ב ב'. 12 משלי ד' ב'.   3 (נימרינהו) ברכות י״א ב' (וצ״ל
שם פפא במקום המנונא), נ״ט ב', ס'
ב'; מגלה כ״א ב'; סוטה מ' א'.   7 (לצדיקים) ב״ר י״ג ו' (וע' ספרי דברים
ל״ב וש״ו ומדרש תהלים קי״ז).   8 (מתוך) ברכות ל״ג א'; ב״ר י״ג ו'.
9 (תחה״מ) ירושלמי ברכות ה' ב'; ב״ר י״ג ו'; ד״ר ז' ו'.   10 (שׁנתנה
תורה) סדרש תהלים קי״ז.   12 (לקח) ספרי דברים שׁ״ו ; מדרש תנאים
האזינו 184.   14 (נתלה) ב״ב י״ב.

Raba pointed out an incongruity: It is written: "My doctrine shall drop as the *rain*," and then: "My speech shall distil as the *dew*"! The explanation is that if the scholar is worthy, the Torah will distil on him like dew, but if he is not, it will drop on him like rain.⁹⁹

We read: R. Bannaah used to say: If one studies the Torah for its own sake, it becomes to him an elixir of life, for it is said (Prov., 3.18): "She is a tree of life to them that lay hold upon her," and it is further said (*ibid.*, 3.8): "It shall be health to thy navel," and again it is said (*ibid.*, 4.22): "For they are life unto those that find them"; but if one studies the Torah not for its own sake, it becomes to him a deadly poison, for it is said (Deut., 32.2): "My doctrine shall drop as the rain," the term used here for dropping (*ya'arof*) being used elsewhere for killing, as it is said (Deut., 21.4): "And they shall break the heifer's neck" (*we-'arefū*).

R. Jeremiah said to R. Zera: Come, Master, teach me something. R. Zera replied: My heart feels faint, and I cannot do it. Then (said R. Jeremiah) tell me something haggadic. R. Zera thereupon said: Why is it written (Deut., 20. 19): "For man is the tree of the field?" Is man, indeed, a tree of the field? But the explanation is this: Having said immediately before: "for thou mayest eat of them, and thou shalt not cut them down," the Bible adds the expression in question to intimate that if a scholar is a worthy

⁹⁹ That is, the learning will harm him, as a heavy rain harms the crop; comp. the Hebrew notes.

רבא רמי כתיב יערף כמטר לקחי וכתיב תזל
כטל אמרתי הא כיצד אם תלמיד חכם הגון הוא
תזל עליו כטל ואם לאו עורפהו כמטר:

תניא היה רבי בנאה אומר כל העוסק בתורה
5 לשמה תורתו נעשית לו סם חיים שנאמר עץ חיים
היא למחזיקים בה ואומר רפאות תהי לשרך ואומר
כי חיים הם למצאיהם וכל העוסק בתורה שלא
לשמה נעשית לו סם המות שנאמר יערף כמטר
לקחי ואין עריפה אלא הריגה שנאמר וערפו שם
10 את העגלה:

אמר ליה רבי ירמיה לרבי זירא ליתי מר וליתני
אמר ליה חליש לבאי ולא יכילנא ולימא מר מלתא
דאגדתא אמר ליה הכי אמר רבי יוחנן מאי דכתיב
כי האדם עץ השדה וכי אדם עץ שדה הוא אלא
15 משום דכתיב ברישא כי ממנו תאכל ואתו לא תכרת

מסרת הש״ס והמדרעים | תורה אור
5 (סם) שבת פ״ח ב׳; ערובין׳ד א׳; | 5 משלי ג׳ י״ח. 6 משלי ג׳ ח׳.
יומא ע׳ב א׳; ספרי דברים ש׳ו; | 7 משלי ד׳ כ״ב. 8 דברים ל״ב ב׳.
מדרש תנאים שם. 9 (עריפה) | 9 דברים כ״א ד׳. 14 דברים כ׳ י״ט.
מדרש תנאים 185. | 15 דברים שם.

man, thou mayest eat (learn) from him and shalt not cut him down, but if not, thou shalt destroy and cut him down.

R. Ḥanina b. Papa pointed out an inconsistency. It is written (Is., 21. 14): "Unto him that is thirsty *bring ye* water," and again it is written (*ibid.*, 55. 1): "Ho, every one that thirsteth, *come ye* to the waters?!" If he is a worthy scholar, then "unto him that is thirsty *bring ye* water," but if he is not worthy, then: "ho, every one that thirsteth, *come ye* to the waters." R. 'Aḥa b. Ḥanina pointed out an inconsistency. It is written (Prov., 5.16): "Let thy springs be dispersed abroad," and directly after it is written: "Let them be only thine own, and not strangers with thee!" If he is a worthy scholar, "let thy springs be dispersed abroad," but if not, "let them be only thine own."

R. Ḥanina b. 'Idi said: Why are the words of the Torah likened unto water, as it is written, "Ho, every one that thirsteth, come ye to the waters"? In order to indicate that just as the water leaves high places and goes to low places, so the words of the Torah leave him who is haughty and stay with him who is humble.

בא לומר לך אם תלמיד חכם הגון הוא ממנו תאכל
ואתו לא תכרת ואם לאו אתו תשחית וכרת:

רבי חנינא בר פפא רמי כתיב לקראת צמא
התיו מים וכתיב הוי כל צמא לכו למים הא כיצד
אם תלמיד חכם הגון הוא לקראת צמא התיו מים
ואם לאו הוי כל צמא לכו למים:

רב אחא בר רב חנינא רמי כתיב יפצו מעינתיך
חוצה וכתיב יהיו לך לבדך הא כיצד אם תלמיד
חכם הגון הוא יפצו מעינתיך חוצה ואם לאו יהיו
לך לבדך:

אמר רבי חנינא בר אידי למה נמשלו דברי
תורה למים דכתיב הוי כל צמא לכו למים לומר
לך מה מים מניחין מקום גבוה והולכין למקום
נמוך אף דברי תורה מניחין מי שדעתו גבוהה
והולכין למי שדעתו שפלה:

תורה אור	מסרת הש״ס והמדרשים

תורה אור: 3 ישעיה כ״א י״ד. 4 ישעיה נ״ה י׳.‏ 8 שם ה׳ י״ו. 12 ישעיה נ״ה א׳.

מסרת הש״ס והמדרשים: 4 (למים) ב״ק י״ז א׳, פ״ב בא׳; עבודה א׳. 7 משלי ה׳ ט״ז. זרה ה׳ ב׳; ירושלמי כאן א׳ א׳; מכילתא בשלח ויסע א׳; מכדרשב״י 72; ספרי דברים מ״ח; ב״ר מ״א ט׳, ס״ו א׳, ס״ט ה׳, פ״ד ט״ז; במ״ר א׳ ז׳; שהש״ר א׳ (פסוק כי טובים) ג׳; תנחומא (הנדפס) ויקהל ח׳, תבוא ג׳; מדרש תנאים 42; מדרש שמואל י״ג; מדרש תהלים (באבער) א׳ סימן י״ח; אדר״נ ספי״א; ד״א זוטא ח׳; אליהו רבא פי״ח (צד 105); אליהו זוטא פי״ג.

R. 'Osha'ya said: Why are the words of the
Torah likened unto these three liquids: water,
wine, and milk?—As to water, it is written (Is.,
55. 1): "Ho, every one that thirsteth, come ye
to the waters"; as to wine and milk, it is written
(*ibid.*): "And he that hath no money come ye,
buy, and eat; yea, come, buy wine and milk
without money and without price"?—To indicate to you that just as these three liquids can
be preserved only in the cheapest kind of vessels,
so will the words of the Torah be preserved only
in him whose mind is lowly. This explains the
story of the daughter of a Roman emperor,[100] who
said to R. Joshua b. Ḥananiah: "What brilliant
wisdom in such an ugly vessel!" Whereupon he
exclaimed: "Oh, you daughter of a man who
puts wine in vessels of clay!" "Wherein should
he put it?" she asked. "You nobles should put
it in vessels of gold and silver!" Whereupon she
went home and told her father, who ordered the
wine to be put into vessels of gold and silver,
and the wine became sour. They then went
to R. Joshua and asked him, "Why did you
give her such advice?" "As she spoke to me,
so I spoke to her," R. Joshua replied. "But
there are also handsome people that are learned!"
they said [fol. 7b]. "If the same people were
ugly, they would be still more learned," was R.
Joshua's answer.

Another explanation:[101] Just as these three

[100] Namely, Hadrian; see Bacher, *J. E., s. v.* Joshua b.
Hananiah.

[101] Why the Torah was likened to the three liquids
mentioned above.

אמר רבי אושעיא למה נמשלו דברי תורה
לשלשה משקין הללו למים וליין ולחלב למים
דכתיב הוי כל צמא לכו למים ליין ולחלב דכתיב
ואשר אין לו כסף לכו שברו ואכלו ולכו שברו
בלוא כסף ובלוא מחיר יין וחלב לומר לך מה
שלשה משקין הללו אין מתקיימין אלא בפחות
שבכלים אף דברי תורה אין מתקיימין אלא במי
שדעתו שפלה והיינו דאמרה ליה ברתיה דקיסר
לרבי יהושע בן חנניה חכמה מפוארה בכלי מכוער
אמר לה אי בת רמי חמרא במאני דפחרא אמרה
ליה אלא במאי כו נרמייה אמר לה אתון דחשיביתו
רמו במאני דהבא וכספא אזלה ואמרה ליה לאבוה
רמייה לחמרא במאני דהבא וכספא ותקיף אתו
ואמרו ליה אמאי אמרת לה הכי אמר להו כי היכי
דאמרה לי אמרי לה והא איכא שפירי דגמירי!
אמר להו אי הוו סנו טפי הוו גמירי דבר אחר מה

מסרת הש"ס והמדרשים

2 (לייין) ד"ר ז' ג';‏ סדרש משלי כ';‏   ד"ר ז' ג' ‏(וע' ערובין נ"ד ב')‏ ושם
אנדת שה"ש לפסוק ישקני;‏ אליהו   נמשלה לדד).   9 (שפלה) ‏ערובין
זוטא שם.   3 (לחלב) ב"ר צ"ט ח';‏   נ"ה א';‏ ד"ר נצבים ח'.   9,‏ ‏(קיסר)
נדרים נ' ב'.

85

liquids become spoiled through neglect, so will the words of the Torah be forgotten through neglect.

Rabbah b. Bar Ḥana said: Why have the words of the Torah been likened unto fire, as it is said (Jer., 23.29): "Is not My word like as fire?" In order to indicate that just as fire does not burn when isolated, so will the words of the Torah not be preserved when studied by oneself, alone. It is in keeping herewith that R. Jose b. Ḥanina said: What is the meaning of the verse (*ibid.*, 50.36): "A sword is upon the boasters, and they shall become fools"? It means: a sword upon the necks of the enemies[102] of the learned who are occupied in the study of the Torah each one by himself. Nay, more, they become dull, as it is said: "And they shall become fools." The same idea may be derived from the following verse (Is., 19.13): "The princes of Zoan[103] are become fools."

R. Naḥman b. Isaac said: Why have the words of the Torah been likened unto a tree, as it is said (Prov., 3. 18): "She is a tree of life to them that lay hold upon her"? In order to indicate

[102] This is a variant of the frequently occurring euphemism שונאיהן של ישראל for Israel (see below, notes 105, 110), and the meaning is that an Israelite who has the chance to enhance the glory of the Torah by joining a multitude in their study, but prefers to study in isolation, deserves punishment (figuratively: The sword). Moreover, study in seclusion dulls one's mind. The word בדים, boasters, is taken in the sense of בודדים, recluses.

[103] The inference is based on the words נואלו, "become fools," used by both Isaiah and Jeremiah, but in the latter

שלשה משקין הללו נפסלין בהסח הדעת אף דברי
תורה משתכחין בהסח הדעת:

אמר רבה בר בר חנה למה נמשלו דברי תורה
לאש שנאמר הלוא כה דברי כאש נאם ה' לומר
לך מה אש אינה דולקת יחידי אף דברי תורה אין
מתקיימין ביחידי והיינו דאמר רבי יוסי בר חנינא
מאי דכתיב חרב אל הבדים ונאלו חרב על צוארי
שונאיהן של תלמידי חכמים שיושבין ועוסקין בתורה
בד בבד ולא עוד אלא שמטפשין שנאמר ונאלו
ואיבעית אימא מהכא נואלו שרי צוען:

אמר רב נחמן בר יצחק למה נמשלו דברי תורה
לעץ שנאמר עץ חיים היא למחזיקים בה לומר לך

מסרת הש"ס והמדרשים	תורה אור

4 ירמיה כ"ג כ"ט.   7 ירמיה נ' ל"ו.   4 (לאש) ספרי דברים שמ"ג; מדרש
10 ישעיה י"ט י"ג.   12 משלי ג' י"ח.   תנאים וזאת הברכה 211; מכילתא
דרשב"י צד 100; אדר"נ (שעכטער)
צד ס"א.   7 (חרב) ברכות ס"ג ב'; מכות י' א'.   12 (לעץ) ערכין ט"ו
ב'; ירושלמי כאן א' א'; מכילתא ויסע א'; ויק"ר ט"ג', ל"ה ו'; תנחומא
(באבער) וישלח ט'; ת"י בראשית ג' כ"ב, כ"ד; מדרש תהלים א' סימן
י"ט; ריש אליהו רבה.

it is not obvious that it refers to scholars unless one accepts
the forced interpretation of בדים, while in Isaiah it is clear
from the context (verses 11 and 12 of the same chapter)
that by princes of Zoan are meant the wise men of Egypt,
though, of course, not students of the Torah; comp.
the Hebrew notes.

that just as a small piece of wood sets on fire a big piece of wood, so minor scholars sharpen the minds of greater ones. It is in harmony with this view that Rabbi said (Makkot, 10a): I learned much from my teachers, more from my colleagues and most of all from my pupils.

R. Ḥama b. Ḥanina said: What is the meaning of the verse (Prov., 27. 17): "Iron sharpeneth iron; so a man sharpeneth the countenance of his friend"? It indicates that just as one piece of iron sharpens the other, so do scholars sharpen one another's minds in the study of the Law.

R. Ḥama b. Ḥanina said: The day of rain is as important as the day on which heaven and earth were created, as it is said (Is., 45. 8): "Drop down, ye heavens, from above, and let the skies pour down righteousness; let the earth open, that they may bring forth salvation, and let her cause righteousness to spring up together: I, the Lord, have created it." It does not say "I have created *them*,"[104] but "I have created *it*."

R.'Osha'ya said: Great is the day of rain, for then even salvation becomes fruitful and multiplies, as it is said: "let the earth open, that they may bring forth salvation."

R.Tanḥum b.Ḥanilai said: No rain falls unless the sins of Israel first have been forgiven, as it is

[104] Which we should expect if the verb referred to "heavens" and "skies." The use of the singular indicates that God prides Himself on having made the heavens to drop rain, saying I have created "it," the rain, thus putting it on the same level with the heavens and the earth.

מה עץ זה הקטן מדליק את הגדול אף תלמידי
חכמים הקטנים מחדדים את הגדולים והיינו דאמר
רבי הרבה למדתי מרבותי ומחברי יותר מרבותי
ומתלמידי יותר מכלם:

5   אמר רבי חמא בר חנינא מאי דכתיב ברזל
בברזל יחד ואיש יחד פני רעהו לומר לך מה ברזל
זה אחד מחדד את חברו אף תלמידי חכמים
מחדדין זה את זה בהלכה:

אמר רבי חמא בר חנינא גדול יום הגשמים כיום

10   שנבראו בו שמים וארץ שנאמר הרעיפו שמים ממעל
ושחקים יזלו צדק תפתח ארץ ויפרו ישע וצדקה
תצמיח יחד אני ה' בראתיו בראתים לא נאמר אלא
בראתיו:

אמר רבי אושעיא גדול יום הגשמים שאפילו

15   ישועה פרה ורבה בו שנאמר תפתח ארץ ויפרו ישע:
אמר רבי תנחום בר חנילאי אין הגשמין יורדין
אלא אם כן נמחלו עונותיהן של ישראל שנאמר

תורה אור

מסרת הש"ס והמדרשים

5 משלי כ"ז י"ג. 10 ישעיה מ"ה ח'.   1 (עץ קטן) מכילתא דרשב"י צד
100.   3 (הרבה) מכות י' א'.
5 (ברזל) ב"ר ס"ט ב'.   9 (גדול) ב"ר י"ג ד'; קה"ר א' ז'; לקמן ט'
ב'.   11 (ישע) ע' ירושלמי כאן א' ג', ט' סה"ב; ברכות ט' ג'; ב"ר י"ג
י"ג.   15 (ישועה) ע' ד"ר ז' ו'.

said (Ps. 85. 2–3): "Lord, Thou hast been favourable unto Thy *land;* Thou hast turned the captivity of Jacob. Thou hast *forgiven* the iniquity of Thy people, Thou hast pardoned all their sin, Selah." Said Ze'iri of Dahabat to Rabina: You derive this teaching from that verse, we derive it from this verse (I Kings, 8. 36): "Then hear Thou in heaven and forgive the sin of Thy servants, and of Thy people Israel, when Thou teachest them the good way wherein they should walk; and send rain upon Thy land, which Thou hast given to Thy people for an inheritance."

R. Tanḥum son of R. Ḥiyya of Kefar 'Akko said: Rain is not withheld unless the enemies[105] of Israel have been condemned to destruction, as it is said (Job, 24, 19): "Drought and heat consume the snow waters, so doth the nether world those that have sinned." Said Ze'iri of Dahabat to Rabina: You derive this teaching from that verse, we derive it from this (Deut., 11. 17): "And He will shut up the heaven, that there be no rain, etc., and ye perish quickly."

R. Ḥisda said: Rain is withheld only on account of the neglect to give the heave-offering and the tithes, as it is said, "Drought and heat consume the snow waters." How do you derive your statement? Answer: A disciple of the school of R. Ishmael said: On account of the things

[105] See above, note 102.

רצית ה' ארצך שבת שבות יעקב נשאת עון עמך
כסית כל חטאתם סלה אמר ליה זעירי מדהבת
לרבינא אתון מהתם מתניתו לה אנן מהכא מתנינן
להו ואתה תשמע השמים וסלחת לחטאת עבדיך ועמך
5   ישראל כי תורם את הדרך הטובה אשר ילכו בה
ונתת מטר על ארצך אשר נתת לעמך לנחלה:
אמר רבי תנחום בריה דרבי חייא איש כפר עכו
אין הגשמין נעצרין אלא אם כן נתחייבו שונאיהן
של ישראל כליה שנאמר ציה גם חם יגזלו מימי שלג
10   שאול חטאו אמר ליה זעירי מדהבת לרבינא אתון
מהתם מתניתו לה אנן מהכא מתנינן לה ועצר את
השמים ולא יהיה מטר וגו':
אמר רב חסדא אין הגשמים נעצרין אלא בשביל
תרומות ומעשרות שנאמר ציה גם חם יגזלו מימי
15   שלג מאי משמע תנא דבי רבי ישמעאל בשביל

מסרת הש"ס והמדרשים	תורה אור
9 (ציה) שבת ל"ב ב'; ירושלמי	4 מ"א ח' 1 תהלים פ"ה ב'–ג'.
רה"ש א' ג' (דף נ"ז ב'); ספרי עקב	11 דברים 9 איוב כ"ד י"ט.
מ'. 14 (תרומות) ירושלמי קדושין	י"א י"ו.
ד' א'; ברכות ט' ג'; אבות ה' ח';	
אדר"נ ל"ח.	

which I have commanded you for the summer
and which you did not carry out, you will be
deprived of the snow waters in the winter.[106]

R.Simeon b. Pazzi said: Rain is withheld only
on account of the slanderers, as it is said (Prov.,
25. 23): "The north wind bringeth forth rain, and
a backbiting tongue an angry countenance."[107]

R. Salla said in the name of R. Hamnuna: Rain
is withheld only on account of the insolent people,
as it is said (Jer., 3. 3): "Therefore the showers
have been withheld, and there hath been no
latter rain; yet thou hadst a harlot's forehead,
thou refusedst to be ashamed."   R. Salla further
said in the name of R. Hamnuna: Everyone who
is insolent will in the end fall a victim to sin,[108]
as it is said: "Thou hadst a harlot's forehead."
R. Naḥman said, it is certain that he has already
fallen a victim to sin, as it is said: "Thou *hadst*
a harlot's forehead," it is not said thou *wilt* have,
but thou *hadst*.

Rabbah b. R. Huna said: A man who is insolent may be called wicked to his face, as it is said
(Prov., 21. 29): "A wicked man hardeneth his

[106] In this interpretation the word ציה, drought, is
read צוה, to command, and חם, heat, is taken as an allusion
to summer, the time of harvesting, when the commands
of heave-offering and tithing are to be carried out.

[107] Here the verb תחולל, bringeth forth, is given a contrary meaning: frustrates, breaks (as יחל in Deut., 30. 3),
the assumption being that north winds prevent rain;
"angry countenance" is taken as denoting divine displeasure caused by the sin of backbiting and slandering.
We thus obtain the meaning: The north wind prevents

דברים שצויתי אתכם בימות החמה ולא עשיתם
יגזלו מכם מימי שלג בימות הגשמים:

אמר רבי שמעון בן פזי אין הגשמין נעצרין אלא
בשביל מספרי לשון הרע שנאמר רוח צפון תחולל
5 גשם ופנים נזעמים לשון סתר:

אמר רב סלא אמר רב המנונא אין הגשמים
נעצרין אלא בשביל עזי פנים שנאמר וימנעו רבבים
ומלקוש לוא היה ומצח אשה זונה היה לך מאנת
הכלם ואמר רב סלא אמר רב המנונא כל אדם
10 שיש בו עזות פנים לסוף נכשל בעברה שנאמר
ומצח אשה זונה היה לך מאנת הכלם רב נחמן אמר
בידוע שנכשל בעברה שנאמר היה יהיה לא נאמר
אלא היה:

אמר רבה בר רב הונא כל אדם שיש בו עזות
15 פנים מותר לקרותו רשע בפניו שנאמר העז איש

תורה אור	מסרת הש״ס והמדרשים

4 משלי כ״ה כ״ג.   7 ירמיה ג' ג'.   7 (רבבים) יבמות ע״ח ב'; ירושלמי
15 משלי כ״א כ״ט.   שם וסנה' ו' ז'; מדרש שמואל כ״ח.

rain, because of the backbiting which causes divine displeasure.

[108] Sin here means in particular adultery, as indicated
by the word harlot.

face."[109]   R. Naḥman b. Isaac said, it is com-
mendable to hate him, as it is said (Eccl., 8. 1):
"And the hardness of his face is changed," do
not read *yeshunne* (is changed), but *yissane* (is
hated).

R. Ḳeṭina said: Rain is withheld only on account of the neglect of the Torah, as it is said
(Eccl., 10. 18): "By slothfulness the rafters
sink in," that is to say on account of the indolence
of the Israelites, who neglect the study of the
Torah, the enemy[110] of the Holy One, blessed be
He, becomes impoverished; for *mak* means poor,
as it is said (Lev., 27. 8): "But if he be poorer
than thy estimation," while *meḳāreh* denotes
the Holy One, blessed be He, as it is said (Ps.,
104. 3): "Who layest the beams of Thine upper
chambers in the waters." R. Joseph said: I derive it from this verse (Job, 37. 21): "And now
men see not the light which is bright in the skies,
but the wind passeth and cleanseth them,"[111]
for *or* (light) means the Torah, as it is said
(Prov., 6. 23): "For the commandment is a lamp
and the law is light."

What is the meaning of "bright in the skies"?
Said a disciple of the school of R. Ishmael: Even

---

[109] Rabbah translates: If a man is insolent (הֵעַז אִישׁ),
call him wicked to his face (רְשָׁע בְּפָנָיו).

[110] See notes 102, 105. In Ps., 104. 3 מקרה, rafter, is
used as an epithet of God (see below, "who layest the
beams"), and the word ימך, sink in, may also mean, as in
Lev., 27. 8, becomes poor. We thus obtain the meaning:
By slothfulness (of Israel and his neglect of the Torah)
God, as it were, becomes poor, that is, powerless to give

רשע בפניו רב נחמן בר יצחק אמר מותר לשנאתו
שנאמר ועז פניו ישנא אל תקרי ישנא אלא ישנא:
אמר רב קטינא אין הגשמים נעצרין אלא בשביל
עצלות תורה שנאמר בעצלתים ימך המקרה בשביל
עצלות שהיתה בהם בישראל שלא עסקו בתורה
נעשה שונאו של הקדוש ברוך הוא מך ואין מך אלא
עני שנאמר ואם מך הוא מערכך ואין מקרה אלא
הקדוש ברוך הוא שנאמר המקרה במים עליותיו
רב יוסף אמר מהכא ועתה לא ראו אור בהיר הוא
בשחקים ורוח עברה ותטהרם ואין אור אלא תורה
שנאמר כי נר מצוה ותורה אור מאי בהיר הוא
בשחקים תנא דבי רבי ישמעאל אפילו בשעה

תורה אור   מסרת הש"ס והמדרשים

2 קהלת ח' א'.   4 שם י' י"ח.   1 (לשנאתו) פסחים קי"ג ב'.
7 ויקרא כ"ז ח'.   8 תהלים ק"ד ג'.   4 (עצלות) מגלה י"א א'. 7 (מקרה)
9 איוב ל"ז כ"א.   11 משלי ו' כ"ג.   מכילתא דשירה בשלח ח';
   מכדרשב"י 67; ב"ר ד' א'; שמ"ר
ט"ו כ"ב.

rain, because of the lack of merit on the part of the Israelites.

III Meaning: Because of their disregard of the light of the Torah, the wind passes and clears away the clouds that were to give them rain.

when the skies are full of cloudy spots,[112] ready to
send down dew and rain, "the wind passeth and
cleareth them."

R. 'Ami said: Rain is withheld only as a punishment for violence, as it is said (Job, 36. 32):
"He covereth His hands with the lightning." Now,
"hands" stands for violence, as it is said (Jon.,
3. 8): "And from the violence, that is in their
hands," and "lightning" signifies rain, as it is
said (Job, 37. 11): "He spreadeth abroad the
cloud of His lightning."[113] What is the remedy?
The people should pray fervently, as it is said
(Job, 36. 32): "And giveth it a charge that it
strike the mark." Now *pegi'ah* means prayer,
as it is said (Jer., 7. 16): "Therefore pray not thou
for this people, neither lift up cry nor prayer
for them, neither make intercession to Me."[114]

R. 'Ami further said: What is the meaning of
the verse (Eccl., 10. 10): "If the iron be blunt
and one do not whet the edge"? If thou seest a
generation over which the heavens are as tough
as iron, sending neither dew nor rain, it is due
to the people's corrupt deeds, as it is said, "and

---

[112] בהיר, bright, is brought in relation to בהרת, white spots
(Lev., 13. 24), here white clouds.

[113] R. Ami thus translates כפים, hands, by "violence of
hands," and takes lightning as the equivalent (forerunner)
of rain. The verse then conveys the meaning: On account of violence God covers (withholds) the rain.

[114] Here again R. Ami plays on the word מפגיע, from
פגע, which means to strike and, as in Jer., 7. 16, to intercede,
and translates: He gives the command that they intercede.

שהשמים עומדין בהורין בהורין להוריד טל ומטר
רוח עברה ותטהרם:

אמר רבי אמי אין הגשמין נעצרין אלא בשביל
גזל שנאמר על כפים כסה אור ואין כפים אלא גזל
שנאמר ומן החמס אשר בכפיהם ואין אור אלא מטר
שנאמר יפיץ ענן אורו מאי תקנתן ירבו בתפלה
שנאמר ויצו עליה במפגיע ואין פגיעה אלא תפלה
שנאמר ואתה אל תתפלל בעד העם הזה ואל תשא
בעדם רנה ותפלה ואל תפגע בי:

ואמר רבי אמי מאי דכתיב אם קהה הברזל
והוא לא פנים קלקל אם ראית דור שהשמים קהין
עליו כברזל מלהוריד טל ומטר בשביל מעשיהן
שהן מקולקלין שנאמר והוא לא פנים קלקל מאי

תורה אור	מסרת הש"ס והמדרשים

תורה אור

4 איוב ל"ו ל"ב.   5 יונה ג' ח'.
6 איוב ל"ו י"א.   7 איוב ל"ו ל"ב.
8 ירמיה ז' ט"ז.   10 קהלת י' י'.
13 קהלת י' י'.

מסרת הש"ס והמדרשים

7 (פגיעה) תענית ח' א' ; ברכות
כ"ו ב' ; סוטה י"ד א' ; סנהדרין צ"ה
ב' ; ירושלמי ברכות ד' א' ; תנחומא
(הנדפס) בשלח סי' ט' ; מכילתא
דויהי בשלח ב' ; מכדרשב"י 45 ;

מדרש תנאים 14.   11 (קהין) במ"ר ג' י"ב ; קה"ר י' י'

one do not whet the edge."[115]   What is the
remedy?   They should pray much, as it is said
(*ibid.*): "Then must he put to more strength,
but wisdom is profitable to direct," the latter
part of which means to say that the additional
praying will prove more profitable if the people's
deeds are still good.[116]   Resh Laḳish explains
it thus: When thou seest a scholar [fol. 8a] to
whom his studies are as tough as iron, it is
because his lesson is not properly ordered in
his mind, as it is said, "and one do not whet the
edge."[116a]   What is his remedy?   He should
attend more diligently the sessions of the scholars,
as it is said, "then must he put to more strength,
but wisdom is profitable to direct," the latter part
of which means to say that increased diligence
will prove still more profitable if the scholar's
studies have always been well ordered.   Resh
Laḳish used to arrange his studies in proper
order forty times, corresponding to the forty
days during which the Torah was given to
Israel, before he appeared before R. Johanan.
R. 'Adda b. 'Ahabah used to arrange his lessons

[115] This interpretation of Eccl., 10. 10 renders the
verse untranslatable.   As is often the case (see above, note
66), the preacher is satisfied with finding some quaint
allusion to his idea and does not care about the construc-
tion of the verse.   Thus, "if the iron be blunt" is turned
into "if the heavens be blunt like iron," giving no rain,
and קלקל, to whet, is given the meaning it has in later
Hebrew: To spoil, to corrupt.   The verb is then used
in the affirmative (the people corrupt their deeds) despite
the negative "not," which precedes it, and which, indeed,

תקנתן יגבירו ברחמים שנאמר וחילים יגבר ויתרון
הכשיר חכמה וכל שכן אם הוכשרו מעשיהן
מעיקרא:

רִישׁ לקיש אמר אם ראית תלמיד חכם
שתלמודו קהה עליו כברזל בשביל משנתו שאינה
סדורה לו שנאמר והוא לא פנים קלקל מאי תקנתיה
ירבה בישיבה שנאמר וחילים יגבר ויתרון הכשיר
חכמה וכל שכן אם משנתו סדורה לו מעיקרא:

רִישׁ לקיש הוה מסדר מתניתיה ארבעין זמנין
כנגד ארבעים יום שניתנה בהן תורה ועייל לקמיה
דרבי יוחנן רב אדא בר אהבא הוה מסדר מתניתיה

מסרת הש״ס והמדרשים	תורה אור
5 (קהה) קה״ר י׳ י׳.	1 קהלת י׳ י׳.

spoils the whole interpretation; comp., however, Lev.,
26. 19, and Targum of Eccl. *ad locum*, which latter
is based on this interpretation.

[116] הכשיר, to direct, is taken in the sense of to improve,
better, as in Eccl., 11. 6; Esth., 8. 5; so also in the following interpretations of Resh Laḳish and Raba.

[116a] Here קלקל retains its meaning, to whet, but in a
somewhat diverted sense, to make clear, lucid, in application to one's learning and ideas, taking פנים, edge, in
the often used sense of method, manner of understanding
and interpreting the Law; comp. *Abot*. iii, 11. Rashi's
explanation here is untenable.

in proper order twenty-four times, corresponding
to the number of the books of the Pentateuch,
Prophets, and Hagiographa, before he appeared
before Raba.

Raba explained the above verse as follows:
If thou seest a disciple to whom his studies are
as tough as iron, it is due to his master's lack
of kindness toward him,[117] as it is said, "and
one do not whet the edge." What is his remedy?
He should send many friends to the master,[118]
as it is said, "then must he put to more strength,
but wisdom is profitable to direct," which means
to say that the intercession of the friends will
prove the more profitable when prior to that
the pupil's ways had been improved before his
master.[119]

R.'Ami further said: What is the meaning of the
verse (Eccl., 10. 11): "If the serpent bite before it is charmed, then the charmer hath no
advantage"? When thou seest a generation over
whom the heavens are rust-colored[120] like copper
and do not let down dew or rain, it is because
there are no whisperers[121] in that generation. What
is their remedy? They should turn to one who
understands to whisper and he shall whisper. But
if he who understands to whisper is unwilling
to do it—what benefit will there accrue to him?[122]

---

[117] Literally: Because of his master who does not show
him a kind face. קלקל = to make bright (cheerful), and
פנים = face.

[118] To intercede for him.

[119] That is to say, when the pupil made efforts on his
part to please the master.

עשרין וארבע זמנין כנגד תורה נביאים וכתובים
ועייל לקמיה דרבא:

רבא אמר אם ראית תלמיד שתלמודו קהה עליו
כברזל בשביל רבו שאינו מסביר לו פנים שנאמר
5 והוא לא פנים קלקל מאי תקנתיה ירבה עליו רעים
שנאמר וחילים יגבר ויתרון הכשיר חכמה וכל שכן
אם הוכשרו מעשיו בפני רבו מעיקרא:

ואמר רבי אמי מאי דכתיב אם ישך הנחש בלוא
לחש ואין יתרון לבעל הלשון אם ראית דור
10 שהשמים משותכין עליו כנחשת מלהוריד טל ומטר
בשביל לוחשי לחישות שאין באותו הדור מאי
תקנתן ילכו אצל מי שיודע ללחוש וילחוש וכל מי
שיודע ללחוש ואינו לוחש מה הנאה יש לו ואם

תורה אור
8 קהלת י' י"א.

---

[120] יָשֵׁךְ, bite, is combined with Aramaic שְׁתַךְ, to get rusty, and נָחָשׁ, serpent, with נְחֹשֶׁת, copper, which alludes also to Lev., 26. 19. Aside from the strangeness of these combinations, the main words, viz. generation and heavens, are not in the text, but see note 115.

[121] לַחַשׁ, to charm, means also to whisper, *i. e.*, to pray.

[122] This purports to interpret the words, "then the charmer (בעל הלשון) has no advantage," as meaning to say that if the one whose prayer might avert the calamity refuses to pray, he will share in the punishment.

Again, if he does whisper and obtains his desire, but then becomes presumptuous, he brings wrath upon the world, as it is said (Job, 36.33): "The cattle also concerning the storm that cometh up."[123]

Raba interprets the latter verse thus: If two scholars living in the same city are unpleasant toward one another because of differences in their interpretations of the law, they solicit wrath and bring it upon themselves, as it is said, "the cattle also concerning the storm that cometh up."[124]

Resh Laḳish said: What is the meaning of the verse (Eccl., 10. 11): "If the serpent bite before it is charmed, then the charmer hath no advantage"? In the time to come all beasts will gather together and approach the serpent, saying to him: A lion attacks with his paws and eats his prey, a wolf tears and eats, but what pleasure hast thou in biting and killing? The serpent will reply: "The charmer hath no advantage."[125]

[123] The verse in Job means to say that the cattle in the field know before a storm comes that it is about to come. R. Ami combines מקנה, cattle, with קנה, to acquire (probably also reading מַקְנֶה in the causative form, to cause to acquire, bring about), takes אף = also, as a noun, meaning wrath, and explains עולה, cometh up, as a haughty person, thus obtaining the sentence: He brings wrath upon the world, who is haughty and overbearing, because of the success of his prayer.

[124] Raba explains מקנה, cattle, as ...התקנא ב, to which the meaning of ....התגרה ב, to provoke, is given; אף

לחש ועלתה בידו והגיס דעתו מביא אף לעולם
שנאמר מקנה אף על עולה:

רבא אמר שני תלמידי חכמים שיושבין בעיר
אחת ואין נוחין זה לזה בהלכה מתקנאין באף
5 ומעלין אותו שנאמר מקנה אף על עולה:

אמר ריש לקיש מאי דכתיב אם ישך הנחש בלוא
לחש ואין יתרון לבעל הלשון לעתיד לבא
מתקבצות כל החיות ובאות אצל הנחש ואומרות
לו ארי דורס ואוכל זאב טורף ואוכל אתה מה
10 הנאה יש לך והוא אומר להם אין יתרון לבעל
הלשון:

תורה אור   מסרת הש״ס והמדרשים
2 איוב ל״ו ל״ג.   3 (שני ת״ח) מגלה ל״ב א'; סוטה
מ״ט א'.   6 (נחש) ערכין ט״ו ב'
ירושלמי פאה א' א' (דף ט״ז ע״א); פסדר״כ פרה (באבער צד ל״ב);
תנחומא (באבער) חקת ח'; ויק״ר כ״ו ב'; במ״ר י״ט ב'; ד״ר ה' י';
קה״ר י' י״א; מדרש תהלים י״ב, ק״כ.

is again a noun, wrath, and על עולה, that cometh up,
is paraphrased by מעלין אותו עליהם, and the total, then, is:
They provoke wrath and bring it upon themselves. For
different readings and interpretations see the Hebrew notes.

125 The Hebrew for charmer in this verse is בעל הלשון,
the man of the tongue, hence, figuratively, also the slanderer.
The serpent's reply thus is that neither has the slanderer
any advantage and yet he slanders. The connection of
the serpent with the slanderer may contain an allusion to
the story in Genesis 3.

R. 'Ami further said: One's prayer is not accepted unless he puts his heart in his hands,[126] as it is said (Lam., 3.41): "Let us lift up our heart with our hands unto God in the heavens." After R. 'Ami had left, R. Samuel b. Nahamani placed an Amora[127] by his side and discoursed as follows: "But they beguiled Him with their mouth, and lied unto Him with their tongue. For their heart was not steadfast with Him, neither were they faithful in His covenant." And yet "He, being full of compassion, forgiveth iniquity" (Ps., 78. 36–38). Do not R. 'Ami and R. Samuel contradict one another? No, one refers to individual, the other to communal, prayers.[128]

R. 'Ami also said: Rain comes down only for the sake of men of faith,[129] as it is said (Ps., 85. 12): "Truth springeth out of the earth and righteousness hath looked down from heaven." R. Ḥanina said: Come and learn the greatness of men of faith from the story about the weasel and

[126] That is to say, he does not merely lift up his hands in prayer but also his heart.

[127] *Amora*, the common designation of the authorities of the Talmud, is sometimes applied to scholars who assisted the lecturers in interpreting their words to the audience; see above, note 53.

[128] Congregational prayers may be accepted even if they do not come up to the standard required by R. 'Ami.

[129] According to Rashi, R. 'Ami means faithfulness and honesty in business, and we should then vocalize אֱמֻנָה (comp. Neh., 10. 1), and the following story of the weasel may also bear out this meaning. Kohut, *s. v.* בעלי, vocalizes אֲמָנָה.

ואמר רבי אמי אין תפלתו של אדם נשמעת אלא

אם כן משים לבו בכפו שנאמר נשא לבבנו אל כפים

אל אל בשמים לבתר דנפק אוקים רבי שמואל בר

נחמני אמורא עליה ודרש ויפתוהו בפיהם ובלשונם

יכזבו לו ולבם לא נכון עמו ולא נאמנו בבריתו

ואף על פי כן והוא רחום יכפר עון קשיין אהדדי

לא קשיא כאן ביחיד כאן בצבור:

ואמר רבי אמי אין הגשמים יורדים אלא בשביל

בעלי אמנה שנאמר אמת מארץ תצמח וצדק

משמים נשקף אמר רבי חנינא בא וראה כמה גדולים

בעלי אמנה מנלן מחולדה ובור ומה המאמין

תורה אור	מסרת הש״ס והמדרשים
2 איכה ג׳ מ״א. 4 תהלים ע״ח	2 (נשא) ירושלמי תענית ב׳ א׳;
ל״ו–ל״ז. 6 תהלים ע״ח ל״ח.	איכ״ר ג׳ פסוק נחפשה (וע׳ לקמן
9 תהלים פ״ה י״ב.	ט״ז א׳). 4 (ויפתוהו) מכילתא
	דרשב״י 148.

faith, but it is quite improbable that while in the Bible the
word is, with very few exceptions, written plene (אמונה),
the Talmud should always have it defective.   At any rate
R. 'Ami takes it as equivalent to אמת, truth, and צדק,
righteousness, as a figure for rain, which is the reward
of righteousness; comp. Is., 45. 8:   "Let the skies pour
down righteousness," quoted above, fol. 7b, top.

the well.[130] If this is the reward of one who
trusts in a weasel and a well, how much more so
when one trusts in God, the Holy One, blessed be
He!

R. Johanan said: He who conducts himself
righteously here below is judged strictly in the
heaven above, as it is said, "Truth springeth out
of the earth and righteousness hath looked down
from heaven."[131] R. Ḥiyya b. 'Abba derives this

[130] The story here alluded to is not found anywhere in
the Talmud or in the Midrashim, although Rashi says that
the story was quite popular (מצוי הוא באגדה). The only
source where it is given in full is the *'Aruk* of Nathan b.
Jehiel of Rome (11th c.), *s. v.* חלד, where, with some omissions, it runs as follows:

A well-dressed, pretty girl going home, lost her way,
and after wandering about in the field for some time and
becoming exhausted, she came near a well that was provided with a rope and a bucket. To slake her thirst, she
slid down on the rope, but was unable to pull herself up
again. Her cries attracted the attention of a young man
who happened to pass by. He offered her help if she prom-
ised to marry him, which she did, whereupon he pulled her
up. As there were no witnesses to testify to the pact of
betrothal, as required by the Jewish law, the girl suggested that the well and a weasel, that was seen near it,
should be invoked as witnesses. This done, the couple
parted. The young man, however, broke his promise and
married another girl, who bore him a son. At the age of
three months the boy was choked to death by a weasel.
Later a second boy was born to the couple, and he fell

בחולדה ובור כך המאמין בהקדוש ברוך הוא על

אחת כמה וכמה:

אמר רבי יוחנן כל המצדיק את עצמו מלמטה

מצדיקין עליו את הדין מלמעלה שנאמר אמת

5   מארץ תצמח וצדק משמים נשקף רבי חייא בר

---

into a well and was drowned. The mother, becoming
alarmed by the peculiar nature of these accidents, urged
her husband for some explanation. He told her the story of
his former breach of promise, whereupon she demanded a
divorce and obtained it. During all that time his former
fiancée was waiting for his appearance, discouraging all
her suitors by simulating epileptic fits. When the young
man, after some search, finally returned to her, she,
not recognizing him, tried to deter him in the same way,
but upon his mentioning to her the weasel and the well,
she at once accepted him. They were married and henceforth lived happily together, their matrimony being
blessed with children. Comp. Rashi and *Tosafot ad
locum*, מדרש הגדול, ed. Schechter, p. 231; ס' המעשיות, ed.
Gaster No. 89.

[131] R. Johanan's thought is that the actions of a prominent man are judged more severely than those of the ordinary man. "Truth springeth out of the earth" is
thus an allusion to the strict conduct of the conscientious,
truthful man on earth, and "righteousness" in the second
half of the verse is to be taken in the sense of strictness,
stern justice, by which such men are treated.

lesson from this verse (Ps., 90.11): "And Thy wrath according to the fear that is due unto Thee."[132] Resh Laḳish derives it from this verse (Is., 64. 4): "Thou didst take away him that joyfully worked righteousness."[133]

R. Joshua b. Levi said: He who accepts gladly the sufferings of this world, brings salvation to the world, as it is said (*ibid.*): "Upon them have we stayed of old, that we might be saved."[134]

Said Resh Laḳish: Why is it written (Deut., 11. 17): "And He will shut up the heavens"? Because when the heavens are prevented from sending down dew and rain, they are to be compared to a woman that travails, but cannot give birth. This is in keeping with what Resh Laḳish said in the name of Bar Ḳappara: The expression "shut up" is used in connection with a woman and in connection with rain; [fol. 8b] the expression "bear" is used in connection with a woman and with reference to the soil; the expression "remember" is also used both in reference to a woman and the soil. "Shutting up" is said with reference to woman (Gen., 20. 18): "For the Lord had fast closed up all the wombs"; and with reference to rain, it is said (Deut., 11. 17): "And He will shut up the heavens"; "bear" is said of a woman, as it is written (Gen., 30. 23): "And she conceived and *bore* a son"; and is also

---

[132] That is to say: The more a person excels in piety and the fear of God the more is he liable to arouse the anger of God by an occasional misdeed.

[133] Bearing out the same idea: God is severe with the righteous.

אבין אמר רב הונא מהכא וכיראתך עברתך ריש
לקיש אמר מהכא פגעת את שש ועשה צדק:

אמר רבי יהושע בן לוי כל השמח ביסורין הבאין
עליו בעולם הזה מביא ישועה לעולם שנאמר בהם
5   עולם ונושע:

אמר ריש לקיש מאי דכתיב ועצר את השמים
בשעה שהשמים נעצרין מלהוריד טל ומטר דומים
לאשה שמחבלת ואינה יולדת והיינו דאמר ריש
לקיש משום בר קפרא נאמרה עצירה באשה
10   ונאמרה עצירה בגשמים ׀ נאמרה לדה באשה חי'
ונאמרה לדה בקרקע נאמרה פקידה באשה ונאמרה ע"ב
פקידה בקרקע נאמרה עצירה באשה דכתיב כי
עצר עצר ה' בעד כל רחם ונאמרה עצירה בגשמים
דכתיב ועצר את השמים נאמרה לדה באשה דכתיב

תורה אור

1 תהלים צ' י"א.   2 ישעיה ס"ד ד'.   6 דברים י"א י"ז.   13 בראשית כ'
י"ח.   14 דברים י"א י"ז.

---

[134] R. Joshua refers "upon them" to the sufferings for
sin (indicated before in the same verse), and explains that
by them the world is saved (עולם ונושע).

said of the soil, as it is written (Is., 55. 10):
"And maketh it bring forth[135] and bud";
"remember" is used in connection with woman,
as it is said (Gen., 21. 1): "And the Lord
remembered Sarah"; and it is said also of the
soil, as it is written (Ps. 65. 10): "Thou hast
remembered the earth, and watered her, greatly
enriching her with the river of God that is full
of water."

What is the meaning of "the river of God"?
It was taught that there is a sort of compart-
ment in heaven, out of which rains descend upon
the world.

R. Samuel b. Nahamani said in the name of
R. Jonathan: What is the meaning of the verse
(Job, 37. 13): "Whether it be for correction,
or for His earth, or for mercy, that He cause it
to come"? If the rain is 'for correction,' it falls
on mountains and hills, but if 'for mercy,' He
causes it to come (where it is needed).

In the days of R. Samuel b. Nahamani there
was a famine accompanied with pestilence. Said
the Rabbis, what are we to do? One cannot pray at once for the cessation of two af-
flictions; let us therefore pray for the staying
of the pestilence and let us suffer famine. But
R. Samuel b. Nahamani advised: Let us pray
for the cessation of the famine, for when the
Merciful gives plenty, He gives it to the living, as it
is said (Ps., 145. 16): "Thou openest Thy hand
and satisfiest every living thing with favour."

[135] To make bring forth = to make bear; in Hebrew the
same root (ילד) is used for both.

ותהר ותלד בן ונאמרה לדה בקרקע דכתיב
והולידה והצמיחה נאמרה פקידה באשה דכתיב
וה' פקד את שרה ונאמרה פקידה בקרקע דכתיב
פקדת הארץ ותשקקה רבת תעשרנה פלג אלהים
מלא מים:

מאי פלג אלהים תנא כמין קבה יש ברקיע
שממנה גשמים יורדין לעולם:

אמר רבי שמואל בר נחמני אמר רבי יונתן מאי
דכתיב אם לשבט אם לארצו אם לחסד ימצאהו
אם לשבט להרים וגבעות אם לחסד ימצאהו:

בימי רבי שמואל בר נחמני הוה כפנא ומותנא
אמרי היכי נעביד אתרתי לא בעינן רחמי אלא
נבעי רחמי אמותנא וכפנא נסבול אמר להו רבי
שמואל בר נחמני נבעי רחמי אכפנא דכי יהיב
רחמנא שבעא לחיי הוא דיהיב דכתיב פותח את
ידך ומשביע לכל חי רצון ומנלן דלא בעינן רחמי

תורה אור   מסרת הש"ס והמדרשים

1 בראשית ל' כ"ג.   2 ישעיה נ"ה י'.   4 (פלג) ב"ר ד' ד'.   6 (תנא) ב"ר
3 בראשית כ"א א'.   4 תהלים ס"ה י'.   ד' ה'.   (ע' טהעאדאר שם הערה
9 איוב ל"ז י"ג.   15 תהלים קמ"ה ט"ז.   9).   9 (לשבט) ע' ירושלמי תענית
                                ג' ג'.   10 (להרים) ירושלמי רה"ש
א' ג' (ע"ז ב').   12 (אתרתי) ירושלמי תענית ד' ד' (ס"ח ב'); איכ"ר א'
                (פסוק על אלה אני בוכיה סימן נ"א).

But whence do we know that it is not proper to pray for two things at the same time? It is written (Ezra, 8. 23): "So we fasted and besought our God for *this*." The word "this" implies that there was yet another thing to pray for. In Palestine it was derived in the name of R. Zera from this verse (Dan., 2. 18): "That they would desire mercies of the God of heaven concerning *this* secret." The implication of "this" is that there was also another thing to be desired.

In the days of R. Zera there was a religious persecution and the Jews were forbidden to fast. R. Zera therefore said: Let us for the present resolve to fast, and when the persecution ceases we will carry out our resolution. On what did he base his opinion? It is written (Dan., 10. 12): "Then said he unto me: Fear not, Daniel; for from the first day that thou didst set thy heart to understand, and to humble thyself before thy God thy words were heard,[136] and I am come because of thy words."

R. Isaac said: Even in years like those in the time of Elijah[137] rain on the eve of Sabbath is but a sign of divine displeasure.[138] This agrees with Rabbah b. R. Shila, who said that a rainy day is as calamitous as a day of judgment.[139] 'Amemar said: Were it not that the rain is a necessity for the world, we would pray and have it abolished.

[136] This proves that a good intention is acceptable before God as an accomplished deed.

[137] That is, years of dearth; see I Kings, 17.

[138] Because it prevents the people from buying food and preparing it for the Sabbath.

תענית

אתרתי דכתיב ונצומה ונבקשה מאלהינו על זאת
מכלל דאיכא אחריתי במערבא אמרי משמיה
דרבי זירא מהכא ורחמי למבעי מן קדם אלה
שמיא על רזא דנה מכלל דאיכא אחריתי:

5 בימי רבי זירא הוה שמדא וגזור דלא למיתב
בתעניתא אמר להו רבי זירא נקבלה עילון ולכי
בטיל שמדא ניתבה אמרו ליה מנא לך הא אמר
להו דכתיב ויאמר אלי אל תירא דניאל כי מן היום
הראשון אשר נתת את לבך להבין ולהתענות לפני

10 אלהיך נשמעו דבריך ואני באתי בדבריך:
אמר רבי יצחק אפילו שנים כשני אליהו וירדו
גשמים בערבי שבתות אינן אלא סימן קללה והיינו
דאמר רבה בר רב שילא קשה יומא דמטרא
כיומא דדינא אמר אמימר אי לא דצריך לבריתא

15 בעינן רחמי ומבטלינן ליה:

תורה אור	מסרת הש"ס והמדרשים

1 עזרא ח' כ"ג.   3 דניאל ב' י"ח.   8 (ויאמר) ע' ירושלמי תענית ג' א'
ור"ה ג' ה'.   11 (שני אליהו) תענית   8 דניאל י' י"ב.
כ"ג א'; ספרא ריש בחקותי; ויק"ר
ל"ה ט'.   13 (יומא) ב"מ פ"ה א'.

---

[139] According to Rashi, Rabbah means the days on which
the people used to come to court to settle their litigations
(every Monday and Thursday), but see מהרש"א, *ad locum.*
The meaning seems to be that rainy days are as bad as
days of punishment.

113

R. Isaac further said: Sunshine on Sabbath
is a benefit to the poor, as it is said (Mal.,
3. 20): "Unto you that fear My name[140] shall
the sun of righteousness arise with healing in
its wings." R. Isaac further said: Great is the
day of rain, for even the money in the purse[141] is
blessed thereby, as it is said (Deut., 28. 12):
"To give the rain of thy land in its season, and to
bless all the work of thy hand." R. Isaac further said: Blessing rests only on a thing which
is hidden from sight, as it is said (*ibid.*, 28. 8):
"The Lord will command the blessing with thee
in thy barns."[142] A disciple of the school of R.
Ishmael taught: Blessing is found only in things
upon which the eye does not rest, as it is said: "The
Lord will command the blessing with thee in thy
barns."[142] The Rabbis teach: One who is about
to measure his grain should say: May it be
Thy will, O Lord our God, that Thou bestow
a blessing upon the work of our hands. As
soon as he has begun to measure, he should
say: Blessed be He who sendeth a blessing upon
this pile. But if he measured first and then
pronounced the benediction, the prayer is in vain,
for a blessing is not bestowed upon anything
that is measured, numbered, or weighed, but
only upon things hidden from sight, as it is said:
"The Lord will command the blessing with thee
in thy barns."[142]

[140] Which includes the observance of the Sabbath.

[141] Figurative expression for industry and commerce.

[142] The biblical word for barns (באסמיך) suggests the
Aramaic verb סמא, to conceal, hide, hence R. Isaac's
interpretation.

ואמר רבי יצחק שמש בשבת צדקה לעניים
שנאמר וזרחה לכם יראי שמי שמש צדקה ומרפא:
ואמר רבי יצחק גדול יום הגשמים שאפילו
פרוטה שבכיס מתברכת בו שנאמר לתת מטר
ארצך בעתו ולברך את כל מעשה ידיך:

ואמר רבי יצחק אין הברכה מצויה אלא בדבר
הסמוי מן העין שנאמר יצו ה' אתך את הברכה
באסמיך:

תנא דבי רבי ישמעאל אין הברכה מצויה אלא
בדבר שאין העין שולטת בו שנאמר יצוה ה' אתך
את הברכה באסמיך:

תנו רבנן ההולך למוד את גרנו אומר יהי רצון
מלפניך ה' אלהינו שתשלח ברכה במעשה ידינו
התחיל למוד אומר ברוך השולח ברכה בכרי הזה
מדד ואחר כך ברך הרי זו תפלת שוא לפי שאין
הברכה מצויה לא בדבר המדוד ולא בדבר המנוי
ולא בדבר השקול אלא בדבר הסמוי מן העין
שנאמר יצו ה' אתך את הברכה באסמיך:

תורה אור   מסרת הש״ס והמדרשים

2 מלאכי ג' כ'.   4 דברים כ״ח   4 (פרוטה) ב״ר י״ג ט״ז; ד״ר ז' ו'.
י״ב.   7 דברים כ״ח ח'.   6 (הברכה) ב״מ מ״ב א'; ב״ר ס״ד
ו'; פסיקתא רבתי כ״ה (הערה ל״א);
פסדר״כ י״א (באבער דף צ״ח).

115

R. Johanan said: The day of rain is as important as that of the gathering of the exiled
(Israelites), for it is said (Ps., 126. 4): "Turn
our captivity, O Lord, as the streams in the dry
land," the word 'afiḳim (streams) meaning
rain, as it is said (Ps. 18. 16): "And the channels[143]
of water appeared." R. Johanan further said:
Great is the day of rain, for then even armies
must stop fighting, as it is said (Ps. 65. 11):
"Watering her ridges abundantly, settling down
the furrows thereof."[144] R. Johanan further said:
Rain is withheld only on account of those who
subscribe to charity in public and refuse to pay,
for it is said (Prov., 25.14): "As vapours and
wind without rain, so is he that boasteth
himself of a false gift." R. Johanan further
said: What is the meaning of the verse (Deut.,
14. 22): [fol. 9a] "Thou shalt surely tithe"?
Tithe, in order that thou mayest become rich.[145]
R. Johanan once met the young son of Resh
Laḳish and said to him: "Tell me thy verse."[146]
"Thou shalt surely tithe," said the boy, "pray,

[143] In the verse from Ps., 126. 4, the turning of the captivity is compared to 'afiḳim, which R. Johanan translates rain, because in Ps., 18. 16, the same word is used
for channels of water, which likewise means rain.

[144] Watering ridges presupposes rain, and the word for
furrows (גדודים) means also armies.

[145] The Talmud often exploits the absolute infinitive
or the following finite verb for halakic or homiletical purposes (comp. note 27). In the passage before us, reading
עשר תעשר, thou shalt surely tithe, תעשר is read (תָּעֲשֵׁר?) תֵּעָשֵׁר
and interpreted תתעשר, thou shalt become rich.

קבוץ גייסות צדקה מעשר פרנס סימן: אמר רבי
יוחנן גדול יום הגשמים כיום קבוץ גליות שנאמר
שובה ה' את שביתינו כאפיקים בנגב ואין אפיקים
אלא מטר שנאמר ויראו אפיקי מים:

5 ואמר רבי יוחנן גדול יום הגשמים שאפילו גייסות
פוסקות בו שנאמר תלמיה רוה נחת גדודה:

ואמר רבי יוחנן אין הגשמין נעצרין אלא בשביל
פוסקי צדקה ברבים ואין נותנין שנאמר נשיאים
ורוח וגשם אין איש מתהלל במתת שקר:

10 ואמר רבי יוחנן מאי דכתיב עשר תעשר עשר ט'
עי"א
בשביל שתתעשר:

רבי יוחנן אשכחיה לינוקיה דריש לקיש אמר
ליה אימא לי פסוקיך אמר ליה עשר תעשר אמר

תורה אור | מסרת הש"ס והמדרשים

3 תהלים קכ"ו ד'.   4 תהלים י"ח   2 (קבוץ גליות) ב"ר י"ג ה'.
ט"ז.   6 תהלים ס"ה י"א.   8 משלי   8 (פוסקי צדקה) סוכה כ"ט ב';
כ"ה י"ד.   10 דברים י"ד כ"ב.   יבמות ע"ח ב'; ירושלמי תענית ג' ג';
   קדושין ד' א'; סנהדרין ז'; מדרש
שמואל כ"ח; מדרש משלי כ"ה.   10 (עשר) שבת קי"ט א'; פדר"כ י"א
(באבער הערה ט"ו וע"ח); תנחומא ראה; שמ"ר ל"א י"ו.

---

[146] That is, the verse the boy was supposed to have
learned on that day in his Bible lesson; comp. Lewy,
Wörterbuch, s. v. פסק.

explain it to me." "Give tithe that thou mayest become rich," said R. Johanan. Whereupon the boy said: "Is man allowed to try God? Is it not written (Deut., 6.16): 'Ye shall not try the Lord'?" "Thus said R. 'Osha'ya," replied R. Johanan, "(trying is forbidden) except in this particular instance, for it is said (Mal., 3.10): 'Bring ye the whole tithe into the store-house, that there may be food in My house, and try Me now herewith, said the Lord of hosts, if I will not open you the windows of heaven, and pour you out a blessing, that there shall be more than sufficiency.'" [What is the meaning of the words: "that there shall be more than sufficiency"? Said Rami son of R. Yud in the name of Rab: It means that your lips will grow tired saying, it is enough].[147] The boy then said to R. Johanan: "If I had come to that verse, I should not have needed either you or 'Osha'ya, your teacher."[148]

Another time R. Johanan again met the same child and said to him: Tell me thy verse! The boy replied: "The foolishness of man perverteth his way; and his heart fretteth against the Lord" (Prov., 19.3). After pondering for a while over the matter R. Johanan said, is it possible that there is something in the Hagiographa to which Moses did not allude in the Pentateuch? Said the boy: "Is not this verse alluded to in the Pentateuch? Is it not written (Gen., 42. 28):

[147] The words in brackets are an insertion by the redactor of the Talmud.

[148] Because that verse would have suggested to him the solution.

ליה לפריש לי מר אמר ליה עשר ליה בשביל שתתעשר

אמר ליה ומי שרי לנסויי לקודשא בריך הוא

והכתיב לא תנסו את ה' אמר ליה הכי אמר רבי

אושעיא חוץ מזו שנאמר הביאו את כל המעשר אל

5 בית האוצר ויהי טרף בביתי ובחנוני נא בזאת אמר

ה' צבאות אם לא אפתח לכם את ארבות השמים

והריקתי לכם ברכה עד בלי די מאי עד בלי די

אמר רמי בר רב יוד אמר רב עד שיבלו שפתותיכם

מלומר די אמר ליה אי מטאי להתם לא הוה צריכנא

10 לך ולאושעיא רבך:

ותו אשכחיה רבי יוחנן לינוקיה דריש לקיש אמר

ליה אימא לי פסוקיך אמר ליה אולת אדם תסלף

דרכו ועל ה' יזעף לבו הוה קא תמה רבי יוחנן

אמר מי איכא מלתא בכתובי דלא רמזה משה

15 באוריתא אמר ליה אטו הא לא רמיזא והכתיב

תורה אור	מסרת הש״ס והמדרשים

3 דברים ו' ט״ז.   4 מלאכי ג' י'.   7 (בלי די) תענית כ״ב ב'; שבת
ל״ב ב'; מכות כ״ג ב'; ירושלמי   12 משלי י״ט ג'.
ברכות ט' ה'; (דף י״ח ג'); תענית
ג' ט'; ויק״ר ל״ה י״ב; במ״ר י״ב י״א; ד״ר י״ב י״א; אסתר רבה ה' ט״ו.

'And their heart failed them, and they turned trembling one to another, saying, what is this that God hath done unto us?' "[149]   R. Johanan lifted his eyes and looked at the boy (in astonishment).   The boy's mother then came in and took him away, saying: "Get away from him, that he may not do to you as he did to your father!"[150]

R. Johanan further said: Rain is granted for the sake of an individual, means of sustenance are granted for the sake of a multitude only. That rain is granted for the sake of an individual we learn from the verse (Deut., 28.12): "The Lord will open unto *thee* His good treasure, the heaven, to give the rain of *thy* land." That means of sustenance are granted for the sake of a multitude only, we learn from the verse (Exod., 16.4): "Behold I will cause to rain bread from heaven for *you*." But are not means of sustenance granted also for the sake of an individual? Do we not read: "R. Jose b. Judah said, three good leaders have arisen for Israel; they are Moses, Aaron and Miriam; and three precious gifts were presented to Israel for their sake. These are, the well, the pillar of cloud and the manna. The well was given for the merits of Miriam, the pillar of cloud for the merits of Aaron, and the manna for the merits of Moses. When Miriam died the well was taken away, for it is said

[149] The verse of the Pentateuch, the boy meant to say, expressed the same truth as Prov., 19. 3, for Joseph's brethren committed a folly in selling their brother and

ויצא לבם ויחרדו איש אל אחיו לאמר מה זאת עשה
אלהים לנו דלי עיניה וחזא ביה אתיא אימיה
אפיקתיה אמרה ליה תא מקמיה דלא ליעביד לך
כדעבד לאבוך:

ואמר רבי יוחנן מטר בשביל יחיד פרנסה בשביל 5
רבים מטר בשביל יחיד דכתיב יפתח ה' לך את
אוצרו הטוב את השמים לתת מטר ארצך פרנסה
בשביל רבים דכתיב הנני ממטיר לכם לחם מן
השמים ופרנסה בשביל יחיד לא והתניא רבי יוסי
ברבי יהודה אומר שלשה פרנסים טובים עמדו להם 10
לישראל ואלו הן משה אהרן ומרים ושלש מתנות
טובות נתנו להם על ידם ואלו הן באר עמוד ענן
ומן באר בזכות מרים עמוד ענן בזכות אהרן ומן
בזכות משה מתה מרים נסתלקה הבאר שנאמר

תורה אור מסרת הש״ס והמדרשים
1 בראשית מ״ב כ״ח. 6 דברים 10 (פרנסים) תוספתא סוטה י״א;
כ״ח י״ב. 8 שמות ט״ז ד'. ס״ע י'; ויק״ר כ״ז ו'; במ״ר א' ב',
י״ג כ'; שהש״ר ד' (פסוק שני
שדיך); תנחומא במדבר א' סימן ב'; מדרש תנאים 227. 12 (באר וכו')
ספרי דברים ש״ד; מכילתא ויסע ה'; מדרש משלי י״ד; ב״ר ס״ב ד' וע'
בכל המקומות שציינתי למלת פרנסים שבסמוך.

then complained about what "God had done" unto them.

[150] This alludes to a story related in Baba Mezi'a,
84a, according to which R. Johanan was the cause of
Resh Laḳish's premature death.

121

(Num., 20. 1): 'And Miriam died there,' and immediately after it is written: 'And there was no water for the congregation.' Subsequently the well came back on account of the merits of Moses and Aaron. When Aaron died the pillar of cloud disappeared, as it is said (*ibid.*, 21.1): 'And the Canaanite, the king of Arad, heard.' What did he hear? He heard that Aaron had died and the clouds of glory were taken away from Israel, so he thought that now permission was given to wage war against them. Therefore it is written (*ibid.*, 20.29): 'And all the congregation *saw* that Aaron was dead,' [concerning which R. 'Abahu said that one should not read 'they saw,' but 'they were seen'[151]—agreeing herein with what Resh Laḳish said, namely, that *ki* (כִּי) has four meanings: *if*, *perhaps* (lest), *but*, *because*]. Both (well and cloud) later came back on account of the merits of Moses, but when Moses died all three disappeared, as it is said (Zech., 11.8): 'And I cut off the three shepherds in one month.' But is it true that they died in one month? Did not Miriam die in Nisan, Aaron in Ab, and Moses in Adar? The meaning therefore can only be that the three precious gifts which had been given to Israel through

---

[151] The text reads וַיִּרְאוּ, they (the congregation) *saw*, which R. 'Abahu vocalizes וַיֵּרָאוּ, they *were seen*, *i. e.*, became visible, because, with the death of Aaron, the clouds, which had hitherto screened them from sight, disappeared, thus bringing the enemy upon them. R. 'Abahu's explanation, however, is only possible when sup-

ותמת שם מרים וכתיב בתריה ולא היה מים לעדה
וחזרה בזכות משה ואהרן מת אהרן נסתלק עמוד
הענן דכתיב וישמע הכנעני מלך ערד מה שמועה
שמע שמע שמת אהרן ונסתלקו ענני כבוד מישראל
וכסבור נתנה רשות להלחם בישראל והיינו דכתיב   5
ויראו כל העדה כי גוע אהרן ואמר רבי אבהו אל
תקרי ויראו אלא ויראו וכדדריש ריש לקיש דאמר
ריש לקיש כי משמש בארבע לשונות אי דילמא
אלא דהא חזרו שניהם בזכות משה מת משה נסתלקו
שלשתן שנאמר ואכחד את שלשת הרעים בירח   10
אחד וכי בירח אחד מתו והלא מרים מתה בניסן
ואהרן באב ומשה באדר אלא מלמד שנסתלקו
שלש מתנות טובות אלו שנתנו לישראל על ידן

מסרת הש"ס והמדרשים	תורה אור
3 (וישמע) רה"ש ג' א'; תוספתא	1 במדבר כ' א'. 3 במדבר כ"א א'.
סוטה ריש פי"א; ספרי בהעלותך	6 במדבר כ' כ"ט. 10 זכריה י"א ח'.
פ"ב; ס"ע ט'; פסדר"כ י"ט;	
8 (כי) פסחים צ"ג ב';	ירושלמי יומא א' א' וסוטה א' י';
12 (באדר) קדושין ל"ח א'; מגלה י"ג ב';	נטין צ' א'; שבועות מ"ט ב'.
סוטה י"ב ב'; תוספתא סוטה י"א; ס"ע י'.	

ported by the statement of Resh Laḳish that *ki* (כי = that)
means also *because*, so that instead of "they say *that*"
we can translate "they were seen *because*", etc.

them were taken away in one month." Now, does it not follow from the foregoing Baraita that means of sustenance are granted also for the sake of an individual?![152] Moses is an exception; since all his requests were for a multitude, he was himself regarded as a multitude.

R. Samuel b. 'Idi, R. Huna b. Manoah and R. Ḥiyya of Vastania used to study under Raba. After Raba's death they studied under R. Papa. Whenever the latter taught them something which did not appeal to them, he noticed that they were winking to one another. R. Papa therefore felt discouraged, [fol. 9b] whereupon he dreamt that he read the verse: "And I cut off the three shepherds in one month." The next morning, when they took leave from him, he said to them: Go ye scholars in peace![153]

R. Shimi b. 'Ashi, studying under R. Papa, used to argue against him very much. One day R. Shimi noticed R. Papa falling on his face[153a] and saying: May the Lord save me from being put to shame through Shimi! R. Shimi then resolved to keep silence, and raised no more questions.

Resh Laḳish was likewise of the opinion that rain is granted also for the sake of an individual,

[152] The manna, a means of sustenance, was granted according to this Baraita solely through the merits of Moses.

[153] In bidding farewell to a dying person one is required to say (according to Talmud *Berakot*, 64a) "go *in* peace" (בשלמא), while on all other occasions one must say "go *to* peace" (לשלמא). R. Papa, thinking, on account

בירח אחד אלמא אשכחן פרנסה בשביל יחיד שאני
משה כיון דלרבים קא בעי כרבים דמי:
רב שמואל בר אידי ורב הונא בר מנוח ורב חייא
מווסתניא הוו שכיחי קמיה דרבא כי נח נפשיה
5 דרבא אתו לקמיה דרב פפא כל אימת דהוה אמר
להו שמעתא ולא הוה מסתברא להו הוו מרמזי
ט׳ בידיהו להדדי חלש דעתיה ׀ ואקריוה בחלמיה
ע״ב
ואכחד את שלשת הרעים בירח אחד למחר כי
הוו מיפטרי מיניה אמר להו זילו רבנן בשלמא:
10 רב שימי בר אשי הוה שכיח קמיה דרב פפא
הוה מקשי ליה טובא יומא חד חזייה דנפל על אפיה
שמעיה דקאמר רחמנא לצלן ככסופא דשימי
קביל עליה שתיקותא ותו לא אקשי ליה:
ואף ריש לקיש סבר מטר בשביל יחיד דאמר

תורה אור   מסרת הש״ס והמדרשים
8 זכריה י״א ח׳.   1 (בשביל יחיד) ירו׳ תענית ג׳ ב׳;
                              ויק״ר ל״ה י״ב.

of his dream, that the three scholars were doomed to die,
used the first formula; comp. C. F. Burney, *Origin of the
Fourth Gospel*, Oxford, 1922, p. 14.

[153a] "Falling on his face" is a technical expression for
the private prayer recited after the *'Amidah*, and known
today also as *tahanun* (supplication).

for he said, whence do we infer that rain is
granted for the sake of an individual? It is
written (Zech., 10. 1): "Ask ye of the Lord rain
in the time of the latter rain, even of the Lord
that maketh lightnings; and He will give them
showers of rain, to every one grass in the field."
Now, from the words "He will give *them*," one
might conclude that He gives it only when
everybody needs it; Scripture therefore adds
"to every *one*"; but if it said only "to every one,"
we might think that He gives it only when that
one needs it for all his fields; Scripture therefore
says "field" (singular); but the word "field"
might still be understood to mean a whole (large)
field; Scripture therefore says "grass."[154] This
finds its illustration in the following case: R.
Daniel b. R. Ketina had a garden which he used
to examine every day, and say: This bed needs
rain, and this one does not need it. The next
day it was found that rain fell upon the one,
but not upon the other.

What is the meaning of "The Lord maketh
lightnings" (Zech., 10. 1)? Said R. Jose b.
Hanina, it teaches us that the Holy One pre-
pares a cloud for every righteous man.
What are *hazizim?*[155] Said R. Judah, *porehot*.
But what are *porehot*. Said R. Papa, a thin
cloud under a thick one. R. Johanan said,
porehot are a sign of coming rain. 'Ulla happened
to be in Pumbedita and, seeing *porehot*, said,

---

[154] Which specification is supposed to indicate that rain
is granted even if it is needed only for one plant in the
entire field.

126

ריש לקיש מנין למטר בשביל יחיד שנאמר שאלו
מה' מטר בעת מלקוש ה' עשה חזיזים ומטר גשם
יתן להם לאיש עשב בשדה יכול לכל תלמוד לומר
לאיש אי לאיש יכול לכל שדותיו תלמוד לומר
שדה אי שדה יכול לכל השדה תלמוד לומר עשב
כי הא דרב דניאל בר רב קטינא הוא ליה ההיא
גנתא כל יומא הוה אזיל וסייר לה אמר האי מישרא
בעי מיא והאי מישרא לא בעי מיא למחר להאי
אתא מטרא ולהאי לא אתא מטרא:

מאי ה' עשה חזיזים אמר רבי יוסי ברבי חנינא
מלמד שכל צדיק וצדיק עושה לו הקדוש ברוך
הוא חזיז בפני עצמו מאי חזיזים אמר רב יהודה
פורחות מאי פורחות אמר רב פפא עיבא קלישא
דתותי עיבא סמיכא אמר רבי יוחנן סימן למטר
פורחות:

עולא איקלע לפומבדיתא חזא פורחות אמר

תורה אור
1 זכריה י' א'.

¹⁵⁵ This is the word used in Zech., 10. 1, for lightnings.
R. Jose, however, translates it clouds, and R. Judah
poreḥot.

move your things, for rain is due to come presently. But rain did not come, whereupon 'Ulla remarked: As the Babylonians are deceivers so are their rains. ['Ulla once happened to be in Pumbedita and seeing that a basketful of dates was selling for a *zuz*,[156] he remarked: A basket of honey for a *zuz* and yet the Babylonians are not studying the Torah! He ate some and became indisposed. He then said: A basketful of knives for a *zuz* and yet the Babylonians study the Torah!].

R. Judah said: A mist before rain is a sign of coming rain; and in order to remember this, think of a sieve.[157] A mist after rain indicates the cessation of rain; and in order to remember this, think of the excrements of goats.[158]

We read in a Baraita ('Erubin, 45b): R. Eliezer said, the whole universe drinks from the ocean, as it is said (Gen., 2. 6): "There went up a mist from the earth,[159] and watered the whole face of the ground." Said R. Joshua to R. Eliezer, is not the water of the ocean salty?! Said R. Eliezer, it gets sweetened in the clouds. R. Joshua said, the whole universe drinks from the

[156] The value of a drachma in ancient Greece, about 20 cents; comp. Zuckermann, *Talmudische Gewichte und Münzen*, Breslau, 1862, pp. 6, 24.

[157] From which the finest flour resembling a mist comes first, and then the heavier, thicker parts, resembling drops of rain.

[158] First the animal discharges with force and then relaxes; comp. the commentaries and *'Aruk, s. v.* חר, No. 5.

[159] "Earth" in the verse is according to R. Eliezer

להו פנו מניכו דהשתא אתי מטרא לסוף לא אתא
מטרא אמר כי היכי דמשקרי בבלאי הכי משקרי
מטריהו עולא איקלע לפומבדיתא חזא מלא צנא
דתמרי בזוזא אמר מלא צנא דדובשא בזוזא ובבלאי
לא עסקי באוריתא אכל מניהו ואצטער אמר
מלא צנא דסכיני בזוזא ובבלאי עסקי באוריתא:

אמר רב יהודה נהילא קמי מטרא אתי מטרא
וסימניך מהולתא נהילא בתר מטרא פסק מטרא
וסימניך חריא דעיזי:

תניא רבי אליעזר אומר כל העולם כלו ממימי
אוקינוס הוא שותה שנאמר ואד יעלה מן הארץ
והשקה את כל פני האדמה אמר לו רבי יהושע
והלא מימי אוקינוס מלוחין הן אמר לו מתמתקין
הן בעבים רבי יהושע אומר כל העולם כלו ממים

תורה אור	מסרת הש"ס והמדרשים

11 בראשית ב' ו'.　　3 (צנא דתמרי) פסחים פ"ח א'.
13 (מימי אוקינוס) עירובין מ"ה ב';
ב"ר ה' ג', י"ג י'; קה"ר א' פסוק כל הנחלים אות א'; תנחומא (הנדפס)
מקץ א'; מדרש תהלים י"ח ט"ז וע' ירושלמי סוכה א' ה').

---

not to be taken literally, but as an expression for this
world below, including the ocean, the real generator
of the mists which gather in the air and turn into rain.

waters above (the firmament),[160] as it is said
(Deut., 11. 11): "A land that drinketh water
as the rain of heaven cometh down." How then
can one explain the verse: "There went up a
mist from the earth"? This verse teaches that
the clouds[161] rise and soar upward, where they
open their mouths like a leathern bottle and receive the rain water, as it is said (Job, 36. 27):
"They distil rain from His vapour." They (the
clouds) are perforated like a sieve and distil
water to the ground, as it is said (II Samuel, 22.
12): "Gathering[162] of waters, thick clouds of the
skies." Between each drop of rain there is no
more space than the breadth of a hair, which is
to impress upon us the truth that the day
of rain is as miraculous a phenomenon as the day
on which heaven and earth were created, for
it is said (Job, 5. 9): "Who doeth great things
and *unsearchable*, marvellous things without
number," and further on (*ib.*, 5. 10): "Who giveth
rain upon the earth, and sendeth waters upon
the fields," and elsewhere (Is., 40. 28): "Hast
thou not known? hast thou not heard that
the everlasting God, the Lord, the Creator of the
ends of the earth, fainteth not, neither is weary?
His discernment is past *searching*[163] out."

[160] See Gen., 1. 6–7.

[161] R. Joshua imagines the clouds as sieve-like vessels
which receive the water from "above the firmament" and
let it come through in the form of rain.

[162] The Hebrew word for "gathering" is the same as
used here by R. Joshua for "distil," so that the verse
reads: "Distilling of waters," bearing out R. Joshua's
idea.

העליונים הוא שותה שנאמר למטר השמים תשתה
מים אלא מה אני מקיים ואד יעלה מן הארץ מלמד
שהעננים מתגברין ועולין לרקיע ופותחין פיהן
כנוד ומקבלין מי מטר שנאמר יזקו מטר לאדו והן
מנוקבין ככברה ומחשרין אותן על גבי קרקע
שנאמר חשרת מים עבי שחקים ואין בין טפה וטפה
אלא כמלא נימא ללמדך שגדול יום הגשמים לפני
הקדוש ברוך הוא כיום שנבראו בו שמים וארץ
שנאמר עשה גדלות ואין חקר נפלאות עד אין מספר
וכתיב הנתן מטר על פני ארץ ושלח מים על
פני חוצות ולהלן הוא אומר הלוא ידעת אם לא
שמעת אלהי עולם ה' בורא קצות הארץ לא ייעף
ולא ייגע אין חקר לתבונתו:

תורה אור   מסרת הש"ס והמדרשים

1 בראשית י"א י"א. 4 איוב ל"ו כ"ז. 7 (יום הגשמים) לעיל ז' ב': ב"ר
6 שמואל ב' כ"ב י"ב. 9 איוב ה'   י"ג ד'; קה"ר שם.
ט'—י'. 11 ישעיה מ' כ"ט.

[163] Job, 5. 10, speaking of rain, makes it evident that
"things unsearchable" (אין חקר) in the preceding verse
likewise refers to the phenomenon of rain. Now the
same expression (אין חקר) is used also in connection with
creation ("past searching out"), which proves that rain
and creation are both equally miraculous; comp. above
note 18.

It has been said above[164]: "R. Eliezer said, it
gets sweetened in the clouds"—whence did he derive this? He derived it in the way reported
by R. Isaac b. Joseph in the name of R. Johanan:
In one passage we find it written (Ps., 18.12):
"darkness (*ḥeshkat*) of waters," in another we
find (II Sam., 22.12): "gathering (*ḥashrat*) of
waters"; take the *kaf* (of ḥeshkat) and add it to
the *resh* (in ḥashrat)[165] and then read *hakshārat*
(=improvement) of waters. What use does R.
Joshua make of these two verses? He explains
the matter on the basis of what was later reported by R. Dimi who, upon returning from
Palestine to Babylon, said that the Palestinians
used to say: when the clouds are dark they contain much water, but when they are light they
contain little water.[166]

Whose view is represented in the following
Baraita (Bereshit Rabba, 4, 3): The upper waters

[164] This paragraph has been transferred here from fol.
10a of the editions; see the Hebrew notes.

[165] Not exactly to the *resh*, but to the word (ḥashrat)
which contains the *resh*. R. Isaac, a Babylonian, performs
two operations on the word חשרת. First he inserts a כ
and then reads a ה for the ח, thus obtaining הכשרת, which
means improvement, namely, the sweetening in the clouds
of the salty water of the ocean, so that it becomes fit to
water the earth. The changing of the ח into ה is nothing
strange, as in Babylon the ח was pronounced like the
ה (the name חונא in the Palestinian Talmud is always
written הונא in the Babylonian, האי (the Gaon) probably for
חי; comp. for other examples Rabbinovicz, *Variae lectiones*,
ad locum). To be sure, R. Isaac reports it in the name

אמר מר אמר לו רבי אליעזר מתמתקין הן
בעבים מנא ליה דכי אתא רב יצחק בר יוסף אמר
רבי יוחנן כתיב חשכת מים וכתיב חשרת מים שקול
כף ושדי אריש וקרי ביה הכשרת מים ורבי יהושע
5 בהני קראי מאי דריש בהו סבר לה כי הא דכי
אתא רב דימי אמר אמרי במערבא חשוך ענני
סגיין מוהי נהור ענני זעירין מוהי:

כמאן אזלא הא דתניא מים העליונים במאמר

תורה אור ⁣ מסרת הש"ס והמדרשים
3 תהלים י"ח י"ב. ⁣ 3 ש"ב כ"ב י"ב. ⁣ 6 (חשוך ענני) מדרש תהלים י"ח
ט"ז. ⁣ 8 (דתניא) ב"ר ד' ג'.

of R. Johanan, a Palestinian, but R. Isaac was often
suspected as to the correctness of his reports (comp.
Yebamot, 64b; Hyman, תולדות תנאים ואמוראים, 794f.). The
insertion of the כ seemed justified by the fact that II
Samuel, 22 and Ps. 18 are duplicates, and hence were
considered as supplements to each other.

[166] This platitude sounds better in the original Aramaic,
where it appears in the form of a popular proverb. The
idea is that R. Joshua does not consider חשכת, darkness,
as a variant of חשרת, gathering, so as to elaborate הכשרת,
but sees in the verse (Ps., 18. 12), "darkness of waters,
thick clouds of the skies" a corroboration of the proverb
that heavy dark clouds are the forebodings of much rain.

are suspended (in the air) by a divine ordinance, and the rain is the fruit thereof, as it is said (Ps., 104.13): "The earth is full of the fruit of Thy work"? Whose view? Answer—that of R. Joshua! [R. Eliezer, however, refers this verse to the handiwork of the Holy One, blessed be He.]

Whose view is expressed in the verse (Ps., 104. 13): "Who waterest the mountains from Thine upper chambers,"—which was interpreted by R. Johanan to mean the upper waters of the Holy One, blessed be He? Whose view?—that of R. Joshua! But how does R. Eliezer explain this verse? He would say that inasmuch as the moisture first rises to the upper regions, it appears as if the rain came from the upper waters.[167]

Whose view does R. Ḥanina follow who, commenting upon the verse (Ps., 33. 7): "He gathereth the waters of the sea together as a heap, He layeth up the deeps in storehouses," says, that it is the deeps that cause the storehouses to fill themselves with grain? Whose view?—that of R. Eliezer! But how does R. Joshua explain this verse? According to him this verse [fol. 10a] refers to the creation of the world.

Our Rabbis have taught: Palestine is watered first, and then the rest of the world; Palestine is watered by rain and the rest of the world by the residue (of the rain) for Palestine, which may be illustrated by the procedure of a man who is making cheese, and in so doing takes up what is eatable and leaves the refuse; Palestine is

[167] Accordingly the "upper chambers" is not to be taken literally.

הם תלויים ופרותיהן מי גשמים שנאמר מפרי מעשיך

תשבע הארץ כמאן כרבי יהושע (ורבי אליעזר

ההוא במעשה ידיו של הקדוש ברוך הוא כתיב):

כמאן אזלא הא דכתיב משקה הרים מעליותיו

5 ואמר רבי יוחנן מעליותיו של הקדוש ברוך הוא

כמאן כרבי יהושע ורבי אליעזר כיון דקסלקי

להתם כמאן דקא אתי מהתם דמי:

כמאן אזלא הא דאמר רבי חנינא כנס כנד מי

הים נתן באוצרות תהומות מי גרם לאוצרות

10 שיתמלאו בר תהומות כמאן כרבי אליעזר ורבי

יהושע ההוא | בבריתו של עולם כתיב: ע״א

תנו רבנן ארץ ישראל שותה תחלה וכל העולם

כולו שותה בסוף ארץ ישראל שותה מי גשמים וכל

העולם כולו שותה מי תמצית משל לאדם שמגבן

15 את הגבינה נוטל את האכל ומניח את הפסלת ארץ

תורה אור
1 תהלים ק״ד י״ג.   4 תהלים ק״ד י״ג.   8 תהלים ל״נ ז׳.

135

watered by God Himself, the rest of the world
by a messenger, as it is said (Job, 5. 10): "Who
giveth rain upon the earth, and *sendeth* waters
upon the fields."[168]

R. Joshua b. Levi said: The whole world is
watered by the residue of the garden of Eden,
for it is said (Gen., 2. 10): "And a river went
out of Eden to water the garden."[169] It was
taught that the residue in a vessel watering a
kor will suffice to water a *tarkab*.[170]

Our Rabbis have taught: Egypt extends over
four hundred square parasangs and is one sixtieth as large as Ethiopia; Ethiopia is one sixtieth as large as the universe, and the universe is
one sixtieth as large as (the Garden of) Eden;
(the Garden of) Eden is one sixtieth as large as
Gehenna, so that in comparison to Gehenna
the whole world is like the lid of a pot. Some
say that neither Eden nor Gehenna has a limit.

[168] ארץ, earth, means also land, here the Holy Land,
while חוצות, (outside) fields, refers to the "rest of the
world."

[169] Which is to prove that Eden was supplied first,
"and from thence it parted and became four heads"
(Gen. 2. 10).

[170] The meaning is that from the residue of water in a
vessel used to irrigate an area requiring a *kor* of seed, one
can irrigate an area requiring a *tarkab* of seed. *Kor*,
a dry measure (I Kings, 5.2), equals thirty *se'ah* (II
Kings, 7,16); *tarkab* = τρίκαβos = three *ḳabs*, is half
of a *se'ah;* comp. above, note 62. The passage gains
some sense only in connection with the Baraita that follows
it. For according to it the whole world is one sixtieth of

ישראל הקדוש ברוך הוא משקה אותה בעצמו וכל
העולם כלו משקהו על ידי שליח שנאמר הנתן
מטר על פני ארץ ושלח מים על פני חוצות:

אמר רבי יהושע בן לוי כל העולם כלו מתמצית
5 גן עדן הוא שותה שנאמר ונהר יוצא מעדן להשקות
את הגן תנא מתמצית בית כור שותה תרקב:

תנו רבנן מצרים ארבע מאות פרסה על ארבע
מאות פרסה ומצרים אחד מששים בכוש וכוש אחד
מששים בעולם ועולם אחד מששים בעדן ועדן אחד
10 מששים בגיהנם נמצא כל העולם כלו ככסוי קדרה
לגיהנם ויש אומרים עדן אין לו שעור וגיהנם אין
לה שעור:

תורה אור   מסרת הש"ס והמדרשים

2 איוב ה' י'.   5 בראשית ב' י'.   1 (בעצמו) ספרי עקב ריש פמ"ב
(וע' מכדרשב"י 168).   6 (תרקב)
ירושלמי ברכות ריש פ"א; ב"ר ט"ו ב'; שהש"ר ו' פסוק ט' אות ג'.
7 (מצרים) פסחים צ"ד א', ובכל המקומות שציינתי למלת תרקב.

the expanse of Eden.   Now, as in the opinion of R. Joshua
the world is watered from the residue of Eden, it follows
that the residue of a *kor* (the quantity which inevitably
remains in the vessel after it has been emptied) is enough
to water a space as large as one watered by a *tarkab*,
which is the sixtieth of a *kor*; see also the Hebrew notes.

R. 'Osha'ya said, what is the meaning of the verse (Jerem., 51. 13): "O thou that dwellest upon many waters, abundant in treasures"? The verse intimates that it is because she (Babylon) dwells upon many waters that her treasures are abundant. Rab said: Babylonia is rich because she harvests without rain.[171] 'Abbayi said, it is generally accepted that a flooded (swampy) land is better than a dry land.

On the third of Marḥeshwan one is to begin praying for rain; Rabban Gamaliel says, on the seventh of that month.

Said R. Eleazar, the law is in accordance with the view of R. Gamaliel.

A Baraita reads: Ḥananiah said, in the diaspora we must wait until the sixtieth day after the autumnal equinox. R. Huna b. Ḥiyya said in the name of Samuel, the law follows Ḥananiah. This cannot be so! For when Samuel was asked when we must begin to say: "And give dew and rain," he replied: From the time when the employees of Ṭabūt the Fowler begin to carry in the twigs![172] Answer: Both of these time-limits may be the same.

The question was raised: Is the sixtieth day to be counted with those that precede it or with those that follow?[173] Rab said, the sixtieth day belongs to the days that succeed it, but

[171] Babylon, being low land, can get along with a minimum of rain.

[172] As fuel for the winter, which was a sign that the rainy season was near.

[173] In the first case praying for rain would have to begin

אמר רבי אושעיא מאי דכתיב שכנת על מים
רבים רבת אוצרות מי גרם לבבל שיתרבו
אוצרותיה מים רבים ששוכנת עליהם אמר רב
עתירה בבל דחצדא בלא מטרא אמר אביי נקיטינן
טובעני ולא יובשני:

בשלשה במרחשון שואלין את הגשמים רבן
גמליאל אומר בשבעה בו: אמר רבי אלעזר הלכה
כרבן מליאל:

תניא חנניה אומר ובגולה עד ששים יום בתקופה

אמר רב הונא בר חייא אמר שמואל הלכה
כחנניה איני והא בעו מיניה משמואל מאימתי
מדכרינן טל ומטר ואמר להו מכי מעיילי ציבי
לבי טבות רישבא דילמא אידי ואידי חד שעורא
הוא:

איבעיא להו יום ששים כלפני ששים או כלאחר
ששים רב אמר יום ששים כלאחר ששים ושמואל

תורה אור   מסרת הש"ס והמדרשים
1 ירמיה נ"א י"ג.   7 (הלכה כר"ג) לעיל ד' ב',
ו' א'; ב"מ כ"ח א'.   9 (חנניה)
ירושלמי תענית א' א'.

on the day following the sixtieth, in the second case on the
sixtieth itself.

Samuel said, the sixtieth day belongs to the days that precede it. Said R. Naḥman b. Isaac, the sign[174] for it should be: Those high up need water, those below need no water. R. Papa said, the law is that the sixtieth day is to be treated like those following it.

If the seventeeth of Marḥeshwan has come, and there has been no rainfall, distinguished individuals begin to fast.

Who is meant by "individuals"? Said R. Huna, Scholars. R. Huna further said, the individuals fast three days, Monday, Thursday and Monday. What does he teach us? Do we not read:[175] Public fasts should not be decreed to begin on Thursday in order not to cause a sudden rise in market prices,[176] but the first three fast-days should be in the order of Monday, Thursday, and Monday? Answer. You might think that this refers only to congregational fasts but not to the fasts of individuals, therefore he teaches us (that it applies also to fasts of individuals). The same is taught in a Baraita: Individuals fast three days, Monday, Thursday and Monday, but must refrain from fasting if these days coincide with the New moon [fol. 10b] or any of the holidays recorded in the Scroll of Fasts.

Our Rabbis have taught: One should not say I am merely a student of the Law and not yet worthy of assuming the rôle of a (distinguished)

[174] To prevent confusion of the statements of Rab and Samuel, R. Naḥman tells us to bear in mind that people living in elevated sections need more rain than those living in valleys, hence Rab, President of the academy of Sura,

אמר יום ששים כלפני ששים אמר רב נחמן בר יצחק
וסימניך עילאי בעו מיא תתאי לא בעו מיא אמר
רב פפא הלכתא יום ששים כלאחר ששים:

הגיע שבעה עשר במרחשון ולא ירדו גשמים
5 התחילו היחידים מתענין:

מאן יחידים אמר רב הונא רבנן ואמר רב
הונא יחידים מתענין שלש תעניות שני וחמישי
ושני מאי קא משמע לן תנינא אין גוזרין תענית על
הצבור בתחלה בחמישי שלא להפקיע את השערים
10 אלא שלש תעניות הראשונות שני וחמישי ושני מהו
דתימא הני מילי צבור אבל יחיד לא קא משמע
לן תניא נמי הכי יחידים מתענין שני וחמישי ושני
ע״ב ומפסיקין בראשי חדשים | ובימים טובים הכתובין
במגלת תענית:

15 תנו רבנן לא יאמר יחיד תלמיד אני איני ראוי

מסרת הש״ס והמדרשים

6 (מאן יחידים) ירושלמי שם א׳   ד׳.   8 (אין גוזרין) לקמן ט״ו ב׳.

a town situated in higher regions, required that the
sixtieth day should mark the beginning of prayer for
rain, while Samuel, President of the academy of Nehardea,
situated in a valley, postponed the prayer to the day after
the sixtieth; see also the Hebrew notes.

[175] See the Mishnah, below, p. 214.9.

[176] See below, note 233.

141

individual, for all students are fit therefor. Who is to be considered as a (distinguished) individual, and who as a student? A distinguished individual is whoever is worthy of being appointed leader of a community, a student is whoever can reply satisfactorily to all questions put before him concerning any subject of halakah within the range of his studies, including even the treatise of the Kallah.[177]

Our Rabbis have taught: Not every one who wants to act as a distinguished individual may do so, but students may; this is the view of R. Meir; R. Jose says, everybody is entitled thereto and deserves to be well thought of, for so acting brings him no distinction, but rather causes him suffering.

Another Baraita reads: Not every one who wishes to act as a distinguished individual is entitled to do so; students, however, are entitled thereto: this is the view of R. Simeon b. Eleazar, Rabban Simeon b. Gamaliel says, if it is a case where acting as a distinguished individual would bring him distinction, he may not do so, if it would bring him suffering, he is well entitled to it.

Our Rabbis have taught: If one is fasting for the recovery of a sick person and in the meantime the person has recovered, or for the

[177] That is, any treatise of the Talmud that happened to be studied during the so-called Kallah months (Adar and Elul) when the academies were open for the public, and the treatises may, therefore, not have been studied with much thoroughness. Others think the Talmud refers

לכך אלא כל התלמידים ראויין לכך איזהו יחיד
ואיזהו תלמיד יחיד כל שראוי למנותו פרנס על
הצבור תלמיד כל ששואלים אותו דבר הלכה
בתלמודו ואומרו ואפילו במסכתא דכלה:

5	תנו רבנן לא כל הרוצה לעשות עצמו יחיד
עושה והתלמידים עושין דברי רבי מאיר רבי יוסי
אומר עושה וזכור לטוב לפי שאין שבח הוא לו
אלא צער הוא לו תניא אידך לא כל הרוצה לעשות
עצמו יחיד עושה והתלמידים עושין דברי רבי
10	שמעון בן אלעזר רבן שמעון בן גמליאל אומר דבר
של שבח אינו עושה דבר של צער עושה:

תנו רבנן הרי שהיה מתענה על החולה ונתרפא

מסרת הש"ס והמדרשים

ע' בכל המקומות שציינתי לאיזהו	2 (איזהו תלמיד) שבת קי"ד א';
הלמיד. 8 (כל הרוצה) תוספתא	קדושין מ"ט ב'; ירושלמי מו"ק ג'
תענית א' ז'. ירושלמי ברכות ב' ט'.	ריש ה"ז (וע' ירושלמי ובבלי ב"מ
12 (חולה) תוספתא שם ג' ג'.	סוף פרק ב'). 4 (מס' כלה)

here to the special tractate known under the name Kallah,
which was not supposed to be studied by everybody;
comp. the commentaries *ad locum*; Rashi to Sabbath, 114a;
Tosafot, ibid. s. v. ואפילו; Bacher, *J. E.*, vii, 423;
Reifmann, בית תלמוד, iv, 84; Halberstam, *ibid.*, p. 256;
Goldberg, *Der Traktat Derek Erez*, Breslau, 1888, p. vii.

relief from some affliction and in the meantime
the affliction has passed, he must nevertheless fast
to the end of the day. One who, while fasting, goes from a place where the people fast to
a place where they do not fast, must fast to
the end of the day; if he goes from a place where
the people do not fast to a place where they
fast, he must fast with the latter. If, for-
getting his fast, he ate or drank, he must not
make it appear before the people, nor must he
indulge himself in delicacies.

"And Jacob said unto his sons, Why do ye
look one upon another?" (Gen., 42. 1). Said
R. Judah in the name of Rab, Jacob said to his
sons, make no show of your plenty before the
sons of Esau and of Ishmael, lest they become
jealous of you.

"See that ye fall not out by the way" (*ib.*,
45.24)—Joseph said to his brethren, Do not engage in discussions of the Law, lest the road
become unsafe for you. This cannot be so!
For R. 'El'ai b. Berechiah said: Two scholars who travel on the road and do not discuss
among themselves the words of the Torah deserve to be burned, as it is said (II Kings, 2. 11):
"And it came to pass, as they still went on, and
talked, that behold, there appeared a chariot of
fire and horses of fire, which parted them both
asunder," which shows that the reason they were
saved (from the fire) was that there was talking
(about the Torah) among them, but had there
been none, they would not have been saved!
This is no contradiction, for in the one case

144

על הצרה ועברה הרי זה מתענה ומשלים ההולך
ממקום שמתענין למקום שאין מתענין הרי זה מתענה
ומשלים ממקום שאין מתענין למקום שמתענין הרי
זה מתענה עמהם שכח ואכל ושתה אל יתראה
בפניהם ואל ינהג עדונין בעצמו:

ויאמר יעקב לבניו למה תתראו אמר רב יהודה
אמר רב אמר להם יעקב לבניו אל תראו עצמכם
בפני בני עשו ובפני בני ישמעאל כאלו אתם שבעין
כדי שלא יתקנאו בכם:

אל תרגזו בדרך אמר להם יוסף לאחיו אל
תתעסקו בדבר הלכה שמא תרגז עליכם הדרך
איני והאמר רבי עילאי בר ברכיה שני תלמידי
חכמים המהלכים בדרך ואין ביניהם דברי תורה
ראויין לישרף שנאמר ויהי המה הלכים הלוך ודבר
והנה רכב אש וסוסי אש טעמא דאיכא דבור הא

תורה אור   מסרת הש"ס והמדרשים

6 בראשית מ"ב א'.   10 בראשית   1 (ההולך) תוספתא שם ג' ה'.
מ"ה כ"ד.   14 מ"ב ב' י"א.   4 (שכח) תוספתא שם ג' ד'.   11
(תתעסקו) ע' ב"ר צ"ד ב'.   12 (שני
ת"ח) סוטה מ"ט א'; ירושלמי ברכות ה' ריש ה"א; תדא"ר ה' (מא"ש צד 23).

reference is had to the mere recitation of one's studies, in the other to the speculation about them.

We read in a Baraita: Joseph instructed his brethren, do not march in wide (hasty) steps, and bring the sun into town. "Do not march in wide (hasty) steps," because it was said a wide step takes away one five-hundredth of one's eye-sight, and "bring the sun into town," because it was said by R. Judah in the name of Rab, one should always enter (town) in day-time and leave it in day-time, for it is said (Gen., 44. 3): "As soon as the morning was light, the men were sent away."

R. Judah said in the name of Rab, who received it from R. Ḥiyya: One who travels on the road must not eat more than one eats in years of famine. What is the reason therefor? Here (in Babylonia) it was explained that it is in order to prevent disorder of the bowels;[178] in Palestine they said that it is in order to prevent shortage of provisions. Does it make any practical difference what reason we adopt? Answer. The difference arises with regard [fol. 11a] to one travelling on a ship,[179] or one travelling from station to station.[180] R. Papa ate a loaf of bread each parasang, for he was of the opinion that the reason for recommending a short diet was to prevent disorder of the bowels (of which he was not afraid).

[178] Which would prevent him from keeping pace with the caravan.

[179] On a ship one need not fear to be left behind, but

ליכא דבור ראוין לישרף לא קשיא הא במגרס
הא בעיוני:

במתניתא תנא אמר להם יוסף לאחיו אל תפסיעו
פסיעה גסה והכניסו חמה לעיר אל תפסיעו פסיעה
גסה דאמר מר פסיעה גסה נוטלת אחד מחמש
מאות ממאור עיניו של אדם והכניסו חמה לעיר
כדרב יהודה אמר רב דאמר רב יהודה אמר רב
לעולם יכנס אדם בכי טוב ויצא בכי טוב שנאמר
הבקר אור והאנשים שלחו:

אמר רב יהודה אמר רב אמר רבי חייא המהלך
בדרך לא יאכל יותר משני רעבון מאי טעמא הכא
תרגימו משום מעיינא במערבא אמרי משום מזוני
מאי ביניהו איכא ביניהו|דיתיב בארבא אי נמי
דקאזיל מאוונא לאוונא רב פפא אכל פרסה ופרסה
הוה אכיל חדא ריפתא קסבר משום מעיינא:

עיא
עייא

תורה אור	מסרת הש״ס והמדרשים
9 בראשית מ״ד ג׳.	4 (פסיעה) ברכות מ״ג ב׳; שבת
	קי״ג ב׳; ב״ר צ״ד ב׳. 6 (מאור)
	פסחים מ״ב א׳. 8 (בכי טוב) פסחים ב׳ א׳; ב״ק ס׳ ב׳.

there is the apprehension of using up the food supply.
[180] In this case the food supply can be renewed.

R. Judah said in the name of Rab, who said it in the name of R. Ḥiyya: He who denies himself food in years of famine will be saved from an unnatural death, for it is said (Job, 5. 20): "In famine He will redeem thee from death, and in war from the power of the sword." Now, for "In famine He shall redeem thee from *death*" he should have said "from *famine*"! The meaning, therefore, is that for denying food to oneself in years of famine one will be saved from an unnatural death.

Resh Lakish said: In years of famine one must refrain from conjugal relations, for it is said (Gen., 41. 50): "And unto Joseph were born two sons before the year of famine came." It was taught, however, that people who have no children may perform their marital duty even in years of famine.

Our Rabbis have taught: If an individual separates from the community when the latter is in distress, the two ministering angels that accompany every man, place their hands upon his head and say, such and such a man who separated himself from the community shall not live to see the comfort of the community. Another Baraita reads: When the community is in distress one should not say, I will go home, eat and drink, and peace will be upon my soul. And if he does so, Scripture says of him (Is., 22.13): "And behold joy and gladness, slaying oxen and killing sheep, eating flesh and drinking wine—'let us eat

ואמר רב יהודה אמר רב אמר רבי חייא כל
המרעיב עצמו בשני רעבון נצל ממיתה משונה
שנאמר ברעב פדך ממות ובמלחמה מידי חרב
פדך ממות פדך מרעב מבעי ליה אלא מתוך
שהרעיב עצמו בשני רעבון נצל ממיתה משונה:

אמר ריש לקיש אסור לאדם לשמש מטתו בשני
רעבון שנאמר וליוסף ילד שני בנים בטרם תבוא
שנת הרעב תנא חשוכי בנים משמשין מטותיהן בשני
רעבון:

תנו רבנן בזמן שהצבור שרויין בצער יחיד
הפורש מהן שני מלאכי השרת המלוין לו לאדם
מניחין ידיהן על ראשו ואומרין פלוני שפרש מן
הצבור אל יראה בנחמת צבור:

תניא אידך בזמן שהצבור שרויין בצער אל יאמר
אדם אלך לביתי ואכל ואשתה ושלום עליך נפשי
ואם עושה כן עליו הכתוב אומר והנה ששון ושמחה
הרג בקר ושחט צאן אכל בשר ושתות יין אכול

תורה אור   מסרת הש״ס והמדרשים

3 איוב ה׳ כ׳.   7 בראשית מ״א נ׳.   6 (לשמש) ירושלמי תענית א׳ ו׳;
16 ישעיה כ״ב י״ג.   ב״ר ל״א י״ב, ל״ד ז׳ וע׳ פדר״א כ״ג
                       א׳.   8 (חשוכי) ירוש׳ תענית א׳
סוף ה״ו (ושם תאבי).   10 (יחיד) תדא״ז ט״ו (הוצאת מא״ש צד 198).
     15 (אלך לביתי) תדא״ר כ׳ (צד 112), כ״ה (128).

149

and drink, for to-morrow we shall die.'" Now, what are the words that follow this verse? "And the Lord of hosts revealed Himself in mine ears, surely this iniquity shall not be expiated by you till ye die." This is the way of the average people, but what is the way of the wicked? "Come ye (say they), I will fetch wine and we will fill ourselves with strong drink; and to-morrow shall be as this day, and much more abundant" (Is., 56.12). But what are the words that follow? "The righteous perisheth, and no man layeth it to heart" (*ibid.*, 57. 1). One should therefore afflict himself with the community, for thus we find that Moses afflicted himself out of sympathy with the community, as it is said (Ex., 17. 12): "But Moses's hands were heavy and they took a stone and put it under him, and he sat thereon." Now, did not Moses have a cushion or a pillow to sit upon? But Moses said to himself, as Israel is in trouble I will also share it with them. If a person should say, however, Who is going to testify against me? Yea, the stones of a man's house and the beams of a man's roof testify against him, as it is said (Hab., 2.11): "For the stone shall cry out of the wall, and the beam out of the timber shall answer it." R. Shila said, the two ministering angels that accompany a man testify against him, for it is said (Ps., 91. 11): "For He will give His angels charge over thee, to keep thee in all thy ways." R. Ḥidḳa says, one's soul testifies against him, for it is said (Micah, 7. 5): "Keep the doors of thy mouth from her that lieth

ושתו כי מחר נמות מה כתיב בתריה ונגלה באזני
ה' צבאות אם יכפר העון הזה לכם עד תמתון זו
מדת בינונים במדת רשעים מהו אומר אתיו אקחה
יין ונסבאה שכר והיה כזה יום מחר גדול יתר מאד
מה כתיב בתריה הצדיק אבד ואין איש שם על לב
אלא יצער אדם את עצמו עם הצבור שכן מצינו
במשה רבנו שצער עצמו עם הצבור שנאמר וידי
משה כבדים ויקחו אבן וישימו תחתיו וישב עליה
וכי לא היה לו למשה כר או כסת לישב עליה אלא
כך אמר משה הואיל וישראל שרויין בצער אף אני
אהיה עמהם בצער ושמא יאמר אדם מי מעיד בי
אבני ביתו של אדם וקורות ביתו של אדם הן מעידין
בו שנאמר כי אבן מקיר תזעק וכפיס מעץ יעננה:
רבי שילא אומר שני מלאכי השרת המלוין לו
לאדם הן מעידין בו שנאמר כי מלאכיו יצוה לך
לשמרך בכל דרכיך רבי חידקא אומר נשמתו של
אדם היא מעידה בו שנאמר משכבת חיקך שמר

תורה אור   מסרת הש״ס והמדרשים

2 ישעיה כ״ב י״ד.   3 ישעיה נ״ו י״ב.   9 (כר) מכילתא בשלח דעמלק
5 ישעיה נ״ז א'.   7 שמות י״ז י״ב.   א'; פס״ר (מא״ש) י״ב אות ס';
13 חבקוק ב' י״א. 15 תהלים צ״א   ריש תדא״ז ופט״ו שם (198). 11
י״א.   17 מיכה ז' ה'.   (ושמא) חגינה ט״ז א'.

in thy bosom." The other sages said, one's own limbs testify against him, for it is said (Is., 43. 12):[181] "Ye are My witnesses, saith the Lord, and I am God."

"A God of faithfulness and without iniquity" (Deut., 32. 4). "A God of faithfulness" means to say that just as the Holy One, blessed be He, pays reward to the righteous in the world to come for every light precept they have performed in this world, so does He pay to the wicked in this world for every light precept they perform in this world.

"Without iniquity" means that just as He punishes the wicked in the world to come for every slight transgression they have committed in this world, so He punishes the righteous in this world for every slight transgression they commit in this world.

"Just and right is He" (ibid.): It was said that when man departs this life, all his deeds are enumerated before him and he is told, thus hast thou done in that place on that day. He, admitting it, says: Yes! and is then told: Sign (the record)! and he signs, as it is said (Job, 37. 7): "He sealeth up the hand of every man." Not only that, but he even acknowledges the justice of the verdict and says, you have judged me rightly, as it is said (Ps., 51. 6): "That Thou mayest be justified when Thou speakest, and be in the right when Thou judgest."

[181] The word "ye" is here referred to the limbs of the human body.

פתחי פיך וחכמים אומרים אבריו של אדם הן
מעידין בו שנאמר ואתם עדי נאם ה' ואני אל:

אל אמונה כשם שהקדוש ברוך הוא משלם שכר
טוב לצדיקים על מצוה קלה שעושין בעולם הזה
5 לעולם הבא כך משלם שכר לרשעים על מצוה
קלה שעושין בעולם הזה בעולם הזה:

ואין עול כשם שהקדוש ברוך הוא נפרע מן
הרשעים על עברה קלה שעושין בעולם הזה
לעולם הבא כך נפרע מן הצדיקים על עברה
10 קלה שעושין בעולם הזה בעולם הזה:

צדיק וישר הוא אמרו בשעת פטירתו של אדם
כל מעשיו נפרטין לפניו ואומרים לו כך וכך עשית
במקום פלוני ביום פלוני והוא אומר הן ואומרים
לו חתום וחותם שנאמר ביד כל אדם יחתום ולא
15 עוד אלא שמצדיק עליו את הדין ואומר יפה דנתוני
שנאמר למען תצדק בדברך תזכה בשפטך:

מסרת הש"ס והמדרשים	תורה אור
3 (כשם) ספרי דברים ש"ז; מדרש	2 ישעיה מ"ג י"ב. 3 דברים ל"ב ד'.
תנאים 187. 12 (נפרטין) ספרי	14 איוב ל"ז ז'. 16 תהלים נ"א ו'.
ומדרש תנאים שם.	

Said Samuel: He that fasts (for self-affliction) is called a sinner, wherein Samuel agrees with this Baraita: R. Eleazar ha-Kappar Berebi[181ᵃ] said: Why is it said (Numbers, 6. 11): "And make atonement of him, for that he sinned by reason of the dead"? Against what soul[182] did he sin? It can only mean that he denied himself the enjoyment of wine.[183] Now, if a person who denies himself only the enjoyment of wine is called a sinner, all the more so one who denies himself all the enjoyments of life.[184]

R. Eleazar says: He that fasts is called holy, for it is said (*ib.*, 6. 5): "He shall be holy." Now, if this man (the Nazirite) who denied himself only the enjoyment of wine is called holy, all the more so one who denies himself all the enjoyments of life.

How does Samuel account for the fact that he (the Nazirite) is called holy? This term is applied to him only in view of his having purified himself (after the defilement). How does R. Eleazar account for the fact that he is also called sinner? This term is applied to him only in view of his having defiled himself (by contact with a dead body). But did R. Eleazar say

[181ᵃ] On Berebi, see L. Ginzberg, *J. E. s. v.*

[182] The word נפש, which in this verse is translated by "dead" (meaning the dead body by which the Nazirite happened to defile himself), is taken by the Talmud in its usual sense of *soul*, hence the question.

[183] Thus sinning against his own soul.

[184] By fasting.

אמר שמואל כל היושב בתענית נקרא חוטא סבר

לה כי הא דתניא רבי אלעזר הקפר ברבי אומר

מה תלמוד לומר וכפר עליו מאשר חטא על הנפש

וכי באיזו נפש חטא זה אלא שצער עצמו מן היין

⁵ והלא דברים קל וחומר ומה זה שלא צער עצמו

אלא מן היין נקרא חוטא המצער עצמו מכל דבר

על אחת כמה וכמה רבי אלעזר אומר נקרא קדוש

שנאמר קדש יהיה והלא דברים קל וחמר ומה זה

שלא צער עצמו אלא מן היין נקרא קדוש המצער

¹⁰ עצמו מכל דבר על אחת כמה וכמה ולשמואל נמי

הא איקרי קדוש ההוא דמדכי נפשיה ולרבי

אלעזר נמי הא איקרי חוטא ההוא דמסאב נפשיה

ומי אמר רבי אלעזר הכי והאמר רבי אלעזר

תורה אור	מסרת הש״ס והמדרשים

3 במדבר ו׳ י״א. 8 במדבר ו׳ ה׳.   1 (חוטא) שבועות ח׳ א׳; נזיר ג׳
א׳; סוטה ט׳ו א׳; כריתות כ׳ו א׳;
ירושלמי נדרים א׳ א׳ ונזיר א׳ ה׳; במ׳ר י׳ ז׳.   3 (וכפר) ב״ק צ״א א׳;
נדרים י׳ א׳; נזיר י׳ט א׳, כ״ב א׳; ספרי במדבר ל׳; במ׳ר י׳ ט׳ו. 7 (קדוש)
במ׳ר י׳ י׳. 11 (דמדכי נפשיה) ע׳ ספרי במדבר כ׳ה וכ׳ו. 12 (דמסאב)
במ׳ר י׳ ט׳ז.

155

so? Did he not say one should always consider oneself [fol. 11b] as if the Holy One were
within him,[185] because it is said (Hos., 11. 9):
"The Holy One in the midst of thee"? This is
no contradiction, for in one instance he has in
mind one who can stand privations, in the other
one who cannot.

Resh Laḳish said: He is called pious, for it
is said (Prov., 11. 17): "The merciful man
doeth good to his own soul."[186]   R. Jeremiah b.
'Abba said in the name of Resh Laḳish, a scholar
is not allowed to impose fasts upon himself,
because it makes him lessen his heavenly
work.   R. Sheshet said, if a student takes
upon himself such a fast, his meal[186] should
be given to the dogs.

If the first day of Kislew has come, etc.
Said R. Jeremiah b. 'Abba: There are no communal fasts in Babylonia except on the Ninth
of Ab.[186ᵇ]

R. Ze'ira said in the name of R. Huna:
If an individual takes upon himself a fast for

---

[185] On account of the presence of the divine within man,
he should not be allowed to afflict himself. How, then,
could R. Eleazar call a man who fasts holy?

[186] Resh Laḳish reads חסיד, pious, for חסד, merciful,
but the commentators differ as to what he intended to say.
According to Hananel and *Tosafot* it is he who does *not*
fast that "doeth good to his soul," while Gershom and
Rashi explain that Resh Laḳish calls pious the man who
does fast, thus chastening his soul. Both explanations
involve certain difficulties, for which see the Hebrew notes.

[186a] The meal by which he was to break his fast.

יא לעולם יראה אדם את עצמו|כאלו קדוש שרוי
עײב
בתוך מעיו שנאמר בקרבך קדוש לא קשיא הא
דמצי מצער נפשיה הא דלא מצי מצער נפשיה:

ריש לקיש אמר נקרא חסיד שנאמר גמל נפשו
5   איש חסד:

אמר רבי ירמיה בר אבא אמר ריש לקיש אין
תלמיד חכם רשאי לישב בתענית מפני שממעט
במלאכת שמים אמר רב ששת האי בר בי רב דיתיב
בתעניתא ליכול כלבא לשירותיה:

10   הגיע ראש חדש כסלו כו': אמר רבי ירמיה בר
אבא אין תענית צבור בבבל אלא אלא תשעה באב
בלבד:

אמר רבי זעירא אמר רב הונא יחיד שקיבל עליו

תורה אור   מסרת הש״ס והמדרשים

2 הושע י״א ט'.   4 כשלי י״א י״ז.   11 (ת״צ) לקמן י״ב ב'; פסחים נ״ד
ב'; ירושלמי תענית ב' א'.

[186b] That is, fasts decreed upon the congregation because
of dearth. These fasts begin the night before and are
subject to all the rigors of the fast on the ninth of Ab
(see the Mishnah above, §§ 6-7). As dearth never
occurred in Babylon (see above, note 171), no such fasts
were ever decreed there; comp. below, note 195.

the next day, he may pray on the following morning the prayer provided for fast days, although he ate and drank during the whole intervening night. If, however, he continued fasting also during the following night, he is not to say on the next morning the prayer provided for fasts.[187] Said R. Joseph: What is the reason of R. Huna? Does he hold that fasting by hours[187a] does not count, or does he hold that fasting by hours does count, but that he who fasts by hours is not supposed to say the prayer provided for fasts? Said Abbayi to R. Joseph: He certainly holds that fasting by hours counts and that he who fasts by hours may also say the prayer provided for fasts; in the case under consideration, however, the matter is different, inasmuch as he had not taken upon himself at all the fasting of that intervening night.[187b]

R. Aḳiba happened to come to Ginzak (Gazaka), where he was asked the following questions:

[187] Because the prayer (beginning עננו) is provided only for a fast that one takes upon oneself on the preceding day. In the case before us, however, the night following the fast was not included in his original vow. He merely volunteered in the evening to continue fasting until next morning. Such voluntary additional fasting without previous binding vow can be broken at will, and therefore is not in the category of fasts for which the prayer 'Anenu was provided. The person, therefore, who so added a night's fasting need not say that prayer on the next morning. The commentators differ considerably in the interpretation of this passage. I followed Rashi and Maimonides, הלכות תעניות, I, 11.

תענית אפילו אכל ושתה כל הלילה כלו למחר
מתפלל תפלת תענית לן בתעניתו למחר אין
מתפלל תפלת תענית אמר רב יוסף מאי קסבר רב
הונא מסבר קסבר אין מתענין לשעות או דילמא
קסבר מתענין לשעות והמתענה לשעות אין מתפלל
תפלת תענית אמר ליה אביי לעולם קסבר מתענין
לשעות והמתענה לשעות מתפלל תפלת תענית
ושאני הכא דלא קבלה עילויה:
רבי עקיבא איקלע לגינוק בעו מיניה מתענין

מסרת הש״ס והמדרשים
4 (לשעות) ע״ז ל״ד א׳; ירושלמי   נדרים ח׳ א׳.   9 (גינוק) ע״ז ל״ד א׳.

187[a] That is, a fast that does not extend over the whole
day; in the case under consideration it lasts over night.
R. Joseph's question is whether in the opinion of R.
Huna such fasting has no obligatory force at all and one
may at any time break it by eating, so that even if he did
not break it, he is not allowed to say 'Anenu, or whether
such partial fasting must be continued to the end of the
stipulated time, but that one need not say 'Anenu, although he may do so if he cares to (so Rashi).

187[b] That is to say: Generally R. Huna is of the opinion
that a fast for a number of hours does count, cannot be
broken, and requires 'Anenu, provided a person took
upon himself such a fast by a vow. In the particular
case before us, however, it is different, as the individual
did not make a vow for the night's fast, hence 'Anenu
is not required (Rashi).

159

Does fasting by hours count or not? When may
the wine-vessels of idolaters be used? In what
garments did Moses officiate during the seven
days of consecration (Lev., 8. 33)? He had no
answer and went to the Bet ha-Midrash for
information, where he was told: The law is
that fasting by hours counts; wine-vessels of
idolaters may be used after twelve months;
Moses officiated during the seven days of consecration in a white frock. R. Kahana's version
is: In a white frock without border.

Said R. Ḥisda [fol. 12a]: The statement that
fasting by hours counts holds good only when
the person in question did not taste any food
during the whole day. Said Abbayi to him: Is
not such a fast a complete one?! The statement
of R. Ḥisda refers to one who only late in the
day made up his mind to fast until evening.[188]
R. Ḥisda further said: A fast upon which the
sun did not set does not deserve the name of
fast. An objection was raised thereto from the
Mishnah (below, p. 210): "The 'priests of the

[188] R. Ḥisda thus gives a different meaning to the phrase
"fasting by hours." It does not mean that a person
fasts some hours and eats during the rest of the day, as
this would not constitute a fast at all, but applies only
to a case in which one happened to be without food till
noon, or later, and then the thought came to his mind that
he might as well continue without food till evening, making
the day a fast day. In such a case R. Hisda maintains that
although the person did not take upon himself the fast
on the preceding day, as required by law, nor was the
fasting during the first part of the day intentional, the

לשעות או אין מתענין לשעות קנקנין של גוים אימתי
מותרין במה שמש משה כל שבעת ימי המלואים
לא הוה בידיה אתא שאיל בי מדרשא אמרו לו
הלכה מתענין לשעות קנקנין של גוים לאחר שנים

5 עשר חדש מותרין ושמש משה כל שבעת ימי
המלואים בחלוק לבן רב כהנא מתני בחלוק לבן
שאין בו אימרא:

אמר רב חסדא|הא דאמרת מתענין לשעות
הוא שלא טעם כלום כל אותו היום אמר ליה אביי

10 הא תעניתא מעליתא היא לא צריכא דאימלך
אימלוכי:

ואמר רב חסדא כל תענית שלא שקעה עליו
חמה לאו שמיה תענית מיתיבי אנשי משמר מתענין

מסרת הש"ס והמדרשים

1 (קנקנין) ע"ז ל"ד א'; ירושלמי ע"ז
ב' ד'.   2 (שמש) ע"ז שם; זבחים
ק"א ב'; ק"ב א'; ספרא מכילתא
דמלואים צו ושמיני (הוצאת אה"ו
צד מ"ב ע"ב ומ"ד ע"ב); שמ"ר ל"ז
א'; שהש"ר א' פסוק ז' אותג'; מדרש
תהלים י"ח (באבער אות קמ"ז) וע'
בכל המקומות למלת חלוק שאח"ז.
6 (חלוק) ע"ז שם; ירושלמי יומא
א' א' (ל"ח ב'); פס"ר פרה
(מא"ש אות צ'); פסדר"כ פרה
סימן קמ"ה; ויק"ר י"א ו': מדרש
תהלים צ"ט.   13 (אנשי) לקמן
ט"ז ב'.

intentional fasting during the later hours of the day makes
of the whole day a fast day, provided he did not eat
until after sunset; comp. Maimonides and his commentators, *l. c.*, § 13.

guard' fast, but not to the end of the day!"
Answer. There they do it merely for the
purpose of undergoing some suffering.

Come and hear: R. Eleazar b. Zadok said:
I am a descendant of Senaah from the tribe of
Benjamin. Once the Ninth of Ab happened to
fall on a Sabbath and we postponed it to the
day after Sabbath. On that day we fasted, but
did not finish the fast, because it was our holiday![189] Answer. There, too, they fasted merely
to inflict pain upon themselves.

Come and hear: R. Johanan used to say: I
am going to fast until I come home! Answer.
There he said so merely to escape invitations
from the house of the Patriarch.

Samuel said: A fast which one did not take
upon oneself before sunset of the preceding day
has not the validity of a fast. But what if one
did fast? Said Rabbah b. R. Shila: Such a one
is comparable to a bellows full of wind.[190] What
is the exact time for one to take a fast upon
himself? Rab says, during the hours of Minḥah
(afternoon); Samuel says, he must insert the
vow in the Minḥah prayer itself. Said R.
Joseph; Samuel's view is reasonable, because it
is written in the Scroll of Fasts—"People for
whom the time of fasting has arrived because of
previous resolutions are required to fast only in

[189] On the tenth of Ab it was the privilege of that family
to offer wood to the altar; see below, the Mishnah of the
fourth chapter, p. 400.

[190] *I. e.*, it amounts to nothing.

162

ולא משלימין התם לצעורי נפשיהו בעלמא הוא
דעבוד:

תא שמע דאמר רבי אלעזר ברבי צדוק אני
הייתי מבני סנאה בן בנימן פעם אחת חל תשעה
5   באב להיות בשבת ודחינוהו לאחר השבת והתע‎נינו
בו ולא השלמנוהו מפני שיום טוב שלנו היה התם
נמי לצעורי נפשיהו בעלמא הוא דעבוד:

תא שמע דאמר רבי יוחנן אהא בתענית עד
שאבוא לביתי התם לשמוטי נפשיה מבי נשיאה הוא
10 דעבד:

אמר שמואל כל תענית שלא קבלה עליו מבעוד
יום לאו שמה תענית ואי יתיב מאי אמר רבה בר
רב שילא דמי למפוחא דמלי זיקא אימת מקבל
לה רב אמר במנחה ושמואל אמר בתפלת המנחה
15 אמר רב יוסף כוותיה דשמואל מסתברא דכתיב
במגלת תענית להן כל איניש דייתי עלוהי מן קדמת

מסרת הש"ס והמדרשים

3 (ראב"צ) ערובין מ"א א'; ירושלמי   א' ריש ו'.   8 (ר' יוחנן) ירוש'
תענית ד' ו' (ושם בטעות ר' אלעזר   נדרים ח' א'.   8 (אהא) מכות
ברבי יוסי); שקלים ד' א'; מגלה   כ"ד א'.

case they bound themselves by a vow *during prayer*." Now, does that not mean that they have bound themselves to fast while praying? No, it means only they have bound themselves.[190a]

R. Ḥiyya and R. Simeon b. Rabbi disagree with regard to this matter. One reads *yēsar* (he bound himself by a vow), the other reads *yě'ĕsar* (is forbidden). If we read *yēsar* we must understand it in the way we explained it above, but if we read *yě'ĕsar*, we must understand it in accordance with the following Baraita: "'People for whom the time of fasting has arrived because of previous resolutions are required to fast only in case they bound themselves by a vow during prayer.' This means that if an individual has taken upon himself to fast on Mondays and Thursdays of the whole year, and it happens that those days conflict with some of the holidays recorded in the Scroll of Fasts, the following rule is to be observed. If his vow preceded our proclamation of the holidays,[191] our proclamation must be disregarded on account of his vow, but if our proclamation preceded his vow, his vow must be disregarded on account of our proclamation."

(*On the nights preceding the fasts*) *they may eat and drink*, etc. The Rabbis have taught: Until what time in the night (preceding a fast) may one eat and drink? Until the morning dawn; this is the opinion of Rabbi. R. Eleazar b.

[190a] But not exactly *while* praying Minḥah. The word בצלו, during prayer, is according to this interpretation

דנא ייסר בצלו מאי לאו ייסר עצמו בצלו לא ייסר
עצמו:

פליגי בה רבי חייא ורבי שמעון ברבי חד אמר
ייסר וחד אמר יאסר מאן דאמר ייסר כדאמרן
ומאן דאמר יאסר מאי היא דתניא להן כל איניש 5
דייתי עלוהי מן קדמת דנא ייסר בצלו כיצד יחיד
שקבל עליו תענית שני וחמשי של כל השנה כלה
ופגעו בו ימים טובים הכתובין במגלת תענית אם
נדרו קודם לגזרתנו תדחה גזרתנו מפני נדרו ואם
גזרתנו קודמת לנדרו ידחה נדרו מפני גזרתנו: 10

אוכלין ושותין משחשיכה כו׳: תנו רבנן עד מתי
אוכל ושותה עד שיעלה עמוד השחר דברי רבי

מסרת הש״ס והמדרשים

1 (ייסר בצלו) ע׳ ירושלמי תענית   נדרים ח׳ א׳ ותענית ספ״ב. 11 (עד
ב׳ י״ג (ס״ו א׳), מגלה א׳ ו׳ (ע׳   מתי) פסחים ב׳ ב׳; ירושלמי תענית
ג׳). 6 (יחיד) מנ״ת י״ב ו ע׳ ירושלמי   א׳ סוף ה״ד; תוספתא תענית א׳.

either regarded as spurious, or taken as a general indica-
tion of the time during which the vow is to be made,
i. e., about the time of the afternoon prayer.

[191] That is, before the issuance of the Scroll of Fasts,
which forbade fasting on the days in question. Regarding
the Scroll see below, note 232.

Simeon says, until one hears the crowing of the
cock. Said Raba, this applies only to one who
has not finished his meal, but if one has finished
his meal, he should not start eating again.
'Abbayi objects hereto from the following Baraita: If one has eaten and gotten up, he may eat
again! Answer. This refers to one who has not
yet put away the table.[192] Some give to the
foregoing passage the following wording: Said
Raba, this applies only to one who has not
yet slept, but if he has slept, he should not
start eating again. In objection hereto 'Abbayi
quoted: If he slept and then got up, he may eat
again! Answer. This refers only to one who
merely dozed. What is meant by dozing?
Said R. 'Ashi [fol. 12b]: Sleep which is no sleep,
a wakefulness which is no wakefulness, so that
if he is called by name he answers, but can
not reply intelligently, though if something is
recalled to his mind, he remembers.

R. Kahana said in the name of Rab: An individual who took upon himself a fast is not
allowed to wear shoes while fasting, because we
apprehend that he might have taken upon
himself a communal fast.[193] What expression must he use in his vow to be allowed to
wear shoes? Said Rabba b. R. Shila: He should
say thus: Tomorrow I shall fast before Thee a
private fast.

[192] So that the meal is not yet to be considered as finished.

[193] Which means to say that when he resolved to fast,
he had in mind to submit to all the rigors of a communal
fast, among which is also the prohibition of wearing shoes;
see the Mishnah, above, p. 6.

רבי אלעזר ברבי שמעון אומר עד קרות הגבר אמר
רבא לא שנו אלא שלא גמר אבל גמר אינו אוכל
איתיביה אביי ישן ועמד הרי זה אוכל התם שלא
סלק:

5 איכא דאמרי אמר רבא לא שנו אלא שלא ישן
אבל ישן אינו אוכל איתיביה אביי ישן ועמד הרי זה
אוכל התם במתנמנם היכי דמי מתנמנם אמר רב
אשי נים ולא נים תיר ולא תיר דקרו ליה ועני ולא
ידע אהדורי סברא וכי מדכרו ליה מדכר:

10 אמר רב כהנא אמר רב יחיד שקבל עליו תענית
אסור בנעילת הסנדל חיישינן שמא תענית צבור
קבל עליו היכי עביד אמר רבה בר רב שילא
דאמר למחר הריני לפניך בתענית יחיד:

מסרת הש"ס והמדרשים

5 (ישן) ירושלמי ותוספתא שם. א'; יבמות נ"ד א'; נדה ס"נ א'.
7 (מתנמנם) פסחים ק"כ ב ; מגלה 11 (ת"צ) לעיל י"א ב'; פסחים נ"ד
י"ח ב'; יבמות נ"ד א'; נדה ס"נ א'. ב'; ירושלמי תענית ב' א' (סוף
8 (נים) פסחים ק"כ ב'; מגלה י"ח דף ס"הב').

R. Sheshet was told that some scholars came to the fast-meeting with their shoes on. R. Sheshet became angry and said: Who knows if they have not also indulged in eating?

'Abbayi and Raba used to wear shoes without soles. Maremar and Mar Zuṭra used to transfer the right shoe to the left foot and the left shoe to the right foot.[194] The scholars of the school of R. 'Ashi, however, wore their shoes in the usual way, agreeing with Samuel, who said, there are no public fasts in Babylonia except the Ninth of Ab.[195]

R. Judah said in the name of Rab: One may borrow a fast and pay it on another day. When I made this statement in the presence of Samuel, he said: Has a resolution to fast the force of a vow, so that one must perforce pay it? It is merely self-affliction that one has taken upon himself. If he feels that he can endure the affliction let him do so, but if he cannot endure it, he need not! Some relate the above in the following form: R. Judah said in the name of Rab: One may borrow a fast and pay it on another day. When I made this statement before Samuel, he said to me: This is a matter of course! Let us assume that his intention has merely the force of a vow, is not one in duty bound to pay a vow the next day or at a later time?

R. Joshua, son of R.'Idi, happened to come to

---

[194] To indicate their being conscious of the fast.
[195] Comp. above, note 186^b; Maimonides, *l. c.*, III, 11.

אמרו ליה לרב ששת קא אתי רבנן לבי תעניתא
כי סיימי מסאני איקפד אמר דילמא מיכל נמי קא
אכלי:

אביי ורבא סיימי אפנתא מרימר ומר זוטרא
מחלפי דימינא לשמאלא ודשמאלא לימינא רבנן
דבי רב אשי סיימי כי אורחיהו סברי לה כשמואל
דאמר שמואל אין תענית צבור בבבל אלא תשעה
באב בלבד:

אמר רב יהודה אמר רב לוה אדם תעניתו ופורע
כי אמריתה קמיה דשמואל אמר לי וכי נדר הוא
דלא סגי דלא משלם צערא הוא דקביל עליה אי
מצי מצער נפשיה אי לא מצי לא מצער נפשיה:

איכא דאמרי אמר רב יהודה אמר רב לוה אדם
תעניתו ופורע כי אמריתה קמיה דשמואל אמר לי
פשיטא לא יהא אלא נדר נדר מי לא משלׁם למחר
וליומא אחרינא:

רב יהושע בריה דרב אידי איקלע לבי רב אשי

מסרת הש"ס והמדרשים

9 (לוה) ירושלמי נדרים ח' א'.   10 (וכי נדר) ירושלמי שם.   17 (רב
יהושע) שבת י"א א'.

R. 'Ashi, where meat of a three-year-old calf[196] was prepared in his honor. They asked him to eat, but he replied, I am keeping a fast. They said to him: Can you not postpone it and make it up another time? Do you not agree with the statement which R. Judah transmitted in the name of Rab, namely, that one may postpone his fast and make it up at another time? "It is a fast on account of a bad dream," he replied, and Raba b. Maḥseya said in the name of R. Ḥama b. Gurya, who reported it in the name of Rab: Fasting is good for a bad dream even as fire is for consuming flax. R. Ḥisda said: But the fast must take place on the same day, to which R. Joseph added: Even if that day is the Sabbath.

If these fast-days are over and the community's prayer has not been answered, etc., *work*, etc., *are forbidden.*

It is right to forbid all the other actions, because they give pleasure, but why should work be forbidden which causes pain? Said R. Ḥisda in the name of R. Jeremiah b. 'Abba: Scripture says (Joel, 1. 14): "Sanctify ye a fast, call a solemn assembly," which indicates that just as on days of a solemn assembly work is forbidden, so also on fast days. If this is the reason, then, just as on days of solemn assembly work must be stopped on the evening before, so it should be stopped on the evening before fast days! Said R.

[196] עגלא תלתא occurs several times in the Talmud (see below, notes 365–366) and is explained by some to mean a calf that is the third born of its dam. Others say that it means a three-year-old calf. Each of the explanations

עבדו ליה עגלא תלתא אמרו ליה לטעום מר מידי
אמר להו בתעניתא יתיבנא אמרו ליה ליזוף מר
וליפרע לא סבר לה מר דהא דאמר רב יהודה
אמר רב לוה אדם תעניתו ופורע אמר להו תענית
5 חלום הוא ואמר רבא בר מחסיא אמר רב חמא
בר גוריא אמר רב יפה תענית לחלום כאש לנערת
ואמר רב חסדא ובו ביום ואמר רב יוסף ואפילו
בשבת:

עברו אלו ולא נענו כו' ואסורין במלאכה: בשלמא
10 כולהו אית בהו תענוג אלא מלאכה צער הוא אמר
רב חסדא אמר רבי ירמיה בר אבא אמר קרא
קדשו צום קראו עצרה מה עצרת אסור בעשית
מלאכה אף צום אסור בעשית מלאכה אי מה עצרת
מאורתא אף צום נמי מאורתא אמר רבי זירא

מסרת הש"ס והמדרשים	תורה אור
6 (יפה) שבת שם; פסדר"כ ל';	12 יואל א' י"ד.

פס"ר הוספה פ"ד; תנחומא (הנדפס)
בראשית סימן ב'; ב"ר מ"ד י"ב; קה"ר ה' פסוק ו'; ביהמ"ד ח"ד צד
קל"ח.   14 (ר' זירא) ירושלמי תענית א' ריש ה'ו (ס"ד ג').

assumes that the meat of such a calf is better than that
of other calves; comp. Kohut, *Aruch*, *s. v.* חלת p. 240, n. 3.
The latter explanation is probably the correct one, and the
phrase corresponds to עולה שלישיה, Gen., 15.9; comp. Is.,
15.5; Jer., 48.34.

Zera, to me the matter was thus explained by R. Jeremiah b. 'Abba: Since Scripture says (*ibidem*): "Gather the elders," the fast must be similar to the gathering of the elders, hence just as the gathering of the elders takes place during the day, so the fast is obligatory only during the day. Said R. Shisha, son of R. 'Idi, this statement supports that of R. Huna, who said: The fast-meeting takes place in the morning. What do they do the whole day?[197] Said 'Abbayi: From morning to midday they consider communal affairs, from midday to evening, one quarter of the day is spent in reading the portions from the Pentateuch and the Prophets and the other quarter in praying and asking for mercy, for it is said (Nehem., 9. 3): "And they stood up in their place, and read in the book of the law of the Lord their God a fourth part of the day; and another fourth part they confessed, and prostrated themselves before the Lord their God." [fol.13a] Why not invert the order of proceedings? No, you should not think of it, for it is written (Ezra, 9. 4–5): "Then were assembled unto me every one that trembled at the words of the God of Israel, because of the faithlessness of them of the captivity; and I sat appalled until the evening offering. And at the evening offering I arose up from my fasting, even with my garment and my mantle rent; and I fell upon my knees, and spread out my hands unto the Lord my God."

[197] Meaning: How does the community that assembles for the fast spend the day?

לדידי מיפרשא ליה מיניה דרבי ירמיה בר אבא
אמר קרא אספו זקנים דומיא דאסיפת זקנים
מה אסיפת זקנים ביום אף צום נמי ביום אמר
רב שישא בריה דרב אידי מסייע ליה לרב
הונא דאמר מצפרא כנופיא היכי עבדי אמר ⁵
אביי מצפרא לפלגיה דיומא מעייני במילי דמתא
מפלגיה דיומא לפניא רבעא דיומא קרו ומיפטרו
ורבעא דיומא מצלו ובעו רחמי דכתיב ויקומו על
עמדם ויקראו בספר תורת ה' אלהיהם רביעית
היום ורביעית מתודים ומשתחוים לה' אלהיהם‖ ¹⁰
איפוך אנא לא סלקא דעתך דכתיב ואלי יאספו ^{ג״י}
^{א״ע}
כל חרד בדברי אלהי ישראל על מעל הגולה ואני
ישב משומם עד למנחת הערב ובמנחת הערב קמתי
מתעניתי ובקרעי בגדי ומעילי ואכרעה על ברכי
ואפרשה כפי אל ה' אלהי: ¹⁵

מסרת הש״ס והמדרשים	תורה אור
5 (כנופיא) מגלה ל' ב'.	8 נחמיה ט' ג'. 11 עזרא ט' ד'–ה'.

Said Rafrem b. Papa in the name of R. Ḥisda:
On every fast which was decreed for the sake of
mourning, like the Ninth of Ab and the fast of a
mourner, both warm and cold baths are forbidden; but on fasts which were decreed merely
to prevent indulgence in pleasure, like the
communal fast, warm, but not cold, baths are
forbidden. Said R. 'Idi b. 'Abin, we indeed, read
in the Mishnah: "the bath-houses must be closed."
Said 'Abbayi to him: Suppose the Mishnah had
meant to forbid also cold baths, how should it
then have expressed itself? Should it have read:
"the rivers must be stopped"? Said R. Shisha,
son of R. 'Idi, my father (in making his statement)
felt this difficulty: Inasmuch as the Mishnah
had said that bathing is forbidden, what was
the idea of adding that the bath-houses must
be closed? Does this not indicate that only
warm baths are forbidden, while cold baths
are allowed? It stands proved.

Shall we say that R. Ḥisda's view is supported
by the following Baraita: "All those bound to
take an immersion,[198] immerse as usual even
on the Ninth of Ab or on the Day of Atonement? What kind of immersion is here intended?
It cannot be in warm water, for such water is
drawn.[199] The Baraita means therefore immersion in cold water and yet it permits it only to
those "bound to take an immersion," while all

[198] As a woman after menstruation or confinement.

[199] The ritual bath can be taken only in water coming
directly from a spring and connected with it. If the water
was separated from the spring, in order to be warmed,

אמר רפרם בר פפא אמר רב חסדא כל שהוא
משום אבל כגון תשעה באב ואבל אסור בין בחמין
בין בצונן כל שהוא משום תענוג כגון תענית צבור
בחמין אסור בצונן מותר אמר רב אידי בר אבין
5 אף אנן נמי תנינא ונועלין את המרחצאות אמר ליה
אביי ואי בצונן אסור סוכרין את הנהרות איבעי
ליה למתני אמר רב שישא בריה דרב אידי אבא
הכי קא קשיא ליה מכדי קתני אסורין ברחיצה
למה לי למתני ונועלין את המרחצאות לאו
10 למימרא דבחמין אסור ובצונן מותר שמע מינה:

לימא מסייע ליה כל חייבי טבילות טובלין
כדרכן בין בתשעה באב בין ביום הכפורים במאי
אילימא בחמין טבילה בחמין מי איכא שאובין
נינהו אלא לאו בצונן וחייבי טבילות אין כולי עלמא

מסרת הש״ס והמדרשים

א'; ירושלמי ברכות ג' ד'; ביצה ב'	3 (בצונן) ע' ירושלמי תענית א'
ב'; יומא ח' א' (מ״ד ד'); תענית א'	ו' (ס״ד ג'); ברכות ב' ז'; מו״ק
ו' (ס״ד ד'). 13 (טבילה בחמין)	ג' ה' (פ״ב ד'). 11 (חייבי) שבת
ברכות כ״ב א'.	קי״א א'; ביצה י״ח ב'; יומא פ״ח

and carried into a tub, it is called "drawn", in contradistinction to "running" water (Num., 19.17), and is
unfit for the purpose.

other people are excluded!²⁰⁰ Said R. Ḥama b. R. Ḳeṭina, the Baraita has reference to the hot springs of Tiberias. If so, how will you understand the following statement that was made with relation to the above Baraita: "R. Ḥanina, the Segan of the priests 200,²⁰⁰ª said, the house of our God is worth that one should give up for its sake one bath in a year"?²⁰¹ If, as you say, the Baraita permits immersion in cold water, they could immerse in cold water (and would not have to give it up even once a year). Said R. Papa, R. Ḥanina refers to a place where there is no cold water (for bathing). Come and hear: "When it was said that bathing on a fast day is forbidden, it was said only with regard to the whole body, but washing the face, hands, and feet is allowed; when it was said that work on a fast day is forbidden, it was said only with regard to the day, but during the preceding night it is allowed; and when it was said that wearing shoes is forbidden, it was said only with reference to the city, but on the road it is allowed. How is it done? When one comes on the road, he puts his shoes on, but as soon as he reaches the city, he must take them off. Thou wilt find the same law applied also to an excommunicated person and to a mourner." Now, does not the last statement (that the same law applies also to mourners) cover all three points (bathing, working, and wearing shoes)? No, it refers only to the latter two.

²⁰⁰ Which would support the view of R. Ḥisda, in whose name Rafrem reported that on fasts of mourning even cold baths are prohibited.

לא אמר רב חנא בר רב קטינא לא נצדכא אלא
לחמי טבריה אי הכי היינו דקתני עלה אמר רבי
חנינא סגן הכהנים כדאי הוא בית אלהינו לאבד
עליו טבילה אחת בשנה ואי אמרת בצונן שרי הא
5 קא טבלי בצונן אמר רב פפא באתרא דלא שכיחי
צונן:

תא שמע כשאמרו אסור ברחיצה לא אמרו אלא
כל גופו אבל פניו ידיו ורגליו מותר וכשאמרו אסור
במלאכה לא אמרו אלא ביום אבל בלילה מותר
10 וכשאמרו אסור בנעילת הסנדל לא אמרו אלא
בעיר אבל בדרך מותר הא כיצד יצא לדרך נועל
הגיע לעיר חולץ וכן אתה מוצא במנודה ובאבל
מאי לאו אכולהו לא אשארא:

מסרת הש"ס והמדרשים

10 (בנעילת הסנדל) תוספתא	3 (כדאי) ירושלמי ביצה ב' ב';
תענית א' ו'; ירושלמי ברכות ב'	פס"ר ריש פכ"ט. 7 (ברחיצה)
ז'; יומא ח' א'; תענית א' ו'.	מו"ק ט"ו ב'; פסחים נ"ד ב'.
11 (בדרך) ירושלמי ברכות ב' ז';	9 (במלאכה) מו"ק ט"ו ב'.
תענית א' ו'; מו"ק ג' ה' (פ"ב ד');	9 (בלילה) תוספתא תענית א' ה';
יומא ח'א'. 13 (אשארא) מו"ק ט"ו ב'.	ירושלמי תענית א' ריש ה'ו.

[200a] On the Segan, see Adolf Schwarz, *Der Segan*, in
Monatsschrift, 64, pp. 30-35.

[201] On the ninth of Ab, on which day the Temple was
destroyed.

Come and hear: "R. 'Abba the Priest said in
the name of R. Jose the Priest, it happened that
when the sons of R. Jose b. R. Hanina died,
he bathed in cold water during all the seven
days of mourning!" Answer: There the deaths
followed closely one after the other, for we read
in a Baraita: If several deaths follow closely
upon one another, the mourner may, if his hair becomes too thick, make it thinner with a clipper
and he may wash his garments in water.
Said R. Hisda: He may cut the hair with a
clipper, but not with scissors; he may wash
his garments in water, but not with natron or
aloe. R. Hisda further said, this Baraita proves
that a mourner is not allowed to wash his
garments.

Raba said, a mourner is not allowed to bathe
in warm water, but he may bathe in cold water.
What is the reason? [fol. 13b] Because it is
something that can be classed with the enjoyment of meat and wine. An objection was
raised against Raba. We read: "A maiden that
has reached maturity should not neglect herself
during the days of her mourning for her father."[202]
This statement indicates that a maiden who did
not reach maturity is in duty bound to neglect
herself. Now, in what respect is she supposed to
neglect herself? By abstaining from warm
baths? And is not a *mature* maiden allowed to
neglect herself in this way? Did not R. Hisda
say, a mourner is not allowed to put even a
finger into warm water? You must therefore

[202] Because it might hurt her in her prospects for mar
riage, her appearance deterring possible suitors.

תא שמע דאמר רבי אבא הכהן משום רבי יוסי

הכהן מעשה ומתו בניו של רבי יוסי ברבי חנינא

ורחץ בצונן כל שבעה התם בשתכפוהו אבליו הוה

דתניא תכפוהו אבליו זה אחר זה הכביד שערו

5 מקל בתער ומכבס כסותו במים אמר רב חסדא

בתער אבל לא במספרים במים אבל לא בנתר

ולא באהל אמר רב חסדא זאת אומרת אבל

אסור בתכבסת:

אמר רבא אבל בחמין אסור ובצונן מותר מאי

10 טעמא מידי דהוה אבשרא וחמרא מיתיבי | אין

הבוגרת רשאה לנול עצמה בימי אבל אביה הא

נערה רשאה במאי אילימא בחמין אין הבוגרת

רשאה והאמר רב חסדא אבל אסור להושיט אצבעו

מסרת הש״ס והמדרשים

4 (תכפוהו) מו״ק י״ז ב׳; ירושלמי ה׳.   8 (תכבסת) תענית י״ג ב׳;
מו״ק נ׳ סוף ה׳א (פ״ב א׳); שמחות   מו״ק ט״ו א׳, י״ז ב׳.

179

admit that the prohibition of self-neglect refers only to bathing in cold water (which proves that to other mourners cold bathing, too, is forbidden)! Answer. No, by neglect is meant only painting the eyelids and fixing the hair.[203]

Some give the passage in the following version: Raba said, a mourner is not allowed to bathe either in warm or in cold water during the seven days. Why should bathing be different from the enjoyment of meat and wine? In the case of meat and wine, indulgence is permitted because it is done merely to lessen the mourner's suffering, while bathing is a matter of (avoidable) pleasure. Is not Raba's statement supported by the following passage: "A maiden that has reached maturity should not neglect herself during the days of her mourning for her father?" This wording certainly indicates that a maiden who did *not* yet reach maturity is in duty bound to neglect herself. Now, what is meant by neglect? Does it mean abstaining from bathing in warm water? Is a maiden of maturity, then, not allowed so to neglect herself? Did not R. Ḥisda say, a mourner is not allowed to put even a finger into warm water? You must therefore admit that the prohibition of neglect refers only to bathing in cold water! Answer. No, by neglect is meant painting her eyelids and fixing her hair.

The law is that a mourner is not allowed to bathe his entire body either in warm or in cold water during the whole week of mourning, but as to face, hands, and feet, he is forbidden to

[203] In this respect she is not allowed to neglect herself, but as to bathing, nothing is said in that passage and no

בחמין אלא לאו בצונן לא כי קתני אכחול ופרכוס:

איכא דאמרי אמר רבא אבל אסור בין בחמין

בין בצונן מאי שנא מבשרא וחמרא התם לפכוחי

פחדיה הכא לתענוג לימא מסייע ליה אין הבוגרת

5 רשאה לנול עצמה בימי אבל אביה הא נערה רשאה

במאי אילימא בחמין אין הבוגרת רשאה והאמר רב

חסדא אבל אסור להושיט אצבעו בחמין אלא לאו

בצונן לא כי קתני אכחול ופרכוס:

והלכתא אבל אסור לרחוץ כל גופו כל שבעה

10 בין בחמין בין בצונן אבל פניו ידיו ורגליו בחמין

---

inference can be drawn therefrom. As to the meaning
of פרכוס, see the dictionaries and Rabbinovicz, *Variae
lectiones, ad locum.*

wash them in warm water, but may wash them in cold water; he is not allowed to anoint his body to any extent whatever, but if he intends only to use the oil in order to remove dirt he may do so.

R. Isaac, with the permission of his father R. Judah, delivered the following discourse:[203a] An individual who has taken upon himself a fast must recite the prayer provided for fasts. Where does he insert it? Between the benediction ending with "Redeemer" and that ending with "Healer" (of Israel).[204] R. Isaac objected: Is an individual entitled to insert a benediction for himself? He should rather, said R. Isaac, include it in the benediction ending with the words: "Who hearest prayer." The same opinion was given also by R. Sheshet. An objection was raised to this view from the following Baraita: There is no difference between an individual and a community, except that the former recites eighteen benedictions, while the latter recites nineteen. Now what is meant by "individual" and "community"? Is "individual" to be understood literally and "community" in the sense of representative of the community? If so, the benedictions here spoken of would not be nineteen, but twenty-four![205] Consequently by "individual" can be meant only one who takes upon himself a fast which is known as a "private fast," while by "community" is meant an

[203a] On the expression אדבריה ודרש, see J. N. Epstein, Monatsschrift, 63, pp. 253–59.

[204] That is, between the seventh and the eighth benedictions.

אסור בצונן מותר ולסוך אפילו **כל שהוא אסור**

ואם להעביר את הזוהמא מותר:

אדבריה רב יהודה לרב יצחק **בריה ודרש**

יחיד שקבל עליו תענית מתפלל תפלת תענית והיכן

אומרה בין גואל לרופא מתקיף לה רב יצחק וכי

יחיד קובע ברכה לעצמו אלא אמר רב יצחק

בשומע תפלה וכן אמר רב ששת בשומע תפלה

מיתיבי אין בין יחיד לצבור אלא שזה מתפלל

שמונה עשרה וזה מתפלל תשע עשרה מאי יחיד

ומאי צבור אילימא יחיד יחיד ממש וצבור שליח

צבור הני תשע עשרה הויין עשרין וארבע הויין אלא

לאו יחיד שקבל עליו תענית יחיד וצבור יחיד

מסרת הש"ס והמדרשים

‏ (ולסוך) ירושלמי תענית א' ו' (גואל לרופא) ירושלמי ברכות ד'
יס"ד ג'); יומא ח' א' (מ"ד ד'); ג'; תענית א' א', ב' ב' (ס"ה ג');
מעשר שני ב' א' (נ"ג ב'). 5 (בין תוספתא תענית א' ט'.

[205] On public fast days six benedictions were added to
the daily eighteen; see the Mishnah below, p. 204, 2.

individual who takes upon himself a "public fast,"²⁰⁶ and yet the Baraita reads: "except that the former recites eighteen benedictions and the latter nineteen," which proves that an individual may insert a benediction for himself! Answer. No, by "community" is no doubt meant its representative, but (as to your objection that in this case twenty-four benedictions are recited, it must be understood that) the Baraita has reference to the first three public fasts, during which the number of benedictions is not increased to twenty-four. Is this true? Is it not stated in a Baraita: "There is no difference between the three first and the three intermediary public fasts, except that during the former work is allowed, while during the latter it is prohibited," from which you must infer that with regard to the number of benedictions they are alike!? Answer. The author of this Baraita mentioned one difference and omitted the other. Is there anything else that he omitted, so that we may be justified in assuming that he omitted this difference? I will say this, then: The teacher of the Baraita was concerned only in pointing out a difference regarding things prohibited on fast days, but did not care to mention a difference in the number of benedictions recited. If you prefer, I may also say that the number of benedictions is not increased to twenty-four even during the intermediary public fasts. Is this true? Is

²⁰⁶ Namely, one that is subject to all the rigors prescribed for public fasts; see above, notes 186^b, 193.

שקבל עליו תענית צבור וקתני שזה מתפלל שמונה

עשרה וזה מתפלל תשע עשרה אלמא יחיד קובע

ברכה לעצמו לא לעולם שליח צבור ובקמייתא

דליכא עשרים וארבע ולא והתניא אין בין שלש

5 ראשונות לשלש אמצעיות אלא שבאלו מותרין

בעשית מלאכה ובאלו אסורין בעשית מלאכה הא

לעשרים וארבע זה וזה שוין תנא ושייר מאי שייר

דהא שייר אלא באסורי קא מיירי בתפלות לא

קא מיירי ואיבעית אימא באמצעייתא נמי ליכא

מסרת הש"ס והמדרשים

7 (תנא ושייר) תענית י"ד א'; סוכה   א', ט"ו א', מ"ג ב', ס"ב ב'; מכות
נ"ד א';יבמות כ"א ב',ע"נ א'.פ"ד ב';   כ"א ב'; ירוש' יבמות ט' א' ב', י"ב
כתובות מ"א א'; קדושין ט"ז א', מ'   ד' (דף ט' ע"ד ושם הלשון לית
א';נזיר ל"ח ב'; סוטה ט"ז א'; ב"ק י'   כללוי דר' כללין).

it not stated in a Baraita: "There is no difference between the three intermediary and the seven (last) public fasts except that during the latter the alarm is sounded and the shops are closed," which proves that with regard to the twenty-four benedictions both groups of fasts are alike? If, however, you should say that here, too, the author of the Baraita mentions one difference and omits the other, what will you do, then, with the explicit words of the Baraita, saying that "there is no difference between them except"? Answer. Do you mean to say that the phrase "there is no difference" is to be taken literally? [fol. 14a] Did not the Baraita omit to mention the procession with the ark?[207] No, this is no omission, because the Baraita meant to point out only things done privately, not such as are done in public.

Said R. 'Ashi: The same view can be deduced from the text of our Mishnah, for it reads: "In what respect are these (seven) fasts more rigorous than the (three) immediately preceding ones? In that on these (seven) fast days the alarm is sounded and the shops are closed," which shows that with respect to the twenty-four benedictions both groups of fasts are alike. If, however, you should say that here, too, the Mishnah mentions one difference and omits another, what will you do with the words of the Mishnah: "In what respect"?[208] Answer. Do you think that the phrase

[207] Which was held publicly during the last seven fasts, but not during the intermediary three; see below, pp. 204, 214.

[208] Which phrase with the following context seems to

186

עשרין וארבע ולא והתניא אין בין שלש אמצעיות

לשבע אחרונות אלא שבאלו מתריעין ונועלין את

החנויות הא לעשרים וארבע זה וזה שוין וכי תימא

הכא נמי תנא ושייר והא אין בין קתני ותסברא אין

5 בין דוקא והא שייר תבה אי משום תבה לאו

שיורא הוא מילי דצנעא קתני מילי דפרהסיא לא

קתני:

אמר רב אשי מתניתין נמי דיקא דקתני מה אלו

יתרות על הראשונות שבאלו מתריעין ונועלין את

10 החנויות הא לעשרים וארבע זה וזה שוין וכי תימא

הכא נמי תנא ושייר והא מה אלו קתני ותסברא מה

מסרת הש"ס והמדרשים

4 (אין בין) תוספתא מגלה א' 11 (ושייר) ע' במסרת הש"ס לעיל
ח'. 8 (מה אלו) תענית י"ב ב'. סוף דף י"ג ב'.

---

emphasize the fact that it is only "in respect" to the
particular points there mentioned (sounding the alarm
and closing the shops) that the last seven fasts differ
from the three intermediary ones.

"in what respect" is to be taken strictly? Did not the Mishnah omit mentioning the ark? No, this is no omission, because the Mishnah mentions it in the next chapter. Now that you have arrived at this point, you may just as well say that failing to mention the increase in the number of benedictions to twenty-four is no omission either, because the Mishnah speaks of it in the next chapter.

What has been decided about the matter? Said R. Samuel b. Sasartai in the name of R. Ḥiyya b. 'Ashi, who said it in the name of Rab: The benediction should be inserted between "Redeemer" and "Healer" (of Israel), but R. 'Asi said in the name of R. Jannai b. Ishmael, it should be included in the benediction: "Who hearest prayer," and this is the accepted law.

One Baraita teaches: Pregnant or nursing women must fast during the first three days, but not during the last seven days; another Baraita teaches that they must fast during the last but not during the first, while a third Baraita teaches, they need not fast either during the first or the last! Said R. Sheshet, take it that the intermediary fast days are meant, which will harmonize all three Baraitot.[209]

[209] The harmonization is brought about by shifting the meanings of the words ראשונות (first) and אחרונות (last) as follows: In the first Baraita ראשונות means the intermediary three fasts, which are called "first" in relation only to the seven last. In the second Baraita אחרונות means intermediary, called "last" in relation to the first three. In the third Baraita the two words are to be taken

אלו דוקא והא שייר תבה אי משום תבה לאו שיורא
הוא דהא קתני לה באידך פרקין השתא דאתית
להכי עשרים וארבעה נמי לאו שיורא הוא דהא
קתני לה באידך פרקין:

5   מאי הוי עלה אמר רב שמואל בר סטרטאי אמר
רב חייא בר אשי אמר רב בין גואל לרופא רבי
אסי משום רבי ינאי בר ישמעאל אמר בשומע תפלה
והלכתא בשומע תפלה:

תני חדא עוברות ומיניקות מתענות בראשונות
10   ואין מתענות באחרונות ותניא אידך מתענות
באחרונות ואין מתענות בראשונות ותניא אידך אין
מתענות לא בראשונות ולא באחרונות אמר רב
ששת נקוט מציעתא בידך (דמיתרצון כולהו):

6 (בין גואל לרופא) ע׳ במסרת   ירושלמי ו.עניית ה׳ ה׳ (ס״ד ג׳);
הש״ס לעיל י״נ ב׳.   9 (עוברות)   תוספתא תעניּת ג׳ ב׳.

---

literally and absolutely, referring respectively to the *first*,
and the *last* group of fasts. The result is that all three
Baraitot agree that the women in question must observe
the intermediary fasts but not the first three, because at
that period the situation of the drought is not yet so
serious as to require feeble women to fast, and not the
last seven, because so many fasts might endanger their
lives; see also the Hebrew note.

In what respect are these fasts more rigorous than the preceding ones? In that on these the alarm must be sounded and the shops must be closed. How is the alarm sounded? R. Judah says, by blowing the shofar; R. Judah, son of R. Samuel b. Shilat says in the name of Rab, by the supplication: "Answer us!" It was thought that the one who advocates blowing the shofar is opposed to the use of the supplication: "Answer us!" and that the one who is in favor of the supplication: "Answer us!" is opposed to blowing the shofar. If so, the latter authority would disagree with this Baraita: No less than seven fast days are enjoined upon the community, and on each of them eighteen alarms are sounded; in order to remember this, take Jericho as a sign. Now, in Jericho it was done by blowing the shofar! You must therefore say that everybody admits that blowing the shofar is a proper means of sounding the alarm, but a difference of opinion exists regarding the supplication: "Answer us!" the one authority considering it a mode of sounding the alarm, the other not considering it as such. But has the supplication: "Answer us!" ever been called alarm-sounding? Does not a Baraita state: "For other calamities that break forth and come upon a community, as epidemic eruptions on the skin, locusts, flies, hornets, mosquitoes and a plague of serpents and scorpions, no alarm was sounded (for their disappearance), but cries were uttered"? Now, crying certainly is by mouth![210] Answer. There

---

[210] Inasmuch as the Baraita is contrasting צועקין (cry-

מה אלו יתרות על הראשונות שבאלו מתריעין
ונועלין את החנויות: במאי מתריעין רב יהודה אמר
בשופרות רב יהודה בריה דרב שמואל בר שילת
משמיה דרב אמר בעננו קא סלקא דעתיה מאן
דאמר בשופרות לא אמר בעננו ומאן דאמר בעננו
לא אמר בשופרות ולא והתניא אין פוחתין משבע
תעניות על הצבור ובהן שמונה עשרה התרעות
וסימן לדבר יריחו ויריחו בשופרות הוה אלא
בשופרות דכולי עלמא לא פליגי דקרי לה התרעה
כי פליגי בעננו מר סבר עננו קרי לה התרעה ומר
סבר לא קרי לה התרעה ועננו מי קרי לה התרעה
והתניא ושאר כל מיני פורעניות המתרגשות ובאות
על הצבור כגון החכוך והגובאי והזבוב והצרעה
והיתושין ושלוח נחשים ועקרבים לא היו מתריעין
אלא צועקין והא צעקה בפה היא תנאי היא דתנן

ing) with מתריעין (sounding the alarm), it obviously disagrees with the authority that considers crying '*Anenu*
(answer us) as a form of sounding the alarm.

are different opinions of teachers in this matter, for we read in the Mishnah:[211] "On the following occasions the alarm is sounded on the Sabbath: When a city is surrounded by troops of the enemy or is threatened by the overflow of a river, and for a ship which is near foundering; R. Jose says, we may do so in order to secure the people's help, but not in the form of crying to God." Now, how is that sounding to be done? By the use of the Shofar? Is it allowed to blow the Shofar on a Sabbath? Undoubtedly, then, the Mishnah means by crying "Answer us!" And yet it terms it "sounding"! It stands proved.[212]

R. Judah Nesiah[213] [fol. 14b] ordained thirteen fast days, but the prayers were not answered. He therefore intended to ordain more fasts, but R. 'Ami said to him, has it not been said that it is not proper to trouble the community too much? Said R. 'Abba son of R. Ḥiyya b. 'Abba: R. 'Ami was thinking of his own convenience (because he did not want to fast), for thus said R. Ḥiyya b. 'Abba in the name of R. Johanan, that statement (quoted by R. 'Ami) applies only to fasts ordained on account of lack of rain, but in the case of other calamities the people must continue fasting until their prayer is answered. The same was taught in a

[211] See below, p. 268.

[212] Viz., that there are two opinions as to whether or not praying 'Anenu is called sounding the alarm, the last quoted Mishnah teaching in the affirmative, while the preceding Baraita holds the opposite view. This being

על אלו מתריעים בשבת על עיר שהקיפוה גוים
או נהר ועל הספינה המטרפת בים רבי יוסי אומר
לעזרה אבל לא לצעקה במאי אילימא בשופרות
שופרות בשבת מי שרי אלא לאו בעננו וקא קרי
5 לה התרעה שמע מינה:

י"ד   רבי יהודה נשיאה ‡ גזר תליסר תעניתא ולא
ע"ב
איעני סבר למגזר טפי אמר ליה רבי אמי הרי אמרו
אין מטריחין על הצבור יותר מדאי אמר רבי אבא
בריה דרבי חייא בר אבא רבי אמי דעבד לגרמיה
10 הוא דעבד הכי אמר רבי חייא בר אבא אמר רבי
יוחנן לא שנו אלא לגשמים אבל לשאר מיני פורעניות
מתענין והולכין עד שיענו:

מסרת הש"ס והמדרשים

תוספתא סוטה ט"ו י'; ירושלמי	1 (עיר) תענית י"ט א',כ"ב ב';
תענית א' ז' (ס"ד ד'); 9 (לגרמיה)	תוספתא תענית ב' י"ב. 2 (ספינה)
ברכות מ"ח א'; שבת ל"ח ב'; מו"ק	ספרי במדבר ע"ו. 3 (לצעקה)
כ"ה ב'.	ירושלמי ג' ח'. 8 (מטריחין)

the case, each of the two contending talmudic authorities
(Amoraim) follows one of the two tannaitic sources
(Mishnah and Baraita).   Otherwise a talmudic authority
is not entitled to contradict either a Mishnah or a Baraita.
213 *Nesiah* (patriarch) was the cognomen of the Patriarch Judah III (end of the third century).

Baraita: When it was ordained that the people should fast (twice) three days and again seven days, it had reference to drought, but in case of other kinds of calamities they must continue fasting until their prayers are answered. Should we say that this Baraita is a refutation of R.'Ami? Answer. R. 'Ami can defend himself by replying that the matter is the subject of dispute between different Tannaim,[214] for a Baraita states: No more than thirteen fasts should be enjoined upon the community, as it is not proper to trouble the community too much; this is the opinion of Rabbi; Rabban Simeon b. Gamaliel says, this is not the reason, but it is because (after the thirteen fasts) the time for rainfall is passed.

The inhabitants of Nawe sent the following question to Rabbi: Inasmuch as we are in need of rain at the time of the solstice of Tammuz, are we to be compared to individuals and hence to include our prayer for rain in the benediction "Who hearest Prayer," or are we regarded as a community and should insert it in the "Blessing of the Years"? Rabbi replied: You are regarded as individuals, and should insert your prayer in the benediction: "Who hearest Prayer." An objection was raised: R. Judah says, the given order of fasts applies only to times when the seasons of the year were divided on the basis of their normal recurrence[215] and Israel was dwelling in its land, but in the present time[216] all depends upon the nature of the seasons and upon the

[214] See note 212.

[215] Namely, that the time for sowing was in Marḥesh-

תניא נמי הכי כשאמרו שלש וכשאמרו שבע לא

אמרו אלא לגשמים אבל לשאר מיני פורעניות

מתענין והולכין עד שיענו לימא תהוי תיובתיה

דרבי אמי אמר לך רבי אמי תנאי היא דתניא אין

5   גוזרין יותר משלש עשרה תעניות על הצבור לפי

שאין מטריחין על הצבור יותר מדאי דברי רבי

רבן שמעון בן גמליאל אומר לא מן השם הוא זה

אלא מפני שיצא זמנה של רביעה:

שלחו ליה בני נוה לרבי כגון אנן דצריכינן

10   למטרא אפילו בתקופת תמוז כיחידים דמינן

ובשומע תפלה או כצבור דמינן ובברכת השנים

שלח להו כיחידים דמיתו ובשומע תפלה מיתיבי

אמר רבי יהודה אימתי בזמן שהשנים כתקנן וישראל

שרויין על אדמתן אבל בזמן הזה הכל לפי השנים

מסרת הש"ס והמדרשים

9 (נוה) ירוש' תענית א' א'; ברכות   ה'·ב' (בשנוי לשון ונינוה שבדפוסים
טעות ע' כאן בהערותי בכרך שני).

---

wan and that of harvesting in Nisan, as was the case in
Palestine.

[216] After the destruction of the Temple, when the Israelites had to settle in other countries with different
climes and seasons.

nature of the localities! What! You quote a Baraita to contradict Rabbi! Rabbi is an authority of the Mishnah and is entitled to differ.[217]

What has been decided in this matter? R. Naḥman said, in such a case the prayer for rain may be inserted in the "Blessing of the Years," but R. Sheshet said, it must be included in "Who hearest Prayer," and the law is that it must be included in "Who hearest Prayer."

On the fasts falling on a Monday the doors of the shops may be slightly opened toward nightfall, while on Thursdays they may be kept open all day for the sake of the approaching Sabbath.

The question was raised: What does this Mishnah teach? Does it mean to say that on Thursdays we leave the doors slightly open all day, or that we may keep them wide open all day for the sake of the Sabbath? Come and hear: A Baraita states: on Mondays toward evening we leave the doors slightly open, but on Thursdays we keep them wide open all day for the sake of the Sabbath; if the shop has two doors, one only should be opened and the other closed; if the owner had a stand before the door, he may open and close the latter as he pleases.[218]

If all these fast days are passed and the community has not been answered, all business transactions, building, planting . . . should be limited. It was

[217] See note 212.

[218] Because the stand renders the opening of the door inconspicuous.

הכל לפי המקומות הכל לפי הזמן מתניתא קא

רמית עליה דרבי רבי תנא הוא ופליג מאי הוי

עלה רב נחמן אמר בברכת השנים רב ששת אמר

בשומע תפלה והלכתא בשומע תפלה:

⁵   בשני מטין עם חשיכה ובחמשי מותרין כל היום

מפני כבוד השבת: איבעיא להו היכי קתני בחמשי

מטין כל היום או דילמא פותחין כל היום מפני כבוד

השבת תא שמע דתניא בשני מטין לעת ערב ובחמשי

פותחין כל היום מפני כבוד השבת יש לו שני פתחים

¹⁰ פותח אחד ונועל אחד ואם יש לו אצטבא כנגד

פתחו פותח ונועל כדרכו ואינו חושש:

עברו אלו ולא נענו ממעטין במשא ומתן בבנין

taught: By building is meant such as is undertaken for pleasure and, likewise, by planting is
meant such as is intended for pleasure. What is
a building for pleasure? A structure that one
erects for the wedding of his son. What are
plantings for pleasure? Bowers, as they are
built by kings.

Greetings. The Rabbis have taught: Schol-
arly people should not greet one another (during
the fast days), and if an uneducated man greets,
the greeting is to be returned in an undertone
and with a serious mien; they should wrap themselves up and sit like mourners and like people
reprimanded by God, (waiting) for heaven to
show them mercy.

R. Eleazar said: A prominent man is not allowed to fall upon his face in prayer unless he knows
that he will be answered, as was Joshua, as it is
said (Josh., 7. 10): "And the Lord said unto
Joshua: 'Get thee up[219]; wherefore, now, art
thou fallen upon thy face?'" R. Eleazar further
said: A prominent man is not allowed to put
on sackcloth unless he knows that he will be
answered, as was Jehoram, as it is said (II
Kings, 6. 30): "And the people looked, and, behold, he had sackcloth within upon his flesh."
R. Eleazar further said: Not all were to fall upon
their faces (for prayer) and not all were to rend
their clothes, but Moses and Aaron were to fall
upon their faces, while Joshua and Caleb were

[219] Which means that his prayer was accepted and he
need not remain prostrated.

198

ובנטיעה: תנא בנין בנין של שמחה נטיעה נטיעה
של שמחה אי זהו בנין של שמחה זה הבונה בית
חתנות לבנו ואיזו היא נטיעה של שמחה זה הנוטע
אכורנקי של מלכים:

5 ובשאילת שלום: תנו רבנן חברים אין שאילת
שלום ביניהן ועם הארץ ששאל מחזירין לו בשפה
רפה ובכבד ראש והן מתעטפין ויושבין כאבלים
וכמנודין כבני אדם הנזופין למקום עד שירחמו
עליהם מן השמים:

10 אמר רבי אלעזר אין אדם חשוב רשאי לפול על
פניו אלא אם כן נענה כיהושע שנאמר ויאמר ה'
אל יהושע קם לך למה זה אתה נפל על פניך:

ואמר רבי אלעזר אין אדם חשוב רשאי לחגור
שק על בשרו אלא אם כן נענה כיהורם שנאמר
15 וירא העם והנה השק על בשרו מבית:

ואמר רבי אלעזר לא הכל בנפילה ולא הכל
בקריעה אלא משה ואהרן בנפילה יהושע וכלב

תורה אור   מסרת הש"ס והמדרשים

12 יהושע ז' י'.   15 מ"ב ו' ל'.   1 (בנין) מגלה ה' ב'; (יבמות
מ"ג א') ירושלמי תענית א' ח';
ד' ט' (ס"ט ב').   7 (רפה) ירושלמי תענית ספ"א, תוספתא תענית ד'
י"ב. 7 (מתעטפין) מו"ק ט"ו א'.   10 (חשוב) מגלה כ"ב ב'; ירושלמי
תענית ב' ו' (ס"ה ד'); ע"ז ד' א' (מ"ג ד').

199

to rend their clothes.²²⁰   As to Moses and Aaron,
it is said (Num., 14. 5–6): "Then Moses and
Aaron fell on their faces"; and as to Joshua
and Caleb, it is said (*ibidem*, 14. 6): "And Joshua
the son of Nun and Caleb the son of Jephunneh,
who were of them that spied out the land, rent
their clothes." R. Zera or, as some say, R.
Samuel b. Naḥamani, raised an objection: If
Scripture had only the word "Joshua," it would
mean what you said, but since it has "*and*
Joshua," Scripture indicates that they (Joshua and Caleb) did both.²²¹

R. Eleazar further said: Not all will have to
rise and not all to prostrate themselves before
the Israelites; but kings will have to rise, and
princes will have to prostrate themselves. "Kings
will have to rise," as it is written [fol. 15a] (Is.,
49.7): "Kings shall see and arise." Princes
will have to prostrate themselves," as it is written (*ibid.*): "Princes and they shall prostrate
themselves." R. Zera or, as some say, R. Samuel
b. Nahamani, raised an objection: If Scripture
said, "*they* shall prostrate themselves," it would
mean what you maintained, but since it says,
"*and* they shall prostrate themselves," it indicates that they will have to do both. Said R.

²²⁰ Rending of the clothes is considered a greater self-
humiliation than prostration. For Moses and Aaron,
being men of great distinction, the latter form was sufficient, but not for Joshua and Caleb.

²²¹ Because the *waw*, meaning and, added to the name of
Joshua indicates that what Joshua and Caleb did, namely,
rending their clothes, was in addition to the prostration

בקריעה משה ואהרן בנפילה דכתיב ויפל משה

ואהרן על פניהם יהושע וכלב בקריעה דכתיב

ויהושע בן נון וכלב בן יפנה מן התרים את הארץ

קרעו בגדיהם מתקיף לה רבי זירא ואיתימא רבי

5 שמואל בר נחמני אי הוה כתיב יהושע כדקאמרת

השתא דכתיב ויהושע הא והא עבוד:

ואמר רבי אלעזר לא הכל בקימה ולא הכל

בהשתחואה אלא מלכים בקימה ושרים בהשתחואה

מלכים בקימה דכתיב | מלכים יראו וקמו שרים
טו׳ו
ע׳א

10 בהשתחואה דכתיב שרים וישתחוו מתקיף לה רבי

זירא ואיתימא רבי שמואל בר נחמני אי הוה כתיב

ישתחוו כדקאמרת השתא דכתיב וישתחוו הא והא

עבוד:

תורה אור
1 במדבר י׳ד ה׳. 3 במדבר י׳ד ו׳. 9 ישעיה מ׳ט ז׳.

---

spoken of in the preceding verse with reference to Moses
and Aaron.   Joshua and Caleb thus did both: They prostrated themselves and rent their clothes.

Naḥman: We say in addition that not all will
share in light and not all in gladness, but the
righteous will have light and the upright will
have gladness. As to the righteous having
light, it is written (Ps., 97.11): "Light is sown
for the righteous," and as for the upright having
gladness, it is written (*ibidem*): "And gladness
for the upright in heart."[222]

[222] This addition of R. Naḥman has here also the
purpose of giving the chapter a cheerful ending, which is
a frequent occurrence in both Mishnah and Talmud, especially at the end of a whole tractate; see below, notes
390, 440.

אמר רב נחמן בר יצחק אף אנו נאמר לא הכל
לאורה ולא הכל לשמחה אלא צדיקים לאורה
וישרים לשמחה צדיקים לאורה דכתיב אור זרע
לצדיק וישרים לשמחה דכתיב ולישרי לב שמחה:

הדרן עלך מאימתי

CHAPTER II

Mishnah: 1. What is the order of procedure on the (last seven) fast days? The ark is carried out into the open place of the town and wood-ashes are strewn upon it, upon the head of the Nasi,[223] and the head of the Ab Bet Din,[223a] and every one present takes and puts some of it upon his own head. The Elder among them addresses them in words of exhortation, saying: Brethren: Of the people of Nineveh it is not said: And God saw their sackcloth and their fasting, but (Jonah, 3. 10): "And God saw their works, that they turned from their evil way," and in the Prophets it is said (Joel, 2. 13): "And rend your heart, and not your garments, and turn unto the Lord your God, for He is gracious and compassionate, long-suffering and abundant in mercy, and repenteth Him of the evil."

2. When they stand up for prayer, they place before the ark an old and experienced man, who has children and whose house is empty, so that his heart may be wholly devoted to his prayer. He recites before them twenty-four benedictions, namely the eighteen that are read every day, to which, he adds six more.

3. These are the additional benedictions: the *Zikrōnōt*,[224] the *Shōfārōt*,[225] and Psalms 120, 121,

---

[223] On the functions of the officials, see Büchler, *Das Synhedrion in Jerusalem*, Vienna, 1902, Index, *s. v.*

[223a] See preceding note.

[224] זכרונות, remembrances, is the name of the second section of the Musaf prayer for New Year, beginning אתה זוכר, Thou rememberest. It consists of nine verses (three each, from the Pentateuch, Prophets, and Hagiographa), in which God's mindfulness of His promises to the pious of every generation (Noah, the Patriarchs, etc.) is praised,

פרק שני

מתניתין: סדר תעניות כיצד מוציאין את
התבה לרחובה של עיר ונותנין אפר מקלה על גבי
התבה ובראש הנשיא ובראש אב בית דין וכל אחד
ואחד נוטל ונותן בראשו הזקן שבהן אומר לפניהם
5 דברי כבושין אחינו לא נאמר באנשי נינוה וירא
האלהים את שקם ואת תעניתם אלא וירא האלהים
את מעשיהם כי שבו מדרכם הרעה ובקבלה
הוא אומר וקרעו לבבכם ואל בגדיכם ושובו אל
ה' אלהיכם כי חנון ורחום הוא ארך אפים ורב
10 חסד ונחם על הרעה עמדו בתפלה מורידין לפני
התבה זקן ורגיל ויש לו בנים וביתו ריקן כדי שיהא
לבו שלם בתפלה ואומר לפניהם עשרים וארבע
ברכות שמונה עשרה שבכל יום ומוסיף עליהן
עוד שש ואלו הן זכרונות ושופרות אל ה' בצרתה

תורה אור   מסרת הש"ס והמדרשים
6 יונה ג' י'.   8 יואל ב' י"ג.   1 (מוציאין) תוספתא תענית א' ח';
14 תהלים ק"כ א';   ב"ר מ"ט י"א. 5 (כבושין) תוספתא
תענית א' ח'. 12 (ואומר) תוספתא
תענית א' ט'.   14 (שש) ירושלמי ברכות ה' ב'; תענית א' א' (ס"ג ד').

winding up with the appropriate prayer that He may be as
mindful of the needs of the present generation.

[225] שופרות, trumpets, the name of the third section,
consisting likewise of nine verses, three from each of the
three parts of the Bible, in which the word *shofar* occurs,
and ending with the prayer that the great horn may be
blown for the redemption of Israel (Is., 27.13).

130, 102. R. Judah said, he does not have to recite the Zikrōnōt and the Shōfārōt, but, instead, he recites the passages: I Kings, 8.37–41, and Jer., 14.1–10. To each of these six he adds the appropriate concluding eulogy.

4. The first[226] benediction he closes with the words: He who answered Abraham on Mount Moriah may answer you and hear the voice of your crying this day, blessed art Thou who redeemest Israel. The second Benediction he closes thus: He who answered our ancestors on the Red Sea, may answer you and hear the voice of your crying this day, blessed art Thou who rememberest things forgotten. The third he closes thus: He who answered Joshua in Gilgal, may answer you and hear the voice of your crying this day, blessed art Thou who hearest the sounding of the trumpet. The fourth he closes thus: He who answered Samuel in Mizpah, may answer you and hear the voice of your crying this day, blessed art Thou who hearest cries. The fifth he closes thus: He who answered Elijah on Mount Carmel, may answer you and hear the

[226] As is explained in the Talmud below, it is not the first of the additional benedictions that is meant here by the Mishnah but one of the regular daily benedictions, namely the seventh (ending with the words גואל ישראל), which is here called the first, because it was the first in which the formula מי שענה (He who answered, etc.) was, on this occasion, to be inserted. This formula was part also of each of the additional six benedictions, as will be seen below, and was thus repeated seven times, which accounts for the Mishnah's enumeration of seven benedictions instead of the expected six.

לי אשא עיני אל ההרים ממעמקים קראתיך ה'
תפלה לעני כי יעטף רבי יהודה אומר לא היה צריך
לומר זכרונות ושופרות אלא אומר תחתיהן רעב
כי יהיה בארץ וגו' אשר היה דבר ה' אל ירמיהו
על דברי הבצרות ואומר חותמותיהן על הראשונה
הוא אומר מי שענה את אברהם בהר המוריה הוא
יענה אתכם וישמע קול צעקתכם היום הזה ברוך
אתה ה' גואל ישראל על השניה הוא אומר מי שענה
את אבותינו על ים סוף הוא יענה אתכם וישמע
קול צעקתכם היום הזה ברוך אתה ה' זוכר
הנשכחות על השלישית הוא אומר מי שענה את
יהושע בגלגל הוא יענה אתכם וישמע קול צעקתכם
היום הזה ברוך אתה ה' שומע תרועה על הרביעית
הוא אומר מי שענה את שמואל במצפה הוא יענה
אתכם וישמע קול צעקתכם היום הזה ברוך אתה
ה' שומע צעקה על החמשית הוא אומר מי
שענה את אליהו בהר הכרמל הוא יענה אתכם

תורה אור

1 תהלים קכ״א א'; 1 תהלים ק״ל א'. 2 תהלים ק״ב א'. 3 ס״א ח'
ל״ז. 4 ירמיה י״ד א'.

voice of your crying this day, blessed art Thou who hearest prayer. The sixth he closes thus: He who answered Jonah in the belly of the fish, may answer you and hear the voice of your crying this day, blessed art Thou who answerest in time of distress. The seventh[227] he closes thus: He who answered David and Solomon, his son, in Jerusalem, may answer you and hear the crying of your voice this day, blessed art Thou who hast mercy on the land.

5. It happened [fol. 15b] in the days of R. Ḥalafta in Sepphoris and R. Ḥanina b. Teradyon in Siknin that one went before the ark, recited the benediction,[228] and the congregation responded Amen.—"Blow, ye priests, blow!"[229] —He who answered Abraham on mount Moriah may answer you and hear the voice of your cry this day.—"Sound the alarm, ye sons of Aaron, sound!"—He who answered our ancestors on the

[227] See the preceding note.

[228] Namely, the seventh of the daily eighteen or, as explained in note 226, the first of the benedictions that received the formula מי שענה. The procedure hereafter described does not apply, however, to this and to the immediately following benediction alone, but also to the remaining five, the Mishnah giving only two as examples.

[229] This admonition to blow the shofar came from the sexton (as given in the Baraita, below, p. 228), who had the order to call upon the priests as soon as the congregation had responded Amen. While he was calling on the priests, the minister said מי שענה, and then the priests blew. The same procedure was observed in the next benediction, except that instead of "blow, ye priests, blow!" the call was

וישמע קול צעקתכם היום הזה ברוך אתה ה' שומע
תפלה על השׁשׁית הוא אומר מי שׁענה את יונה במעי
הדגה הוא יענה אתכם וישמע קול צעקתכם היום
הזה ברוך אתה ה' העונה בעת צרה על השׁביעית
5 הוא אומר מי שׁענה את דוד ושׁלמה בנו בירושלם
הוא יענה אתכם וישמע קול צעקתכם היום הזה
ברוך אתה ה' המרחם על הארץ: מעשה ׀ בימי רבי
חלפתא בצפורי ורבי חנינא בן תרדיון בסיכני
שׁעבר אחד לפני התבה וגמר את כל הברכה וענו
10 אחריו אמן תקעו הכהנים תקעו מי שׁענה את אברהם
בהר המוריה הוא יענה אתכם וישמע קול צעקתכם
היום הזה הריעו בני אהרן הריעו מי שׁענה את

(marginal: ט"ו ע"ב)

"sound the alarm, ye sons of Aaron, sound!", and so al-
ternately till the end of the six and seven benedictions
respectively. The reason for the change in the calls was
that the one had to be a תקיעה (*blowing* of one tune) and the
other a תרועה (*sounding* of several tunes in quick succession,
as for alarm). The Rabbis disapproved of this procedure,
and the medieval authorities differ widely as to the reasons therefor. Nor do they agree in the interpretation
of the Mishnah as given above, but space forbids to enter
upon details, for which see the Hebrew notes; comp.,
Büchler, *Types of Jewish-Palestinian Piety*, London, 1922,
pp. 223, 245.

Red Sea, may answer you, and hear the voice of
your cry this day; and so after each benediction.
When the matter came up before the Sages they
said this procedure was customary only before
the eastern gates (of the Temple).

6. On the first three fast days the priests of
the guard[230] fast, but not to the end of the
day, while the priests of the sub-division do
not fast; on the second (intermediary) three
fast days the priests of the guard fast to the
end of the day, while those of the sub-division
fast but part of the day; on the seven last fast

[230] The whole people of Israel was divided into 24
sections. The priests (and Levites) within each section
formed each a special division (משמר = guard; comp. Num.
18. 1–7), which had to do service in the Temple of Jerusalem
one full week every half year; 48 weeks of the year were
thus distributed between the 24 divisions, the remaining
weeks being festival weeks (Passover, Pentecost, Tabernacles) during which all Israel had to make a pilgrimage
to Jerusalem (Ex. 34.23); and owing to the multitude of
the visitors and their sacrifices, the priests of all divisions
had to be present. Each division of priests was subdivided into seven smaller groups (בתי אבות, fathers,
houses, families), each one of which had to do service one
day of the respective week which was assigned to their
division (comp. I Chron., 24. 4–18).

As the law required that owners of sacrifices be present
while the latter were being offered up (see the Mishnah, below, p. 396, 2) and as it was, of course, impossible that every
offering Israelite should go to Jerusalem for that purpose,
it was arranged that with each of the 24 priestly divisions
there should go also a corresponding division of some lay-

אבותינו על ים סוף הוא יענה אתכם וישמע קול
צעקתכם היום הזה וכן בכל ברכה וברכה וכשבא
דבר אצל חכמים אמרו לא היו נוהגין כן אלא
בשערי מזרח שלש תעניות הראשונות אנשי משמר
מתענין ולא משלימין אנשי בית אב לא היו מתענין
שלש שניות אנשי משמר מתענין ומשלימין אנשי בית
אב מתענין ולא משלימין שבע אחרונות אלו ואלו

מסרת הש"ס והמדרשים

2 (וכשבא) ר"ה כ"ז א'; תוספתא (ס"ה ד') ומו"ק ריש פ"ג (וע'
תענית א' י"ד.   4 (אנשי משמר) לקמן כ"ו ב', כ"ט ב' ויבמות מ"ג א'
מו"ק י"ד א'; ירושלמי כאן ב' י"ב ווירושלמי כאן ד' ט' (ס"ט ב')
ויבמות ספ"ו.

---

men to act as representatives of their respective Israelitish
section. Their action consisted in standing by during
the sacrificial ceremonies and reciting prayers, that the
offerings of their brethren at home, whom they represented,
might be accepted. They too, like the division of priests to
which they were attached, had to change off every week.
These lay representatives were called אנשי מעמד, men of
the (lay)-post, in contradistinction to the אנשי משמר,
men of the (priestly) guards, while the sub-divisions of
priests, doing one day's service, were called אנשי בית אב,
men belonging to a father's house, a family. However,
the terms אנשי משמר and אנשי מעמד, especially the former,
are sometimes used promiscuously; see below, notes
318, 397; comp. Müller, *Masechet Soferim*, Leipzig, 1878,
pp. 236ff., and the Hebrew notes to the Mishnah, below,
p. 397, 2.

211

days both divisions fast to the end of the day;
this is the opinion of R. Joshua, but the Sages
say: On the first fast days none of the divisions
fasts; on the second fast day the priests of the
guard fast but part of the day, while the sub-
division does not fast at all; on the seven last
fast days the priests of the guard fast to the
end of the day, while the sub-division fasts but
part of the day.

7. Members of the priests of the guard may
drink wine at night, but not during the day,[231]
while the members of the sub-division should not
drink either during the day or at night; the
priests of the guard and the members of the lay
division are not allowed to cut their hair or to
wash their clothes; on Thursday, however, they
are allowed to do so for the honor of the
Sabbath.

8. Wherever the "Scroll of Fasts"[232] records
a day as one on which mourning is forbidden,
it is not allowed to mourn even on the preceding
day; on the day following, however, it is allowed; R. Jose says, it is forbidden both on the
preceding and on the following day. Wherever a
day is recorded in the "Scroll of Fasts" as one
on which fasting is forbidden, fasting is allowed
both on the preceding and on the following day;
R. Jose says, it is forbidden on the preceding,
but allowed on the following day.

[231] This has no reference to the public fast days, but is
a general law forbidding priests to drink wine during the
days on which they were stationed in Jerusalem for Temple
services. The same thing applies to the law forbidding

מתענין ומשלימין דברי רבי יהושע וחכמים אומרים
שלש תעניות הראשונות אלו ואלו לא היו מתענין
שלש שניות אנשי משמר מתענין ולא משלימין אנשי
בית אב לא היו מתענין שבע אחרונות אנשי משמר
5 מתענין ומשלימין אנשי בית אב מתענין ולא משלימין
אנשי משמר מותרין לשתות יין בלילות אבל לא
בימים אנשי בית אב לא ביום ולא בלילה אנשי
משמר ואנשי מעמד אסורין לספר ולכבס ובחמשי
מותרין מפני כבוד השבת כל הכתוב במגלת תענית
10 דילא למספד לפניו אסור לאחריו מותר רבי יוסי
אומר בין לפניו בין לאחריו אסור דילא להתענאה
בין לפניו בין לאחריו מותר רבי יוסי אומר לפניו

מסרת הש״ס והמדרשים

8 (ובחמשי) תענית י״ב ב׳, כ״ו ב׳, כ״ט א׳; יבמות מ״נ א׳; ירושלמי
בכל המקומות הנ״ל.

---

cutting the hair and washing clothes.   See below, p. 240f.

[232] The Scroll of Fasts (מגלת תענית) is a list of 35 days.
on which fasting and, in some instances, also public mourning, were forbidden, in commemoration of certain joyous
events that took place on those days during the past history of the Jewish people.   For details regarding this
Scroll see the recent work of S. Zeitlin, *Megillat Taanit
as a Source for Jewish Chronology and History in the Hel-
lenistic and Roman Periods*, Philadelphia, 1922.

9. Fasts should not be decreed so as to begin
on a Thursday,[233] in order not to cause a sudden
rise in market prices; thus the first three fasts
should be in the order of Monday, Thursday,
and Monday, while the second three may be in
the order of Thursday, Monday and Thursday;
R. Jose says, just as the first three fasts are not
to begin on a Thursday, so also should the
second three and the last seven not begin on
that day.

10. No fasts should be enjoined upon the
community on the days of the New Moon,
Ḥanukkah, and Purim, but if the fasts began
prior to these days, they should not be inter-
rupted; this is the opinion of R. Gamaliel.
Said R. Meir: Although R. Gamaliel said that if
the fasts had begun they should not be inter-
rupted, he admitted that one should not fast
to the end of the respective days. The same
rule applies to the Ninth of Ab that happens
to be on a Friday.[234]

Gemara: *What is the order of procedure on
the fast days? The ark is carried out*, etc. Does
this order of procedure apply also to the first
six fasts? This would contradict a Baraita which
reads: On the first three and the second three

[233] Because on Thursday the people begin to buy food
for Sabbath (above, note 10). If a fast is held on the same
day, they would have to buy also for the breaking of the
fast in the evening, and the unexpected rush for larger
quantities of food would induce the vendors to raise the
prices. During the intermediary and last groups of
fasts this was not to be feared, as by that time the vendors

אסור לאחריו מותר אין גוזרין תענית על הצבור

בתחלה בחמשי שלא להפקיע את השערים אלא

שלש תעניות הראשונות שני וחמשי ושני שלש שניות

חמשי ושני וחמשי רבי יוסי אומר כשם שאין

5 הראשונות בחמשי כך לא שניות ולא אחרונות אין

גוזרין תענית על הצבור בראשי חדשים בחנוכה

ובפורים ואם התחילו אין מפסיקין דברי רבן

גמליאל אמר רבי מאיר אף על פי שאמר רבן

גמליאל אין מפסיקין מודה היה שאין משלימין וכן

10 תשעה באב שחל להיות בערב שבת:

גמרא: סדר תעניות כיצד מוציאין את התבה

כו': ואפילו בקמייתא והתניא שלש תעניות ראשונות

מסרת הש"ס והמדרשים

1 (גוזרין) תענית י' א'.   6 (גוזרין)   עירובין מ'א א'.

_____

were supposed to be prepared for the occasion. R. Jose,
however, makes no distinction between the various groups
of fasts in this respect.

[234] Because one should not begin the Sabbath (Friday
evening) while weak and hungry.

fast days the people go to the synagogue and
pray in the same way as they do during the whole
year, but on the seven last fast days the ark is
carried into the open place of the town and
ashes are strewn on it (on the head of the Nasi,
and on the head of the Ab Bet Din, and
everyone else takes ashes and puts on his head;
R. Nathan said, it was wood-ashes that were
used)!²³⁵   Said R. Papa: Our Mishnah also has
reference to the last seven fasts only.

*On the head of the Nasi and the head of the
Ab Bet Din.*   And then "everyone present
takes some of it and puts upon his own head"?
Does not a Baraita state: Rabbi said: For distinction the most important person comes
first, but for degradation the least important
comes first; for distinction the most important
person comes first, because it is said (Levit.,
10. 6): "And Moses spake unto Aaron and
unto Eleazar and unto Ithamar his son." For
degradation the least important comes first
because the serpent was degraded first, then
Eve, and then Adam?!   Answer.   In our case,
too, it is a sign of distinction for them,²³⁶ for we
thus demonstrate to them that they are the men
to pray for mercy for all of us.

*And everyone present takes some of it and puts
upon his own head.*   Why do not the Nasi and

---

²³⁵ The Hebrew text of the words in parentheses is not in
the Munich MS. and is indeed superfluous, as the contradiction is contained only in the statement that the ark was
carried out only during the seven last fasts.

²³⁶ Namely, for the *Nasi* and the *Ab Bet Din.*

ושניות נכנסין לבית הכנסת ומתפללין כדרך
שמתפללין כל השנה כלה ובשבע אחרונות מוציאין
את התבה לרחובה של עיר ונותנין אפר על גבי
התבה ובראש הנשיא ובראש אב בית דין וכל אחד
ואחד נוטל ונותן בראשו רבי נתן אומר אפר מקלה
היו מביאין אמר רב פפא כי קתני מתניתין נמי
אשבע אחרונות קתני:

ובראש הנשיא ובראש אב בית דין: והדר כל
אחד ואחד נוטל ונותן בראשו והתניא רבי אומר
בגדולה מתחילין מן הגדול ובקלקלה מתחילין מן
הקטן בגדולה מתחילין מן הגדול שנאמר ויאמר
משה אל אהרן ולאלעזר ולאיתמר בניו ובקלקלה
מתחילין מן הקטן שבתחלה נתקלל נחש ואחר כך
נתקללה חוה ואחר כך נתקלל אדם הא נמי
חשיבותא היא לדידהו דאמרינן להו אתון חשיביתו
למבעי עלן רחמי:

וכל אחד ואחד נוטל ונותן בראשו: נשיא ואב

תורה אור   מסרת הש"ס והמדרשים

11 ויקרא י' ו'.   10 (מתחילין) ספרא שמיני
דמלואים; ברכות ס"א א'; ב"ר
כ' ג'.   13 (שבתחלה) ספרא וברכות וב"ר שם; ערובין י"ח א'; מדרש
תהלים קל"ט.   17 (בראשו) ב"ר מ"ט י"א וירושלמי תענית ב' ריש ה"א
(בשם ר"י בן פזי).

217

the Ab Bet Din take the ashes themselves and put them on their heads? Why is it that someone else has to take them and put them on their heads? Said R. 'Abba of Cæsarea: Because self-humiliation is not the same as [fol. 16a] being humiliated by others. On what part of the head are the ashes put? Said R. Isaac: On the place of the phylacteries, as it is said (Isaiah, 61. 3): "To appoint unto them that mourn in Zion, to give unto them a garland[237] for ashes."

Why did they go out for these ceremonies to the open place of the town? Said R. Ḥiyya b. 'Abba: Because they wished to say thereby: We have cried privately and were not answered, now let us humiliate ourselves publicly. Resh Laḳish said, they meant to say: We have exiled ourselves from our synagogues, and exile atones for sin. Does it make any practical difference what reason we adopt? The difference arises with regard to a case where the community leave one synagogue and enter another.[238]

Why is the ark carried into the open place of the town? Said R. Joshua b. Levi, this is to say: We had a vessel that we kept hidden, and it has been thus exposed on account of our sins.

---

[237] The word פאר, garland, is taken by the Talmud (*Berakot*, 11a) in explanation of Ez., 24.17 (comp. Targum *ad locum*) as referring to the phylacteries, which are here contrasted with ashes.

[238] To such a case you may apply the word "exiled," but it is not a humiliation in public.

בית דין נמי נשקלו אינהו וננחו בראשיהו מאי שנא
דשקיל איניש אחרינא ומנח להו אמר רבי אבא דמן
קסרי לפי שאינו דומה מתבייש מעצמו ۱ למתבייש ‏ע"א
מאחרים היכא מנח ליה אמר רבי יצחק במקום
5 תפלין שנאמר לשום לאבלי ציון לתת להם פאר
תחת אפר:

(רחוב תיבה ושקים אפר אפר קבורה ומוריה
סימן) למה יוצאין לרחובה של עיר אמר רבי חייא
בר אבא לומר צעקנו בצנעא ולא נענינו נבזה
10 עצמינו בפרהסיא ריש לקיש אמר גלינו וגלותנו
מכפרת עלינו מאי ביניהו איכא ביניהו דגלו מבי
כנשתא לבי כנשתא:

למה מוציאין את התבה לרחובה של עיר אמר
רבי יהושע בן לוי לומר כלי צנוע היה לנו ונתבזה
15 בעוננו:

תורה אור	מסרת הש"ס והמדרשים
5 ישעיה ס"א ג'.	3 (מתבייש) סנהדרין מ"ב א';

ב"ב ס' ב'; מדרש תהלים קל"ז. 4 (מנח)
ירושלמי תענית ב' א'. 9 (בצנעא) ירושלמי תענית ב' א'
(בשם ריב"ל). 10 (גלינו) ירוש' שם (בשם ר"ח בר בא). 14 (כלי)
ירושלמי שם (בשם ר"ח ב"ב).

Why did they cover themselves in sackcloth? Said R. Ḥiyah b. Abba, it is as though they said: We regard ourselves before Thee as beasts.[239]

Why do they put wood-ashes on the Torah scroll? Said R. Judah b. Pazzi, this means to say: "I will be with him in trouble" (Ps., 91. 15);[240] Resh Laḳish said, it means to say: "In all their affliction He was afflicted" (Is., 63. 9). Said R. Zera: When I saw wood-ashes put on the Torah. I trembled in my whole body.

Why does everyone put ashes on his head? R. Levi b. Laḥma and R. Ḥama b. Ḥanina differ as to the reason therefor, the one maintains that it signifies: We regard ourselves before Thee as dust, while according to the other it means: That Thou mayest remember in our favor the ashes of Isaac and have mercy upon us. Does it make any difference what reason we adopt? The difference arises with regard to ordinary dust.[241]

[239] Which are protected against the weather by ordinary sackcloth. See, however, R. Gershom and Rashi, who explain that sackcloth was to remind one of beasts, because it is made of the hair of animals; comp. חדושי אגדות, *ad locum.*

[240] This verse is often explained as saying that while God punishes His people on account of their sins, He at the same time sympathizes with them and says: I am with them in trouble. The Torah-scroll represents God, and the ashes strewn on it symbolize His sympathy.

[241] To indicate that we regard ourselves as dust (R. Levi), any kind of dust will do, but to remind us of Isaac, who was to be burnt on the altar (R. Ḥama), ashes are required.

למה מתכסין בשקים אמר רבי חייא בר אבא
לומר הרי אנו חשובין לפניך כבהמה:

למה נותנין אפר מקלה על גבי ספר תורה אמר
רבי יהודה בן פזי כלומר עמו אנכי בצרה ריש
5 לקיש אמר בכל צרתם לו צר אמר רבי זירא כי
הוה חזינא דיהבי אפר מקלה על גבי ספר תורה
הוה מזדעזע כוליה גופאי:

למה נותנין אפר בראש כל אחד ואחד פליגי
בה רבי לוי בר לחמא ורבי חמא בר חנינא חד
10 אמר הרי אנו חשובין לפניך כעפר וחד אמר כדי
שיזכור לנו אפרו של יצחק וירחם עלינו מאי ביניהו
איכא ביניהו עפר סתם:

מסרת הש"ס והמדרשים	תורה אור

4 תהלים צ"א ט"ו. 5 ישעיה ס"ג ט'. 4 (בצרה) מגלה כ"ט א'; ירושלמי
כאן א' סה"א (ס"ד א') ב' ריש
ה"א, סוכה ד' סוף ה"ג ע"ד ג'); מכילתא בא פי"ד, בשלח דשירה
ג'; ספרי בהעלותך פיסקא פ"ד, מסעי קס"א; שמ"ר פט"ו סימן ט"ז,
פכ"ג ה'; במ"ר ז' ט'; איכ"ר א' י"ט; שהש"ר ד' ח' אות א'; אגדת
שה"ש ד' ח'. 5 (ר' זירא) ירושלמי תענית ב' א'. 11 (יצחק) ספרא
בחקותי פ"ב ח'; ירושלמי שם (בשם ריב"מ ורשב"נ); ב"ר מ"ט י"א;
ויק"ר ל"ו ה' (ע' ברכות ס"ב ב' וב"ר צ"ד ה').

221

Why do they go to the cemetery? R. Levi b. Laḥma and R. Ḥama b. Ḥanina differ as to the reason, the one maintains that it signifies: We are before Thee as dead, while according to the other it is in order that the departed ones should pray for mercy in our behalf. What practical difference is there? The difference arises with regard to non-Jewish cemeteries.²⁴²

What is the meaning of "Mount Moriah" (II Chron., 3. 1)?²⁴³ R. Levi b. Laḥma and R. Ḥama b. Ḥanina differ, the one saying it means a mount from which instruction (*horaah*) went forth to Israel, while the other says it means a mount which imposed fear (*mora*) upon the nations of the world.²⁴⁴

The Elder among them addresses them in words of exhortation. The Rabbis have taught: If there was an elder among them, he addresses them, if not, a scholar addresses them. Are we to assume that the term "elder" here used applies also to one who is not a scholar? Said 'Abbayi, the Rabbis mean to say this: If there is an elder who at the same time is a scholar, this elder and scholar addresses them; if there is not such an elder, a (younger) scholar addresses them, but if there is neither an elder nor a scholar, some man of imposing presence addresses them, saying: Brethren, it is neither sackcloth nor fast-

²⁴² Where only the first reason holds good.

²⁴³ This passage is placed here because it records a difference of opinion between the same two Rabbis, R. Levi and R. Ḥama; comp. below, note 417.

²⁴⁴ Both interpretations play on the name מוריה (the

למה יוצאין לבית הקברות פליגי בה רבי לוי
בר לחמא ורבי חמא בר חנינא חד אמר הרי אנו
חשובין לפניך כמתים וחד אמר כדי שיבקשו מתים
רחמים עלינו מאי ביניהו איכא ביניהו קברי גוים:

5   מאי הר המוריה פליגי בה רבי לוי בר לחמא
ורבי חמא בר חנינא חד אמר הר שיצאה ממנו
הוראה לישראל וחד אמר הר שיצא ממנו מורא
לאומות העולם:

הזקן שבהן אומר לפניהן דברי כבושין: תנו
10   רבנן יש שם זקן אומר זקן אין שם זקן אומר חכם
אטו זקן דקאמרינן אף על גב דלאו חכם הוא אמר
אביי הכי קאמר יש שם זקן והוא חכם אומר זקן
והוא חכם אין שם זקן והוא חכם אומר חכם אין שם
לא זקן ולא חכם אומר אדם של צורה אחינו לא שק

1 (הקברות) ירוש' ב' א' (ע' הנהות   ברכות ד' ה'; פס"ר מ' (מ"ע שם
רצ"ה חיות). 7 (הוראה) ירושלמי   סימן מ"ה); ב"ר נ"ה ז'; שהש"ר ד'
ד' סוף אות ו'.

mount on which the Temple was built), the one connecting
it with הורה, from ירה, to teach, and the other with מורא
from ירא, to fear, to revere.

ing that brings about God's favor, but it is repentance and good deeds, for thus we find that in the case of the people of Nineveh it was not said: And God saw their sackcloth and their fasting, but (Jonah, 3.10): "And God saw their works, that they turned from their evil way."

"Let them be covered with sackcloth, both man and beast" (Jonah, 3. 8). What did they do (with the beasts)? Said Samuel, they separated the dams from their sucklings, saying: Master of the world, if Thou wilt have no mercy upon us, we will have none upon these. "And let them cry mightily unto God" (*ibidem*). What did they say? Said Samuel, they said: Master of the world, if one is humbled and the other is not, if one is mighty and the other is not, if one is righteous and the other is wicked, which one should yield?[245]

"Let them turn every one from his evil way, and from the violence that is in their hands" (*ibidem*). What is meant by "the violence in their hands"? Said Samuel, if one had stolen a joist, even though he had used it in the building of a fort, he should pull down the entire fort and restore the joist to its owner.

Our Rabbis have taught: If a man is guilty of a sin and confesses it, but does not change his way, unto what is he like? He is like a man who holds a reptile in his hand, to whom,

[245] Meaning: God who cannot be affected ("humbled") by the actions of men, God the mighty and the righteous, should be generous and yield to the entreaties of the humbled, the weak, and the wicked.

ותענית גורמין אלא תשובה ומעשים טובים גורמין
שכן מצינו באנשי נינוה שלא נאמר בהם וירא אלהים
את שקם ואת תעניתם אלא וירא האלהים
את מעשיהם כי שבו מדרכם הרעה:

5   ויתכסו שקים האדם והבהמה מאי עבוד אמר
שמואל אסרו את הבהמות לחוד ואת הולדות
לחוד   אמרו לפניו רבונו של עולם אם אין אתה
מרחם עלינו אין אנו מרחמים על אלו:

ויקראו אל אלהים בחזקה מאי אמור אמר
10   שמואל אמרו לפניו רבונו של עולם עלוב ושאינו
עלוב יכול ושאינו יכול צדיק ורשע מי נדחה מפני מי:

וישבו איש מדרכו הרעה ומן החמס אשר
בכפיהם מאי ומן החמס אשר בכפיהם אמר שמואל
אפילו גזל מריש ובנאו בבירה מקעקע כל הבירה
15   כלה ומחזיר מריש לבעליו:

תנו רבנן אדם שיש בידו עברה ומתודה עליה
ואינו חוזר בו למה הוא דומה לאדם שתופש שרץ

תורה אור   מסרת הש"ס והמדרשים

3 יונה ג' י'.   5 יונה ג' ח'.   9 יונה   2 (נינוה) ב'ר מ"ד ב"י. 6 (הבהמות)
ג' ח'.   12 יונה ג' ח'.   ירושלמי כאן ב' א'; פסדר"כ כ"ה
                                              (באבער צד קס"א).   9 (בחזקה)
                                    ע' ירוש' ופסדר"כ שם.   10 (עלוב) מגלה כ"ט א'.   12 (וישבו) ע' ירוש'
                                    שם ובאבער בפסדר"כ שם אות צ'.   17 (שרץ) ירושלמי שם ופסחים ו'
                                    א'; איכ"ר ג' פסוק נחפשה.

though he should immerse himself in all the waters of the world, it will avail nothing; but as soon as he throws away the defiling reptile, an immersion in forty *se'ah* of water will be accounted to him as a cleansing bath, as it is said (Prov., 28.13): "But whoso confesseth and forsaketh them shall obtain mercy," and as it is further said (Lament., 3. 41): "Let us lift up our heart with our hands unto God in the heavens."

When they stand up for prayer, they place before the ark an old and experienced man, etc. The Rabbis have taught: When they stand up for prayer, even if there is among them an elder and a scholar, they send to the ark only one who is experienced; R. Judah said, they send up one who toils without success, who has his labor invested in the field,[246] and whose house is empty;[247] an elderly person whose youth was spent decently, who is modest and agreeable to the people, who knows how to chant and has a sweet voice; one who is well versed in the Scriptures, the Mishnah, the Talmud, Halakot and Haggadot and in all the prayers. The Rabbis (after this description) fixed their eyes upon R. Isaac of the school of R. 'Ami.

[fol. 16b] It was said above: "Who labors without success and whose house is empty."

[246] Because that will make him pray for rain with more fervor and devotion, since his own welfare depends upon the success of his prayer.

[247] The Talmud below explains ריקן (empty) as *free* from sin, which is interpreted by Rashi to mean one who has not stolen or otherwise unjustly acquired goods in

בידו שאפילו טובל בכל מימות שבעולם לא עלתה
לו טבילה זרקו מידו כיון שטבל בארבעים סאה
מיד עלתה לו טבילה שנאמר ומודה ועזב ירחם
ואומר נשא לבבנו אל כפים אל אל בשמים:

5 עמדו בתפלה מורידין לפני התבה זקן כו': תנו
רבנן עמדו בתפלה אף על פי שיש שם זקן וחכם
אין מורידין לפני התבה אלא אדם רגיל רבי יהודה
אומר מטפל ואין לו ויש לו יגיעה בשדה וביתו ריקן
זקן ופרקו נאה ושפל ברך ומרוצה לעם ויש לו
10 נעימה וקולו ערב ורגיל לקרות בתורה בנביאים
ובכתובים ולשנות במשנה ובתלמוד בהלכות
ובאגדות ובקי בכל הברכות כלן ויהבו ביה רבנן
עיניהו ברבי יצחק דבי רבי אמי:

ט"ז
ע"ב אמר מר מטפל ואין לו וביתו ריקן היינו מטפל

תורה אור   מסרת הש"ס והמדרשים

3 משלי כ"ח י"ג.   4 איכה ג' מ"א.   4 (לבבנו) ע' לעיל ח' א'.   7 (רגיל)
ירושלמי כאן ב' ריש ה"ב (סוף
ד' ס"ה ב').   11 (ולשנות) לקמן ל' א'; ברכות כ"ב א'; מו"ק ט"ו א', כ"א א';
ירושלמי ברכות ג' ד', מו"ק ג' ה' (דף פ"ב ד'); תוספתא ברכות ב' י"ג;
שמחות פ"ו.

his possession. This seems far fetched and the meaning
is obviously that he has nothing in the house, all his pos-
sessions consisting in what he expects to harvest in the field.
This seems to be also the interpretation of R. Gershom,
as against that of the Talmud.

Are not both the same thing? Said R. Ḥisda, the latter phrase means one whose house is free of sin.

What is the meaning of "an elderly person whose youth was spent decently"? Said 'Abbayi, it means one who had no evil reputation in his younger years.

"My heritage is become unto Me as a lion in the forest; she has uttered her voice against Me; therefore have I hated her" (Jerem., 12. 8). Said R. Zuṭra b. Tobiah in the name of Rab or, as some report, said R. 'Aḥa in the name of R. Eleazar: This verse applies to an unworthy person, who goes before the ark as a messenger of the congregation.

He recites before them twenty-four benedictions, namely, the eighteen that are read every day, to which he adds six more. You say six, are they not seven, as we read in the Mishnah: "The *seventh* he closes thus"? Said R. Naḥman b. Isaac: Do you know what "seventh" means? It means the seventh of the longer[248] benedictions, as it is stated in a Baraita: The reader must prolong the benediction: "Redeemer of Israel" and, in closing it, he is to say: "He who answered Abraham our ancestor on mount Moriah, may answer you and hear the voice of your crying this day, blessed art Thou, O Lord, redeemer of Israel"; the congregation responds: Amen! and the sexton of the synagogue says, "Blow,

---

[248] That is, the benediction ending גואל ישראל (Redeemer of Israel, the seventh in the eighteen daily benedictions), in which on public fast days the formula מי שענה was

ואין לו היינו ביתו ריקן אמר רב חסדא ביתו ריקן
מעברה:

מאי זקן ופרקו נאה אמר אביי שלא יצא עליו
שם רע בילדותו:

5 היתה לי נחלתי כאריה ביער נתנה עלי בקולה
על כן שנאתיה אמר רב זוטרא בר טוביה אמר רב
ואמרי לה אמר רבי אחא אמר רבי אלעזר זה שליח
צבור היורד לפני התבה שאינו הגון:

ואומר לפניהם עשרים וארבע ברכות שמונה
10 עשרה שבכל יום ומוסיף עליהן עוד שש: הני שש
שבע הוין כדתנן על השביעית הוא אומר אמר רב
נחמן בר יצחק מאי שביעית שביעית לארכות
כדתניא בגואל ישראל מאריך ובחותמה הוא אומר
מי שענה את אברהם בהר המוריה הוא יענה אתכם
15 וישמע קול צעקתכם היום הזה ברוך גואל ישראל
והן עונין אחריו אמן וחזן הכנסת אומר להם תקעו

תורה אור   מסרת הש״ס והמדרשים

5 ירמיה י״ב ח׳.   13 (מאריך) ירושלמי ברכות א׳ ח׳.
                       16 (חזן) תוספתא תענית א׳ י״ד.

inserted, thus making it longer than usual and increasing
the number of long benedictions to seven; comp. above,
note 228.

ye priests, blow! He[249] who answered our
fathers on the Red Sea, may answer you and
hear the voice of your crying this day, blessed
art Thou, O Lord, who rememberest things
forgotten!" The congregation answers: Amen!
and the sexton of the synagogue says, "Sound
the alarm, ye sons of Aaron, sound!" The same
order was observed in all other benedictions,
namely, that in one case he would say "blow!"
and in the other "sound the alarm!" However,
the rule (of responding *Amen*) applies only
to services in the country, but in the Sanctuary
it was not so, because it was not customary to
respond Amen in the Sanctuary. Whence do
we know that they did not respond Amen in the
Sanctuary? It is said (Nehem., 9. 5): "Stand
up and bless the Lord your God from everlasting
to everlasting; and let them say: 'Blessed be
Thy glorious Name, that is exalted above all
blessing and praise.' "[250] One might think that
after all the benedictions there was one doxology, Scripture therefore says: "exalted above
all blessing," which means to say: Give praise
after each blessing (benediction). What then
was said in the Sanctuary? The reader said:
"Blessed is the Lord, Our God, the God of

---

[249] This is the continuation by the reader, who repeats
the formula "He who answered" in connection with the
second benediction, which is the first of the six additional
ones; see note 228.

[250] The words וברכו שם כבודך in Neh., 9. 5, are taken as
a proof that in the Sanctuary they did not respond briefly
Amen! but he had to say, ברוך שם כבוד מלכותו לעולם ועד

הכהנים תקעו מי שענה את אבותינו על ים סוף
הוא יענה אתכם וישמע קול צעקתכם היום הזה
ברוך זוכר הנשכחות והן עונין אחריו אמן וחזן
הכנסת אומר להם הריעו בני אהרן הריעו וכן
בכל ברכה וברכה באחת אומר תקעו ובאחת אומר
הריעו במה דברים אמורים בגבולין אבל במקדש
אינו כן לפי שאין עונין אמן במקדש ומנין שאין עונין
אמן במקדש שנאמר קומו ברכו את ה' אלהיכם
מן העולם עד העולם ויברכו שם כבדך ומרומם
על כל ברכה ותהלה יכול על כל הברכות כלן
תהלה אחת תלמוד לומר ומרומם על כל ברכה
ותהלה על כל ברכה וברכה תן לו תהלה ואלא
במקדש מהו אומר ברוך ה' אלהינו אלהי ישראל

5

10

תורה אור · מסרת הש"ס והמדרשים

8 נחמיה ט' ה'. · 7 (אמן במקדש) ברכות ס"ג א';
סוטה מ' ב'; ירושלמי ברכות ספ"ט
וכאן ב' י"א; תוספתא תענית א' י"א.

(blessed be His glorious kingdom for ever and aye). As
to the reason why Amen was not said in the Temple, the
commentators differ widely without producing anything
satisfactory; see the commentaries to the Mishnah, *Sotah*,
VII, 6, and Solomon ʻAdeni (16th cent), מלאכת שלמה, to
Sotah, *l. c.*, and to *Tamid* VII, 2; *Tosafot Sotah*, 40b, top;
comp. Büchler, *Types of Jewish-Palestinian Piety*, p. 239.

Israel from everlasting to everlasting, blessed art Thou O, Lord, redeemer of Israel," to which the congregation responded: "Blessed be the Name of His glorious kingdom for ever and ever!" The sexton of the synagogue then said: "Blow, ye priests, blow!" whereupon the reader again said: "He who answered Abraham on mount Moriah, may answer you and hear the voice of your crying this day, blessed art Thou who rememberest things forgotten," to which they responded: "Blessed be the Name of His glorious kingdom for ever and aye!" The sexton of the synagogue then said: "Sound the alarm, ye sons of Aaron, sound!" The same procedure was observed in all other benedictions, namely, that in connection with the one he would say "blow!" and with the other, "sound the alarm!" until he had finished them all. This procedure was introdueed also by R. Halafta in Sepphoris and by R. Hanina b. Teradyon in Siknin, but when the matter came before the other Sages they said, this was customary only before the Eastern Gates and on the Temple Mount.

Some give the foregoing passage in the following version: As is stated in a Baraita, he recites before them twenty-four benedictions, namely, the eighteen daily benedictions, to which he adds six more. Where are the latter inserted? Between "Redeemer" and "Healer."[251] The benediction of redemption is prolonged and

---

[251] That is, between the seventh and the eighth benedictions.

מן העולם עד העולם ברוך גואל ישראל והן עונין

אחריו ברוך שם כבוד מלכותו לעולם ועד וחזן

הכנסת אומר להם תקעו הכהנים תקעו חזר ואומר

מי שענה את אברהם בהר המוריה הוא יענה אתכם

5 וישמע קול צעקתכם היום הזה ברוך זוכר

הנשכחות והן עונין אחריו ברוך שם כבוד מלכותו

לעולם ועד וחזן הכנסת אומר להם הריעו בני

אהרן הריעו וכן בכל ברכה וברכה באחת אומר

תקעו ובאחת אומר הריעו עד שגומר את כלן וכן

10 הנהיג רבי חלפתא בצפורי ורבי חנינא בן תרדיון

בסיכני וכשבא דבר אצל חכמים אמרו לא היו

נוהגין כן אלא בשערי מזרח ובהר הבית:

ואית דאמרי כדתניא אומר   לפניהן   עשרים

וארבע   ברכות שמונה עשרה   שבכל יום   ומוסיף

15 עליהן עוד שש והיכן אומרן בין גואל לרופא ומאריך

Amen is responded after each benediction. This
was the custom in the country, but in the Sanctuary they used to say: "Blessed is the Lord our
God, the God of Israel, from everlasting to everlasting, blessed art Thou, O Lord, who redeemest Israel," whereupon the congregation responded: "Blessed is the Name of His glorious kingdom
for ever and aye," because it was not customary
to respond Amen in the Sanctuary. And whence
do we know that it was not customary to respond Amen in the Sanctuary? For it is said
(Neh., 9. 5): "Stand up and bless the Lord
your God from everlasting to everlasting; and
let them say: 'Blessed be Thy glorious Name,
that is exalted above all blessing and praise.'"
One might think that there was one general
doxology pronounced after all the benedictions,
Scripture therefore says, "exalted above all blessing and praise", which means to say: Give praise
after each blessing (benediction). Thus before
closing the first he says: Blessed is the Lord
our God, the God of Israel, from everlasting
to everlasting, blessed art Thou, O Lord, who
redeemest Israel, to which the congregation
responds: "Blessed be the Name of His glorious kingdom for ever and aye!" The sexton
of the synagogue then says: "Blow, ye priests,
blow!", whereupon the reader repeats: "He
who answered Abraham on mount Moriah",
etc. They then blow, sound the alarm and
blow again. The second he closes by saying:
"Blessed is the Lord our God, the God of Israel,
from everlasting to everlasting, blessed art Thou

בגאולה והן עונין אחריו אמן על כל ברכה וברכה
וכן היו נוהגין בגבולין אבל במקדש היו אומרים
ברוך ה' אלהינו ואלהי ישראל מן העולם עד
העולם ברוך גואל ישראל והן עונין אחריו ברוך
5   שם כבוד מלכותו לעולם ועד לפי שאין עונין אמן
במקדש ומנין שאין עונין אמן במקדש שנאמר קומו
ברכו את ה' אלהיכם מן העולם עד העולם ויברכו
שם כבדך ומרומם על כל ברכה ותהלה יכול על
כל הברכות כלן תהלה אחת תלמוד לומר ומרומם
10 על כל ברכה ותהלה על כל ברכה וברכה תן לו
תהלה על הראשונה אומר ברוך ה' אלהינו אלהי
ישראל מן העולם עד העולם ברוך גואל ישראל
והן עונין אחריו ברוך שם כבוד מלכותו לעולם
ועד וחזן הכנסת אומר תקעו הכהנים תקעו חזר
15 ואומר מי שענה את אברהם בהר המוריה הוא יענה
אתכם וישמע קול צעקתכם היום הזה ותוקעין
ומריעין ותוקעין ועל השניה הוא אומר ברוך ה'
אלהינו אלהי ישראל מן העולם עד העולם ברוך

who rememberest things forgotten," to which the congregation responds: "Blessed be the Name of His glorious kingdom for ever and aye," whereupon the sexton of the synagogue says: "Sound the alarm, ye sons of Aaron, sound!" The reader then repeats: "He who answered our fathers on the Red Sea", etc. This order is observed in all benedictions, namely that in connection with one he would say first "blow!" and with the other "sound the alarm," until he had finished them all. R. Ḥalafta in Sepphoris and R. Ḥanina b. Teradyon in Siknin introduced the same order, but when the matter came before the other Sages they said, this was customary only before the Eastern Gates and on the Temple mount.[252]

R. Judah said, he does not have to recite the Zikronot and the Shofarot, etc. Said R. 'Adda of Joppa: What is R. Judah's reason? He is of the opinion that *Zikronot* and *Shofarot* [fol. 17a] are recited only on New Year's day, on the Day of Atonement of the Jubilee year, and in time of war.

The first benediction he closes with the words: He who answered Abraham, etc. It was taught: There are some that reverse the order, putting the word "crying" in the benediction referring to Elijah, and the word "prayer" in the one referring to Samuel. This would be correct so far as Samuel is concerned, because in connection with him crying as well as prayer are found in

[252] For all details relating to these Baraitot see the Hebrew notes. For the place Siknin, see Neubauer, *Géogr. du Talmud*, p. 204; Hirschenson, שבע חכמות, p. 179.

זוכר הנשכחות והן עונין אחריו ברוך שם כבוד
מלכותו לעולם ועד וחזן הכנסת אומר הריעו בני
אהרן הריעו חוזר ואומר מי שענה את אבותינו על
ים סוף הוא יענה אתכם וישמע קול צעקתכם היום

5 הזה ומריעין ותוקעין ומריעין וכן בכל ברכה וברכה
באחת אומר תקעו ובאחת אומר הריעו אומר עד שיגמור
את כלן וכן הנהיג רבי חלפתא בצפורי ורבי
חנינא בן תרדיון בסיכני וכשבא דבר אצל חכמים
אמרו לא היו נוהגין כן אלא בשערי מזרח ובהר

10 הבית:

רבי יהודה אומר לא היה צריך לומר זכרונות
ושופרות: אמר רבי אדא דמן יפו מאי טעמיה דרבי
יהודה לפי שאין אומרים זכרונות ושופרות ואלא   ע״א
בראש השנה וביובל ובשעת מלחמה:

15 על הראשונה הוא אומר מי שענה את אברהם
כו': תנא יש מחליפין צעקה לאליהו ותפלה לשמואל
בשלמא גבי שמואל כתיב תפלה וכתיב צעקה אלא

the Bible,[253] but in the case of Elijah, the expression used is 'prayer', not 'crying'. Answer. The words (I Kings, 18. 37) "Hear me, O Lord, hear me," are equivalent to crying.

The sixth he closes thus: He who answered Jonah, etc. *The seventh he closes thus: He who answered David,* etc. Did not Jonah live after David and Solomon? Why then is he mentioned first? Because it is intended that the last closing should be: "Blessed be He who has mercy upon the land." It was taught: It is reported in the name of Symmachos that the seventh benediction is closed with the words: "Blessed be He who lowereth the haughty."

On the first three fast days the priests of the guard fast, but not to the end of the day, etc. The Rabbis have taught: Why was it decreed that the priests of the guard might drink wine by night, but not by day? Because the day-work might become too heavy for those in the sub-division, so that the priests of the guard would have to assist them; why was it decreed that the members of the sub-division should not drink either by day or by night? Because they are usually at work.[254] On the basis of this law it was decreed that every priest who can trace his pedigree to his division and sub-division and knows that the members of

[253] I Samuel, 7. 5, 9; comp. also 15. 11.

[254] So that even if they should happen to have some free hours during the day on which they are on duty, they must refrain from drinking, as they might be called upon at any minute; see above, note 230; Maimonides הלכות ביאת

גבי אליהו תפלה כתיב צעקה לא כתיב עני ה'
עני לשון צעקה היא:

על הששית הוא אומר מי שענה את יונה כו' על
השביעית הוא אומר מי שענה את דוד וכו': מכדי
יונה בתר דוד ושלמה הוה מאי טעמא מקדים ליה
ברישא משום דבעי למחתם ברוך מרחם על הארץ:
תנא משום סומכוס אמרו על השביעית הוא
אומר ברוך משפיל רמים:

שלש תעניות הראשונות אנשי משמר מתענין
ולא משלימין וכו': תנו רבנן מפני מה אמרו אנשי
משמר מותרין לשתות יין בלילות אבל לא בימים
שמא תכבד העבודה על אנשי בית אב ויבואו ויסייעו
אותן ומפני מה אמרו אנשי בית אב לא ביום ולא
בלילה מפני שהן רגילין בעבודה מכאן אמרו כל
כהן המכיר משמרתו ומשמרת בית אב שלו ויודע

תורה אור   מסרת הש"ס והמדרשים

1 מ"א י"ח ל"ז.   6 (למחתם) ירושלמי תענית ב' ט'.
                   7 (סומכוס) שם ב' י';   תוספתא
תענית א' י'. 10 (מפני מה) שם ב· י"ב. 10 (א"מ) תענית ט"ו ב'; תוספתא
                   שם ב' ב'—ג'.

מקדש, I, 6, and the annotations of Abraham b. David
to the passage; comp. also Gershom's commentary.

that sub-division were appointed to the work, is
not allowed to drink wine during that particular
day, but if he can trace his pedigree to the
chief division, but not to the sub-division, while
knowing that the latter was appointed to the
work, he is not allowed to drink wine during that
entire week;[255] if, however, he is unable to trace
his pedigree either to the chief division or the
sub-division, but knows that the latter was
appointed to the work, he is not allowed to
drink wine during that entire year. Rabbi says:
I say that from this point of view the priest
should never be allowed to drink wine, but what
can I do (in favor of such an injunction) seeing
that his misfortune[256] has turned out to his
benefit. Said 'Abbayi: In accordance with
whose view do the priests drink wine now-a-days?
According to whose opinion? Of course according to that of Rabbi!

*The priests of the guard and the members of the
lay division are not allowed to cut their hair or
to wash their clothes; on Thursday, however, they
are allowed to do so for the honor of the Sabbath.*
What is the reason? Said Rabba bar Ḥana in
the name of R. Johanan: In order that they may
not enter their division looking neglected.

Our Rabbis have taught: A king should have
his hair trimmed every day, a high priest every

[255] Because he cannot tell on what day of the week his
sub-division is on duty.

[256] The destruction of the Temple, which made the
services of the priests unnecessary, thus making it possible
for them to drink.

שבתי אבותיו קבועין הן אסור לשתות יין כל אותו

היום מכיר משמרתו ואינו מכיר משמרת בית אב

שלו ויודע שבתי אבותיו קבועין הן אסור לשתות

יין כל אותה שבת אינו מכיר משמרתו ומשמרת

5 בית אב שלו ויודע שבתי אבותיו קבועין הן אסור

לשתות יין כל השנה כלה רבי אומר אני

כהן אסור לשתות יין לעולם אבל מה אעשה

שתקנתו קלקלתו אמר אביי כמאן שתו האידנא

כהני חמרא כמאן כרבי:

10   אנשי משמר ואנשי מעמד אסורים לספר ולכבס

ובחמשי מותרין מפני כבוד השבת: מאי טעמא

אמר רבה בר בר חנה אמר רבי יוחנן כדי שלא

יכנסו למשמרתם כשהן מנוולין:

תנו רבנן מלך מסתפר בכל יום כהן גדול מערב

מסרת הש"ס והמדרשים

2 (מכיר) ירושלמי שם ב' י"ב.   ריש ה"ו.   12 (שלא יכנסו) טו"ק
8 (קלקלתו) סנהדרין כ"ב ב';   י"ד א'; ירושלמי תענית ב' י"ב;
תוספתא תענית ב' ב'; ירושלמי   טו"ק ג' א'. 14 (מלך) סנהדרין
תענית ב' י"ב; ירושלמי מגלה א'   כ"ב ב' (כל הענין שם).

Friday, an ordinary priest once a month. A
king everyday—what is the reason? Said R.
'Abba b. Zabda in the name of Rab, because it
is written (Is., 33. 17): "Thine eyes shall see
the king in his beauty." A high priest every
Friday—what is the reason? Said R. Samuel b.
R. Isaac, because new divisions of priests come
in every Saturday. An ordinary priest once a
month—what is the reason? This rule is derived from the occurrence of the word *pera'* (lock)
both in connection with the Nazirite and the
priest, for it is written in one place (Ez., 44. 20):
"Neither shall they (the priests) shave their heads
nor suffer their *locks* to grow long," and it is written in another place (Num., 6. 5): "He (the
Nazirite) shall let the *locks* of the hair of his head
grow long," which leads us to the analogy that
just as there (in the instance of the Nazirite)
the growing of the locks is meant for a period
of thirty days, so also here (in the instance of
the priests).[257] But whence do you know it to be
so in the case of the Nazirite himself? Scripture
(*ibid.*) uses the word *yihyeh* (יהיה = he shall be),
the numerical value of which is thirty.[258] Said R.
Papa to 'Abbayi: Is it not possible that the verse
(in Ezekiel) means to say that they should not
suffer their locks to grow at all? If it were written, Abbayi replied, "they shall not suffer locks
to grow long," your interpretation might be
correct, but since it is written, "the locks they
shall not suffer to grow long", it indicates that

[257] Thus when in Ezekiel the priests are enjoined not
to let the locks grow long, the idea is that they should

242

תענית

שבת לערב שבת כהן הדיוט אחד לשלשים יום
מלך מסתפר בכל יום מאי טעמא אמר רבי אבא
בר זבדא אמר רב אמר קרא מלך ביפיו תחזינה
עיניך כהן גדול מערב שבת לערב שבת מאי טעמא
אמר רב שמואל בר רב יצחק הואיל ומשמרות   5
מתחדשות כהן הדיוט אחד לשלשים יום מנלן
אתיא פרע פרע מנזיר כתיב הכא וראשם לא יגלחו
ופרע לא ישלחו וכתיב התם גדל פרע שער ראשו
מה להלן שלשים אף כאן שלשים והתם מנלן
אמר קרא יהיה יהיה בגימטריא תלתין הוו אמר   10
ליה רב פפא לאביי ודילמא הכי קאמר רחמנא לא
לרבו כלל אמר ליה אי הוה כתיב לא ישלחו פרע
כדקאמרת השתא דכתיב ופרע לא ישלחו פרע

תורה אור   מסרת הש״ס והמדרשים

3 ישעיה ל״ג י״ז.   7 יחזקאל מ״ד   10 (יהיה) נזיר ה׳ א׳; מו״ק י״ט ב׳;
כ׳.   8 במדבר ו׳ ה׳.   ירושלמי נזיר א׳ ג׳.

---

not let them grow beyond the time limit prescribed for
the Nazirite, that is, 30 days.

²⁵⁸ The letter י, the tenth in the alphabet, equals 10,
while the ה, the fifth, equals 5; the word יהיה thus makes
10+5+10+5 = 30.

they may have locks, must but not let them grow too long. If so, the law ought to apply also to the priests of the present time! No, the prohibition of growing the hair is analogous to that of drinking of wine, so that just as the latter applies only to the time when they enter the Temple for service, so also the former applies only to the time when they might enter the Temple, but when there is no Temple which they might enter, they may let the hair grow. But is it true that wine is permitted when there is no Temple to enter? Does not the following Baraita intimate the contrary? Rabbi says, I would say that a priest should never drink wine, but what can I do, seeing that his misfortune has turned out to be his benefit, whereupon 'Abbayi asked according to whose view the priests of our time drink wine [fol. 17b] and was told that they do so in accordance with the view of Rabbi. This proves that the other scholars forbade it, their reason being that the Temple might soon be rebuilt, and we should have no priest fit for the service.[259] Now, does not the same reason hold good also here (in the case of the priests growing their hair long)? No, in this case the priest may have his hair cut and then enter upon his duty. If so, an intoxicated priest might likewise sleep a while and then go to his duty, as Rami b. 'Abba said, a walk of a mile, or a little sleep causes the wine to evaporate? No, for did not R. Naḥman say in the name of Rabbah b. 'Abuha, this holds good only if one

[259] This is, of course, formal casuistry, as no matter how rapidly the building of the Temple, or even the finishing

244

ליהוי שלוחי הוא דלא לשלחו אי הכי האידנא נמי
דומיא דיין מה יין בזמן ביאה הוא דאסור שלא
בזמן ביאה שרי אף גדול‎,שער נמי בזמן ביאה הוא
דאסור שלא בזמן ביאה שרי ויין שלא בזמן ביאה
5 שרי והתניא רבי אומר אני כהן אסור לשתות
יין לעולם אבל מה אעשה שתקנתו קלקלתו ואמר
אביי כמאן שתו האידנא כהני חמרא כמאן‎|כרבי
עי"ב
מכלל דרבנן אסרי התם מאי טעמא מהרה יבנה
בית המקדש ובעינן כהן הראוי לעבודה וליכא הכא
10 נמי מהרה יבנה בית המקדש ובעינן כהן הראוי
לעבודה וליכא הכא אפשר דמספר ועייל אי הכי
שתוי יין נמי אפשר דגני פורתא ועייל דאמר רמי
בר אבא דרך מיל ושנה כל שהו מפיגין את היין
לאו איתמר עלה אמר רבנחמן אמר רבה בר אבוה

מסרת הש"ס והמדרשים

8 (מהרה) סנהדרין כ'ב ב'. 13 (דרך) ערובין ס'ד ב'; סנהדרין
כ'ב ב'; ירושלמי ע"ז א' ט'.

touches thereof, should proceed (unless a miracle is here
thought of), there ought to be enough time for any intoxicated priest to sober up, but see below; comp. Derenbourg, *Essai sur l'hist. et la géogr. de la Palestine*, Paris
1867, p. 403.

drank about a fourth (of a *log*), but if he drank more than that, walking makes him still more weary and sleep makes him still more drunk? R. 'Ashi said, in the case of intoxicated priests the Rabbis were apprehensive,[260] because they desecrate the service, but priests with long hair do not desecrate the service, hence the Rabbis felt no apprehension. Rabina raised an objection from the following Baraita (Tosefta, Zebaḥim, 12.17): 'The following priests die a premature death, those who perform their service while drunk, and those who perform it with long (neglected) hair." As regards drunken priests it is explicitly stated (Levit., 10.9): "Drink no wine nor strong drink, thou, nor thy sons with thee, when ye go into the tent of meeting, that ye die not." And how do we know that long hair is in the same category? It is written (Ezek., 44.20): "Neither shall they shave their heads, nor suffer their locks to grow long," and immediately following it is written (*ib.*, 44.21): "Neither shall any priest drink wine, when they enter into the inner court." Priests with long hair are thus compared to priests who are drunk, and we conclude that just as drunken priests die prematurely, so also priests with long hair. Now, does it not follow from this that the reason is because long hair is a desecration of the service as well as drink? Said R. 'Ashi in reply to Rabina: (this analogy based on Ezekiel has no force, for) who knew of it prior to the time of Ezekiel? If you use

---

[260] Of the unavailability of a sober priest.

לא שנו אלא ששתה רביעית אבל שתה יותר
מרביעית כל שכן שדרך מטרידתו ושנה משכרתו:

רב אשי אמר שתויי יין דמחלי עבודה גזרו בהו
רבנן פרועי ראש דלא מחלי עבודה לא גזרו בהו
5 רבנן מתיב רבינא ואלו שבמיתה שתויי יין ופרועי
ראש שתויי יין בהדיא כתיב בהו יין ושכר אל תשת
אתה ובניך אתך בבאכם אל אהל מועד ולא תמתו
פרועי ראש מנלן דכתיב וראשם לא יגלחו ופרע
לא ישלחו וכתיב בתריה ויין לא ישתו כל כהן
10 בבואם אל החצר הפנימית ואיתקוש פרועי ראש
לשתויי יין מה שתויי יין במיתה אף פרועי ראש
במיתה ומינה מה שתויי יין דמחלי עבודה אף פרועי
ראש דמחלי עבודה אמר ליה רב אשי לרבינא והא
מקמי דאתא יחזקאל מאן אמרה אמר ליה ולטעמיך

תורה אור   מסרת הש״ס והמדרשים

6 ויקרא י׳ ט׳.   8 יחזקאל מ״ד   2 (רביעית) ערובין ס״ד ב׳;
כ׳.   9 שם מ״ד כ״א.   סנהדרין כ״ב ב׳; תוספתא כריתות
א׳ כ׳.   5 (שבמיתה) תוספתא
זבחים י״ב י׳; תוספתא כריתות א׳ ה׳; סנהדרין כ״ב ב׳, פ״ג א׳;
שבועות ל״ו ב׳.

247

such argument, retorted Rabina, you must apply it also to the statement of R. Ḥisda (Zebaḥim, 22b): This law (that an uncircumcised priest is not fit for service) we do not derive from the Torah of our teacher Moses, but from the words of Ezekiel the son of Buzi (44.9): "No alien, uncircumcised in heart and uncircumcised in flesh, shall enter into my sanctuary." How could any one have knowledge of this law before Ezekiel? You will have to say therefore that the law in question was a tradition and Ezekiel expressed it in a verse; why not say the same in our case, namely, that the law (of long hair desecrating the service) was known by tradition and that Ezekiel expressed it in a verse? No, the burden of that tradition was only that long-haired priests die prematurely, but not that they desecrate the service.

Wherever the "Scroll of Fasts" records a day as one on which mourning is forbidden, it is not allowed to mourn even on the preceding day; on the day following, however, it is allowed. The Rabbis have taught: On the following days fasting, and on some of them also mourning, is forbidden: From the first until the eighth day of the month of Nisan, during which time the Daily Offering was established, mourning is forbidden; from the eighth thereof until the close of the festival (of Passover), during which the date for the Feast of Weeks was fixed (in accordance with the Pharisaic view), mourning is likewise forbidden.[261]

[261] For details regarding these rules, see Zeitlin (above, note 232), pp. 65ff.

הא דאמר רב חסדא דבר זה מתורת משה רבנו לא
למדנו מדברי יחזקאל בן בוזי למדנו כל בן נכר
ערל לב וערל בשר לא יבוא אל מקדשי מקמי
דאתא יחזקאל מאן אמרה אלא גמרא גמירי לה
ואתא יחזקאל ואסמכה אקרא הכא נמי גמרא גמירי
לה ואתא יחזקאל ואסמכה אקרא כי גמירי הלכה
למיתה לאחולי עבודה לא גמירי:

כל הכתוב במגלת תענית דילא למספד לפניו
אסור לאחריו מותר: תנו רבנן אלין יומיא דילא
להתענאה בהון ומקצתהון דילא למספד בהון מריש
ירחא דניסן ועד תמניא ביה אתוקם תמידא דילא
למספד מתמניא ביה ועד סוף מועדא אתותב חגא
דשבועיא דילא למספד:

תורה אור	מסרת הש"ס והמדרשים
2 יחזקאל מ"ד ט'.	1 (משה) יומא ע"א ב'; מו"ק ה'
	א'; סנהדרין כ"ב ב', פ"ג ב'; זבחים
	י"ח ב', כ"ב ב' 6. (הלכה) סנהדרין כ"ב ב'. 9 (ת"ר) מנחות ס"ה א';
	מג"ת ס"א.

It is said above, "from the first day of the month of Nisan", etc.—why from the first? Why does he not say from the second day of Nisan, since the first day of Nisan is a holiday, on which mourning is anyhow forbidden? Said Raba: The first of Nisan is mentioned in order that the prohibition may include also the preceding day.[262] But could not this be inferred from the fact that the day following is New Moon? The New Moon is of biblical origin, and biblical laws require no reënforcement, for it is stated in a Baraita: The prohibition (of fasting and mourning) on the days recorded in the Scroll of Fasts includes also, in each case, the preceding as well as the following day; as regards, however, the Sabbaths and holidays, fasting on these days is forbidden, but is permitted on the days preceding or following them. Why is such a difference made between the two? Because these (Sabbaths and holidays) are biblical laws, which need no reënforcement, while the others are soferic laws, which need reënforcement.[263]

[262] By expressly forbidding mourning on the first of Nisan, the day preceding it will, according to the rule of the Mishnah (above, p. 106), also be included, while on the basis of the first of Nisan being New Moon, the preceding day, it is assumed, could not be affected.

[263] By extending the prohibition of fasting and mourning to the days immediately preceding and following a rabbinically instituted holiday, its importance is impressed upon the people. This is not necessary in the case of biblical laws, as they are generally known and respected anyhow.

אמר מר מריש ירחא דניסן ועד תמניא ביה
אתוקם תמידא דילא למספד למה לי למימר מריש
ירחא דניסן לימא מתרי בניסן וראש חדש גופיה
יום טוב הוא אמר רבא לא נצרכא אלא לאסור
יום שלפניו שלפניו נמי תיפוק לי דהוה ליה יום
שלפני ראש חדש ראש חדש דאוריתא הוא
ודאוריתא לא בעי חזוק דתניא הימים האלה הכתובין
במגלת תענית הן ולפניהם ולאחריהם אסורין
שבתות וימים טובים הן אסורין לפניהן ולאחריהן
מותרין ומה הפרש בין זה לזה הללו דברי תורה
והללו דברי סופרים הללו דברי תורה ודברי תורה
אין צריכין חזוק והללו דברי סופרים ודברי
סופרים צריכין חזוק:

מסרת הש"ס והמדרשים

תענית כ"ח א' ; רה"ש י"ט א' ; יבמות
פ"ה ב' ; תוספתא תענית ב' ו' ;
ירושלמי תענית ב' י"ג ; מגלה א'
ו' ; יבמות ט' ה' ; כתובות ספי"א.

2 (ל"ל למימר) ירושלמי תענית ב'
י"ב (דף ס"ו א' ונוסח הקושיא שם:
בלא כך) ; מגלה א' ו' (דף ע' ע"ג).
7 (הימים) רה"ש י"ט א'. 10 (הללו)

"From the eighth thereof until the close of
the festival, etc." Why did he not say, "until
the festival", since the festival is a holiday (on
which fasting and mourning are anyhow forbidden)? Said R. Papa, Raba's statement above
[fol. 18a] will apply here. There the first of Nisan
was mentioned to extend the prohibition to the
day preceding. Here the festival is included in
order to extend the prohibition to the day following. With whose view does this tally?
With that of R. Jose, who said that the prohibition includes "both the preceding and the following day?" If so, why base the inclusion of
the twenty-ninth of Adar on the fact that
it is the day preceding the first of Nisan, on
which day the Daily Offering was established,
when the prohibition might have been derived
from the fact that it follows upon the twenty-
eighth of Adar (which was likewise proclaimed a holiday) as we read[264]: On the twenty-
eighth of Adar the good news reached the
Jews that they were no longer to be restrained
from the study of the Torah? [It had namely
happened that the wicked government issued a
decree against Israel, that they should not study
the Torah nor circumcise their children, and
that they should profane the Sabbath, whereupon
Judah b. Shammu'a and his colleagues took
counsel with a prominent lady with whom all the
noblemen of Rome associated, who advised them
to make an appeal during the night; they made
the appeal during the night, saying: "O Heavens!

[264] In the same Scroll of Fasts.

מתמניא ביה ועד סוף מועדא אתותב חגא
דשבועיא דילא למספד למה לי למימר עד סוף
מועדא לימא עד מועדא ומועד גופיה יום טוב
חא הוא אמר רב פפא כדאמר רבא ׀ לאסור יום שלפניו
עא

5 הכי נמי לאסור יום שלאחריו כמאן כרבי יוסי
דאמר בין לפניו בין לאחריו אסור אי הכי עשרים
ותשעה נמי מאי איריא דהוה ליה יומא דמקמי
דאתוקם תמידא תיפוק לי דהוה ליה יומא דבתר
עשרין ותמניא ביה דתניא בעשרין ותמניא ביה אתת

10 בשורתא טבתא ליהודאי דלא יעידון מן פתגמי
אוריתא שפעם אחת גזרה מלכות הרשעה שמד על
ישראל שלא יעסקו בתורה ושלא ימולו את בניהם
ושיחללו שבתות מה עשה יהודה בן שמוע וחבריו
הלכו ונטלו עצה ממטרונית אחת שכל גדולי רומי

15 מצויין אצלה אמרה להם באו והפגינו בלילה עמדו
והפגינו בלילה אמרו אי שמים לא אחיכם אנחנו לא
בני אב אחד אנחנו לא בני אם אחת אנחנו מה

מסרת הש״ס והמדרשים

9 (בעשרין) רה״ש י״ט א׳.   11 (פעם   אחת) מג״ת פי״ב׳.

253

Are we not your brethren, are we not the sons of one father and one mother? Wherein do we differ from all other nations and tongues, that you issue such cruel decrees against us?", whereupon the decrees were annulled and the day was declared a holiday.] Said 'Abbayi in reply to the above: The twenty-eighth of Adar would be of no avail for the last day if it were a full month.[265] R. 'Ashi said, the same thing would be true if Adar was deficient,[266] for on a day following immediately upon a holiday only fasting is forbidden, while mourning is allowed, whereas the twenty-ninth of Adar, being placed between two holidays, has been made as important as if it were itself a holiday.[267]

"From the eighth thereof until the close of the festival", etc. Why does he say "from the eighth thereof", why not from the ninth thereof, since the eighth is anyhow a holiday?[268] Because if for some reason we should have to abolish the first seven days of Nisan as holidays, mourning would still be forbidden on the eighth[268a] because it immediately precedes the days on which the date for the Feast of Weeks was legally fixed.[269] Now that you have

[265] Counting 30 instead of 29 days, in which case the 30th day could only be included in the prohibition because it precedes the first of Nisan, but not because it follows the 29th of Adar, as it does not follow upon it immediately.

[266] Counting only 29 days.

[267] The character of the 29th of Adar, being a day on which mourning too is forbidden, is thus defined not only

נשתנינו מכל אומה ולשון שאתם גוזרין עלינו גזירות
קשות ובטלום ואותו היום עשאוהו יום טוב אמר
אביי לא נצרכה אלא לחדש מעובר רב אשי אמר
אפילו תימא חדש חסר כל שלאחריו בתענית אסור
בהספד מותר וזה הואיל ומוטל בין שני ימים ⁵
טובים עשאוהו כיום טוב עצמו:

מתמניא ביה ועד סוף מועדא אתותב חגא
דשבועיא דילא למספד למה לי למימר מתמניא
ביה לימא מתשעה ביה ותמניא גופיה יום טוב הוא
דאי מקלעא מלתא ובטלניה לשבעה תמניא גופיה ¹⁰
אסור דהוה ליה יומא דמקמי דאתותב ביה חגא

מסרת הש"ס והמדרשים
4 (שלאחריו) ירושלמי תענית ב'   י"נ; מגלה א' ו'.

by its following upon the 28th of Adar, but also by its
preceding the first of Nisan.

[268] Being the last of the eight holidays at the beginning
of Nisan (1–8), as mentioned before.

[268a] Although the reason for the abolishing of the preceding seven days would naturally hold good for the abolition
also of the eighth day, inasmuch as it is part of the same
group of holidays. By "something should happen"
the Talmud has in mind persecutions by an inimical government, which would turn these holidays into days of public
mourning and fasting.

[269] The days from the ninth of Nisan till the close of
Passover.

arrived at this point, the matter becomes clear
also regarding the twenty-ninth of Adar, for if it
happened that we should have to abolish the
twenty-eighth of Adar as a holiday, fasting on
the twenty-ninth would still be prohibited on the
ground that it immediately precedes the time
during which the Daily Offering was established.

It was reported: R. Ḥiyya b. 'Ashi said in the
name of Rab, the law is in accordance with R.
Jose,[270] but Samuel said, it is in accordance with
R. Meir.[271] Did Samuel say so? Is it not stated
in a Baraita: R. Simeon b. Gamaliel said:
Why is the word *behon* (בהון = on them) used
(in the Scroll of Fasts) twice in succession? In
order to indicate that the prohibition applies
only to the days specified, but not to the days
immediately preceding or following them—
to which Samuel remarked that the law is in
accordance with R. Simeon b. Gamaliel! Answer.
Originally Samuel was of the opinion that there
was no authority as lenient in the matter as was
R. Meir, and therefore he said that the law is in
accordance with R. Meir, but when he heard of
the view of R. Simeon b. Gamaliel, who is
still more lenient, he said, the law is in accordance with R. Simeon b. Gamaliel. Bali, too, said
in the name of R. Ḥiyya b. 'Abba, who had it
from R. Johanan: The law is in accordance with
R. Jose, whereupon R. Ḥiyya b. Abba said to

[270] Who holds that both the day preceding and the day
following a holiday are included in the prohibition.

[271] Who includes only the preceding, not the following
day. R. Meir's name is not given in the Mishnah, the

דשבועיא השתא דאתית להכי עשרים ותשעה נמי
דאי מקלעא מלתא ובטלניה לעשרים ותמניא
עשרין ותשעה גופיה אסור דהוה ליה יומא דמקמי
דאתוקם תמידא:

5   איתמר רב חייא בר אשי אמר רב הלכה כרבי
יוסי ושמואל אמר הלכה כרבי מאיר ומי אמר
שמואל הכי והתניא רבן שמעון בן גמליאל אומר
מה תלמוד לומר בהון בהון שני פעמים לומר לך הן
אסורין לפניהן ולאחריהן מותרין ואמר שמואל
10   הלכה כרבן שמעון בן גמליאל מעיקרא סבר רבי
מאיר הוא דמיקל אמר הלכה כרבי מאיר כיון
דשמעיה לרבן שמעון בן גמליאל דמיקל טפי אמר
הלכה כרבן שמעון בן גמליאל וכן אמר באלי אמר
רבי חייא בר אבא אמר רבי יוחנן הלכה כרבי יוסי
15   אמר ליה רבי חייא בר אבא לבאלי אסברה לך כי

statement here referred to being given there anonymously,
but it is a talmudic rule that anonymous opinions occurring
in a Mishnah, unless there is proof to the contrary, are
based on the authority of R. Meir (סתם מתניתין כרבי מאיר).

257

Bali, I must inform you that when R. Johanan
said the law is in accordance with R. Jose, he
referred only to those days on which the Scroll
of Fasts forbids fasting (but not mourning).
Did R. Johanan say so? Did he not say, the
law always follows the anonymous opinion of a
Mishnah?[272] Now, we read in an anonymous
Mishnah: Although it has been decided that
under certain circumstances the Megillah of
Esther should be read several days before, instead
of after, Purim [fol. 18b], mourning and fasting during these days is allowed. Now, which of these
days is here meant? If you say that the Mishnah
refers to those people who under ordinary circumstances would have to read the Megillah
on the fifteenth of Adar but, as it happens,
read it on the fourteenth,[273] the question must
be asked, is it true that in this event mourning
and fasting are allowed on the fourteenth? Is
it not written in the Scroll of Fasts that the fourteenth and fifteenth must be celebrated as
Purim days, on which mourning is forbidden—,
a rule on which Raba commented, saying that
their listing in the Scroll was needed only for the
purpose of emphasizing that whatever was prohibited on the one day should be prohibited also
on the other?[274] If, however, you say that the

[272] Which is that of R. Meir, see the preceding note.

[273] And the Mishnah thus means that fasting on the
fourteenth is permitted, because the actual Purim day
for these people was to be on the fifteenth.

[274] The 14th and 15th of Adar are given in the Bible as
Purim days, and there was no need for their being especially

קאמר רבי יוחנן הלכה כרבי יוסי אדילא להתענאה
ומי אמר רבי יוחנן הכי והאמר רבי יוחנן הלכה
כסתם משנה ותנן אף על פי שאמרו מקדימין ולא

י״ח
ע״ב מאחרין ‖ מותרין בהספד ובתענית אימת אילימא

5 בני חמיסר דקא קרו באר בסר ומי שרי והכתיב
במגלת תענית את יום ארבעה עשר בו ואת יום
חמשה עשר בו יומי פוריא אינון דילא למספד
ואמר רבא לא אנצרכה אלא לאסור את של זה בזה

מסרת הש״ס והמדרשים

3 (כסת״מ) שבת מ״ו א׳, פ״א ב׳,
קי״ב ב׳, קמ״ז ב׳, קמ״ח ב׳, קנ״ו
ב׳; ערובין צ״ב א׳; ביצה ל״ז ב׳;
יבמות ט״ז ב׳, מ״ב א׳; נטין פ״א ב׳;
ב״ק כ״ט ב׳, ל״ב א׳, ס״ט א׳, צ״ד
ב׳; ב״מ ל״ג ב׳; סנהדרין ל״ד ב׳;
8 (לאסור) מגלה ה׳ ב׳.

שבועות ג׳ ב׳; מנחות נ״ב ב׳; חולין
ל״א ב׳, מ״ג א׳; נדה נ׳ א׳, נ״ו ב׳;
ירושלמי תענית ב׳ י״ד; מגלה א׳ ז׳.
3 (אע״פ) מגלה ה׳ א׳.   7 (פוריא)
מגלה ה׳ ב׳; ירושלמי תענית ב׳ י״ג
(ס״ז א׳); מגלה א׳ ו׳ (דף ע׳ ג׳).

mentioned in the Scroll as holidays. Raba therefore
says that by this special mention it was intended to emphasize that both days are of equal importance as holidays,
a fact which is not stated in the Bible. Consequently
fasting and mourning are forbidden on the 14th as well as
on the 15th. How then could the Mishnah have differen-
tiated between the two?

Mishnah refers to those who would have to
read the Megillah on the fourteenth, but for
given reasons are to read it on the thirteenth,
you then face the difficulty that the thirteenth
is Nicanor Day (on which fasting is likewise
forbidden); if, finally, you say that the Mishnah
refers to those who would have to read the
Megillah on the fourteenth but, as it happens,
have to read it on the twelfth, you face again
the difficulty that the twelfth is Trajan Day (on
which, too, fasting is forbidden).   You will therefore have to say that the Mishnah refers to
those that would have to read the Megillah on
the fourteenth but happen to be compelled to
read it on the eleventh, and it is thus with reference to this day that the anonymous Mishnah
teaches that mourning and fasting thereon are
allowed!²⁷⁵   No, the Mishnah, no doubt, refers
to those who would ordinarily have to read the
Megillah on the fourteenth but who by reason
of circumstances are permitted to read it on the
twelfth, and as to your objection that the twelfth
is Trajan Day, the festive character of that
day was later abolished, as is instanced by R.
Naḥman who ordered a public fast on the
twelfth, and when the Rabbis objected thereto,
pointing out that it was Trajan Day, he replied
that Trajan Day had been abolished, because
on that day Shemaiah and Ahijah were ex-
ecuted.²⁷⁶   But ought not fasting on that day
be prohibited on the ground that it precedes

²⁷⁵ Accordingly, the prohibition of fasting and mourning
on a holiday—in this case Trajan day—does not apply

260

ואת של זה בזה ואלא בני ארבסר דקרו בתליסר

יום נקנור הוא ואלא בני ארבסר דקרו בתריסר

יום טורינוס הוא ואלא בני ארבסר דקרו בחד סר

וקתני מותרין בהספד ובתענית לא לעולם בני

5 ארבסר דקרו בתריסר ודקאמרת יום טורינוס הוא

יום טורינוס בטולי בטלוה כי הא דרב נחמן גזר

תעניתא בתריסר אמרו ליה רבנן יום טורינוס הוא

אמר להו יום טורינוס בטולי בטלוה הואיל ונהרגו

בו שמעיה ואחיה ותיפוק לי דהוה ליה יום שלפני

---

to the day preceding it. Now, if it is true that R. Johanan
agrees with this view of the Mishnah, how could he have
said that the law follows R. Jose, who does include in the
prohibition of fasting also the day preceding a holiday?

[276] Comp. M. Joel, *Blicke in die Religionsgeschichte*,
Breslau, 1880, pp. 17ff.; see also the Hebrew notes.

Nicanor Day? Said R. 'Ashi, if Trajan Day itself was abolished, should we declare it a holiday because it comes before Nicanor Day?

What was Nicanor Day? It is taught in a Baraita: Nicanor was one of the Greek generals. Every day he used to wave his hand in the direction of Judah and Jerusalem saying, when will that nation fall into my hands that I might crush it! When the Hasmonean Kings prevailed and defeated the Greeks, they broke through his legions, cut off his thumbs and big toes, hung them at the gates of Jerusalem and said: Upon the mouth that spoke so haughtily and the hands that waved against Judah and Jerusalem such vengeance is executed.

What was Trajan Day? It was reported that when Trajan had ordered the execution of Lulianus (Julianus) and his brother Pappos in Laodicea (Lydia), he said to them, if you are of the people of Hananiah, Mishael, and Azariah, let your God come and save you from my hands, as He saved them from the hand of Nebuchadnezzar; to which they replied: Hananiah, Mishael, and Azariah were wholly righteous men and worthy of a miracle being performed for their sake; Nebuchadnezzar, too, was

נקנור אמר רב אשי השתא איהו גופיה בטולי בטלוה
משום יום שלפני נקנור ניקום ונגזור:

מאי נקנור דתניא נקנור אחד מהפרכי יונים היה
ובכל יום ויום היה מניף ידו על יהודה וירושלם
5 ואומר מתי תפול בידי וארמסנה וכשגברו מלכי
בית חשמונאי ונצחוהו נכנסו לחילות שלו וקצצו
בהנות ידיו ורגליו ותלאום בשערי ירושלם אמרו
פה שהיה מדבר בגאות וידים שהיו מניפות על
יהודה וירושלם תעשה בהם נקמה זאת:

10 מאי טורינוס אמרו כשהרג טורינוס את לוליְנוס
ואת פפוס אחיו בלודקיא אמר להם אם מעמו של
חנניה מישאל ועזריה אתם יבא אלהיכם ויציל אתכם
מידי כדרך שהציל את חנניה מישאל ועזריה מיד
נבוכדנצר אמרו לו חנניה מישאל ועזריה צדיקים
15 גמורים היו (וראויין היו ליעשות להם נס) ונבוכדנצר

מסרת הש"ס והמדרשים

2 (נקנור) ירושלמי תענית ב' י"ג;
מגלה א' ו'.   10 (לולינוס) ספרא
אמור פרשה ח' פ"ט מ"ה, בחקתי
פרשה ב' פ"ה מ"ב; ירושלמי שביעית
ד' ב' (ל"ה א'), תענית ב' י"ג,
מגלה א' ו', סנהדרין ג' ו' (כ"א
ב'); מכילתא דרשב"י 125; ב"ר
הוצאת אלבעק באבער הערה ת"כ).

ס"ד ט'; קה"ר ג' פסוק י"ז (ונם
קהלת זוטא שם) וט' פסוק י';
שמחות פ"ח; מג"ת פי"ב (וע'פסחים
נ' א' וב'ב' ב' אבל באיכ"ר א' סימן
נ' ותדא"ר פ'לויילקוט תבוא תתקל"ח
מוסב כל הספור על מאורע אחר
ובפס"ר מ"נ הוא מקוצר ע' באיכ"ר

a respectable king, worthy of being the medium through which a miracle should be performed, but you are a wicked and ignoble man, not deserving that a miracle should be performed through you. Now, we have been found guilty of death in the eyes of God, and if you do not slay us, God has enough other slayers; He has plenty of bears and leopards and lions to attack and kill us, and the only reason for God's delivering us into your hand is that He intends to avenge our blood on you. It is reported that he had not yet moved from the place, when two deputies arrived from Rome and split his skull with clubs.[277]

Fasts should not be decreed so as to begin on a Thursday, etc. *No fasts should be enjoined upon the community on the days of New Moon, Hanukkah and Purim, but if the fasts began*, etc. What constitutes a beginning? R. Aḥa said, three fasts, R. Jose said, even one fast. R. Judah said in the name of Rab, this view (that one should not fast to the end of the day) is the view of R. Meir, who offered it in the name of Rabban Gamaliel, but the other Sages say, one must fast to the end of the day. Mar Zuṭra lectured in the name of R. Huna that the law is, one must fast to the end of the day.

[277] As to the historicity of these stories about the Nicanor and Trajan days, see Zeitlin (above, note 232), pp. 82, 108ff., and my Hebrew notes.

מלך הגון היה וראוי ליעשות נס על ידו ואותו רשע
הדיוט הוא ואינו ראוי ליעשות נס על ידו ואנו נתחייבנו
הריגה למקום ואם אין אתה הורגנו הרבה הורגים יש
לו למקום הרבה דבים הרבה נמרים והרבה אריות
5 יש לו שפוגעין בנו והורגין אותנו אלא לא מסרנו
הקדוש ברוך הוא בידך אלא שעתיד ליפרע דמנו
מידך אמרו לא זז משם עד שבאו דיופלי מרומי
ופצעו את מוחו בגזירין:

אין גוזרין תענית על הצבור בתחלה בחמשי
10 כו' אין גוזרין תענית על הצבור בראשי חדשים
בחנכה ובפורים ואם התחילו כו': וכמה הוא
התחלה רבי אחא אמר שלש רבי יוסי אמר אחת
אמר רב יהודה אמר רב זו דברי רבי מאיר שאמר
משום רבן גמליאל אבל חכמים אומרים מתענה
15 ומשלים דרש מר זוטרא משמיה דרב הונא הלכה
מתענה ומשלים:

הדרן עלך סדר תעניות כיצד

מסרת הש"ס והמדרשים

12 (התחלה) ירושלמי תענית ב'   א'.   15 (הלכה) ערובין מ"א ב';
ט"ו.   13 (זו דר"מ) ערובין מ"א   ירושלמי תענית ספ"ב.

CHAPTER III

Mishnah: 1. The order of these fasts, as given above, applies only to (a drought) during the first season,[278] but if the sprouts show signs of decay, the alarm must be sounded at once. And if there was absence of rain for forty days between the first and second rainfall, the alarm is likewise sounded at once, because this is a calamity of drought.

2. If rains came down which benefited the plants, but not the trees, or the trees but not the plants, or so as to benefit both but not in a measure to fill the cisterns, ditches and caves, the alarm must also be sounded at once.

3. Similarly if it did not rain upon a certain city, as it is written (Amos, 4. 7): "And I caused it to rain upon one city, and caused it not to rain upon another city; one piece was rained upon, and the piece whereupon it rained not withered", [fol. 19a] that city should fast and sound the alarm, while the people of surrounding places should fast, but not sound the alarm: R. 'Aḳiba says, they should sound the alarm but not fast.

4. Similarly if a city is visited by an epidemic or its houses are falling in,[279] that city should fast and sound the alarm, while the surrounding places should fast but should not sound the

[278] The rains due during the month of Marḥeshwan are called in the Bible יורה (former rain) and in the Talmud רביעה ראשונה, the first (season of) fructification; comp. below, note 291.

[279] When the falling cannot be attributed to any natural cause, as earthquake or general deterioration by time, and the like, but must be taken as a divine punishment; see below, p. 292.

פרק שלישי

מתניתין: סדר תעניות האלו האמור ברביעה

ראשונה אבל צמחים ששנו מתריעין עליהן מיד

וכשפסקו גשמים בין גשם לגשם ארבעים יום מתריעין

עליהן מיד מפני שהיא מכת בצרת ירדו לצמחים

5 אבל לא לאילן לאילן אבל לא לצמחין לזה ולזה

אבל לא לבורות ולא לשיחין ולא למערות מתריעין

עליהן מיד וכן עיר שלא ירדו עליה גשמים כדכתיב

והמטרתי על עיר אחת ועל עיר אחת לא אמטיר

חלקה אחת תמטר וחלקה אשר לא תמטיר עליה

10 תיבש | אותה העיר מתענה ומתרעת וכל סביבותיה

מתענות ולא מתריעות רבי עקיבא אומר מתריעות

ולא מתענות וכן עיר שיש בה דבר או מפלת אותה

העיר מתענה ומתרעת וכל סביבותיה מתענות ולא

תורה אור	מסרת הש"ס והמדרשים
8 עמוס ד' ז'.	8 (והמטרתי) לעיל ו' ב'; ירושלמי
	תענית ג' ג' (ס"ו ג'). 10 (סביבותיה)
ירושלמי כאן ג' סה"ד.   12 (דבר) תוספתא תענית ב' ט'.

alarm. R. 'Aḳiba says, they should sound the alarm, but need not fast. What is considered an epidemic? When, in a city capable of furnishing five hundred foot soldiers, three men[280] die in succession within three successive days.[281]

5. On the following occasions the alarm must be sounded everywhere. If there appeared a plague of blast, mildew, locust, cricket, wild beasts, and also when armies are passing through the country,[282] because they are all moving plagues.

6. It happened that certain elders as they travelled from Jerusalem to their home cities ordered a fast because there was seen in Ashkelon a blast injuring a quantity of grain sufficient to fill an oven (with bread made thereof). They further decreed a fast, because wolves had devoured two children beyond the Jordan; R. Jose said, it was not because the wolves had devoured children, but because they (the wolves) had appeared there.

7. On the following occasions the alarm is sounded even on the Sabbath: When a city is surrounded by troops of the enemy, or is threatened with a flood, and when a ship is foundering on the sea; R. Jose says, in this case the alarm may be sounded only as a signal

[280] Of normal health, to the exclusion of old decrepit men, or women after confinement, whose death is not due to an epidemic; comp. Maimonides, הלכות תעניות II, and his commentators.

[281] That is, one each day, but three on one day is considered merely an accident; see below, p. 306.

[282] Even peaceful armies; see below, p. 324.

מתריעות רבי עקיבא אומר מתריעות ולא מתענות

איזהו דבר עיר המוציאה חמש מאות רגלי ויצאו

ממנה שלשה מתים בשלשה ימים זה אחר זה ועל

אלו מתריעין בכל מקום על השדפון ועל הירקון

על הארבה ועל החסיל ועל חיה רעה ועל החרב

מתריעין עליהן מפני שהיא מכה מהלכת מעשה

שירדו זקנים מירושלם לעריהם וגזרו תענית על

שנראה כמלא תנור שדפון באשקלון ועוד גזרו תענית

על שאכלו זאבים שני תינוקות בעבר הירדן רבי

יוסי אומר לא על שאכלו אלא על שנראו על אלו

מתריעין בשבת על עיר שהקיפוה גוים או נהר ועל

הספינה המטרפת בים רבי יוסי אומר לעזרה

מסרת הש"ס והמדרשים

4 (שדפון) ספרי בהעלותך ע"ו.   11 (בשבת) לעיל י"ד א'. 12 (ספינה)

5 (חרב) תוספתא תענית א' י'.   ספרי שם.

for help, but not as a form of supplication;
Simeon the Temanite said (the alarm is sounded on the Sabbath) also on account of an epidemic, but the other Sages did not agree with him.

8. The alarm is sounded on account of any
calamity that comes[283] upon the community,
except that of excessive rain.[284] It happened
that Ḥoni (Onias) the Circle-drawer was asked
to pray for rain. He replied: Go and take
in the Passover ovens, so that they should
not be dissolved.[285] He then prayed, but no
rain came down. He therefore drew a circle
and placed himself in the center of it. Then
he said: Master of the world! Thy children
have set their faces on me, because I am looked
upon as one of Thy household. Now, I swear
by Thy great Name that I will not move
from here until Thou have mercy upon Thy
children. The rain began to trickle. Ḥoni,
however, said, not for such rain did I pray, but for
a rain that would fill the cisterns, ditches, and
caves. The rain then came down with vehemence. Ḥoni again said, not for such rain
did I pray, but for a rain of benevolence, blessing
and graciousness. The rain then continued
coming down in proper fashion until the Israelites
had to go up from Jerusalem to the Temple mount
on account of the flood. They then said to him,

[283] The phrase שלא תבוא, that does *not* come, is a euphemism for שתבוא, that comes. It is also possible that the
phrase is parenthetical: May it not come!

[284] See below, p. 330, where Rab interprets the Mishnah
as referring only to Palestine, which is hilly and dry, so

אבל לא לצעקה שמעון התימני אומר אף על הדבר
ולא הודו לו חכמים על כל צרה שלא תבא על
הצבור מתריעין עליהן חוץ מרוב גשמים מעשה
שאמרו לחוני המעגל התפלל שירדו גשמים אמר
להם צאו והכניסו תנורי פסחים בשביל שלא ימקו
התפלל ולא ירדו גשמים עג עוגה עמד בתוכה
ואמר לפניו רבונו של עולם בניך שמו פניהם עלי
שאני כבן בית לפניך נשבע אני בשמך הגדול שאיני
זז מכאן עד שתרחם על בניך התחילו גשמים מנטפין
אמר לא כך שאלתי אלא גשמי בורות שיחין ומערות
ירדו בזעף אמר לא כך שאלתי אלא גשמי רצון
ברכה ונדבה ירדו כתקנן עד שעלו ישראל
מירושלם להר הבית מפני הגשמים אמרו לו כשם

מסרת הש"ס והמדרשים

1 (לצעקה) ירושלמי תענית ג' ח'.   א'; ירושלמי תענית ג' י'—י"ב;
2 (צרה שלא תבא) ספרי שם.   מו"ק ג' א'; מנ"ת י"ב וע' ב"ר
4 (חוני) לקמן כ"ג א'; ברכות י"ט   י"ג ז' ותוספתא כאן ג' א'.

that abundant rain does no harm, while in low countries,
like Babylon, the alarm must be sounded also in cases
of excessive rain.

[285] Because they were made of clay. They were por-
table, and in order to harden were kept in the courtyard
when not used. As regards Onias the Circle-drawer, see
note 327.

just as thou hast prayed for the rain to come
down, so pray now that it should stop. He replied: "Go out and see whether the stone of
losers[286] has been washed away." Simeon b. Sheṭaḥ then sent word to him saying, thou deservest
to be excommunicated, but what can I do to thee
since thou art petulant before God like a son
that is petulant toward his father and the latter
does his will. With regard to thee Scripture says
(Proverbs, 23.25): "Let thy father and thy mother
be glad, and let her that bore thee rejoice."

9. If the people begin to fast and then rain
begins to fall, if this happens before sunrise,
they need not continue the fast to the end of
the day,[287] but if it was after sunrise they must
complete the fast; R. Eliezer said, (if the rain
came) before noon they need not complete the
fast, but[288] (if it came) after noon they must
complete it. It happened that a fast was ordered in Lydda and the rain came before noon; R.
Tarfon then said to the people: Go out, eat and
drink and make a holiday. They went out,
ate and drank and made a holiday. In the afternoon they assembled and recited the great hallel.[289]

[286] A high stone on which the recovery of lost articles
was proclaimed. According to the commentators Ḥoni
(Onias) meant to say that just as it is impossible that this
high stone should be washed away or, according to others
(Hananel, *ad locum;* see also *Yerushalmi Ta'anit*, III, 11),
to be covered by the flood, so it is impossible to pray
for the cessation for rain, as taught above; see below, p. 330.

[287] Because people do not eat so early, and the fast has
therefore not yet begun.

שהתפללת עליהם שירדו כך התפלל עליהם שילכו
להן אמר להם צאו וראו אם נמחית אבן הטועים
שלח לו שמעון בן שטח צריך אתה לנדות אבל מה
אעשה לך שאתה מתחטא לפני המקום כבן שמתחטא
לפני אביו ועושה לו רצונו ועליך הכתוב אומר
ישמח אביך ואמך ותגל יולדתך היו מתענין וירדו
להם גשמים קודם הנץ החמה לא ישלימו לאחר
הנץ החמה ישלימו רבי אליעזר אומר קודם חצות
לא ישלימו לאחר חצות ישלימו מעשה שגזרו תענית
בלוד וירדו להם גשמים קודם חצות אמר להם
רבי טרפון צאו ואכלו ושתו ועשו יום טוב ויצאו
ואכלו ושתו ועשו יום טוב ובאו בין הערבים וקראו
הלל הגדול:

תורה אור	מסרת הש"ס והמדרשים
6 משלי כ"ג כ"ה.	6 (מתענין) לקטן כ"ה ב'; ירושלמי
	תענית ג' י"ג. 8 (קודם חצות)
ירושלמי נדרים ח' א'.	11 (ויצאו) ירושלמי פסחים ה' ז'.

[288] R. Eliezer goes by the time of the main meal, which is at noon.

[289] Psalm 136, which is so called in contradistinction to Psalms 112–118, the usual Hallel; comp. Dünner, הגהות on Sukkah, p. 144.

Gemara: *The order of these fasts as given above applies only to a drought during the first season*, etc.   A contradiction was pointed out from a Baraita: If the rain fails to come in its first and second season, we should pray for it, but if it fails to come also in its third season, we should begin to fast.[290]   Said R. Judah in the name of Rab, our Mishnah must be understood as follows: The order of these fasts, as enumerated above, applies only when the first, second and third seasons had passed without rain,[291] but if there was rain in the first season and the seeds sprouted, but then changed for the worse, the alarm must be sounded at once.   Said R. Naḥman, the alarm should be sounded only if they changed, but not if they dried up.   This is self-evident, since the Mishnah says explicitly "changed!"   No, this remark (of R. Naḥman) is needed in case the seeds recovered (so far as to) produce stalks; you might then think that this producing of stalks is something to rely on for a full recovery; he therefore informs you that producing of stalks is nothing to count upon.

If there was absence of rain for forty days between the first and second rainfall, the alarm is likewise sounded at once because this is a calamity of drought, etc.   What is to be

[290] This contradicts the Mishnah, which teaches that the fasts should commence right after the first failure (17th of Marḥeshwan); but see the following note.

[291] Rab thus corrects the impression one gets by reading in the Mishnah the phrase רביעה ראשונה.   The Mishnah,

גמרא: סדר תעניות האלו האמור ברביעה
ראשונה וכו': ורמינהי רביעה ראשונה ושניה לשאול
שלישית להתענות אמר רב יהודה הכי קאמר סדר
תעניות האלו האמור אימתי בזמן שיצתה רביעה
ראשונה ושניה ושלישית ולא ירדו גשמים אבל ירדו   5
גשמים ברביעה ראשונה וצמחו וחזרו ושנו מתריעין
עליהן מיד אמר רב נחמן דוקא שנו אבל יבשו לא
פשיטא שנו תנן לא צריכא דהדר אקון מהו דתימא
אקנתא מלתא היא קא משמע לן דאקנתא לאו
מלתא היא: 10

וכשפסקו גשמים בין גשם לגשם ארבעים יום
מתריעין עליהן מיד מפני שהיא מכת בצרת: מאי

---

he says, does not mean the first rainfall, but means the whole
season during which the first rainfall (the biblical יורה,
former rain) is due. Within this season three dates are
set for the rainfall; The third, the seventh, and the
seventeenth of Marḥeshwan (so R. Meir, above, fol.
6a), or the seventh, seventeenth, and twenty-third of
the same month (so R. Judah, *ibid.*), or the seventeenth
and twenty-third of that month, and the first of Kislew
(R. Jose). There is accordingly no contradiction between
the quoted Baraita and the Mishnah, for the Baraita
uses the word רביעה, fructification, rainfall, for each of
the three dates within the season, while the Mishnah
applies it to all three together; comp. note 278.

understood by a calamity of drought (מכת בצרת)?
Said R. Judah in the name of Rab, a calamity
that is the cause of scarcity.   Said R. Naḥman,
when provision has to be imported from one city
to another by water, [fol. 19b] it is scarcity, but
when from one country to another, it is famine.
R. Ḥanina said, if a *Se'ah* (measure of grain[292]) is
sold for one *Sela'*,[293] and is obtainable, it is
scarcity; if four measures are sold for a Sela',
but are obtainable with difficulty, it is famine.
(Said Rabbah bar b. Ḥana in the name of R.
Johanan, this applies only to a time when money
is plentiful but food is dear, but if money
is scarce and food is plentiful, the alarm must be
sounded at once.)   Said R. Johanan, I clearly
remember when four Se'ah stood at a Sela', and
yet many people were swollen from starvation
in Tiberias, because there was not a coin (lit.
'asarion') to be had.

*If rains came down which benefited the plants
but not the trees, etc.*   It is quite possible that
a rain may be good for plants but not for trees;
when, for example, it comes down gently; it may
be good for trees but not for plants, when it
comes down vehemently; it may be good for
both, but not for cisterns, ditches and caves,
when it comes down in both forms, but not in
abundance.   But when do you find that, as is
stated in a Baraita, there is rain for cisterns,

[292] See above, note 170.

[293] *Sela'* = the biblical *Shekel*; see, however, below, note
300.

מכת בצרת אמר רב יהודה מכה המביאה לידי

בצרת אמר רב נחמן נהרא אנהרא ובצרתא   יט״
   ע״ב

מדינתא אמדינתא כפנא אמר רבי חנינא סאה בסלע

ושכיחא בצרתא ארבעה ולא שכיחי כפנא (אמר

5   רבי יוחנן לא שנו אלא בזמן שמעות בזול ופרות

ביקר אבל מעות ביקר ופרות בזול מתריעין

עליהן מיד ו)אמר רבי יוחנן נהירנא כד הוו קיימן

ארבע סאין בסלע והוו נפישי נפיחי כפן בטבריא

מדלית איסר:

10   ירדו לצמחין אבל לא לאילן וכו׳: בשלמא

לצמחים ולא לאילן משכחת לה דאתיא ניחא לאילן

ולא לצמחין דאתיא רזיא לזה ולזה אבל לא

לבורות ולא לשיחין ולא למערות דאתיא הכי והכי

מיהו טובא לא אתיא אלא הא דתניא לבורות לשיחין

5 (לא שנו) ב״ב צ״א ב׳.   7 (נהירנא)   תענית ג׳ ב׳.   12 (רזיא) לעיל ג׳
ב״ב שם.   11 (לצמחים) ירושלמי   ב׳.

ditches and caves, and not for plants or trees?
This happens when the rain comes down in a
cloudburst.

Our Rabbis have taught: The alarm for rain
for the trees must be sounded in the middle of the
Passover season,²⁹³ᵃ while the alarm for rain for
cisterns, ditches, and caves must be sounded
in the middle of the Tabernacles season²⁹³ᵃ: if
there is no water for drinking purposes, the
alarm is to be sounded at once. What is meant
by "at once"? The first Monday, Thursday, and
Monday. In all these cases the alarm is sounded
only in the province concerned. If there is an
epidemic of croup the alarm is sounded, provided
the disease proves fatal, but if it is not fatal,
the alarm is not sounded. The alarm is sounded
on account of the appearance of locusts, no
matter in what numbers; R. Simeon b. Eleazar
said, the alarm is sounded also on account of
grasshoppers.

Another Baraita teaches: The alarm is
sounded for rain for the trees during the six
years of the Septenary (but not during the Sabbatical year); for the cisterns, ditches, and caves
it is sounded also during the Sabbatical year;
Rabban Simeon b. Gamaliel said, for the trees
also we sound during the Sabbatical year,
because they furnish a livelihood to the poor.
Another Baraita teaches: The alarm is sounded
for the trees during the six years of the Septen-

---

²⁹³ᵃ According to traditional explanation, the expression
means 15 days before the festival. Cf. Tal. Yer. Shekalim,
ch. 3, beg.

ולמערות אבל לא לזה ולא לזה היכי משכחת לה
דאתיא בשפיכותא:

תנו רבנן מתריעין על האילנות בפרס הפסח
על הבורות על השיחין ועל המערות בפרס החג
5 ואם אין להם מים לשתות מתריעין עליהן מיד
ואיזהו מיד שלהן שני וחמשי ושני וכלן אין מתריעין
עליהן אלא בהפרכיא שלהן ואסכרא בזמן שיש
בה מיתה מתריעין עליה בזמן שאין בה מיתה אין
מתריעין עליה ומתריעין על הגובאי בכל שהו רבי
10 שמעון בן אלעזר אומר אף על החגב:

תניא אידך מתריעין על האילנות בשאר שני
שבוע על הבורות על השיחין ועל המערות אפילו
בשביעית רבן שמעון בן גמליאל אומר אף על
האילנות בשביעית מפני שיש בהן פרנסה לעניים:

15   תניא אידך מתריעין על האילנות בשאר שני

מסרת הש"ס והמדרשים

2 (בשפיכותא) ב"ב כ"ה ב'.   ירושלמי שם ג' א'.   7 (אסכרא)
3 (בפרס) ירושלמי תענית ג' ב';   ירושלמי שם ג' ה'. 13 (בשביעית)
תוספתא תענית ב' ח'.   6 (איזהו)   ירושלמי שם ג' א'.

ary (but not during the Sabbatical year); for cisterns, ditches, and caves, it is sounded even during the Sabbatical year; R. Simeon b. Eleazar said, also for what grows of itself we sound during the Sabbatical year, because it furnishes a livelihood to the poor.

It is taught in a Baraita: Said R. Eleazar b. Peraṭa: Ever since the Temple was destroyed rain is diminishing in the world; there are years with abundant rain and years with but little rain; there are years in which the rain comes in its proper season and years in which it comes out of season. A year with seasonable rains may be compared to the treatment of a slave by his master who gives him his weekly fare on the first day of the week; the result then is that the dough is properly baked and palatable. A year with unseasonable rains may be compared to the treatment of a slave by his master who gives him his weekly fare on the eve of the Sabbath; the result is that the dough is not well baked and not palatable. In a year with abundant rain the situation is like that of a slave to whom his master gives his provision for the whole year at once; the waste in the mill in grinding a kor is the same as in grinding a *kab;* likewise the waste in the trough in kneading the dough of a *kor* is the same as in kneading the dough of a *kab.* In a year with but little rain the situation is like that of a slave to whom his master gives his provision little by little. The waste in grinding a *kab* is the same as in grinding a *kor*, and the waste in kneading a *kab* is the same as in kneading a *kor*.

שבוע על הבורות על השיחין ועל המערות אפילו
בשביעית רבי שמעון בן אלעזר אומר אף על
הספיחין בשביעית מפני שיש בהן. פרנסה לעניים:
תניא אמר רבי אלעזר בן פרטא מיום שחרב

5 בית המקדש נעשו גשמים סקימיון בעולם יש שנה
שגשמיה מרובין ויש שנה שגשמיה מועטין יש שנה
שגשמיה יורדין בזמנן ויש שנה שאין גשמיה יורדין
בזמנן שנה שגשמיה יורדין בזמנן למה הוא דומה
לעבד שנותן לו רבו פרנסתו באחד בשבת נמצאת

10 עסה נאפת כתקנה ונאכלת כתקנה שנה שאין
גשמיה יורדין בזמנן למה הוא דומה לעבד שנותן
לו רבו פרנסתו בערב שבת נמצאת עסה נאפת
שלא כתקנה ונאכלת שלא כתקנה שנה שגשמיה
מרובין למה הוא דומה לעבד שנותן לו רבו פרנסתו

15 בבת אחת נמצאות רחים כמה שאוכלות מן הקב
אוכלות מן הכור נמצאת עסה כמה שאוכלת מן
הקב אוכלת מן הכור שנה שגשמיה מועטין למה
הוא דומה לעבד שנותן לו רבו פרנסתו מעט מעט
נמצאות רחים כמה שאוכלות מן הכור אוכלות מן

20 הקב נמצאת עסה כמה שאוכלת מן הכור אוכלת

Another version compares the situation to
that of a man moulding clay. If the water is
abundant, it will not give out and the moulding
will proceed well, but if the water is scanty, it
will soon give out and the moulding will not
proceed well.

Our Rabbis have taught: It once happened
that the Israelites went up to Jerusalem for the
festival and there was not enough water in the
city for drinking purposes. Naḳdimon (Nicode-
mos) b. Gorion therefore betook himself to a
general who possessed water and said to
him: Lend me twelve wells of water and I
will return to you twelve wells of water or,
in case I cannot do so, I will give you twelve
talents of silver. He stipulated the sum of
money and fixed the day for payment. When
the time arrived, the general sent word to Naḳdimon that he should deliver either the water
or the money. The latter replied, the day
is not yet over. At noon he sent to him
again saying, deliver the water or the money.
Naḳdimon again replied, I have still time.
In the afternoon the general sent again the
demand that either the water or the money
be delivered and Naḳdimon again replied, the
day is not yet over. The general said: There
has been no rain for a whole year [fol. 20a]
and you expect it to come now? He then went
in good spirits to the bath-house. But while the
general was on his way to the bath-house,
Naḳdimon went to the Temple, wrapped himself
in his cloak and prayed; Master of the world!
It is well known before Thee that I did not do it

282

מן הקב דבר אחר משל לאדם שהיה מגבל את
הטיט מימיו מרובין מים אינן כלין וטיט מתגבל יפה
מימיו מועטין מים כלין וטיט אינו מתגבל יפה:

תנו רבנן פעם אחת עלו ישראל לרגל לירושלם
5   ולא היה להם מים לשתות הלך נקדימון בן גוריון
אצל הגמון אחד שהיה לו מים אמר לו הלוני שתים
עשרה מעינות מים ואני אתן לך שתים עשרה מעינות
מים ואם לאו הריני נותן לך שנים עשר ככרי כסף
קצץ לו מעות וקבע לו זמן כיון שהגיע הזמן שלח
10 לו שגר לי מים או מעות שלח לו עדין יש לי שהות
ביום בצהרים שלח לו שגר לי מים או מעות שלח
לו עדין יש לי שהות ביום במנחה שלח לו שגר
לי מים או מעות שלח לו עדין יש לי שהות ביום
אמר אותו הגמון כל השנה כלה לא ירדו גשמים
15 ‏‏ועכשו ירדו גשמים נכנס לבית המרחץ בשמחה
עד שהגמון נכנס לבית המרחץ נקדימון בן
גוריון נכנס לבית המקדש נתעטף ועמד בתפלה
אמר לפניו רבונו של עולם גלוי וידוע לפניך

מסרת הש"ס והמדרשים

5 ‹נקדימון› כתובות ס"ה א‹, ס"ו ב‹;   פס"ר כ"ט; כ"ר מ"ב א‹; איכ"ר
נטין נ"ו א‹; ע"ז כ"ה א‹; תוספתא   א‹ סימן מ"ח ‹באבער העראה
כתובו‹ ה‹ ט‹; ספרי דברים ש"ה;   תל"א› אדר"ן ו‹, שם י"ז.

for my own glory or for that of my father's house, but for Thy glory, that the pilgrims should have water. Immediately the skies became clouded and rain began to fall, so that all wells over-flowed with water. While the general was coming from the bath-house, Nakdimon came from the Temple, and when they met, the former said to the latter: I know that it is for you alone that your God disturbed His world. How-ever, I can still maintain my claim against you, so as to get my money from you, for the sun had set and the rain came during the time that belonged to me. Nakdimon returned to the Temple, wrapped himself and again stood in prayer, saying: Master of the world! As Thou hast performed a miracle for me before, do it also now! Immediately the wind blew, the clouds were dispersed and the sun shone. The general then said: Were it not that the sun shone, I would have had a claim against you, to collect my money from you.

It has been taught that his name was not Nakdimon but Bunai. Why then was he sur-named Nakdimon? Because the sun shone for him.[294]

The Rabbis have taught: There were three men for whom the sun shone, namely Moses, Joshua, and Nakdimon b. Gorion. The case of Nakdimon was mentioned before; as to Joshua, it is written (Joshua, 10.13): "And the sun stood still, and the moon stayed," etc., but whence do

[294] The Hebrew verb for shining is nakad (נקד); see Kohut, *Aruch, s. v.*

שלא לכבודי עשיתי ולא לכבוד בית אבא
עשיתי אלא לכבודך עשיתי כדי שיהו מים מצויין
לעולי רגלים מיד נתקשרו שמים בעבים וירדו
גשמים עד שנתמלאו כל המעינות מים והותירו עד
5 שיצא הגמון מבית המרחץ נקדימון בן גוריון יצא
מבית המקדש כשפגעו זה בזה אמר לו יודע אני
שלא הרעיש אלהיך את העולם אלא בשבילך אלא
עדיין יש לי פתחון פה עליך שאוציא ממך את מעותי
שכבר שקעה חמה ומים ברשותי ירדו חזר נקדימון
10 בן גוריון ונכנס לבית המקדש נתעטף ועמד בתפלה
אמר לפניו רבונו של עולם כשם שעשית לי נס
בראשונה כך עשה לי נס באחרונה מיד נשבה הרוח
ונתפזרו העבים וזרחה החמה באותה שעה אמר
אותו הגמון אלו לא נקדה חמה היה לי פתחון פה
15 עליך שאוציא ממך את מעותי:

תנא לא נקדימון שמו אלא בוני שמו ולמה נקרא
שמו נקדימון שנקדה חמה בעבורו:

תנו רבנן שלשה נקדה להם חמה משה ויהושע
ונקדימון בן גוריון בשלמא נקדימון בן גוריון הא
20 דאמרן יהושע דכתיב וידם השמש וירח עמד וגו'

תורה אור   מסרת הש"ס והמדרשים
20 יהושע י' י"ג.   14 (חמה) ע"ז כ"ה א'.

we know it as regards Moses?   Said R. Eleazar,
it is derived from the analogous use of *'āḥêl*
(אחל = I will begin), for it is written with reference to Moses (Deut., 2. 25): "*I will begin*
to put the dread of thee" (upon the peoples), and
it is written with reference to Joshua (Josh., 3. 7):
"*I will begin* to magnify thee."   R. Samuel b.
Naḥamani said, it is derived through the analogous use of *têt* (תת = to give, put, deliver), for it is
written (Deut., 2. 25): "I will begin to *put* the
dread of thee," and again (Josh., 10. 12): "In the
day when the Lord *delivered* up the Amorites."
R. Johanan said, it can be derived from the
content of that verse (Deut., 2. 25) itself: "(the
peoples) who shall hear the report of thee, shall
tremble, and be in anguish because of thee;" when
did it happen that they trembled and were in
anguish?   At the time the sun was delayed for
Moses.

Similarly, if it did not rain upon a certain city,
etc.   Said R. Judah in the name of Rab: Both
cities are here (in the verse of Amos quoted in
the Mishnah) pointed out as being punished.[295]
"Jerusalem is among them as one unclean"
(Lament., 1. 17).   Said R. Judah in the name of
Rab, this verse contains a promise of (future)
blessing, for just as an unclean (menstruating)
woman becomes clean again, so also Jerusalem.
"She is become as a widow" (*ib.*, 1. 1).   Said
R. Judah in the name of Rab, this verse also is
meant as a blessing, for Scripture says, '*as a*

---

[295] The one by want of rain and the other by an excess
of it.

תענית

אלא משה מנלן א מר רבי אלעזר אתיא אחל אחל

כתיב הכא אחל תת פחדך וכתיב התם אחל גדלך

רבי שמואל בר נחמני אמר אתיא תת תת כתיב

הכא תת פחדך וכתיב התם ביום תת ה' את האמרי

5 רבי יוחנן אמר אתיא מגופיה דקרא אשר ישמעון

שמעך רגזו וחלו מפניך אימתי רגזו וחלו מפניך

בשעה שעמדה לו חמה למשה:

וכן עיר שלא ירדו עליה גשמים וכו': אמר רב

יהודה אמר רב שתיהן לקללה היתה ירושלם לנדה

10 ביניהם אמר רב יהודה אמר רב לברכה כנדה מה

נדה יש לה היתר אף ירושלם יש לה היתר היתה

כאלמנה אמר רב יהודה אמר רב לברכה כאלמנה

מסרת הש״ס והמדרשים		תורה אור
9 (שתיהן) לעילו׳ב׳. 10 (כאלמנה)		2 דברים ב׳ כ״ה. 2 יהושע ג׳ ז׳.
סנהדרין ק״ד א׳; איכ״ר א׳ סימן ג׳		4 דברים ב׳ כ״ה. 4 יהושע י׳ י״ב.
(באבער צד כ״ג).		9 איכה א׳ י״ז. 11 איכה א׳ א׳.

widow', not a 'widow', but as a woman whose husband went to a country beyond the sea and intends to come back to her. "Therefore have I also made you contemptible and base before all the people" (Malachi, 2. 9). Said R. Judah in the name of Rab, this is also meant as a blessing, for (in thus despising us) they do not appoint us as overseers of rivers, and as bailiffs. "The Lord will smite Israel, as a reed is shaken in the water" (I Kings, 14. 15). Said R. Judah in the name of Rab, this too is meant in a good sense, for R. Samuel b. Naḥamani said in the name of R. Jonathan: What is the meaning of the verse (Prov., 27. 6): "Faithful are the wounds of a friend; but the kisses of an enemy are importunate"? It means to say that the curse uttered by Ahijah the Shilonite against Israel was better than the blessing given them by the wicked Balaam; Ahijah the Shilonite cursed them by comparing them to a reed; now the reed rises in water, always drives young shoots and has many roots, so that even if all the winds of the world come and blow against it, the reed will move with the winds hither and thither, and when the winds have subsided the reed still stands firm in its place. Not so wicked Balaam. He blessed them by comparing them to a cedar tree, as is said (Numbers, 24. 6): "As cedars beside the waters;" now the cedar tree does not grow in water, does not drive young shoots and its roots are not many, and when the winds come and blow against it, it does not yield to them; hence when a strong southern wind arises, it uproots it and turns it upside down.

288

ולא אלמנה ממש אלא כאשה שהלך בעלה למדינת
הים ודעתו לחזור אליה וגם אני נתתי אתכם נבזים
ושפלים אמר רב יהודה אמר רב לברכה דלא
מוקמי מינן לא רישי נהרי ולא גזירפטי והכה ה׳
את ישראל כאשר ינוד הקנה במים אמר רב יהודה
אמר רב לברכה דאמר רבי שמואל בר נחמני אמר
רבי יונתן מאי דכתיב נאמנים פצעי אוהב ונעתרות
נשיקות שונא טובה קללה שקלל אחיה השילוני
את ישראל מברכה שברכן בלעם הרשע אחיה
השילוני קללן בקנה מה קנה זה עומד במקום מים
וגזעו מחליף ושרשיו מרובין   ואפילו כל הרוחות
שבעולם באות ונושבות בו הולך   ובא עמהן דממו
הרוחות קנה עומד במקומו אבל בלעם הרשע
ברכן בארז שנאמר כארזים עלי מים מה ארז זה
אינו עומד במקום מים ואין גזעו מחליף ואין שרשיו
מרובין וכשהרוחות באות ונושבות בו אינו הולך
ובא עמהן כיון שנשבה בו רוח דרומית עוקרתו
והופכתו על פניו:

5, 10, 15 (שורות)

תורה אור
2 מלאכי ב׳ ט׳.   4 מ״א י״ד ט״ו.
7 משלי כ״ז ו׳.   14 במדבר כ״ד ו׳.

מסרת הש״ס והמדרשים
8 (השילוני) סנהדרין ק״ה ב׳.
11 (רוחות) ד״א רבה ד׳.   14 (ארז)
לקמן כ״ה ב׳.

Our Rabbis have taught: It happened that R.
Simeon b. Eleazar once came from the house
of his teacher at Migdal-Geder.[295a] He was riding leisurely on an ass along the lake-shore and
felt greatly elated over the fact that he had
acquired so much learning. [fol. 20b]. While in
this mood he chanced upon a man who was
extremely ugly. "Raca!" R. Simeon said, "Are
all the people of thy town as homely as thou
art?" "Go to the artisan, who made me," the
man replied, "and say to him: 'How ugly is
this vessel which thou hast made'!" As soon
as R. Simeon realized his error he alighted
from the ass and bowing before the man
said: "I submit myself to thee, forgive me!"
"No!" the man replied, "I will not forgive thee,
until thou goest to the artisan who made me
and sayest unto him, 'O how ugly is this vessel
which thou hast made'!'" R. Simeon followed
him until he reached his town. When he arrived
there, people of the town came to meet R.
Simeon and greeted him with the words, "Peace
be with thee, Master!" The man then asked
them, "Whom do you address as Master?"
"Him that follows thee," they replied. "If this
man is a Master," he said, "may there not be
many like him in Israel!" "Why? God beware!"
they exclaimed, "What did he do to you?" "So
and so he behaved toward me," he answered.
"Nevertheless, forgive him," the people pleaded,
"for he is a great scholar." "I will forgive
him," the man said, "but on condition that he

[295a] See the Hebrew Note to this passage.

תנו רבנן מעשה ברבי שמעון בן אלעזר שבא
ממגדל גדר מבית רבו והיה רוכב על החמור
ומטייל על שפת הים והיה שמח שמחה גדולה על
שלמד תורה הרבה ׀ נזדמן לו אדם אחד שהיה
מכוער ביותר אמר לו ריקה שמא כל בני עירך
מכוערין כמותך אמר לו לך ואמור לו לאומן
שעשאני כמה מכוער כלי זה שעשית כיון שידע
בעצמו שחטא ירד מן החמור ונשתטח לפניו ואמר
לו נעניתי לך מחול לי אמר לו איני מוחל לך עד
שתלך לאומן שעשאני ותאמר לו כמה מכוער כלי
זה שעשית היה מטייל אחריו עד שהגיע לעירו כיון
שהגיע לעירו יצאו אנשי עירו לקראתו אמרו לו
שלום עליך רבי אמר להם למי אתם קורין רבי
אמרו לו לזה שמטייל אחריך אמר להם אם זה
רבי אל ירבו כמותו בישראל אמרו לו חס ושלום
מה עשה לך אמר להם כך וכך עשה לי אמרו לו
אף על פי כן מחול לו שאדם גדול בתורה הוא
אמר להם הריני מוחל לו ובלבד שלא יהא רגיל

מסרת הש״ס והמדרשים

1 (מעשה) אדר״ן מ״א; ד״א רבה   9 (נעניתי) ברכות כ״ח א׳; כתובות
ד׳; מס׳ כלה דפוס קוריניל צד י״ג.   ס״ז ב׳; אדר״ן מ״א; ד״א רבה ד׳;
מס׳ כלה הוצאת קורוניל צד י״ג.

should never act in this manner again." R. Simeon b. Eleazar thereupon entered the Bet Hamidrash and lectured: "A man should always be soft as a reed and not hard as a cedar tree. And it is because of its softness that the reed was privileged to be used for the making of pens with which Torah scrolls, phylacteries and *mezuzot* are written".

Similarly if a city is visited by an epidemic, or its houses are falling in, etc. It was taught: The falling in of houses here spoken of refers to sound houses and not shaky ones, to such as are not liable to fall in and not to such as are liable to fall in. Are not "sound" and "not liable to fall in," the same? And are not "shaky" and "liable to fall in," the same? No, we must needs distinguish between the two, as for instance in a case where the walls (were sound but) fell, because they were too high or stood on the banks of a river.

There was a ruinous wall in Nehardea near which Rab and Samuel would not pass, although it had stood on its place for thirteen years. One day R. 'Adda b. 'Ahabah came to that place. On their way Samuel said to Rab, "Let us go roundabout," to which the latter replied: "Now it is not necessary, as we have R. Adda b. 'Ahabah with us, whose merits are very great (and will protect us), hence I am not afraid."

R. Huna had wine in a ruinous house and wanted to remove it. He therefore engaged R. Adda b. 'Ahabah in a learned discussion until

לעשות כן מיד נכנס רבי שמעון בן אלעזר לבית
המדרש ודרש לעולם יהא אדם רך כקנה ואל יהא
קשה כארז לפיכך זכה קנה לטול ממנו קולמוס
לכתוב בו ספר תורה תפלין ומזוזות:

5 וכן עיר שיש בה דבר או מפלת כו': תנא מפלת
שאמרו בריאות ולא רעועות שאינן ראויות ליפול
ולא שראויות לפול הינו בריאות והינו שאינן
ראויות לפול הינו רעועות והינו ראויות לפול
לא צריכא דנפלו מחמת גובהיהו אי נמי דקימן
10 אגודא דנהרא:

ההיא אשיתא רעיעתא דהות בנהרדעא דלא
הוה חליף רב ושמואל תחותה אף על גב דקימא
באתרה תליסר שנין יומא חד איקלע רב אדא בר
אהבה להתם אמר ליה שמואל לרב ניתי מר נקיף
15 אמר ליה לא צריכנא האידנא איכא רב אדא בר
אהבה בהדן דנפישא זכותיה ולא מסתפינא:

רב הונא הוה ליה חמרא בההוא ביתא דהוה
רעיע בעא לפנויה משכיה לרב אדא בר אהבה

2 (לעולם) אדר"ן וד"א וכלה שם.   17 (ביתא רעיעא) ירושלמי שבת
3 (לפיכך) סנהדרין ק"ו א'.   ב' ג'; תעניית ג' י"ג (ס"ז א');
6 (בריאות) ירושלמי כאן ג' ה'.   תנחומא (הנדפס) וישלח סימן ח'.
(וע' שם ריש וינש וב"ר צ"א ט').

the wine was removed. As soon as they left the house, it fell in. When R. Adda b. 'Ahabah noticed that he was used for such a purpose, he became angry, saying, "Is not this an instance with regard to which R. Jannai said, one should never stay in a place of danger and say, I shall be saved by a miracle, for it might be that no miracle will be performed for him, and even if one should be performed, such performance would be charged against his merits?" Said R. Hanan, where is the biblical verse to prove it? "I am not worthy²⁹⁶ of all the mercies, and of all the truth" (Gen., 32. 11).

What were the meritorious deeds of R. Adda b. 'Ahabah? They are as follows: R. Adda b. 'Ahabah's pupils once asked him, "Through what merits was such long life granted you?" He replied to them: I never lost my temper in my house, never walked in front of one who was my superior in learning, never thought of sacred subjects in filthy alleys, never walked four ells without meditating about the Torah or without the phylacteries, never slept or took a nap in the house of learning, never rejoiced in the misfortune of a fellow-man, and never called my neighbor by an opprobrious surname, which I gave him. Some say R. Adda said, "which others gave him."

---

²⁹⁶ R. Hanan translates קטנתי (I am not worthy) literally: I have become smaller, *i. e.*, poorer in merits, on account of all the mercies, miracles, etc., which Thou hast performed for me.

בשמעתא עד דפנייה בתר דנפק נפל ביתא ארגיש

רב אדא בר אהבה איקפד אמר לאו היינו דרבי

ינאי דאמר רבי ינאי לעולם אל יעמוד אדם במקום

סכנה ויאמר עושין לי נס שמא אין עושין לו נס ואם

5 עושין לו נס מנכין לו מזכיותיו אמר רבי חנין מאי

קראה קטנתי מכל החסדים ומכל האמת:

מאי הוה עובדיה דרב אדא בר אהבה כי הא

דאתמר שאלו תלמידיו את רב אדא בר אהבה

במה הארכת ימים אמר להם מימי לא הקפדתי

10 בתוך ביתי ולא צעדתי בפני מי שגדול ממני ולא

הרהרתי במבואות המטונפות ולא הלכתי ארבע

אמות בלא תורה ובלא תפלין ולא ישנתי בבית

המדרש לא שנת קבע ולא שנת ארעי ולא ששתי

בתקלת חברי ולא קראתי לחברי בחניכתי ואמרי

15 לה בחניכתו:

תורה אור	מסרת הש"ס והמדרשים
6 בראשית ל"ב י"א.	4 (סכנה) שבת ל ב א'. 5 (חנין)
	שבת שם. 9 (הקפדתי) מגלה
	כ"ח א'; ירושלמי תענית ג' י"ג. 14 (בחניכתי) מגלה שם.

Raba said to Rafrem b. Papa, tell me some of
the noble deeds performed by R. Huna. Said
Rafrem, of his earlier days I remember nothing;
as to his later years I remember that after
cloudy (stormy) days he used to be taken out in
a gilt carriage, in which he inspected the whole
city, and wherever there was a damaged wall,
he ordered it to be torn down. If the owner was
in a position to build a new wall, he had to
do so, if not, R. Huna would have it built at his
own expense. Every Friday toward evening
R. Huna would send a servant to the market who
would buy up all the vegetables left over with
the gardeners and throw them into the river.
Why did he not rather give them to the poor?
Because they would sometimes rely on these gifts
and fail to provide themselves for the Sabbath.
Why did he not throw it to the animals? He
was of the opinion that food proper for human
beings should not be given to animals. Why
did he buy them at all? Because if he had
not done so, it would lead the gardeners to
sin in the future (by failing to provide the community with vegetables).

When R. Huna was in possession of some
medicament, he would take a pitcherful thereof,
hang it on the door-post and say: "Whoever
wishes to have some, let him come and take it."
Some report that he knew of a medicine against
a disease called *shibta*,[297] and he would place it on

[297] The meaning of the word is disputed; see the dictionaries, especially *Aruch s. v.* שבתא. According to the
commentary of Hananel it is the name of a liquid medicine.

אמר ליה רבא לרפרם בר פפא לימא לן מר
מהנך מילי מעליתא דהוה עביד רב הונא אמר
ליה בינקותיה לא דכירנא בסיבותיה דכירנא ביומא
דעיבא הוו מפקין ליה בגוהרקא דדהבא והוה סייר
לה לכולה מתא כל אשיתא דהות רעיעא הוה   5
סתר לה אי אפשר למרה בני לה ואי לא בני לה
איהו מדידיה כל בהדי פניא דמעלי שבתא הוה
משדר שליחא לשוקא וכל ירקא דהוה יתיר להו
לגנאי זבין ליה ושדי ליה לנהרא וליהביה לעניים
אמר זמנין דסמכא דעתיהו ולא אתו למזבן ולשדייה   10
לבהמה קסבר מאכל אדם אין מאכילין אותו
לבהמה ולא לזבניה כלל נמצאת מכשילן לעתיד
לבא כי הוה ליה מלתא דאסותא הוי מלי כוזא דמיא
ותלי ליה בסיפא דביתא ואמר כל דבעי ליתי
ולשקול ואיכא דאמרי מלתא דשיבתא הוה גמיר   15

מסרת הש"ס והמדרשים

12 (מכשילן) רה"ש כ"א ב', ל"א   ב', יומא ע"ז ב'; כתובות צ"ז א'.

a jug of water, hang the latter outside and say: "Anyone who needs it, let him come (and use it) to avoid danger (of contagion)." When he was about to sit down to a meal, he would open the doors, saying: "Anyone who desires to eat, let him come in and eat." Said Raba, I could do all these things myself, except this last one, [fol. 21a] for there are too many soldiers in Maḥoza.²⁹⁸

'Ilfa and R. Johanan were greatly distressed by poverty and therefore said to one another, let us go into business and thus make true in our own lives the words (Deut., 15. 4): "Howbeit there shall be no needy among you." They then went and sat down under a ruined wall. While eating, R. Johanan overheard one angel saying to another, "Let us throw down the wall upon them and kill them, for they are going to neglect the life everlasting and busy themselves with the life of the moment." The other angel, however, replied, "Let them alone, for one of them has a great future before him." Said R. Johanan to 'Ilfa: "Did you hear anything?" 'Ilfa replied, "No." R. Johanan then said to himself, "I must be the one with the great future before him; I will therefore go back (to my studies) and make true of myself the words (Deut., 15. 11): "For the poor shall never cease out of the land." Before 'Ilfa returned to the city, R. Johanan had been appointed head of the academy, and when 'Ilfa came, the people of the town said to him: "Had you remained here and devoted yourself to study,

²⁹⁸ A city on the Tigris where Raba lived; comp. Neubauer, *La Géographie du Talmud*, Paris, 1868, p. 356. See the Hebrew Note here.

והוה מנח לה אכוזא דמיא ותלי ליה אמר כל
דצריך ליתי וליעול דלא לסתכן כי הוה כריך
ריפתא הוה פתח לבביה אמר כל מאן דצריך ליתי
וליכול אמר ליה כולהו מצינא מקיימנא להו לבר
מהא | משום דנפישי בני חילא במחוזא:

אילפא ורבי יוחנן הוה דחיקא להו מילתא טובא
אמרי ניקום ניזיל נעביד עסקא ונקיים בנפשין אפס
כי לא יהיה בך אביון אזלו איתיבו   תחותי ההיא
אשיתא רעיעתא הוו קא כרכי ריפתא שמעיה רבי
יוחנן למלאך דקאמר ליה לחבריה תא נשדייה
עליהו ונקטלינהו שמניחין חיי עולם ועוסקין בחיי
שעה אמר ליה אידך שבקינהו דחד מיניהו קיימא
ליה שעתא אמר ליה רבי יוחנן לאילפא שמע מר
מידי אמר ליה לא אמר שמע מינה אנא הוא דקיימא
לי שעתא אידהר אזיל אנא אקיים בנפש כי לא יחדל
אביון מקרב הארץ עד דאתא אילפא מלך רבי יוחנן
כי אתא אילפא אמרו ליה אי הוה יתיב מר וגריס לא

תורה אור

8 דברים ט״ו ד׳.   15 דברים ט״ו   11 (שמניחין) שבת י׳ א׳, ל״ג ב׳;
י״א.   ביצה ט״ו ב׳.

מסרת הש״ס והמדרשים

you would have been made the head."²⁹⁹   'Ilfa
thereupon climbed up to the top of the mast and
said: "If any one will put to me a question regarding a Baraita handed down by R. Ḥiyya and R.
'Osha'ya and I will be unable to answer it by
quoting a corroborating parallel from the Mishnah,
I will throw myself from the mast into the
water and drown."   An old man appeared and
recited to him the Baraita: If a dying man says
(to the trustees of his estate),   "Give to my
children one sheḳel a week," and it happens
that the children need a *sela*',³⁰⁰ the trustees
may give them a sela', but if he said, "Do
not give them more than a sheḳel a week," the
trustees are not allowed to give them more than a
sheḳel; if the father adds: "In case my children
die, others shall inherit the amount in their
place," they should give them only a sheḳel, no
matter whether the father said, "give them a
sheḳel" or "Do not give them more than a
sheḳel."   "The authority of this Baraita,"
exclaimed 'Ilfa, "is none other than R. Meir,
who holds that it is a religious duty to carry out
the request of the dead."

It was told of Nahum of Gamzo that he was
blind in both eyes, stumped in both hands,
crippled in both legs, that his whole body was

²⁹⁹ Because 'Ilfa had greater talents and would have
been elected in place of R. Johanan; see also *Tosafot, ad
locum.*

³⁰⁰ Which is twice the amount of a *shekel*.   The Talmud
here refers to the so-called *common* shekel used in talmudic
times, while the *holy* shekel of the Bible corresponds to a

מר הוה מליך אזל תלא נפשיה באסקריא דספינתא

אמר כל מאן דשאיל לי מלתא בדבי רבי חייא

ובדבי רבי אושעיא ולא פשיטנא ליה ממתניתין

נפילנא מאסקריא וטבענא אתא ההוא סבא תנא

5 ליה האומר תנו שקל לבני בשבת וראויין לתת להם

סלע נותנין להם סלע ואם אמר אל תתנו להם אלא

שקל אין נותנין להם אלא שקל ואם אמר אם מתו

יירשו אחרים תחתיהם בין שאמר תנו בין שאמר אל

תתנו אין נותנין להם אלא שקל הא שקל הא מני רבי מאיר

10 היא דאמר מצוה לקיים דברי המת:

אמרו עליו על נחום איש גם זו שהיה סומא בשתי

עיניו גדם בשתי ידיו קטע בשתי רגליו והיה כל

מסרת הש״ס והמדרשים

כתובות ו' ז' (ל' סוף ע״ד).	1 (תלא) כתובות ס״ט ב'; ירושלמי
10 (מצוה) כתובות ע' א'; נטין י״ד	כתובות ו' ז' (ל״א ריש ע״א);
ב', ט״ו א', מ' א'. 11 (נחום) חגינה	קדושין א' א' (ע״ח ד'). 5 (האומר)
י״ב א'; שבועות כ״ו א'; תוספתא	כתובות ס״ט ב'; ב״ב קכ״ט א';
שבועות א' ז' (וע' בציונים להלן).	תוספתא כתובות ו' י'; ירושלמי

sela'; see Zuckermann, *Talmudische Gewichte und Münzen*,
Breslau, 1862, pp. 9ff.; above, note 293.

covered with sores and his bed stood in four basins
of water to prevent ants climbing up (the legs of
the bed). Once he was lying in a ruinous house
and his disciples desired to remove him, but he
said to them: "Remove first the furniture and
then remove my bed, for you can be sure that
as long as I am in the house, the house will
not fall in." They removed the furniture
and then the bed, and immediately after
the house fell in. His disciples then asked
him: "Master! Since thou art so wholly
righteous, why did all this come upon thee?"
"I caused it myself", he replied. "Once I was
going to the house of my father-in-law and had
with me a load carried by three asses, one part
consisting of food, another of drinks and the
third of all sorts of delicacies. Suddenly there
appeared before me a man, who said to me:
'Master, give me something to eat.' I said to him,
'Wait until I alight from the ass.' After I had
alighted, I turned around and found that the man
was dead. I then threw myself upon him and
said: 'My eyes that had no pity upon thine eyes
shall become blind; my hands that had no pity
upon thy hands shall become stumped; and my
feet that had no pity upon thy feet shall become
crippled.' But even then my mind was not set
at rest until I said: 'May my body become covered with sores.'" Said they to him: "Woe unto
us that we must see thee in such a condition!"
Nahum, however, replied: "Woe would it be
to me if you did *not* see me in this condition."

גופו מלא שחין והיתה מטתו מונחת על גבי ספלים
של מים כדי שלא יעלו אליו נמלים פעם אחת
היתה מטתו מונחת בבית רעוע ובקשו תלמידיו
לפנותה אמר להם פנו את הכלים ואחר כך פנו
את מטתי שכל זמן שמטתי בתוך הבית מובטח
לכם שאין הבית נופל פנו את הכלים ואחר כך פנו
את מטתו מיד נפל הבית אמרו לו תלמידיו רבנו
וכי מאחר שצדיק גמור אתה למה עלתה בך כך
אמר להם אני עשיתי בעצמי פעם אחת הייתי
מהלך לבית חמי עמי והיה משוי שלשה חמורים
אחד של מאכל ואחד של משתה ואחד של מיני
מגדים נזדמן לי אדם אחד אמר לי רבי פרנסני
אמרתי לו המתן עד שאפרק מן החמור לאחר
שפרקתי חזרתי לאחורי ומצאתיו מת נפלתי עליו
ואמרתי עיני שלא חסו על עיניך יסומו ידי שלא
חסו על ידיך יתגדמו רגלי שלא חסו על רגליך
יתקטעו ולא נתקררה דעתי עד שאמרתי יהיה כל
גופי מלא שחין אמרו לו אוי לנו שראינוך בכך אמר
להם אוי לי אם לא ראיתוני בכך:

מסרת הש״ס והמדרשים

2 (פעם אחת) ירושלמי סוף פאה;   שקלים ספ״ה.

Why was he called Nahum of Gamzo?[301] Because whenever something untoward happened to him he would say: "This, too, is for a good purpose." Once the Rabbis wished to send a present to the Emperor and they deliberated through whom they should send it. They then said: Let us send it through Nahum of Gamzo, because he is one to whom miracles always happen. So they sent the present through him. On the way, Nahum stopped at an inn over night. During the night the occupants (of the inn) got up, took out everything that was in the bags and filled the bags with dust. When he arrived at his destination, the bags were untied and it was found that they were filled with dust. The emperor, insulted, said, the Jews are mocking me, and gave an order to have Nahum executed. Nahum, however, said: "This too is for the good." Thereupon the prophet Elijah appeared in the disguise of one of them and said to the emperor: This is perhaps some of the dust of Abraham, for when Abraham threw dust against an enemy it turned into swords, and when he threw stubble it turned into arrows, as it is written (Isaiah, 41.2): "His sword maketh them as the dust, his bow as the driven stubble."[301a] Now, there was a certain province which they had

[301] גמזו is a place mentioned in II Chronicles, 28. 18. The legend tries to explain the word as a combination of גם (also) and זו (this); comp. Rapoport, בכורי העתים, 1829, pp. 71f. (reprinted by B. Tursch in the collection יריעות שלמה, Warsaw, 1904, p. 120); Kohut, *s. v.* גם זו.

ואמאי קרו ליה נחום איש גם זו דכל מאי דהוה
סליק ביה הוה אמר גם זו לטובה זמנא חדא בעו
רבנן לשדורי דורון לקיסר אמרו בהדי מאן נשדר
נשדר בהדי נחום איש גם זו דמלומד בנסין הוא
שדור בהדיה אזל גנא בההוא דורא קמו בליליא 5
הנך דיוראי שקלו כל מה דהוה בספטיהו ומלונהו
עפרא כי מטא להתם שרונהו לספטיהו חזנהו דמלו
עפרא אמר קיסר אחוכי קא מחכו בי יהודאי
פקיד עליה למקטליה אמר גם זו לטובה אתא
אליהו אידמי ליה כחד מינייהו אמר ליה דילמא 10
האי עפרא מעפרא דאברהם אבוהון הוא דהוה
שדי מיניה והוו חרבי גילי והוו גירי דכתיב יתן כעפר
חרבו כקש נדף קשתו הויא ההיא מדינתא דלא הוו

תורה אור מסרת הש"ס והמדרשים

12 ישעיה מ"א ב'. 3 (דורון) סנהדרין ק"ח ב'.
11 (עפרא דאברהם) סנהדרין
ק"ט א'; ב"ר מ"ג ג'; תנחומא לך ט"ו (באבער סימן י"ט); מדרש תהלים
ק"י א.

301[a] This verse is explained by the Talmud (*Baba Batra* 15a) as referring to Abraham, who fought the four kings (Gen. 14). The Talmud translates: He maketh of something that is like dust—his sword, of something that is like stubble—his bow.

been thitherto unable to conquer. They tried some of the dust against this province and succeeded in conquering it. Thereupon the emperor took Nahum into the treasury, filled his bags with precious stones and pearls, and dismissed him with great honors. When on his way back he came again to the same inn, the occupants asked him: "What did you bring with you for the emperor that they honored you so?" "I brought them what I took from here," replied Nahum. Thereupon the occupants of the inn took some of the same dust and brought it to the emperor. It was tried, but did not turn into swords and arrows. All the inhabitants were then executed.

What is considered an epidemic? When in a city capable of furnishing five hundred foot-soldiers etc. The Rabbis taught: If in a small town capable of furnishing five hundred foot-soldiers as, for instance, Kefar 'Imḳi, three men died within three successive days, it is to be considered an epidemic, but if the three men died in one day or in four days, it does not constitute an epidemic; if in a larger city, capable of furnishing fifteen hundred men as, for instance, Kefar 'Akko,[302] nine men died successively within three days, it constitutes an epidemic [fol. 21b], but if they died in one day or in four days, it is not an epidemic.

[302] For Kefar 'Akko and Kefar 'Imḳi see Neubauer, *l. c.* p. 272; Hirschenson, שבע חכמות, Lemberg, 1883, pp. 145f.

מצי למכבשה בדקו מיניה עלה וכבשוה עייליה

לבי גנזא ומלינהו לספטיהו אבנים טובות ומרגליות

ושדרוה ביקרא רבא כי אתא בההוא דיורא אמרו

ליה מאי אמטית בהדך לבי מלכא דעבדו לך יקרא

5 כולי האי אמר להו מאי דשקלי מהכא קמו אינהו

נמי אמטו מההוא עפרא בדקו מיניה ולא הוו חרבי

וגירי וקטלינהו לכולהו דיוראי:

איזהו דבר עיר המוציאה חמש מאות רגלי כו':

תנו רבנן עיר קטנה המוציאה חמש מאות רגלי כגון

10 כפר עמיקו ויצאו ממנה שלשה מתים בשלשה ימים

זה אחר זה הרי זה דבר ביום אחד או בארבעה

ימים אין זה דבר עיר גדולה המוציאה אלף וחמש

מאות רגלי   כגון כפר עכו ויצאו ממנה תשעה

מתים בשלשה ימים זה אחר זה הרי זה דבר

כא^א
ע״ב   15 | ביום אחד או בארבעה ימים אין זה דבר:

מסרת הש״ס והמדרשים

11 (דבר) תוספתא תענית ב' ט' א.   12 (עיר גדולה) ירושלמי תענית
נ' ה' (ס״ו ד').

In Droķeret,[302a] a town of five hundred men, there died once three men in one day, wherefore R. Naḥman b. R. Ḥisda intended to decree a public fast., R. Naḥman b. Isaac, however, said to him: In accordance with whose view do you intend to do this? That of R. Meir, who said, if an ox that gores at long intervals (three times in three days) has to pay the full damage, all the more so one that gores at short intervals (three times in one day)? Said R. Naḥman b. R. Ḥisda to R. Naḥman b. Isaac: "Come and take a seat beside me,"[303] to which the latter replied: I hold to what is taught in a Baraita: R. Jose said: It is not the place that honors the man, but it is the man that honors the place, for thus we find that as long as the Shekinah was present on Sinai, the law was (Exod., 34. 3): "Neither let the flocks nor herds feed before that mount," but as soon as the Shekinah departed from there, the Torah prescribed (ib., 19.13): "When the ram's horn soundeth long, they shall come up to the mount." The same, we find, was the case with the tent of meeting, namely, when the tent was pitched, the order of the Torah was (Numbers, 5. 2): "They shall put out of the camp every leper, and every one that hath an issue," but as soon as the curtains were folded up (for removing the tent), those that had an issue as well as lepers were permitted to enter. "Then I shall come to your place," said Naḥman

---

[302a] According to Kohut, *Aruch*, *s. v.* דרוקרת, it is a corruption from דיוקרת (below, note 336), which he identifies with Idikara or Diakara on the Euphrates; comp.

דרוקרת עיר המוציאה חמש מאות רגלי הוא‸
ויצאו ממנה שלשה מתים ביום אחד סבר רב נחמן
בר רב חסדא למגזר תעניתא אמר ליה רב נחמן
בר יצחק כמאן כרבי מאיר דאמר רחק נגיחותיו חייב
5 קרב נגיחותיו לא כל שכן אמר ליה רב נחמן בר רב
חסדא לרב נחמן בר יצחק ליקום מר להכא אמר ליה
תנינא רבי יוסי אומר לא מקומו של אדם מכבדו אלא
הוא מכבד את מקומו שכן מצינו בסיני שכל זמן
שהשכינה שרויה עליו אמרה תורה גם הצאן והבקר
10 אל ירעו אל מול ההר ההוא נסתלקה שכינה ממנו
אמרה תורה במשך היבל המה יעלו בהר וכן
מצינו באהל מועד שכל זמן שאהל מועד נטוי אמרה
תורה וישלחו מן המחנה כל צרוע וכל זב הוגללו
הפרכות הותרו זבין ומצורעין ליכנס לשם אמר ליה

תורה אור	מסרת הש״ס והמדרשים
9 שמות ל״ד ג׳. 11 שמות י״ט י״ג. 4 (רחק) ב״ק כ״ד א׳; ב״ב כ״ח ב׳.	7 (תנינא) מכילתא דבחדש יתרו
13 במדבר ה׳ ב׳.	ג׳; מכדרשב״י 97. 10 (נסתלקה)

מכילתא שם (וע׳ ביצה ה׳ ב׳). 13 (הוגללו) מנחות צ״ה א׳; ירושלמי
יומא ספ״ד.

Rapoport, ערך מלין, pp. 33 ff. *s. v.* איהי; Hirschenson,
שבע חכמות, pp. 100, 125, and my Hebrew Notes.

303 Impressed by the ingenious comparison, R. Naḥman b. R. Ḥisda invited R. Naḥman b. Isaac to take a
more prominent seat, near his own.

b. R. Ḥisda. R. Naḥman b. Isaac, however, replied, "It is proper that an eminent man who is the son of one less eminent, should go to one who is eminent and is the son of an eminent man, but it is not proper that a man of eminence who is the son of an eminent man should go to an eminent man who is the son of one less eminent."[304]

An epidemic once broke out in Sura, but in the neighborhood of Rab's residence the epidemic did not appear. The people thought that this was due to Rab's merits, but in a dream they were told that the miracle was too slight to be attributed to Rab's great merit and that it happened because of the merits of a man who willingly lent hoe and shovel to a cemetery (for the digging of graves).

A fire once broke out in Droḳeret, but the neighborhood of R. Huna was spared. The people thought that it was due to the merit of R. Huna, but they were told in a dream that R. Huna's merits were too great and the sparing of his neighborhood from fire too small a matter to attribute it to him, and that it was due to the merits of a certain woman who used to heat her oven and place it at the disposal of her neighbors.

[304] It will be noticed that Isaac, the father of this R. Naḥman, did not have the title "R." (which stands for Rab, scholar, master) before his name, which means that he was not a man of distinction, while the other R. Naḥman was the son of the distinguished Amora, R. Ḥisda. R. Naḥman b. Isaac, using the name of a money-weight (מנה =

אזיל אנא לגבי מר אמר ליה כותב שיבא מנה בן
פרס אצל מנה בן מנה ואל יבא מנה בן מנה אצל
מנה בן פרס:

בסורא הוות דברתא בשיבבותיה דרב לא הוות
5 סבור מינה משום זכותיה דרב אתחזי להו בחלמא
רב נפישא זכותיה טובא והא זוטרא ליה לרב אלא
משום ההוא גברא דקא מושיל מרא וזבילא לבי
קבורה:

בדרוקרת הוות דליקתא בשיבבותיה דרב הונא
10 לא הוות סבור מינה משום זכותיה דרב הונא אתחזי
להו בחלמא רב הונא נפישא זכותיה טובא והא
זוטרא ליה לרב הונא אלא משום ההיא אתתא
דמחממא תנורא ומשיילא לשיבבתא:

מסרת הש"ס והמדרשים
4 (דברתא) ירושלמי תענית ג' ד'.

μνᾶ, mina) as a figure for the weightiness and importance
of men, refers to himself as מנה בן פרס, literally, mina,
the product of half a mina, while the other R. Naḥman
is designated by him as מנה בן מנה.

R. Judah was apprised of the appearance of locusts and ordered a public fast. The people, however, told him that the locusts were not doing any damage, whereupon he remarked, "Did the locusts bring along provisions?"

R. Judah was once informed that a pest broke out among the swine and he ordered a public fast. Are we to say that R. Judah was of the opinion that an epidemic which breaks out among one kind (of living beings) is liable to spread also among the other kinds? No, it is different in the case of swine, because their intestines are similar to those of human beings.

Samuel was told that there was an epidemic among the people of Khuza.[305] He ordered a public fast. The people objected, saying that the place was far off, whereupon Samuel said, "Do you think that the (absence of a) ferry will prevent the epidemic from spreading?"

R. Naḥman was told that there was an epidemic in Palestine, so he ordered a fast, saying, "If the mistress is stricken, how much the more so her servant!"[306] Is the fact that the one is mistress and the other servant the reason for ordaining a fast? Suppose both were servants, would we not order a fast? Is it not a fact that when Samuel was told of an epidemic among the people of Khuza, he ordered a fast (in Neharde'a)?

[305] A city east of the Tigris; comp. Neubauer, *Géogr. du Talm.*, p. 380; Kohut, *Aruch*, *s. v.* בי חוזאי; Hirschenson, שבע חכמות, p. 68.

[306] Palestine is figuratively called mistress, while Babylon, the country of R. Naḥman, is named servant.

312

אמרו ליה לרב יהודה אתו קמצי גזר תעניתא

אמרו ליה והא לא קא מפסדין אמר להו זודי אייתו

בהדיהו:

אמרו ליה לרב יהודה איכא מותנא בחזירי גזר

⁵ תעניתא נימא קסבר רב יהודה מכה משולחת במין

אחד משולחת בשאר מינין לא שאני חזירי דדמיין

מעייהו לדבשרא ודמא:

אמרו ליה לשמואל איכא מותנא בי חוזאי גזר

תעניתא אמר ליה והא מרחק אמר להו וכי מברי

¹⁰ פסקי ליה:

אמרו ליה לרב נחמן איכא מותנא בארעא

דישראל גזר תעניתא אמר גבירה לוקה שפחה לא

כל שכן טעמא דגבירה ושפחה הא שפחה ושפחה

לא והא אמרו ליה לשמואל איכא מותנא בי חוזאי

מסרת הש"ס והמדרשים

9 (מברי פסקי) נדרים כ"ז ב'.

In that case it was different, for caravans were
frequently travelling between the two places
and might have carried the infection (to Neharde'a).

'Abba the Bleeder received every day a greeting from the heavenly academy while 'Abbayi
received one every Friday, and Raba every year
on the eve of the Day of Atonement. 'Abbayi
felt discouraged on account of the greater distinction of 'Abba the Bleeder. 'Abbayi was therefore
told, "Thou canst not perform deeds like those of
'Abba the Bleeder!" What were the deeds of
'Abba the Bleeder? When he performed the operation (of bleeding), he had a separate place
for men and another for women. He had a
garment ready in which there were numerous
slits, and when a woman came, he made her put
it on, so that he should not have to look upon
her bare body.[307] Outside of his office he had a
place (box) where his fees were to be deposited.
Whoever had money could put it in, but those
who had none could come in without feeling
embarrassed. When he saw a person who was
in no position to pay, he would offer him some
money, saying to him: "Go, strengthen thyself."[308] One day 'Abbayi sent a pair of
scholars to him to find out the truth about
him. When they came to his house, he gave
them to eat and to drink and laid cushions

[307] As he could insert the instrument anywhere through
one of the little slits in the garment, without having to
bare the body.

[308] Which was necessary after the operation of bleeding.

314

וגזר תעניתא שאני התם כיון דשכיחן שיירתא דאזלן
ואתין מיגרי:

אבא אומנא הוה אתי ליה שלמא ממתיבתא
דרקיעא כל יומא לאביי ממעלי שבתא למעלי
⁵ שבתא לרבא ממעלי יומא דכפורי למעלי יומא
דכפורי הוה קא חלשא דעתיה דאביי על דאבא
אומנא אמרו ליה לא מצית למיעבד כעובדיה
מאי עובדיה דאבא אומנא כי הוה עביד מלתא
הוה עביד ליה דוכתא דגברי לחודיהו ודנשי
¹⁰ לחודיהו והוה ליה לבושא דאית ביה בזעי
בזעי דכי הוות אתיא אתתא הוה מלביש לה
כי היכי דלא לסתכל בה והוה ליה דוכתא
מאבראי למרמי ביה פריטי דאית ליה רמי
דלא אית ליה הוה אתי יתיב ולא מיכסיף וכד
¹⁵ הוה חזי אינש דלא אפשר ליה הוה יהיב ליה פריטי
אמר ליה זיל איברי נפשך זמנא חדא שדר אביי
זוגא דרבנן למבדקיה אזול לביתיה אוכלינהו

315

before them to sleep on [fol. 22a]. The next
morning the scholars took the cushions with them
and brought them to the market place. 'Abbayi
then sent for.'Abba, and the scholars requested
him to appraise the value of the cushions. 'Abba
said, they are worth so and so much. "But,
perhaps, they are worth more?" the scholars
inquired. "This is what I paid for them," he
replied. "Of what did you suspect us?" the
scholars asked. "I thought," he said, "the
gentlemen happened to be in need of money for
some charitable purpose and were ashamed to
tell me." "Take them back now," they said.
"No," he replied, "from that moment I diverted
my mind (from them), considering them con-
secrated to charity."

Raba felt discouraged on account of 'Abbayi's
greater distinction; he was therefore told: "It is
honor enough to you that your merits protect
the whole city."

R. Beroḳah of Khuza frequented the market
of Lapet.[309] One day Elijah appeared to him
there, and R. Beroḳah asked him: "Is there
among the people of this market any one that is
destined to share in the world to come?" Elijah
replied, "There is none." In the meantime there
came a man who wore black shoes and had
no fringes on his garment. "This man," Elijah
remarked, "is one who will share in the world
to come." R. Beroḳah thereupon called to the
man, but the latter did not heed the call, so
R. Beroḳah went over to him and asked him

[309] See Neubauer, *l. c.*, Kohut, *s. v.* בי לפט; Hirschenson, שבע חכמות, p. 70.

316

כ״ב ואשקינהו ומך להו בסתרקי|לצפרא כרכינהו
ע״א
ואיתינהו לשוקא שדר אביי וקרייה אמרו ליה

לשימינהו מר אמר להו הכי והכי שוו אמרו ליה

דילמא שוו טפי אמר להו בהכי שקלי להו אמרו

5 ליה במאי חשדתינן אמר להו אמינא מלתא דמצוה

איזדמנא להו לרבנן וכסיפא להו מלתא למימר

לי אמרו ליה לשקלינהו מר אמר להו מההיא

שעתא אסחתה לדעתאי לצדקה:

הוה קא חלשא דעתיה דרבא על דאביי אמרו

10 ליה מסתיך דקא מגנא זכותך אכוליה כרכא:

רב ברוקא חוזאה הוה קאי בשוקא דבי לפט

אתא אליהו אתחזי ליה אמר ליה מי איכא בהאי

שוקא בר עלמא דאתי אמר ליה לא איניש אדהכי

והכי אתא ההוא גברא דהוה סיים מסאני אוכמי

15 ולא הוה רמי חוטי אמר ליה האי בר עלמא דאתי

הוא קרא ליה ולא אתא לגביה אזל בתריה אמר

317

what his occupation was. "I am a jailer," the man declared, "and I keep men and women separate. At night I place my bed between the men and the women, so that no wrong be committed. When I see among the prisoners a Jewish woman, upon whom the Gentiles around her have fixed their eyes, I risk my life for her and save her. One day a betrothed maiden happened to be placed in my prison and the Gentiles were about to assault her, so I took lees of red wine and put them around the lower part of her skirt, saying to them that she was menstruating." R. Berokah then asked him, "Why do you wear black shoes?"[310] "Because I mourn for Jerusalem." "And why did you not put fringes on your garment?" "In order that the people should not recognize me as a Jew, so that when they have some secret plot against us and are about to issue hard decrees, they may reveal it to me and I would advise the Rabbis thereof, in order that they may pray to God and avert the menace." "But why did you not come when I called you?", R. Berokah continued. "At that moment," he replied, "they had just issued a decree, and I thought I must first find out what it was and send word to the Rabbis, in order that they may pray to God (and thus frustrate the plan)."

In the meantime two other men appeared on the scene, and Elijah said to R. Berokah, these two will also share in the world to come. R. Berokah then asked them, "What is your occu-

---

[310] See *Tosafot*, Synhedrin 74b, *s. v.* אפילו.

ליה מאי עובדך אמר ליה זנדוקנא אנא ואסרנא

גברי לחודיהו ונשי לחודיהו ובליליא רמינא פוריי

בין גברי לנשי כי היכי דלא לתעבד אסורא כי

חזינא בת ישראל דיהבי גוים עיניהו עלה מסרנא

5 נפשי ומצילנא לה זמנא חדא אתרמאי נערה

מאורסה בעו למנסה שקלי דורדיא דחמרא שדאי

לה בשפולה ואמינא להו דשתנא היא מאי טעמא

סיימת מסאני אוכמי דקא מתאבלנא על ירושלם ומאי

טעמא לא רמית חוטי כי היכי דלא לידעו דיהודאה

10 אנא דכי הויא מלתא דצנעא ובעו למגזר גזירתא

מגלו לי ואמינא להו לרבנן ובעו רחמי ומבטלי לה

מאי טעמא כי קריתך לא אתית בההיא שעתא הוו

קא גזרי גזירתא אמינא ברישא אשמעה ואשלח להו

לרבנן דלבעו רחמי עלה דמלתא אדהכי והכי

15 אתו הנך בי תרי אחריני אמר ליה הני נמי בני עלמא

דאתי נינהו אמר להו מאי עובדיכו אמרו ליה

מסרת הש״ס והמדרשים

8 (מתאבלנא) ב״ק נ״ט ב׳.

pation?" "We are merry-makers; when we see a man who is down-cast we cheer him up; also when we see two people quarrelling with one another, we endeavor to make peace between them."

On the following occasions the alarm must be sounded, etc. Our Rabbis have taught: In case of blast and mildew, the alarm must be sounded in whatever quantity they appear; in case of locust and crickets, the alarm must be immediately sounded, even if only one of these winged creatures appeared in the whole land of Palestine.

Wild beasts, etc. Our Rabbis have taught: In cases of wild beasts the alarm must be sounded only when they appear as a visitation, but if they do not appear as a visitation, we do not sound the alarm. How are we to know whether it is the one or the other? If the wild beasts appear in the town, it is a visitation, but if only in the fields, it is not a visitation; if by day, it is a visitation, if by night it is not a visitation; if a beast saw two men together and ran after them, it is a visitation, but if on seeing them it fled, it is not a visitation; if it tore two persons but devoured only one of them, it is a visitation,[311] but if it devoured both of them, it is not a visitation; if it climbed upon the roof and took a child out of the cradle, it is a visitation.

[311] That is to say, it tore one person and devoured him and tore another without devouring him. This is considered a visitation, because the animal tore the second person after it had stilled its hunger.

אינשי בדוחי אנן כי חזינן איניש דעציבא דעתיה
מבדחינן ליה אי נמי בי תרי דאית להו תיגרא בהדי
הדדי טרחינן ועבדינן להו שלמא:

ועל אלו מתריעין כו׳: תנו רבנן שדפון וירקון כל
5 שהוא ארבה וחסיל אפילו לא נראה אלא כנף אחד
בכל ארץ ישראל מתריעין עליהן מיד:

ועל חיה רעה: תנו רבנן חיה רעה בזמן שהיא
משולחת מתריעין עליה בזמן שאינה משולחת אין
מתריעין עליה כיצד נראתה בעיר משולחת בשדה
10 אינה משולחת נראתה ביום משולחת בלילה אינה
משולחת ראתה שני בני אדם ורצתה אחריהם
משולחת ברחה מפניהם אינה משולחת טרפה שני
בני אדם ואכלה אחד מהם משולחת שניהם אינה
משולחת עלתה לגג ונטלה תינוק מעריסה משולחת

מסרת הש״ס והמדרשים

5 (כנף) ירושלמי תענית ג׳ ו׳.   7 (חיה) ירושלמי שם.

Is not the foregoing Baraita contradictory?
First it says: If the beasts appear in the towns
it is a visitation, making no distinction between
day and night, later again it says that it is
a visitation only when they appear by day and
not when they appear by night. It is no contradiction, and the meaning is this: If the beasts
appear in the town by day, it is a visitation, if
by night, it is not. "If the beast saw two people
and ran after them it is a visitation." This
would imply that if the beast remained standing
in its place it is not a visitation, and yet in the
following clause it is taught that "if the beast
fled it is not a visitation," which implies that if
it remained standing in its place, it is a visitation! This too is no contradiction, because in
the one case the reference is to a beast standing
in a field that is near reedland, in the other, to
one standing in a field that is not near reedland.[312]
"If it tore two persons and devoured only one of
them, it is a visitation." But just above it was
said that even if it only ran after them it is a
visitation! Answer. This sentence refers to
a beast standing in the very midst of the
reeds.[313] "If it climbed upon the roof and took
a child out of a cradle, it is a visitation." Is
this not a matter of course? Said R. Papa, the
statement is needed in order to include the case
of a beast taking a child out of a cradle standing
in a hunter's cave.[314]

[312] If the animal stands near a place that affords it protection (as reedland) and, in the sight of approaching
people, remains still, it is not to be taken as a sign that

הא גופא קשיא אמרת נראתה בעיר משולחת ואפילו
בלילה והדר תני ביום ולא בלילה הכי קאמר
בעיר ביום משולחת בלילה אינה משולחת ראתה
שני בני אדם ורצתה אחריהם משולחת הא עמדה
אינה משולחת והא קתני סיפא ברחה מפניהם אינה   5
משולחת הא עמדה משולחת לא קשיא כאן בשדה
הסמוכה לאגם כאן בשדה שאינה סמוכה לאגם
טרפה שני בני אדם ואכלה אחד מהם משולחת
והא אמרת אפילו רצתה כי תניא ההיא באגם גופיה
עלתה לגג ונטלה תינוק מעריסה משולחת פשיטא   10
אמר רב פפא לא צריכא דאפילו בכוכא דצייד:

---

it makes ready for attack, for it feels instinctively that
it is secure, having a place of escape. Not so when it stands
in an open field.

313 For in such a place of security the animal would run
after people even if it had no desire to devour them. Its
pursuing the people, unless it actually attacks them,
is therefore no proof of its viciousness, and is not visitation.

314 Upon which the hunters erect a little hut for protection against the weather. As it is a very low building,
an animal need not be vicious in order to climb up for its
prey.

When armies are passing, etc. Our Rabbis
have taught: Not only when a hostile army
is invading the country (must the alarm be
sounded), which is a matter of course, but also
when a friendly army is passing through the
country; for there was no more friendly army
than that of Pharaoh-necoh, and yet king Josiah
met his doom through it, as it is said (II Chron.,
35.21): [fol. 22b] "He sent ambassadors to him,
saying, what have I to do with thee, thou king
of Judah? I come not against thee this day,
but against the house wherewith I have war;
and God hath given command to speed me; for-
bear thee from meddling with God, who is
with me, that He destroy thee not." [What God
(did Pharaoh refer to)? Said R. Judah in the
name of Rab, he referred to his idol. Josiah
therefore thought, since Pharaoh relies on his
idol, I shall prevail over him.] And it is further
written (*ib.*, 35. 23): "And the archers shot at
king Josiah." [Said R. Judah in the name of Rab:
This verse teaches us that they made his body
(perforated) like a sieve.[315] And R. Judah further
said in the name of Rab: Why was Josiah so
punished? Because he should have taken counsel
with Jeremiah, but failed to do so.] On what
verse did he base his attitude? On the verse
(Lev., 26. 6): "And the sword shall not go through
your land." What sword, Josiah asked himself,
can here be meant? Does Scripture refer to the

---

[315] He assumes that וירו הירים (the shooters shot)
indicates repeated shooting; comp. for a similar use
above, note 145; see also the Hebrew Notes.

ועל החרב: תנו רבנן אין צריך לומר חרב שאינה
של שלום אלא אפילו חרב של שלום שאין לך חרב
של שלום יותר משל פרעה נכה ואף על פי כן נכשל
בה יאשיהו המלך שנאמר וישלח אליו מלאכים
לאמר מה לי ולך מלך יהודה לא עליך אתה היום
כי אל בית מלחמתי ואלהים אמר לבהלני חדל
לך מאלהים אשר עמי ואל ישחיתך מאן אלהים
אמר רב יהודה אמר רב זו עבודה זרה אמר הואיל
וקא בטח בעבודה זרה יכילנא ליה וכתיב ויֹרו
הֹירים למלך יאשיהו אמר רב יהודה אמר רב
מלמד שעשו כל גופו ככברה אמר רב יהודה אמר
רב מפני מה נענש יאשיהו מפני שהיה לו לימלך
בירמיהו ולא נמלך מאי דרש וחרב לא תעבר
בארצכם מאי חרב אילימא חרב שאינה של שלום

כ״ב
ע״ב

5

10

תורה אור   מסרת הש״ס והמדרשים

4 דה״י ב' ל״ה כ״א.   9 דה״י ב'   1 (חרב) ירושלמי שם; תוספתא
ל״ה כ״ג.   13 ויקרא כ״ו ו'.   תענית ב' י'.   11 (ככברה) מו״ק
כ״ח ב'; סנהדרין מ״ח ב'; פסדר״כ
ריש כ״ז; ירושלמי קדושין א' ז'; תוספתא תענית ב' י'; תנחומא (הנדפס)
מסעי י״ב (באבבר סימן ט') ריש ואתחנן (באבער); במ״ר כ״ג י״ג; איכ״ר
א' י״ח; מדרש שמואל כ״ה.   12 (לימלך) תרגום איכה א' י״ח.   14 (של
שלום) תוספתא כאן ב' י״א; איכ״ר (באבער) א' י״ח.

sword of an enemy? This can not be the case, because it is written (in the same verse), "And I will give peace in the land;" it must therefore mean even the sword of a friend. He did not realize, however, that his generation did not appear good enough (in the eyes of God).[316] When Josiah was expiring, Jeremiah came to inquire about him. He then noticed that Josiah's lips were moving, wherefore he said, is it possible that in his agony he is uttering some blasphemy against God! He therefore bent over him and heard him justify God's verdict against him, saying (Lament., 1. 18): "The Lord is righteous; for I have rebelled against His word." Jeremiah then said of him: "The breath of our nostrils, the anointed of the Lord" (*ib.*, 4.20).

It happened that certain elders, as they travelled from Jerusalem to their home cities, etc. The question was raised: Does the Mishnah mean a quantity of grain sufficient to fill an oven, or a quantity of grain sufficient to fill an oven with bread? Come and hear: A Baraita teaches, "A quantity sufficient to close the opening of an oven" (which can refer only to loaves of bread). The question still remains whether this means as many loaves as would cover the opening (on top) of the oven or a row of loaves reaching up to the opening of the oven? This remains undecided.

[316] He did not realize that God's promise (to prevent even friendly armies from passing through the Holy Land) did not apply to an unrighteous generation like his. Josiah's attempt against Pharaoh was thus a mistake.

והכתיב ונתתי שלום בארץ אלא אפילו חרב של

שלום והוא אינו יודע שאין דורו דומה יפה כי הוה

קא ניחא נפשיה אתא ירמיהו לשיולי ביה חזייה

דקא מרחשן שפותיה אמר דילמא חס ושלום אגב

5 צעריה קאמר מלתא כלפי שמיא נחין עליה שמעיה

דקא מצדיק עליה דינא וקאמר צדיק הוא ה' כי

פיהו מריתי פתח עליה רוח אפינו משיח ה':

מעשה שירדו זקנים מירושלם לעריהם כו':

איבעיא להו כמלא תנור תבואה או דילמא כמלא

10 תנור פת תא שמע כמלא פי תנור ועדין תבעי לך

כמלא פי תנור ככסויא דתנורא או דילמא כי דרא

דריפתא דהדר ליה לפומיה דתנורא תיקו:

תורה אור   מסרת הש"ס והמדרשים

6 איכה א' י"ח.   7 איכה ד' כ'.   4 (שפותיה) תרגום איכה א' י"ח.

8 (מעשה) מנחות ס"ט ב'.

This last sentence forms the climax of the proof that the
Mishnah refers also to friendly armies.   All the preceding
sayings and the immediately following passages in brackets
are incidental comments on other points of the Baraita.

They further decreed a fast because wolves had devoured, etc. 'Ulla said in the name of R. Simeon b. Jehozadak, it once happened that wolves devoured two children beyond the Jordan and discharged them through the excretory canal. When the fact came before the Sages, they declared the excreted (digested) flesh as clean, but the excreted bones as unclean.[317]

On the following occasions the alarm is sounded even on the Sabbath, etc. Our Rabbis have taught: When a city is surrounded by enemy troops, or is threatened with a flood; when a ship is foundering on the sea; when a person is pursued by Gentiles or by wild beasts or by bandits, the alarm is sounded even on the Sabbath. For any of these things individuals may volunteer to afflict themselves by fasting; R. Jose said, an individual is not allowed to afflict himself by fasting, for he might become dependent upon the public [by reason of incapacity for work] and find no mercy on their part. Said R. Judah in the name of Rab, what is R. Jose's (Scriptural) reason? It is written (Gen., 2. 7): "And man became a living soul;" the Torah means to say, keep alive the soul which I gave you.

Simeon the Temanite said (the alarm is sounded on the Sabbath) also on account of an epidemic, but the other Sages did not agree with him, etc. The question was raised: Did the Rabbis disagree with Simeon only so far as the Sabbath was concerned, but agreed with him with regard

[317] Defiling persons that come in contact with them (according to Lev., chs., 5, and 22).

ועוד גזרו תענית על שאכלו זאבים כו׳: אמר
עולא משום רבי שמעון בן יהוצדק מעשה ובלעו
זאבים שני תינוקות בעבר הירדן והקיאום דרך בית
הרעי ובא מעשה לפני חכמים וטהרו את הבשר
וטמאו את העצמות: ⁵

על אלו מתריעין בשבת כו׳: תנו רבנן עיר
שהקיפוה גוים או נהר וספינה המטרפת בים ויחיד
הנדדף מפני גוים או מפני חיה רעה או מפני לסטים
מתריעין עליהן בשבת ועל כלן יחיד רשאי לסגף
את עצמו בתענית רבי יוסי אומר אין היחיד רשאי ¹⁰
לסגף את עצמו בתענית שמא יצטרך לבריות ואין
הבריות מרחמות עליו אמר רב אמר רב יהודה אמר רב
מאי טעמיה דרבי יוסי דכתיב ויהי האדם לנפש
חיה אמרה תורה נשמה שנתתי בך החייה:

שמעון התימני אומר אף על הדבר ולא הודו לו ¹⁵
חכמים: איבעיא להו לא הודו לו בשבת אבל בחול

תורה אור   מסרת הש״ס והמדרשים
13 בראשית ב׳ ז׳.   6 (עיר) תענית י״ד א׳; תוספתא
                        כאן ב׳ י״ב.   7 (ספינה) ספרי
            במדבר ע״ו.   9 (לסגף) תוספתא כאן ב׳ י״ב.

to week-days, or did they disagree with him in both? Come and hear: Simeon the Temanite said, the alarm is sounded on the Sabbath for an epidemic, and all the more so on week days; Hanan b. Phineas, the disciple of R. 'Aḳiba, said in the name of R. 'Aḳiba, the alarm is not to be sounded either on the Sabbath or on week days.

The alarm is sounded on account of any calamity that comes upon the community, except that of excessive rain. What is the reason? Said R. 'Abba in the name of Samuel, because it is not allowed to pray for the cessation of too much good. R. 'Abba further said in the name of Samuel, whence do we learn that one is not to pray for the cessation of too much good? From the statement (Malachi, 3. 10): "Bring ye the whole tithe into the store-house, that there may be food in My house, and try Me now herewith, saith the Lord of hosts, if I will not open you the windows of heaven, and pour you out a blessing, that there shall be more than sufficiency." What is the meaning of "that there shall be more than sufficiency?" Said Rami b. R. Yud in the name of Rab, it means that your lips will grow tired saying, "it is enough".

R. Judah said in the name of Rab, in the Exile we do sound the alarm at once (for excessive rain). The same is taught in a Baraita: When there was excessive rain, the people belonging to the division (of that week)[318] would send word to their delegates in Jerusalem: "Look

---

[318] Here אנשי משמר refers not to the priests but to the lay Israelites of one of the twenty-four sections, whose

הודו לו או דילמא לא הודו לו כלל תא שמע דתניא
שמעון התימני אומר מתריעין על הדבר בשבת
(ואין צריך לומר בחול) רבי חנן בן פנחס תלמידו
של רבי עקיבא משום רבי עקיבא אומר אין מתריעין
5 על הדבר כל עקר:

על כל צרה שלא תבא על הצבור מתריעין
עליה חוץ מרוב גשמים: מאי טעמא אמר רבי אבא
אמר שמואל לפי שאין מתפללין על רוב הטובה
ואמר רבי אבא אמר שמואל מנין שאין מתפללין
10 על רוב הטובה שנאמר הביאו את כל המעשר אל
בית האוצר וגו' והריקתי לכם ברכה עד בלי די
מאי עד בלי די אמר רמי בר רב יוד אמר רב עד
שיבלו שפתותיכם מלומר די אמר רב יהודה אמר
רב ובגולה מתריעין עליהן מיד תניא נמי הכי שנה
15 שנשמיה מרובין אנשי משמר שולחין לאנשי מעמד

תורה אור   מסרת הש"ס והמדרשים
10 מלאכי ג' י'.   8 (רוב הטובה) לקמן כ"ג א';
מנ"ח י"ב.   11 (די) לעיל ט' א';
שבת ל"ב ב'; מכות כ"ג ב'; ירושלמי ברכות ט' ה' ותענית ג' ט'; ויק"ר
ל"ה י"ב; במ"ר י"ב א'; ד"ר י"ב י"א; אסתר רבה י' ט"ו.

representatives (אנשי מעמד) happen to be on duty with
the corresponding division of priests; see above, note 230,
and below, note 397.

ye out for your brethren in the Exile, that
their houses should not become their graves!"

R. Eleazar was asked, how long must a rainfall
last without our being allowed to pray for its
cessation? "Until," he replied, "a man can sit
on the *Keren 'Ofel*[319] and have his foot dabble in
the water." Did not another Baraita teach
"hand" (instead of feet)? Said 'Abbayi, by
saying "foot" the situation is so conceived that
the man could also wash his hands while sitting
there. Said Rabbah b. Bar Ḥanah: I saw that
place, and [while I was standing on it], an Arab
riding on a camel and holding a spear in his hand
passed beneath me, and he looked to me as small
as a flax worm.

Our Rabbis have taught: "I will give your
rains in their season" (Lev., 26. 4) means that the
soil will be neither soaked nor thirsty, for whenever
the rain is excessive it washes away the soil, so
that it yields no fruit. Another interpretation
[fol. 23a] is that "in their season" means that the
rain will fall only on the eves of Wednesday
and Friday, for thus we find that in the time of
Simeon b. Shetaḥ the rain fell on the eves

---

[319] אפל, no doubt the same as the biblical עפל (see
Gesenius, *s. v.*), a high place, especially the one on the brook
Kidron, near the Olive mount. In *Yerushalmi Ta'anit*,
III, 11, the reading is indeed העפל, with the article, and
there, as well as in the *Tosefta*, Ta'anit, 3,1, it is said
explicitly that when the brook Kidron rose, one could sit
on the 'Ofel, having his feet in the water and reaching it
also with his hands.

תנו עיניכם באחיכם שבגולה שלא יעשו בתיהם
קבריהם:

שאלו את רבי אלעזר עד מתי גשמים יורדין ולא

יהו מתפללין עליהם שלא ירדו אמר להם כדי

5 שישב אדם על קרן אפל וישכשך רגלו במים והתניא

ידו אמר אביי רגלו כידו אמר רבה בר בר חנה

לדידי חזיא לי ההיא דוכתא וחליף טייעא כי

רכיב גמלא ונקיט רומחא בידיה ומתחזי כיאניכא:

תנו רבנן ונתתי גשמיכם בעתם לא שכורה ולא

10 צמאה אלא בינונית שבזמן שהגשמים מרובין

מטשטשין את הארץ ואינה עושה פירות דבר אחר ׀

כ״ג בעתם בלילי רביעיות ובלילי שבתות שכן מצינו
ע״א

בימי שמעון בן שטח שירדו להם גשמים בלילי

תורה אור	מסרת הש״ס והמדרשים
9 ויקרא כ״ו ד׳.	2 (קבריהם) ירושלמי יומא ה׳ ג׳.
	3 (שאלו) ירושלמי תענית ג׳ י״א.
	5 (אפל) ירושלמי שם; תוספתא ג׳ א׳. 9 (בעתם) ספרי דברים מ״ב;
	ספרא ריש בחקותי; ויק״ר ל״ה ט׳.

of Wednesday and Friday with the result
that the wheat grains became as big as kidneys,
and the barley grains as big as the kernels of
olives, and the lentils as big as gold dinars.
The Sages have preserved samples of them for
future generations in order to demonstrate how
much loss is caused by sin, as it is said (Jerem.,
5. 25): "Your iniquities have turned away
these things, and your sins have withholden
good from you." Similarly, we find that in the
days of Herod, when they were rebuilding
the Temple, rain fell during the night, and
in the morning the wind blew, the clouds dispersed, and the sun shone, so that everyone
would rise early for his work—all of which
demonstrated to the people that their work
was for the sake of Heaven.

*It happened that Ḥoni, the Circle-drawer, was
asked to pray for rain*, etc. Our Rabbis have
taught: It happened once that the greater part
of the month of Adar had passed and no rain had
yet fallen. Ḥoni the Circle-drawer was therefore
asked to pray that rain should fall. He did
so, but rain did not fall. He then drew a circle
and placed himself in its center, as did the prophet Habakkuk, who said (Habakkuk, 2. 1): "I
will stand upon my watch," and said before
God: "Master of the world! Thy children have
set their face upon me, because I am, as it were,
Thy intimate. I swear by Thy great Name
that I will not move from here until Thou
showest mercy to Thy children." Rain began to
trickle. The people therefore said to him:
Master, we see thee, and this is a warranty to us

334

רביעיות ובלילי שבתות עד שנעשו חטים ככליות
ושעורים כגרעיני זיתים ועדשים כדינרי זהב וצררו
מהם חכמים דוגמא לדורות להודיע כמה חטא
גורם שנאמר עונותיכם הטו אלה וחטאותיכם מנעו
הטוב מכם וכן מצינו בימי הורודוס בזמן שהיו
עוסקין בבנין בית המקדש ירדו להם גשמים בלילות
למחר נשבה הרוח ונתפזרו העבים וזרחה החמה
וכל אחד ואחד משכים למלאכתו להודיע שמלאכת
שמים בידיהם:

מעשה שאמרו לחוני המעגל וכו': תנו רבנן פעם
אחת יצא רוב אדר ולא ירדו גשמים שלחו לחוני
המעגל התפלל וירדו גשמים התפלל ולא ירדו
גשמים עג עוגה ועמד בתוכה כדרך שעשה חבקוק
הנביא שנאמר על משמרתי אעמדה ואתיצבה על
מצור וגו' אמר לפניו רבונו של עולם בניך שמו
פניהם עלי שאני כבן בית לפניך נשבע אני בשמך
הגדול שאיני זז מכאן עד שתרחם על בניך התחילו
גשמים מנטפין אמרו לו רבי ראינוך ולא נמות

תורה אור   מסרת הש"ס והמדרשים

4 ירמיה ה' כ"ה.   14 חבקוק ב' א'.   5 (הורודוס) ספרא שם; ויק"ר ל"ה
י'.   10 (מעשה) ירושלמי תענית
ג' י'; מנ"ת י"ב.

that we shall not die,[320] but it seems to us that
this rain comes only in order to free thee from
thy oath. "Ye have seen me and ye shall not
die," Ḥoni replied, and continuing his prayer
said, "Not for such rain did I pray, but for rain
sufficient to fill the cisterns, ditches and caves."
The rain then came down with vehemence, each
drop as big as the opening of a barrel, and the
Rabbis estimated that none of them contained
less than a *log*.[321] The people again said to him:
Master, we see thee, and this is a warranty that
we shall not die, but it seems to us that this rain
comes only to destroy the world. "Ye have
seen me and ye shall not die," he replied, and
then continued: "Not for such rain did I pray,
but for a rain of benevolence, blessing and
graciousness!" The rain then continued coming
in proper measure so that the Israelites had
to go up from the streets of Jerusalem to the
Temple Mount on account of the rain. They
then said to him: "Just as thou hast prayed for
the rain to come, so pray now that it should stop."
He, however, replied: "I have a tradition that it
is not proper to pray for the cessation of too
much good; however, bring ye to me a bullock
for the confession of my sins!"[322] They brought

[320] The exact meaning of this, as it seems, idiomatic
phrase is somewhat doubtful. See the commentaries of
R. Gershom and Rashi and the Hebrew Notes.

[321] Leviticus, 14. 12.

[322] So Rashi, but perhaps it means a bullock for a thanks-
giving-offering; comp. the commentary קרבן עדה on the
parallel passage in *Yerushalmi Ta'anit*, III,   11.

כמדומין אנו שאין הגשמים יורדין אלא להתיר

שבועתך אמר להם ראיתוני לא תמותו אמר לא

כך שאלתי אלא גשמי בורות שיחין ומערות ירדו

בזעף כל טפה וטפה כמלא פי חבית ושערו חכמים

5 אין טפה פחותה מלוג אמרו לו רבי ראינוך ולא

נמות כמדומין אנו שאין הגשמים יורדין אלא לשחת

את העולם אמר להם ראיתוני לא תמותו אמר לא

כך שאלתי אלא גשמי רצון ברכה ונדבה ירדו

כתקנן עד שעלו ישראל מירושלם להר הבית

10 מפני הגשמים אמרו לו כשם שהתפללת עליהם

שירדו כך התפלל עליהם שילכו להם אמר להם

כך מקובלני שאין מתפללין על רוב הטובה אף על

פי כן הביאו לי פר הודאה הביאו לו פר הודאה

מסרת הש"ס והמדרשים

1 (להתיר) ירושלמי שם ג' י"א;   תוספתא תענית ג' א'.   12 (רוב
מנ"ת שם. 10 (כשם) לעיל י"ט א';   (הטובה) לעיל כ"ב ב'.   13 (פר)
ירושלמי שם ג' י"א; מג"ת שם.

337

him a bullock, upon which Ḥoni laid both his
hands and said: "Master of the world! Thy
people Israel, whom Thou hast brought out of
Egypt, can stand neither too much good, nor too
much punishment; when Thou becamest wroth
(withholding rain), they could not stand it, and
now that Thou hast showered much good upon
them, they again cannot stand it; let it be Thy
will that there be ease in the world." Immediately the wind blew, the clouds dispersed and
the sun began to shine and the people went out
into the field and brought home morils and
truffles. Thereupon Simeon b. Shetaḥ sent word
to Ḥoni saying: "Wert thou not Ḥoni I would
order thy excommunication; if these years
were like those of Elijah, would not the name of
God be profaned through thee?[323] However,
what can I do since thou behavest petulantly
before God as a son behaves before his father,
who then grants the son's desire, so that if the
son says to him, bathe me in warm water, the
father bathes him in warm water; wash me with
cold water, he washes him in cold water; give
me nuts, peaches, almonds and pomegranates,
he gives him nuts, peaches, almonds and pomegranates. With regard to one like thee Scripture
says (Proverbs, 23.25): 'Let thy father and thy
mother be glad, and let her that bore thee
rejoice.'"

[323] Elijah swore in the name of God that there would
be no rain for years (I Kings, 17. 1ff.). In Ḥoni's time,
too, God might have decreed drought and it would therefore be sinful to importune God to break His oath.

סמך שתי ידיו עליו ואמר רבונו של עולם עמך
ישראל שהוצאת ממצרים אינן יכולין לעמוד לא
ברוב טובה ולא ברוב פורענות כעסת עליהם אינן
יכולין לעמוד השפעת להם טובה אינן יכולין לעמוד
5 יהי רצון מלפניך שיהא רוח בעולם מיד נשבה
הרוח ונתפזרו העבים וזרחה החמה ויצאו העם
לשדה והביאו להם כמהין ופטריות שלח לו שמעון
בן שטח אלמלא חוני אתה גוזרני עליך נדוי שאלו
שנים כשני אליהו לא נמצא שם שמים מתחלל על
10 ידיך אבל מה אעשה שאתה מתחטא לפני המקום
כבן שמתחטא לפני אביו ועושה לו רצונו אומר לו
רחצני בחמין רוחצו שטפני בצונן שוטפו תן לי
אגוזים אפרסקים שקדים ורמונים נותן לו עליך
הכתוב אומר ישמח אביך ואמך ותגל יולדתך:

תורה אור	מסרת הש״ס והמדרשים

14 משלי כ״ג כ״ה.   2 (לעמוד) ירושלמי וסנ״ת שם.
7 (שלח) לעיל י״ט א׳; ברכות י״ט
א׳; ירושלמי שם ג׳ י״ב; מו״ק ג׳ א׳; סנ״ת שם.   9 (שני אליהו) לעיל ח׳
ב׳; ספרא ריש בחקותי; ויק״ר ל״ה ט׳; ירושלמי שם ג׳ י״ב; מו״ק ג׳ א׳;
סנ״ת שם.   10 (סתחטא) לעיל י״ט א׳; ירושלמי וסנ״ת שם.   12 (בחמין
צונן) סנ״ת שם.

R. Naḥman b. R. Ḥisda discoursed: What message did the Synhedrin of the Hewn-Stone-Hall[324] send to Ḥoni the Circle-drawer? (They expounded to him the verses) (Job, 22. 28–30): "Thou shalt also decree a thing and it shall be established unto thee, and light shall shine upon thy ways. When they cast thee down, thou shalt say: 'There is lifting up'; for the humble person He saveth. He shall deliver even him that is not innocent, yea, thou shalt be delivered through the cleanness of thy hands."—"Thou shalt also decree a thing, and it shall be established unto thee," that is, thou hast decreed here below and the Holy One, blessed be He, established thy decree there above. —"And light shall shine upon thy ways," that is, a generation that was in gloom, thou hast brightened by thy prayer—"When they cast thee down, thou shalt say: 'There is lifting up'", that is, a generation that was cast down, thou hast lifted up by thy prayer. "For the humble person He saveth," that is, a generation whose eyes drooped down, thou hast saved by thy prayer. "He shall deliver even him that is not innocent," that is, a generation that is *not*[325] innocent, thou hast saved

[324] The hall in which the Synhedrin used to hold their sessions; see Mishnah *Middot*, V. 4.

[325] This agrees with the traditional translation of אי־נקי: *not* innocent, so also the Revised Version. The recent Jewish version issued by the Jewish Publication Society of America, Philadelphia, 1917, translates: That *is* innocent, taking אי as a particle (so also, perhaps, *Yerushalmi Ta'anit*, III, 12, and the Munich MS.; see the Hebrew

דרש רב נחמן בר רב חסדא מאי שלחו ליה בני

לשכת הגזית לחוני המעגל ותגזר אמר ויקם לך ועל

דרכיך נגה אור כי השפילו ותאמר גוה ושח עינים

יושע ימלט אי נקי ונמלט בבר כפיך ותגזר אמר

5 ויקם לך אתה גזרת מלמטה והקדוש ברוך הוא

קיים אמרך מלמעלה ועל דרכיך נגה אור דור

שהיה אפל האֹרתו בתפלתך כי השפילו ותאמר

גוה דור שהיה שפל הגבהתו בתפלתך ושח עינים

יושע דור שהיו עיניו שחות הושעתו בתפלתך ימלט

תורה אור	מסרת הש"ס והמדרשים
2 איוב כ'ב כ'ח.	5 (גזרת) מו'ק ט'ז ב'; שבת ס'ג א';
	ב'מ פ'ה א'; ירושלמי שם; ד'ר י'
ב' ג' (וע' ב'ר ע'ז א'); מדרש שמואל כ'ט; אגדת בראשית כ'ב.	
6 (דרכיך השפילו ימלט) ירושלמי תענית ג' י'ב.	

Notes), which, however, for obvious reasons, could not
be adopted here.

by thy prayer. "Yea, thou shalt be delivered
through the cleanness of thy hands," that is,
through the work of thy clean hands.[326]

Said R. Johanan: All his life long this righteous
man (Ḥoni) was troubled about this verse
(Psalms, 126. 1): "When the Lord brought back
those that returned to Zion, we were like unto
them that dream." Did anybody ever sleep
seventy[327] years (without interruption)? One day
while walking on the road he noticed a man
planting a carob-tree. Said Ḥoni to the man:
"You know that it takes seventy years before
a carob-tree bears fruit; are you so sure that
you will live seventy years and eat therefrom?"
"I found this world provided with carob-trees,"
the man replied, "as my ancestors planted

[326] It is not clear whether the Talmud refers ונמלט to
a third person (so the R. V.: *He* shall be delivered), here
the Israelites, who were delivered from dearth through
Ḥoni, or to Ḥoni himself (for ונמלטת, so Saadia and Abraham
Ibn Ezra, followed by the aforementioned Jewish Version:
Thou shalt be delivered; see the preceding note). In
the latter case the Talmud may allude to Ḥoni's escape
from the punishment which Simeon b. Sheṭaḥ said he
deserved, while if the word is referred to a third person,
the talmudic interpretation, "through the work of thy
clean hands," has no point, as it adds nothing to the verse;
comp. Büchler, *Types of Jewish-Palestinian Piety*, pp.
255ff.

[327] The Babylonian captivity referred to in this verse
lasted 70 years (Jer., 25. 11; 29. 10). The story about
Ḥoni (Onias), as given below, is a Jewish elaboration of

342

אי נקי דור שהיה לא נקי מלטתו בתפלתך ונמלט
בבר כפיך במעשה ידיך הברורים:

אמר רבי יוחנן כל ימיו של אותו צדיק היה מצטער
על מקרא זה שיר המעלות בשוב ה' את שיבת ציון
היינו כחלמים אמר שבעין שנין כחלמא יומא חד הוה
קא אזיל באורחא חזא ההוא גברא דקא נטע חרובא
אמר ליה מכדי חרובא עד שבעין שנין לא טעין פשיטא
לך דחיית שבעין שנין ואכלת מיניה אמר ליה אנא
עלמא בחרובא אשכחתיה כי היכי דשתלו לי אבהתי

תורה אור	מסרת הש"ס והמדרשים
4 תהלים קכ"ו א'.	5 (שבעין שנין) ירושלמי שם ג' י'.

similar stories current among other nations. Well known
is the legend about Epimenides of Crete, poet and prophet
of the 6th century B. C., who, tending his father's sheep,
is said to have fallen asleep in a cave near Cnossus, from
which he did not awake for 57 years. When the Athenians
were visited by pestilence, Epimenides was invited by
Solon to purify the city, which is a striking parallel to
what is told here of Ḥoni's invitation to pray for rain.
The Christian story of the Seven Sleepers is equally famous
and forms the subject of the eighteenth Surah of the Ḳorân;
comp. Burton's *Thousand Nights and a Night*, III, 128,
note 2; see also Rapoport, בכורי העתים, 1929, p. 74; יריעות
שלמה, p. 122; Büchler, *Types of Jewish-Palestinian Piety*,
pp. 196ff., 247ff.

them for me, so I plant them for my progeny."
Thereupon Ḥoni sat down to eat and was
overcome by sleep. As he slept, a grotto
was formed around him, so that the was screened
off from the human eye, and thus he slept for
seventy years. When he awoke, he saw a man
gathering carobs from the carob-tree and eating
them. "Do you know who planted this carob-
tree?" Honi asked. "My grandfather," the
man replied. "I must have slept seventy
years!" Ḥoni exclaimed. (He saw the many
herds that had descended from his she ass.)[327a]
He then went to his house and inquired whether
the son of Ḥoni the Circle-drawer was still a!ive.
He was told that the son was no longer among
the living, but that his grandson was still alive.
"I am Ḥoni," he said, but the people did not
believe him. He betook himself to the Bet ha-
Midrash where he heard the scholars say, "Our
studies are as clear to us today as they used to
be in the times of Ḥoni the Circle-drawer, for
when he came to the Bet ha-Midrash he used
to explain to the scholars all their difficulties."
He then said to them: "I am Ḥoni," but they
would not believe him nor would they show him
the respect due him. [This grieved him very
much], and he therefore prayed to God (that he
should die), and he died. Said Raba, hence
comes the popular proverb, "either a companion
or death!"

'Abba Hilkiah was the grandson of Ḥoni the
Circle-drawer. Once the Rabbis sent to him

[327a] Seems a later addition, see the Hebrew Notes.

אנא נמי אשתיל לבראי איתיב קא כריך ריפתא
אתיא ליה שנתא נים אהדרא ליה משוניתא איכסי
מעינא נים שבעין שנין כי קם חזא גברא דקא מנקיט
חרובי מההוא חרובא וקא אכיל אמר ליה ידעת
5 מאן שתליה להאי חרובא אמר ליה אבוה דאבא
אמר ודאי שבעין שנין כחלמא (חזא לחמרתיה
דילדא ליה רמכי רמכי) אזל לביתיה אמר להו
בריה דחוני המעגל מי קיים אמרו ליה בריה ליתיה
בר בריה איתיה אמר להו אנא הוא לא הימנוה
10 אזל לבי מדרשא שמעינהו לרבנן דקאמרי נהירן
שמעתתין האידנא כבשני חוני המעגל דכי הוה עייל
לבי מדרשא כל קושיא דהוה להו לרבנן הוה מפרק
לה אמר להו אנא הוא לא הימנוה ולא נהגו ביה
יקרא כדמבעי ליה בעא רחמי ונח נפשיה אמר
15 רבא היינו דאמרי אינשי או חברא או מיתותא:

אבא חלקיה בר בריה דחוני המעגל הוה זמנא
חדא אצטריך עלמא למטרא שדור רבנן זוגא דרבנן
מסרת הש"ס והמדרשים

a pair of scholars that he should pray for rain.
When they came to his house they did not find
him at home. They went to see him in the
field and found him ploughing the ground. They
greeted him [fol. 23b], but he did not heed them.
Towards evening he was picking up chips of wood
and, on his way home, carried the chips on one
shoulder and his cloak on the other. The whole
way long he did not put on his shoes, but when
he had to cross the water he put them on. When
he came across thorns and shrubs he lifted up his
garments, and when he reached the city, his wife
came to meet him bedecked with her finery.
When he arrived at the door of his house, he let her
enter first, then he followed. He sat down to eat,
but did not invite the scholars to join him. Dis-
tributing cakes to the children, he gave to the older
child one and to the younger two. Turning to his
wife, he said: "I know that these scholars came
to see me on account of rain; let us go up to the
roof and pray; the Holy One, blessed be He, will,
perhaps, accept our prayer and there will be
rain." When on the roof, he stood praying
in one corner and she in another. The clouds
appeared first over the corner where his wife
stood. He came down and asked the scholars:
"Why did the Rabbis come?" "The Rabbis
sent us to the Master, that you might pray for
rain to come," they replied. Said he: "Blessed
be the Lord who put you beyond the need of
Abba Hilkiah's prayer!" They, however, replied:
"We know well that this rain is come through
you, but be that as it may, we should like
you to explain to us those actions of yours that

לגביה למבעי רחמי ומיתי מטרא אזלו לביתיה לא
אשכחוה אזלו לגביה לדברא אשכחוה דהוה קא
רפיק רפקא יהבו ליה שלמא ולא אסבר להו   ^{כ"ג}
^{ע"ב}
אפי בפניא הוה קא מנקט ציבי כי קא אתי דרא
5   ציבי אחד כתפיה וגלימיה אחד כתפיה כולה
אורחא לא סיים מסאניה כי מטא למיא סיים
מסאניה כי מטא להיזמי והיגי דלינהו למניה כי
מטא למתא נפקא דביתהו לאפיה כי מקשטא כי
מטא לביתיה עיילא דביתהו ברישא והדר עייל איהו
10   אבתרה יתיב כרך ריפתא ולא אמר להו לרבנן תו
כרוכו פלג ריפתא לינוקי לקשישא יהב ליה חדא
ולזוטרא תרתי אמר לה לדביתהו ידענא דרבנן
אמטול מטרא אתו להו קום ניסק לאיגרא ונבעי
רחמי אפשר דמרצי קודשא בריך הוא ואתי מטרא
15   קם איהו בחדא זויתא ודביתהו בחדא זויתא קדים
סליק עננא מזויתא דדביתהו נחית אמר להו אמאי
אתו רבנן אמרו ליה שדרונן רבנן לגביה דמר למבעי
רחמי ומיתי מטרא אמר להו ברוך המקום שלא
הצריך אתכם לאבא חלקיה אמרו ליה ידעינן
20   דמטרא מחמת מר הוא דאתא אלא לימא לן מר

347

greatly surprised us: Why, when we greeted
you, did you not heed us?" "I hired myself out
for the day, so I thought I had no right to
interrupt my work." "Why did you carry the
chips of wood on one shoulder and your cloak
on the other?" "It is a borrowed garment,"
he said, "and it was loaned to me for the
purpose of wearing, but not for the purpose of
placing wood on it." "Why did you not put
on your shoes the entire way," the scholars continued, "but when you had to cross the water
you put them on?" "Because the entire way,"
he replied, "I could see (what I was stepping on),
in the water I could not see." "Why did you
lift up your garments when you came upon thorns
and shrubs?" "Because the one (a scratch on the
body) heals up, the other (a rent in the garment)
does not heal up." "Why did your wife come
to meet you so well dressed?" "In order that
I should not cast an eye upon another woman."
"Why did your wife enter the house first and you
after her?" "Because ye are not known to me.³²⁸"
"Why did you not invite us to eat with you?"
"Because there was not enough food and I
did not want to get your thanks for nothing."
"Why did you give one cake to the older child
and two to the younger?" "The older one stays
at home, while the younger goes to school."³²⁹

³²⁸ And he would not leave his wife behind him
unguarded.

³²⁹ בי כנשתא usually stands for synagogue; here, however,
study and not prayer was the object. One of the MSS.
has indeed בי מדרשא, but it may be a scribal change.

הני מלי דתמיהא לן מאי טעמא כי יהבין ליה

שלמא למר לא אסבר לן מר אפי אמר להו אגיר

יומא הואי ואמינא לא איפגר מאי טעמא דרא מר

ציבי אחד כתפיה וגלימיה אחד כתפיה טלית

שאולה היא להכי שאולה לי להכי לא שאולה לי 5

מאי טעמא כולה אורחא לא סיים מר מסאניה

כי מטא למיא סיים מסאניה כולה אורחא קא חזינא

במיא לא קא חזינא מאי טעמא כי מטא מר להיזמי

והיגי דלינהו למניה זה מעלה ארוכה וזה אינו מעלה

ארוכה מאי טעמא נפקא דביתהו דמר לאפיה כי 10

מקשטא שלא אתן עיני באשה אחרת מאי טעמא

עיילא איהי ברישא ומר אבתרה לא בדיקיתו לי

מאי טעמא לא אמר לן מר כרוכו ריפתא לא הוה

נפישא ריפתא ואמינא לא אחזיק בהו ברבנן טובת

חנם מאי טעמא יהב מר לקשישא חדא ולזוטרא 15

תרתי האי קאי בביתא והאי קאי בבי כנשתא מאי

מסרת הש"ס והמדרשים
9 (ארוכה) ב'ק צ'א ב'.

"Why did the clouds appear first over the corner where your wife was standing?" "Because the woman is usually in the house, and the good she does is direct.[330] (Or it may be because there were some highwaymen living in my neighborhood; I prayed that they should die, while she prayed that they should improve their ways)."[331]

Hanin Ha-Neḥba was the son of the daughter of Ḥoni the Circle-drawer. When the world needed rain, the Rabbis would send schoolchildren to him, who would pull him by the corners of his garments and say to him: "Father, Father! Give us rain!" Said Hanin: "Master of the world! Do it for the sake of these, who do not distinguish between the Father Who gives rain and a father who does not give rain." And rain came. Why was he named Hanin ha-Neḥba? Because (in his modesty) he used to hide himself.[332]

Said R. Zeriḳa to R. Safra: Come and see the difference between the imperious men of Palestine and the pious men of Babylonia. The pious men of Babylonia (namely R. Huna and R. Ḥisda), when there was need of rain, would say: "Come let us meet together in prayer; perad-

[330] That is, the hungry find immediate relief by her supply of food. The editions add, "But I give money, which is an indirect help," as the poor have to wait until they obtain food for the money. This is no doubt an explanatory note taken from Rashi.

[331] A later insertion based on Talmud *Berakot*, 10a; see the Hebrew Notes.

[332] Comp. Rapoport, *l. c.*, p. 73, and the Hebrew Notes.

טעמא קדים סליק עננא מההיא זויתא דהות קימא
דביתהו דמר משום דאתתא שכיחא בביתא ומקרבא
אהניתה (אי נמי הנך בריוני דהוו בשיבבותן אנא
בעינא רחמי דלימתו והיא בעיא רחמי דלהדרו
בתיובתא):

חנין הנחבא בר ברתיה דחוני המעגל הוה כי
הוה מצטריך עלמא למטרא הוו משדרי רבנן ינוקי
דבי רב לגביה (ונקטי ליה בשפולי גלימיה) ואמרי
ליה אבא אבא הב לן מטרא אמר לפניו רבונו של
עולם עשה בשביל אלו שאין מכירין בין אבא דיהיב
מטרא לאבא דלא יהיב מטרא ואתי מטרא ואמאי
קרי ליה חנין הנחבא שהיה מחביא עצמו בבית
הכסא:

אמר ליה רבי זריקא לרב ספרא תא חזי מה
בין תקיפי דארעא דישראל לחסידי דבבל חסידי
דבבל (רב הונא ורב חסדא) כי הוה מצטריך עלמא
למטרא אמרי נכניף לגבי הדדי ונבעי רחמי אפשר

מסרת הש״ס והמדרשים

3 (אהניתה) כתובות ס״ז ב׳.   14 (תא חזי) מגלה כ״ח ב׳; חולין
4 (דלהדרו) ברכות י׳ א׳.   קכ״ב א.

351

venture the Holy One, blessed be He, will accept
our prayer and rain will come;" but as to the
imperious men of Palestine, there is, for example, R. Jonah, the father of R. Mani, who,
when they needed rain, would go into the
house and say: "Get me my haversack and
I will go and buy grain for a *zuz*,"[333] whereupon
he would go to some cave-like, hidden place,
cover himself in sackcloth and pray until rain
came. When he came back he was asked, "Did
you bring anything?" "No," he answered, "I
thought that after this rainfall there would be
relief everywhere."

R. Mani, the son of R. Jonah, was annoyed by
members of the Patriarchal house, so he went and
prostrated himself upon the burial cave of his
father. One day when members of the Patriar-
chate happened to pass before the cave, the
legs of their horses were caught in the ground
and they could not move until they took upon
themselves not to annoy R. Mani again.

R. Mani used to attend the lectures of R.
Isaac b. Eliashib. Once he complained before the
latter that the rich members of his father-in-
law's house annoyed him. Said R. Isaac: "May
they become poor!" and they became poor.
(R. Mani then complained):[334] "They press
me for support" (whereupon R. Isaac said):
"May they become rich again!" and they became rich. (R. Mani then complained): "I am
not pleased with my wife."[335] (Whereupon R.

[333] See above, note 156.
[334] All the words in parentheses to the end of the para-

דמרצי קודשא בריך הוא ואתי מטרא תקיפי
דארעא דישראל כגון רבי יונה אבוה דרבי מני
כי הוה מצטריך עלמא למטרא הוה עייל לביתיה
ואמר להו הבו לי גואלקי אזיל אייתי בזוזא עבורא
5 אזל קאים בדוכתא עמיקתא וצניעא מכסי שקא
ובעי רחמי ואתי מטרא כי הוה אתי אמרי ליה אייתי
מר מידי אמר להו אמינא הואיל ואתא מטרא רווח
עלמא:

רבי מני בריה הוו קא מצערי ליה דבי נשיאה
10 אזל אשתטח אמערתא דאבוה יומא חד הוו קא חלפי
התם אינקוט כרעי דסוסותייהו עד דקבילו עליהו
דלא לצערו ליה:

הוה שכיח קמיה דרבי יצחק בן אלישיב אמר
ליה עתירי דבי חמי קא מצערו לי אמר ליענו איענו
15 קא דחקו לי ליעתרו איעתרו לא מקבלי אינשי

Isaac asked him): "What is her name?" "Hannah" (was the reply). "May Hannah become beautiful!" and Hannah became beautiful. "Now she lords it over me;" (whereupon R. Isaac said): "May Hannah become ugly again!" and Hannah became ugly again.

Two disciples, who used to attend the lectures of R. Isaac b. Eliashib, once said to him: "Pray for us that we may become more learned!" R. Isaac replied, "This power was once in my possession, but I have given it up."

R. Jose b. 'Abin used to attend the lectures of R. Jose of Yodḳart,[336] later he left him and went over to R. 'Ashi [fol. 24a]. One day he heard R. 'Ashi teaching in the name of Samuel: He that takes a fish out of the water on Sabbath is guilty of having desecrated the Sabbath (by killing) as soon as a piece (of the fish's body) as large as a *sela'* has become dry. To this statement R. Jose remarked that the dry spot must be between the fins. Said R. 'Ashi: Are you not aware of the fact that what you remarked was said by Jose b. 'Abin? "I am Jose b. 'Abin", he replied. "But were you not studying under R. Jose of Yodḳart?" "Yes, I was." "Why did you leave him and come here?" "How should a man who has no pity for his son and his daughter have any for me?" replied R. Jose b. 'Abin.

To what circumstance did he refer? He referred to the following event: One day R. Jose of Yodḳart had employed some laborers in the field.

[336] See above, note 302a.

ביתאי עלאי מה שמה חנה תתיפה חנה נתיפתה
חנה קא מגנדרא עלי תחזור חנה לשחרירותה חזרה
חנה לשחרירותה:

הנהו תרי תלמידי דהוו שכיחי קמיה דרבי יצחק

5 בן אלישיב אמרו ליה לבעי מר רחמי עלן דנחכים
טפי אמר להו עמי היתה ושלחתיה:

רבי יוסי בר אבין הוה שכיח קמיה דרבי יוסי
כ״ד
ע״א דמן ידקרת שבקיה ואתא לקמיה דרב אשי ׀ יומא
חד שמעיה דקא גריס אמר שמואל השולה דג מן
10 הים בשבת כיון שיבש בו כסלע חייב אמר ליה
איהו ובין סנפיריו אמר ליה ולא סבר לה מר דההיא
רבי יוסי בר אבין אמרה אמר ליה אנא הוא יוסי
בר אבין ולאו קמיה דרבי יוסי דמן ידקרת הוה
שכיח מר אמר ליה אין ומאי טעמא שבקיה מר
15 ואתא אמר ליה גברא דעל בריה ועל ברתיה לא
חס עלי דידי חייס:

בריה מאי היא יומא חד הוו אגירי ליה אגירי

מסרת הש״ס והמדרשים
9 (השולה) שבת ק״ז ב׳.

It became dark before R. Jose brought them
something to eat. The laborers therefore complained to R. Jose's son that they were hungry.
A fig-tree happened to be in the neighborhood, so
the son of R. Jose turned to that tree saying,
"Fig-tree, fig-tree! bring forth thy fruit, in order
that the laborers of my father may eat." The
tree immediately brought forth fruit and the
laborers ate. In the meantime his father (R.
Jose) arrived and, addressing the laborers,
said, "Do not bear me a grudge, the reason I
came late is because I was occupied by a matter
of charity, and it is only now that I was able
to come." They replied: "May the Merciful
satisfy thy hunger as thy son has satisfied ours!"
Said R. Jose, "What do you mean by that?"
They told him what had happened, whereupon
R. Jose said, "My son! Thou hast troubled thy
Creator to make the fig-tree yield fruit before
its time, so mayest thou be gathered in before
thy time."

What was the incident with his daughter? It
was the following: R. Jose of Yodḳart had a
beautiful daughter. One day he noticed a man
making a hole in the fence and gazing at her. R.
Jose asked him why he did that, whereupon the
man said, "If I had not the good fortune to marry
her, may I not have at least the privilege of
looking at her?" R. Jose then said: "Daughter,
daughter! Thou art a cause of trouble to hu-
manity, return to thy dust, in order that the
people should not stumble on thy account".

The same R. Jose had a she-ass which he
used to hire out. Those who hired her would

בדברא נגה ולא אייתי להו ריפתא אמרו ליה
לבריה כפנינן הוה תמן תאנה אמר תאנה תאנה
הוציאי פרותיך ויאכלו פועלי אבא אפקא ואכול
אדהכי והכי אתא אבוה אמר להו לא תנקטו
בדעתיכו דהאי דנגהנא אמצוה טרחנא ועד השתא
הוא דסגאי אמרו ליה רחמנא לשבעך כי היכי
דאשבען ברך אמר להו היכי הוה אמרו ליה הכי
והכי הוה אמר ליה בני אתה הטרחת את קונך
להוציא פרות תאנה שלא בזמנה תאסף שלא בזמנך:

ברתיה מה היא הויא ליה ברתא בעלת יופי יומא
חד חזייה לההוא גברא דהוה קא כרי בהוצי וקא
חזי לה אמר ליה מאי האי אמר ליה אם ללקחה
לא זכיתי לראותה לא אזכה אמר לה ברתי קא
מצערת לברייתא תובי לעפריך ואל יכשלו ביך
בני אדם:

הוייא ליה ההיא חמרא דכד הוו אגרי לה הוו

place the hire upon her back, and she would
walk home. If the amount was too much or
too little, the ass would not move from the
spot. One day a pair of sandals was forgotten
on the ass, and she refused to proceed until the
shoes were taken off.

The collectors of charity funds used to hide
themselves whenever they saw Eleazar of the
village of Bartota, because he was in the habit
of giving them everything he happened to possess.
One day he was going to the market in order to
buy a wedding outfit for his daughter, when
the collectors espied him and tried to hide
themselves. Eleazar, however, followed them
and said: "I adjure you to tell me for what
purpose you are collecting?" "For a marriage
between an orphaned boy and an orphaned
girl," they replied. "By the Service of the
Temple! they have precedence over my daughter," exclaimed he, and putting together all
that he had, he gave it to them, except one
zuz that remained in his possession. For this
he bought wheat and deposited it in the granary. Thereupon his wife inquired of her daughter what her father had brought her. "All
that he brought he took up to the granary,"
the daughter replied. The wife then went up to
the granary and found it full of wheat, to the
extent that it came through the door hinges.
When Eleazar returned from the Bet ha-Midrash,
she said to him, "Come and see what thy Friend
(God) has done for thee!" Said he: "By the

מותבי אגרא עילוה ואתיא לבי מרה ואי טפו לה או

בצרו לה לא אתיא יומא חד אינשי זוגא דסנדלי

עלה ולא אזלה עד דשקלוה מנה:

אלעזר איש כפר ברתותא כד הוו חזו ליה גבאי

5   צדקה הוו טשו מיניה דכל דהוה נקיט הוה יהיב להו

יומא חד סליק לשוקא למזבן נדוניא לברתיה

חזיוה גבאי צדקה טשו מיניה אזל בתריהו אמר

להו אשבעתיכו במאי עסקיתו אמרו ליה ביתום

ויתומה אמר להם העבודה שהן קודמין לבתי שקל

10   כל דהוה בהדיה ויהב להו פש בהדיה חד זוזא אזל

זבן ביה חטי ואסיק ואסיק שדייה באכלבא אתאי דביתהו

אמרה לה לברתה מai איתי לך אבוך אמרה לה

כל דאייתי לאכלבא אסקיה סלקא חזיא לאכלבא

דמליא חטי וקא נפקא בצנורא דדשא כי אתא מבי

15   מדרשא אמרה ליה בא וראה מה עשה לך אוהבך

359

service of the Temple! This wheat shall be sacred property and thy share in it shall not be more than that of any among the poor of Israel."[337]

R. Judah Nesiah (Patriarch) once ordained a fast during which he prayed for rain, but rain did not come. Said he: "What a difference between Samuel the Ramathite and Judah b. Gamaliel! [Samuel the Ramathite did not decree any fast and yet rain fell, while Judah decrees a fast and no rain comes!] Woe unto a generation that is placed in such a position! Woe unto him in whose lifetime such a thing happens!" and became very much discouraged, whereupon rain came.

The Patriarchal house once ordered a public fast, without informing R. Johanan and Resh Laḳish thereof. They informed them, however, the next morning. Resh Laḳish therefore said to R. Johanan: "How can we observe the fast, since we did not take it upon ourselves yester-night?"[338] Said R. Johanan, "We must follow their (the Patriarchs') ordinances."

The Patriarchal house once ordered a fast (during which they prayed for rain), but rain failed to come. 'Osha'yah, the younger from Ḥabraya, therefore, quoted to them the verse (Num., 15. 24): "Then it shall be, if it be done in error by the congregation, it being hid from their eyes," and illustrated it by the following simile:

[337] The reason given by the commentaries is that one should avoid deriving benefit from miracles (אין נהנין ממעשה נסים), see below, note 346.

[338] See above, notes 187–190a.

אמר לה העבודה הרי הן הקדש עליך ואין לך בהם

אלא כאחד מעניי ישראל:

רבי יהודה נשיאה גזר תעניתא בעא רחמי ולא

אתא מטרא אמר (כמה) משמואל הרמתי ליהודה

5 בן גמליאל אוי לו לדור שנתקע בכך אוי לו למי

שעלתה בימיו כך חלש דעתיה אתא מטרא:

דבי נשיאה גזור תעניתא ולא אודעינהו לרבי

יוחנן ולריש לקיש לצפרא אודעינהו אמר ליה ריש

לקיש לרבי יוחנן הא לא קבלינן עלן מאורתא

10 אמר ליה אנן בתריהו גרירינן:

דבי נשיאה גזור תעניתא בעו רחמי ולא אתא

מטרא תנא להו אושעיא זעירא דמן חברייא והיה

אם מעיני העדה נעשתה לשגגה משל לכלה בזמן

תורה אור

13 במדבר ט״ו כ״ד.

As long as a bride (in her paternal house) has beautiful eyes, the rest of her body needs no examination, but if her eyes are not beautiful, her entire body must be examined.[339] Hearing this, the servants of the Patriarch seized 'Osha'ya, put a towel (sudary) around his neck and began to choke him, but some townspeople who saw it said to them: "Let him go, for he used to harass us too, but when we saw that all his deeds were for the sake of Heaven we let him alone."

Rabbi once ordered a fast, and 'Ilfa or, as some say, R. 'Ilfi, went down at Rabbi's request to the praying desk, and as soon as he said the words, "He causes the wind to blow," a wind blew, and when he said, "He causes the rain to come down," rain fell. Rabbi thereupon asked him, "What is thy occupation?"[340] to which he replied: "I live in a poverty-stricken place (where there is no wine for Kiddush and Habdalah), but I make efforts and obtain wine for Kiddush and Habdalah and thus make the community discharge their duty."

Rab happened to come to a certain place, where he ordered a fast. The reader of the congregation then went down to the praying desk and recited, "He causes the wind to blow," and immediately a wind blew, and when he recited, "He causes the rain to fall," rain fell. Rab therefore asked him: "What is thy occupation?"[340] "I am a teacher of young children," he replied, "and I teach the children of the

[339] 'Osha'ya hinted that the patriarchal house, the

362

שעיניה יפות אין כל גופה צריך בדיקה אין עיניה
יפות כל גופה צריך בדיקה אתו עבדי ורמו ליה
סודרא בצואריה וקא מצערו ליה אמרו להו בני
מאתיה שבקוה דהא נמי מצער לן כיון דחזינן דכל
5 מליה לשום שמיא לא אמרינן ליה ולא מידי:

רבי גזר תעניתא נחית קמיה אילפא ואמרי לה
רבי אילפי אמר משיב הרוח נשא זיקא אמר מוריד
הגשם אתא מטרא אמר ליה מאי עובדך אמר ליה
דיירנא בקוסא רחיקא טרחנא ומיתינא קדושא
10 ואבדלתא ומפיקנא להו לצבורא ידי חובתיהו:

רב איקלע לההוא אתרא גזר תעניתא נחית קמיה
שליחא דצבורא אמר משיב הרוח נשא זיקא אמר
מוריד הגשם אתא מטרא אמר ליה מאי עובדך
אמר ליה מקרי ינוקי אנא ומקרינא לבני עניי כבני

מסרת הש״ס והמדרשים
3 (סודרא) ע״ז ד׳ א׳.   7 (נשא)   לקמן כ״ה ב׳; ב״מ פ״ה ב׳.

---

leaders (figuratively the "eyes") of the community, were
at fault, their sins causing suffering to the whole people.
[340] Or what are thy meritorious deeds? See above,
p. 318.

poor as well as those of the rich, and if any one is so poor that he is unable to pay, I take no fee from him. I possess a fish-pond, and if a child is careless in his studies, I bribe him by giving him some of the fish and thus win him over to study."

R. Naḥman once ordered a public fast, during which he prayed for rain, which, however, failed to come. He therefore said: "Take Naḥman and throw him down from the wall!" He felt greatly discouraged, and then rain came.

Raba ordered a fast, prayed for rain, but rain did not come. He was therefore asked: "Why is it that when R. Judah ordered a fast rain came?" "What can I do?" replied Raba. "As far as learning goes, we are superior to them; for in his time all studies [fol. 24b] were confined to the Section *Neziḳin* (Damages), while our studies embrace much more; when R. Judah reached in his studies the Mishnah (Ṭeharot, II, 1): 'If a woman was pressing vegetables in a pot,' or, as some say, the Mishnah ('Uḳḳaẓin, II, 1): 'Olives which have been pressed with their leaves are clean,' he would say: 'I see here problems as difficult as the discussions of Rab and Samuel,' while we to-day teach the tractate 'Uḳḳaẓin in thirteen different recensions.³⁴¹ [And yet when R. Judah took

---

³⁴¹ So Rashi on the parallel passage in *Berakot* 20a, while *Tosafot, ibid.*, declare it as a mere form of parlance, meaning we study it more thoroughly. Rashi, *Shabbat*, 119a, *s. v.* תריסר, quotes several passages of the Talmud, where thirteen is used to express an indefinite number, a multitude. In *Berakot, l. c.*, and in *Synhedrin,*

עתירי וכל דלא אפשר ליה לא שקילנא מיניה מידי
ואית לי פירא דכוורי וכל מאן דפשע בינוקי
משחידנא ליה בכוורי ‹ומשדלנא ליה ומפייסנא
ליה› עד דאתי וקרי:

5   רב נחמן גזר תעניתא בעא רחמי ולא אתא מטרא
אמר שקלוה לנחמן טריוה מגודא לארעא חלש
דעתיה אתא מטרא:

רבא גזר תעניתא בעא רחמי ולא אתא מטרא
אמרו ליה והא רב יהודה גזר תעניתא ואתא מטרא
10   אמר להו מאי אעביד אי משום תנויי אנן עדיפינן
מינייהו דבשני דרב יהודה כולהו תנויי בנזיקין הוה
ואנן קא מתנינן טובא וכי הוה מטי רב יהודה האשה
שכובשת ירק בקדירה ואמרי לה זיתים שכבשן
בטרפיהן אמר הויי דרב ושמואל קא חזינא הכא
15   ואנן קא מתנינן בעוקצין תליסר מתיבתא ‹ואלו

מסרת הש״ס והמדרשים

10 ‹תנויי› ברכות כ' א';   ק״ו ב';   סנהדרין   12 ‹האשה› טהרות ב' א'.
13 ‹זיתים› עוקצין ב' א'.

106b, however, Rashi (and so also pseudo-Rashi to our
passage) explains it to mean thirteen colleges that existed
in the place of Raba.

off one of his shoes[342] rain fell, while we cry (for rain) the whole day and nobody heeds us! Should it be because of our conduct—if there is anybody who has noticed anything wrong, let him testify against me.][343] However, what can the leaders do when the generation does not appear good enough in the eyes of God!"

R. Judah, seeing two men who were using bread in a wasteful manner, said: "It seems that there is too great plenty in the world." He cast an angry look about him and a famine came. Said the Rabbis to R. Kahana, son of R. Nehunya, the disciple of R. Judah: "Try thou, who art his disciple, to prevail upon him (R. Judah) that he should go out to the market-place."[344] He (R. Kahana) prevailed upon him. R. Judah went to the market, and noticing people crowding together, he asked: "What is the matter?" He was told that they were standing around a mass of offals of ground dates which was for sale. "There is evidently a famine in the country," said R. Judah, and ordered his disciple to pull his shoes from his feet. The disciple pulled off one of his master's shoes, and when he was about to pull off the other, Elijah appeared to him saying: "If you pull off the other shoe, you will destroy the world."[345]

[342] With the beginning of a fast the shoes had to be taken off; see above, fol. 12b; comp. also the Mishnah, above, p. 6, 12.

[343] For this addition see the Hebrew Notes.

[344] So that he might see with his own eyes the suffering that he brought upon the people by causing the famine.

[345] This is not quite clear. It may have been meant

366

רב יהודה כי הוה שליף חד מסנא אתי מטרא ואנן
קא צוחינן כולי יומא וליכא דמשגח בן אי משום
עובדא אי איכא דחזא מידי לימא) אלא מה יעשו
פרנסי הדור שאין דורן דומה יפה:

רב יהודה חזנהו להנהו בי תרי דהוו קא פרצי 5
בריפתא אמר שמע מינה איכא שבעא בעלמא יהב
עיניה הוה כפנא   אמרו ליה רבנן לרב כהנא בריה
דרב נחוניא שמעיה מר דשכיח קמיה נעשייה
דליפוק לשוקא עשייה נפק לשוקא חזא כנופיא
אמר להו מאי האי אמרו ליה אכוספא דתמרי 10
דקא מזדבן אמר שמע מינה איכא כפנא בעלמא
אמר ליה לשמעיה שלוף לי מסאני שלף ליה חד
מסנא כי מטא למשלף אחרינא אתא אליהו אתחזי
ליה אמר ליה אי שלפת אחרינא מחרבת ליה
לעלמא: 15

מסרת הש"ס והמדרשים
1 (שליף) ברכות כ' א'; סנהדרין   4 (דומה) לעיל כ"ב ב'; ירושלמי
ק"ו ב'; ירושלמי תענית ג' י"ג.   תענית ג' ד'.   14 (שלפת אחרינא)
ירושלמי תענית ג' י"ג.

as a warning that he should not importune God too much
by self-humiliation, as rain was about to come (as above
in the story of R. Judah, who brought rain by pulling off
one shoe), or because rain was *not* to come, as seems to be
borne out by the following story of R. Mari that the sand
turned into flour, etc.

Said R. Mari, son of the daughter of Samuel: I was standing (on the day the miracle was performed by R. Judah) on the bank of the River Papa, and saw angels, disguised as sailors, filling ships with sand, which turned into fine flour. Everybody tried to obtain some, but they were told that they should not buy that kind of flour, because it was the product of a miracle.[346] The next morning ships laden with wheat arrived from Parzina.[347]

Raba once came to Hagrunya, where he ordered a fast and prayed for rain, but rain did not come. He therefore advised the people to continue their fast over night. The next morning he said to them: "Is there any one among you who saw something in a dream last night?" Said to him R. Eleazar of Hagrunya, I dreamed that I read the following words: "Good health to the good master from the good Lord, who will grant of His goodness to His people." Raba then said: "It is evident that the time is propitious;" accordingly he prayed and rain fell.

A certain man was sentenced in the court of Raba to be lashed because he had sexual intercourse with a Gentile woman. Raba had the lashing administered to him, and the man died of the effects. The matter came to the hearing of king Shabur (Sapor), who wanted to punish Raba for the deed, but 'Ifra 'Ormuzd, mother

[346] See above, note 337.
[347] The sources differ as to the name of the place (?); comp. Kohut, *Aruch*, *s. v.* ארזן, and the Hebrew Notes.

אמר רב מרי ברה דבת שמואל אנא הוה קאימנא

אגודא דנהר פפא חזאי למלאכי (דאידמו למלחי)

דאיתי חלא ומלונהו לארבי והוה קמחא וסמידא

אתו כולי עלמא למזבן אמרי להו מהא לא תזבנון

5 דמעשה נסים הוא למחר אתיאן חטי דפרזינאי:

רבא איקלע להגרוניא גזר תעניתא בעא רחמי

ולא אתא מטרא אמר להו ביתו כולי עלמא

בתעניתיכו למחר אמר להו מי איכא דחזא מידי

בחלמא אמר ליה רב אלעזר מהגרוניא לדידי

10 אקריון בחלמא שלם טב לרב טב מרבון טב

דמטוביה מיטיב לעמיה אמר שמע מינה עת רצון

היא בעא רחמי ואתא מטרא:

ההוא גברא דאיחייב נגדא בי דיניה דרבא דבעל

גויה נגדיה רבא ומית אשתמעא מלתא בי שבור

15 מלכא בעו לצעוריה אמרה ליה איפרא הורמיז

מסרת הש"ס והמדרשים

11 (עת רצון) ברכות ח' א'; יומא   ס"ט א'; יבמות ע"ב א'; סנהדרין
ס"ד א'.

369

of king Shabur, said to him: "Have no quarrels
with the Jews, because anything they ask of
their God, He does for them." Said he: "What,
for instance?" "They pray for rain," she replied, "and rain comes." Said he: "That is
because it is the season when rain is due, let
them pray for it now, in the equinox of Tammuz, and bring down rain!" 'Ifra 'Ormuzd
thereupon sent word to Raba that he should
concentrate his mind and pray for rain. Raba
did so, but no rain came. Said he: "Master
of the world! 'O God, we have heard with our
ears, our fathers have told us, what work Thou
didst in their days, in the days of old' (Ps.,
44.2), but we did not see it with our own
eyes." Immediately a heavy rain fell, so that the
gutters of Maḥuza carried the water into the
Tigris. Thereupon Raba's father appeared to
him in a dream, saying: "Is there another man
who puts Heaven to so much trouble! Change
thy place."[348] (He did so and) the next morning
he found that his bed was scratched with knives.

R. Papa ordered a fast but, feeling very weak,
took some food. He then prayed, but no rain
came. R. Naḥman b. 'Ish Prati (of the Euphrates) then said to him: "If you had swallowed a plate of grit, rain would have come."
R. Papa felt humiliated, and then rain came.

[348] It was a general belief that by changing one's place
(here the bed in which Raba was to sleep) one might escape
the evil that was to befall him.

370

אימיה דשבור מלכא לברה לא ליהוי לך פיקר
בהדי יהודאי דכל דבעין ממריהו עביד להו אמר
לה מאי היא בעון רחמי ואתי מטרא אמר לה ההוא
משום דזמנא דמטרא הוא לבעי רחמי האידנא
בתקופת תמוז וליתי מטרא שלחה ליה לרבא כוין
דעתך ובעי רחמי דליתי מטרא בעא רחמי ולא
אתא מטרא אמר לפניו רבונו של עולם אלהים
באזנינו שמענו אבותינו ספרו לנו פעל פעלת בימיהם
בימי קדם אבל אנו בעינינו לא ראינו אתא מטרא
עד דשפוך מרזבי דמחוזא לדיגלת אתחזי ליה
אבוה בחלמיה אמר ליה מי איכא דמטרח קמי
שמיא כולי האי שני דוכתיך שני דוכתיה למחר
אשכחיה לפורייה דמרשם בסכיני:

רב פפא גזר תעניתא חלש לביה טעים מידי
בעא רחמי ולא אתא מטרא אמר ליה רב נחמן בר
איש פרתי אי שריף מר חדא פנכא דדיסא הוה אתי
מטרא חלש דעתיה אתא מטרא:

תורה אור

7 תהלים מ״ד ב׳.

371

R. Ḥanina b. Dosa once travelled on the road,
when it began to rain. Said he: "Master of
the world! The whole world is at ease, but
Ḥanina alone is in distress!" The rain stopped.
When he came home, he said again: "Master
of the world! The whole world is in distress,
while Ḥanina alone is at ease!" The rain
came again. Said R. Joseph, what good did the
prayer of the high priest do if R. Ḥanina could
make it to naught? For we read in a Mishnah
that the high priest used to recite a short prayer
in the outer hall. What was the prayer?
R. 'Abin b. R. 'Adda and Raba b. R. 'Adda said,
both in the name of R. Judah, the prayer ran
thus: "May it be Thy will, Lord our God,
that this year be one of heat and rain." Is
a hot year of any benefit? On the contrary,
it is a calamity! But the prayer read thus: "If
the year is to be hot, let it also be blessed with
ample rain, and may the prayers of travellers
find no hearing before Thee." R. Aḥa the son of
Raba reported in the name of R. Judah the
following conclusion(of the prayer): "May the
rulership never depart from the house of Judah
and may Thy people Israel never be in need
of supporting one another or of assistance from
other people."³⁴⁹

Said R. Judah in the name of Rab: Every
day a Heavenly Voice comes forth and says: "The
whole world is supplied with food only on account

³⁴⁹ See Targum to Genesis, 49. 10.

רבי חנינא בן דוסא הוה קא אזיל באורחא אתא
מטרא אמר לפניו רבונו של עולם כל העולם כלו
בנחת וחנינא בצער פסק מטרא כי מטא|לביתיה
אמר רבונו של עולם כל העולם כלו בצער וחנינא
בנחת אתא מטרא אמר רב יוסף מאי אהניא ליה
צלותיה דכהן גדול לגבי רבי חנינא בן דוסא דתנן
מתפלל תפלה קצרה בבית החיצון מאי מצלי רבין
בר רב אדא ורבא בר רב אדא תרויהו משמיה
דרב יהודה אמרי יהי רצון מלפניך ה' אלהינו
שתהא שנה זו שחונה וגשומה שחונה מעליותא היא
אדרבא גריעותא היא אלא אם שחונה תהא גשומה
ולא תכנס לפניך תפלת עוברי דרכים רב אחא
בריה דרבא מסיים בה משמיה דרב יהודה לא
יעדי עביד שולטן מדבית יהודה ולא יהיו עמך
ישראל צריכין לפרנסה זה מזה ולא לעם אחר:
אמר רב יהודה אמר רב בכל יום ויום בת קול
יוצאת ואומרת כל העולם כלו אינו נזון אלא

מסרת הש"ס והמדרשים

1 (חנינא) יומא נ"ג ב'.   7 (מתפלל)   ג'.   16 (בת קול) ברכות י"ז ב';
יומא נ"ב ב'; ירושלמי יומא ה'   חולין פ"ו א'.

of my son Ḥanina, while he is satisfied with one *ḳab*[350] of carobs from one Sabbath eve to the other." Every Friday R. Ḥanina's wife would throw some smoke-producing matter into the oven [fol. 25a], because she was ashamed (to have it known that she had nothing to bake for the Sabbath). She had, however, a certain neighbor who said: "I surely know that she has nothing (to bake), let me go and see what causes that smoke." She went in and found the stove full of bread and a kneading-trough full of dough. She therefore exclaimed: "Hear! Hear! Bring a shovel, for your bread is getting charred!" It is taught in a Baraita that R. Ḥanina's wife actually went for a shovel, because she was used to miracles (and therefore did not assume that the woman was mocking her).

Once the wife of R. Ḥanina said to her husband: "Pray that some of the good which is stored up for the righteous in the world to come may be given to you here." He prayed and a leg of a golden table was swung into his house, but subsequently he saw in a dream that all other people would dine on a table with three legs, while he would dine on a table with two legs. She then said to him: "Pray that they should take it (the golden leg) back." He did so and it was taken back. It was taught in a Baraita that the latter miracle was greater than the former, for there is a tradition that things prayed for may be granted, but (when granted) are never taken back.

[350] See above, note 62.

בשביל חנינא בני וחנינא בני דיו קב חרובים מערב
שבת לערב שבת:

כל מעלי שבתא הות רגילא דביתהו דשדיא
אקטרתא בתנורא | משום כסופא הות לה ההיא
שיבבתא אמרה מכדי ידענא דמידי לית לה איזיל
אחזי מאי האי אזלא אשכחתיה לתנורא דמלי ריפתא
ואגנא דמלי לישא אמרה לה פלניתא פלניתא איתא
מסא דחריכא ליך ריפתיך תנא אף היא להביא
מרדא נכנסה מפני שמלומדת בנסין:

אמרה ליה דביתהו מטיבותא דגניזא להו לצדיקי
לעלמא דאתי בעי רחמי דלתנון לך מידי בעא
רחמי שדו ליה חד כרעא דכואנא דדהבא חזא
בחלמא דכולי עלמא קא אכלי אכואנא דתלתא
כרעי ואיהו על דתרתין כרעי אמרה ליה בעי
רחמי דלשקלוה בעא רחמי ושקלוה תנא גדול
נס האחרון יותר מן הראשון דגמירי מיהב יהבי
משקל לא שקלי:

11 (לעלמא דאתי) שמ"ר נ"ב ג'; ‏ בר"ש.) ‏ 16 (נס האחרון) שמ"ר
רות רבה ג' ד' (ושם העובדא ‏ ורות רבה שם; שהש"ר ה' פסוק
י"ד אות ב'.

One Friday eve Ḥanina saw that his daughter
was sad. He asked her, "Why are you so down-
cast?" "Because I mistook a vessel containing
vinegar for a vessel containing oil and poured
the vinegar into the lamp." "My daughter,"
said Ḥanina, "He who ordained that oil should
burn, will ordain that vinegar should burn." It
was reported that the lamp continued burning,
so that on Saturday evening they still used its
light for *Habdalah*.

R. Ḥanina had some goats and was told that
they were damaging people's property. Said he:
"If they really do damage, may bears devour
them, but if not, may they bring the bears im-
paled on their horns." In the evening each of
the goats brought a bear on its horns.

R. Ḥanina had a neighbor who once said to
him: "I have built a house for myself and
the joists are not long enough to reach from
one wall to the other." Said he: "What is
thy name?" "My name is 'Eiku," she replied.
Said he: "'Eiku, 'Eiku! May thy joists reach
the walls."[351]

It was taught: Pelimo said, I saw that house;
its beams protruded an ell on each side,
and people told me: This is the house which
R. Ḥanina b. Dosa covered with beams through
his prayer. Some say that joints were added
to the beams by a miracle.[352]

---

[351] The name אַיְכוּ suggested to him the Greek εἶκε =
would that! (*sc.* the joists may reach the walls); see the
Hebrew Notes.

[352] That is, instead of the original short joists getting

חד בי שמשי חזייה לברתיה דהות עציבא אמר
לה אמאי עצבת דאיחלף לי מנא דמשחא במנא
דחלא ורמאי בשרגא אמר לה בתי מי שאמר לשמן
שידלוק יאמר לחמץ וידלוק תנא היה דולק והולך
5 עד שנטלו ממנו אור להבדלה:

הוין ליה הנך עיזי אמרו ליה קא מפסדן אמר
אי קא מפסדן ניכלינהי דובי ואי לא ליתיין דובי
בקרניהי לאורתא אתיא כל חדא וחדא דובא
בקרנה:

10 הויא ליה ההיא שיבבתא אמרה ליה בנאי לי ביתא
ולא קמטו כשורי אמר לה מה שמיך אמרה ליה
איכו אמר איכו נימטו כשוריך תנא פלימו אומר אני
ראיתי אותו הבית והיו קורותיו יוצאות אמה לכאן
ואמה לכאן ואמרו לי זהו הבית שקרה רבי חנינא
15 בן דוסא בתפלתו ויש אומרין סניפין עשאום:

4 (דולק והולך) ב״ר י״א ב׳; פס״ר   כ׳ג פסוק על כן ברך ה׳.   6 (עיזי)
ב״מ ק״ו א׳.

---

longer by a miraculous stretching, new pieces were added
by a miracle. For the story about the goats which follows
here in the editions of the Talmud, see the Hebrew Notes.

R. Eleazar b. Pedat was greatly distressed by poverty. One day he was bled, and after the operation had nothing to eat. He found some garlic and swallowed it, whereupon he fainted. Some of the Rabbis went to visit him and noticed that he was weeping and laughing, and that a ray of light proceeded from his forehead. When he awoke, they asked him: "Why did you weep and laugh, and why did a ray of light proceed from your forehead?" "I saw the Shekinah," he replied, "and complained before her, saying, 'how long shall I continue to live in this poverty?' and the Shekinah replied to me: 'Would it be acceptable to thee that I should destroy the world and create it anew? Perhaps thou wilt then be born in an hour that will betoken plenty for thee.' I said, 'So much trouble for a mere *perhaps?*' [I further said: 'Is the time which I have already lived greater than the time I am yet to live, or the reverse?' I was told: 'The time thou hast lived is greater.' 'If so,' said I, 'I do not care to be reborn.'] I then asked: 'What wilt thou give me in the world to come?' 'Thou wilt be given,' the answer was, 'thirteen rivers flowing with balsam oil, in which thou wilt find pleasure.' Said I, 'Is that all?' [The Shekinah replied: 'What am I to give to thy fellowmen if thou takest everything?' But I said: 'Do I ask it of one who is not in a

רבי אלעזר בן פדת הוה דחיקא ליה מלתא
טובא עבד מלתא ולא הוה ליה מידי למטעם
אשכח ברה דתומא שדא פומיה חלש לביה עיילי
רבנן לשיולי ביה חזיוה דבכא וחייך ונפק צוציתא
5 דנורא מאפותיה כי אתער אמרו ליה מאי טעמא
בכא מר וחייך ונפק צוציתא דנורא מאפותיה
אמר להו דחזאי שכינה ואמרי קמיה עד אימת
אידבר ואיזיל בהאי דוחקא אמר לי ניחא לך
דאחרביה לעלמא והדר אבריה אפשר דנפלת
10 בשעתא דמזוני אמרי קמיה כולי האי ואפשר (דחיי
נפיש או דחיינא אמר לי דחיית אמרי קמיה אי הכי
לא בעינא) אמרי קמיה לעלמא דאתי מאי יהבת לי
אמר לי יהיבנא לך תליסר נהרי דמשכי אפרסמא
דמעגנת בהו אמרי קמיה ותו לא (אמר ליולחברך
15 מאי יהיבנא אמרי קמיה ואנא מגברא דלית ליה קא

מסרת הש״ס והמדרשים

13 (תליסר נהרי) ירושלמי ע״ז ג'   בראשית סימן א' (ועיי״ש ויחי ד'
א'; ב'ר ס״ב ב'; תנחומא (הנדפס)   ושמ״ר נ״ב ג'); פסדר״כ סוף ברכה.

position to give?"].³⁵³ I was then struck on my
forehead by the snapping of a thumb and was
asked: 'Eleazar my son, do my arrows irritate
thee?' "³⁵⁴

R. Ḥanina b. Ḥama ordered a fast, but no
rain came. The people asked, "Why is it that
when R. Joshua b. Levi orders a fast rain does
fall?" R. Ḥanina replied: "I am I (Ḥanina) and
he is the son of Levi!"³⁵⁵ They sent for him (R.
Joshua), and R. Ḥanina said to him: "Come let
us put our minds in the right spirit of prayer;
perchance the community too will become con-
trite and pray, and rain will come." They all
prayed, but there was no rain. R. Ḥanina then
said: "Is it your desire that rain shall descend
for our sake?" They said "Yes!" R. Ḥanina
then called: "Sky! sky! cover thy face (with
clouds)!" But the sky did not cover itself.
Then he said: "How impudent art thou, O sky!"
The sky thereupon covered itself and rain came.

Levi ordered a fast, prayed for rain, but none
came. Said he: "Master of the world! Thou
hast gone up and taken Thy seat in heaven and
showest no consideration for (the suffering of)
Thy children." Rain fell, but Levi became lame.
Said R. Eleazar, one must never reproach God,

³⁵³ Regarding the passages in brackets, see the Hebrew
Notes.

³⁵⁴ The meaning of this question is not quite clear. The
various interpretations (see the Hebrew Notes) are un-
satisfactory.

³⁵⁵ Meaning: I am not so great a man as R. Joshua b.
Levi. According to Dr. Louis Ginzberg the words of R.

בעינא) טרק לי באסקוטלא באפותאי ואמר לי

אלעזר ברי איגרו בך גירי:

רבי חנינא בר חמא גזר תעניתא בעא רחמי ולא

אתא מטרא אמרו ליה והא רבי יהושע בן לוי גזר

5   תעניתא ואתא מטרא אמר להו הא אנא והא בר

ליואי שלחו וקרו ליה אמר ליה ניתי ונכוין דעתין

אפשר דתברי צבורא לביהו ובעו רחמי ואתי

מטרא בעון רחמי ולא אתא מטרא אמר להם

רצונכם שיבא מטר בשבילנו אמרו לו הין אמר

10   רקיע רקיע כסה פניך לא איכסי אמר כמה עזין

פני רקיע איכסי ואתא מטרא:

לוי גזר תעניתא בעא רחמי ולא אתא מטרא

אמר לפניו רבונו של עולם עלית וישבת במרום ואי

אתה משגיח על בניך אתא מטרא ואטלע:

15   אמר רבי אלעזר לעולם אל יטיח אדם דברים

מסרת הש״ס והמדרשים

3 ⟨ר״ח בר חמא⟩ ע' ירושלמי כאן   תענית ג' ח'.   15 ⟨לעולם⟩ מגלה

ג' ד'.   13 ⟨אמר לפניו⟩ ע' ירושלמי   כ״ב ב'; סוכה נ״ג א'; ירושלמי

סוכה ה' ד'.

Hanina expressed his doubts as to the efficacy of R.
Joshua b. Levi's prayers, and consequently the passage
should be translated: "Here am I and here is the son of
Levi", *i. e.* let us see whether he will succeed where I failed.

for a great man once reproached God and became lame. Was that the cause thereof? Was
it not stated that Levi showed to Rabbi how
to make a certain kind of prostration[356] and on
that occasion became lame? Both incidents were
the cause of his lameness.[357]

R. Ḥiyya b. Luliani overheard the clouds
saying: "Let us pour rain on Ammon and
Moab." Said he to them: When the Holy One,
blessed be He, offered His Torah to the various
nations and tongues they did not accept it, until
Israel came and accepted it. Now ye are ready
to pass over Israel and pour your rain upon
Ammon and Moab! Pour down the rain on
the spot below you! And they did so.

R. Ḥiyya b. Luliani once discoursed: Why is it
written (Ps., 92. 13): "The righteous shall flour-
ish like the palm-tree; he shall grow like a
cedar in Lebanon?" If the righteous is compared to a palm-tree, why is he compared to
a cedar, and if he is compared to a cedar why
should he be compared to a palm-tree? Because
if Scripture had only mentioned the palm-tree
and not the cedar, one might have said that just
as a palm-tree [fol. 25b] does not produce young
shoots, so neither does the righteous. Scripture

[356] He prostrated himself and tried to get up by supporting himself on his toes, without using his hands, thus
dislocating his thigh.

[357] That is, his attempt to rise in the manner described
was made the occasion for his punishment (for reproaching
God).

כלפי למעלה שהרי אדם גדול הטיח דברים כלפי
למעלה ואטלע ומנו לוי והא גרמא ליה והאמר מר
לוי אחוי קדה קמיה דרבי ואטלע הא והא גרמא
ליה:

5 רבי חייא בר לוליני שמעינהו לענני דקאמרי
ניזיל נשדי מטרא בעמון ומואב אמר להו כשהחזיר
הקדוש ברוך הוא את התורה על כל אומה ולשון
ולא קבלוה עד שבאו ישראל וקבלוה ואתון שבקתון
ישראל ושדיתון בעמון ומואב שדו אדוכתיכו שדונהו

10 אדוכתיהו:

דרש רבי חייא בר לוליני מאי דכתיב צדיק
כתמר יפרח כארז בלבנון ישגה אם נאמר תמר
למה נאמר ארז ואם נאמר ארז למה נאמר תמר
אלו נאמר תמר ולא נאמר ארז הייתי אומר מה תמר

כה"ג
ע"ב 15 | אין גזעו מחליף אף צדיק אין גזעו מחליף לכך

<table>
<tr><td>תורה אור</td><td>מסרת הש"ס והמדרשים</td></tr>
</table>

11 תהלים צ"ב י"ג.   3 (קדה) מגלה כ"ב ב'; סוכה נ"ג
א'; ב"ר ל"ט י"ב.   12 (תמר ארז)
ב"ב פ"ב'; ב"ר מ"א א'; במ"ר ג' א'; תנחומא (באבער) לך לך אות ט'
(בנדפס ה'), במדבר אות י"ז (ט"ו); מדרש תהלים מזמור צ"ב.

therefore compares him also to a cedar; if, on the other hand, Scripture only mentioned the cedar and not the palm-tree, one might have said that just as a cedar bears no fruit, so neither does the righteous, therefore Scripture has both palm-tree and cedar.

Does a cedar produce young shoots? Do we not read in a Baraita: He who buys a tree from his neighbor in order to fell it, must cut it a hand-breadth above the ground;[358] if the tree is a virgin-sycamore, he must cut it three hand-breadths above the ground;[358] and if it is a truncated sycamore, he must cut it two hand-breadths above ground;[358] if he buys reeds and vine, he must cut them above the knot;[359] in case of palm-trees and cedars he may dig deep in the ground and uproot them, because they do not produce young shoots! Answer. In the passage above (of R. Ḥiyya) reference is had to different kinds of cedars, which is in keeping with a statement of Rabbah b. R. Huna; for Rabbah b. R. Huna said that it was taught in the School of Rab: There are ten kinds of cedars, as it is said (Is., 41. 19): "I will plant in the wilderness the cedar, the acacia-tree, and the myrtle, and the oil-tree; I will set in the desert the cypress, the plane-tree and the larch together."[360]

[358] So that the piece remaining above ground may send out new shoots.

[359] Where the plant begins to branch out.

[360] In the parallel passage in *Rosh ha-Shanah*, 23a, the question is raised that Isaiah counts only *seven*, and in reply three more are quoted from a Baraita.

נאמר ארז ואלו נאמר ארז ולא נאמר תמר הייתי

אומר מה ארז אין עושה פרות אף צדיק אין עושה

פרות לכך נאמר תמר ונאמר ארז וארז גזעו מחליף

והתניא הלוקח אילן מחברו לקוץ מגביה מן

הקרקע טפח וקוצץ בתולת השקמה שלשה טפחים

סדן שקמה שני טפחים בקנים ובגפנים מן הפקק

ולמעלה בדקלים ובארזים חופר ומשרש לפי שאין

גזעו מחליף הכא במאי עסקינן בשאר מיני ארזים

כדרבה בר רב הונא דאמר רבה בר רב הונא אמרי

בי רב עשרה מיני ארזים הם שנאמר אתן במדבר

ארז שטה והדס ועץ שמן אשים בערבה ברוש תדהר

ותאשור יחדו:

תורה אור	מסרת הש״ס והמדרשים

10 ישעיה מ״א י״ט.

2 (אין עושה פרות) ב״ר מ״א א'
במ״ר ג' א'.   4 (הלוקח) ב״ב פ
ב'; שביעית ד' ה' ו'.   7 (ארזים) ר״ה כ״ג א'; סוכה ל״ז א'; ב״ב פ
ב'; ירושלמי כתובות ספ״ז'; ב״ר ט״ו א'; ש״ר ל״ה א'; תנחומא תרומה
ט' (באבער נ״ו).

Our Rabbis have taught: It happened once that R. Eliezer decreed thirteen fast days for the community and yet no rain came. Finally, the people began to leave the synagogue. Said he to them: "Did you prepare graves for yourselves?" All the people burst forth crying, whereupon rain descended.

Another time it happened again that R. Eliezer went before the ark and said the twenty-four benedictions,[361] but his prayer was not answered. R. 'Akiba then succeeded him before the ark and said: Our Father, our King! We have sinned before Thee, our Father, our King, we have no king beside Thee. Our Father, our King! have compassion upon us! His prayer was answered, and the Rabbis therefore began to utter suspicion against R. Eliezer. However, a heavenly voice came forth and proclaimed: Not that R. 'Akiba is greater than R. Eliezer, but the one is of a forbearing disposition, while the other is not.

Our Rabbis have taught: How much rain must fall in order that the congregation may stop fasting? There must be rain enough to penetrate the cavity made by the plough; this is the opinion of R. Meir; R. Judah said, if the soil is dry (hard), it is enough if the rain penetrates to the depth of a hand-breadth, in moderately soft soil the penetration of two hand-breadths is required, and in tilled (loose) ground three hand-breadths.

[361] The eighteen daily benedictions and the six additional ones prescribed for public fasts; see above, p. 204.2.

תנו רבנן מעשה ברבי אליעזר שגזר שלש עשרה
תעניות על הצבור ולא ירדו גשמים באחרונה
התחילו הצבור לצאת אמר להם תקנתם קברים
לעצמכם געו כל העם בבכיה וירדו גשמים שוב

5 מעשה ברבי אליעזר שירד לפני התבה ואמר עשרים
וארבע | ברכות ולא נענה ירד אחריו רבי עקיבא
ואמר אבינו מלכנו חטאנו לפניך אבינו מלכנו אין
לנו מלך אלא אתה אבינו מלכנו רחם עלינו ונענה
הוו קא מרני רבנן יצתה בת קול ואמרה לא מפני

10 שזה גדול מזה אלא שזה מעביר על מדותיו וזה
אינו מעביר על מדותיו:

תנו רבנן עד מתי יהיו גשמים יורדין ויהיו צבור
פוסקין מתעניתם כמלא ברך המחרשה דברי רבי
מאיר רבי יהודה אומר בחרבה טפח בבינונית

15 טפחים ובעבודה שלשה טפחים:

מסרת הש״ס והמדרשים

6 (ר׳ עקיבא) ירושלמי ־ ־־ ג׳   לעיל כ״ב ב׳.   13 (פוסקין) ע׳
ד׳.   12 (עד מתי) ב״ר י״נ י״נ;   ירושלמי ברכות ט׳ סוף ג׳
(הפלוגתא אם להפסק נאמרה).

We read in a Baraita: R. Simeon ben
Eleazar said, Not a hand-breadth of rain
comes from above, but that the deep[362] below
comes up to meet it with two hand-breadths.
But did we not read three hand-breadths
(instead of two)? There is no contradiction,
for one passage refers to tilled ground[363] and
the other to fallow ground.

R. Eleazar said: When the libation is offered during the Feast of Tabernacles, one deep
says to the other:[364] "Let thy water spring forth,
I hear the voice of two comrades," for it is said
(Ps., 42. 8): "Deep calleth unto deep at the
voice of Thy cataracts." Said Rabbah bar Bar
Ḥanah, I saw that Ridya;[365] he resembles a heifer
of three years old;[366] his lip is split and he is
stationed between the upper and the lower deep;

[362] It was assumed that the abyss sends up its water
through the earth to meet the water of the rain; comp.
above, note 97.

[363] In tilled, loose ground even a smaller quantity of
rain may penetrate a hand-breadth and, correspondingly,
the deep below also sends up less water, that is, two hand-
breadths; but if the rain penetrates a hand-breadth of
fallow, hard ground, the deep must respond with three
hand-breadths; comp. S. Strashun's Annotations.

[364] According to the commentaries, R. Eleazar speaks
here of the two vessels from which wine and water were
drawn respectively for libation during the feast of Tabernacles (above, fol. 3a). They are called comrades and
symbolize the two deeps spoken of by R. Simeon. The
voice of the cataracts is the noise produced by the water
and the wine rushing through the pipes attached to the

תניא רבי שמעון בן אלעזר אומר אין לך טפח
שיורד מלמעלה שאין תהום עולה לקראתו טפחים
והא תניא שלשה טפחים לא קשיא כאן בעבודה
כאן בשאינה עבודה:

אמר רבי אלעזר בשעה שמנסכין מים בחג תהום   5
אומר לחבירו אבע מימיך קול שני רעים אני שומע
שנאמר תהום אל תהום קורא לקול צנוריך:

אמר רבה בר בר חנה לדידי חזי לי האי רידיא
דמי לעגלא תלתא ופריטא שפתיה וקאים בין
תהומא עילאה לתהומא תתאה לתהומא עילאה   10

תורה אור	מסרת הש״ס והמדרשים
7 תהלים מ׳ב ח׳.	1 (תניא) תוספתא תענית א׳ ד׳;
	ירושלמי ברכות ט׳ סוף ג׳ (ב׳)
	ותענית א׳ ד׳; ב׳ר י׳ג י׳ג; ע׳ ש׳ר ה׳ ט׳.

---

vessels; comp. R. Hananel's commentary and *Aruch, s. v.* שת.

[365] In Persian mythology the name of an angel appointed
as a dispenser of rain; see Kohut, *Aruch, s. v.*—Rabbah b.
bar Ḥanah, the famous fabulist of the Talmud, places
this angel between the two deeps, which he urges to pour
out their contents. The verse from Canticles is supposed
to indicate the revival of nature as a result of the rain, and
תור, turtle, its taken as the Aramaic for שור, ox, thus alluding
to the resemblance of the angel to a three year old heifer,
as visualized by Rabbah.

[366] See above, note 196.

to the upper deep he says: "Pour down thy water,"
and to the lower deep: "Let thy water spring
up," as it is said (Cant., 2. 12): "The flowers
appear on the earth; the time of the singing is
come, and the voice of the turtle is heard in
our land."

*If the people begin to fast and then the rain begins
to fall, if this happens before sunrise,* etc. Our
Rabbis have taught: If while the people are
fasting rain falls, if it is before sunrise,
they need not finish the fast, but if it
is after sunrise, they must finish the fast.
This is the opinion of R. Meir; R. Judah said, if
it rains before noon they need not finish, but
if it rains after noon they must finish; R. Jose
said, if it rains before three o'clock in the afternoon, they need not finish, if after three, they
must finish; for thus we find that Ahab fasted
after three, as it is said (I Kings, 21.29): "Seest
thou how Ahab humbleth himself before Me?
Because he humbleth himself before Me, I will
not bring the evil in his days; but in his son's
days will I bring the evil upon his house."[367]

[367] Kings, according to the Talmud (comp. *Pesaḥim*,
107b; Derenbourg, *Essai sur l'hist. et la géogr. de la
Palestine*, p. 254), used to dine at three o'clock in the
afternoon. It is further assumed that Ahab "humbled
himself," that is, fasted, on the day he heard his
verdict from Elijah. This can only mean that he decided
not to take his dinner, which proves that such a late
resolve, provided one did not eat before that time, namely
at three o'clock, is counted as a fast; comp. above, note 188.

אמר ליה חשור מימך לתהומא תתאה אמר ליה

אבע מימך שנאמר הנצנים נראו בארץ עת הזמיר

הגיע וקול התור נשמע בארצנו:

היו מתענין וירדו להם גשמים קודם הנץ החמה:

5 תנו רבנן היו מתענין וירדו להם גשמים קודם הנץ

החמה לא ישלימו לאחר הנץ החמה ישלימו דברי

רבי מאיר רבי יהודה אומר קודם חצות לא ישלימו

לאחר חצות ישלימו רבי יוסי אומר קודם תשע

שעות לא ישלימו לאחר תשע שעות ישלימו שכן

10 מצינו באחאב שהתענה מתשע שעות ולמעלה

שנאמר הראית כי נכנע אחאב מלפני יען כי נכנע

מפני לא אביא הרעה בימיו בימי בנו אביא הרעה

על ביתו:

מסרת הש"ס והמדרשים   תורה אור

2 שיר השירים ב' י"ב. 11 מלכים   4 (מתענין) ירושלמי תענית ג' י"ג.
א' כ"א כ"ט.

R. Judah Nesiah (Patriarch) ordered a fast,
and rain came after sunrise. He then thought
to finish the fast, but R. 'Ami said to him, in
our Mishnah we read about "forenoon" and
"afternoon."[368]

Samuel the Little ordered a fast and rain came
before sunrise. The people therefore thought
that it was due to the merit of the congregation,
but Samuel said, I will illustrate the event to
you by a simile: The situation is to be compared
to that of a slave who asks reward of his master,
and the master says to his servants, "Give it to
him so that I may hear his voice no more."
Another time Samuel the Little ordered a fast
and rain came after sunset. The people again
thought that it was due to the merits of the congregation, but Samuel said to them, I will explain the matter by a simile: The situation is to
be likened unto that of a slave who asks the master
for his reward, and the latter says to his servants:
"Wait until he shows contrition and is worried,
and then you can give it to him." But if
this interpretation of Samuel the Little is accepted, how will it ever be possible to recognize
the merit of a congregation? It can be recognized if when the reader recites: "He causes the
wind to blow," a wind blows, and when he recites:
"He causes the rain to descend," rain descends.

It happened that a fast was ordered in Lydda, etc.
Why did they not recite the great Hallel before

---

[368] But no distinction is made between before and after
sunrise. R. Judah was therefore entitled to give up the
fast.

רבי יהודה נשיאה גזר תעניתא ירדו להם גשמים
לאחר הנץ החמה סבר לאשלומה אמר ליה רבי
אמי קודם חצות ואחר חצות שנינו:

שמואל הקטן גזר תעניתא ירדו להם גשמים קודם

5 הנץ החמה כסבורין העם לומר שבח צבור הוא
אמר להם אמשול לכם משל למה הדבר דומה
לעבד שמבקש פרס מרבו אמר להם תנו לו ואל
אשמע קולו שוב פעם אחת שמואל הקטן גזר תעניתא
ירדו להם גשמים לאחר שקיעת החמה כסבורין

10 העם לומר שבח צבור הוא אמר להם אמשול לכם
משל למה הדבר דומה לעבד שמבקש פרס מרבו
אמר להם המתינו לו עד שיתמקמק ויצטער ואחר
כך תנו לו אלא לשמואל הקטן שבח צבור היכי
משכחת לה דאמר משיב הרוח ונשא זיקא אמר מוריד

15 הגשם ואתא מטרא:

מעשה וגזרו תענית בלוד וכו': ולימרו הלל הגדול

מסרת הש"ס והמדרשים

1 (ר"י נשיאה) ע' ירוש' שם.   (בשם ר"ע ובאופן אחר). 14 (ונשא)
6 (משל) ירושלמי תענית נ' ד'   לעיל כ"ד א'; ב"מ פ"ה א'.

393

they ate and drank?   Both 'Abbayi and Raba said,
the great Hallel must be read only [fol. 26a] when
the appetite is satisfied and the stomach filled.
This is not so, for did not R. Papa once chance
to be in the synagogue of 'Abi Gubar,[369] where he
ordered a fast and rain fell before noon-time
(of the fast-day), yet he advised them: "Read the
great Hallel and then eat and drink!"   With
city people it is different, as drunkenness is a
frequent occurrence among them.[370]

[369] Name of a person or a place near Pumbedita in
Babylonia; Comp. Neubauer, *Géographie*, 358; Kohut,
Aruch, *s. v.* בי גובר.

[370] And one cannot trust them to postpone the Hallel
until after they had eaten and drunk.

מעיקרא אביי ורבא דאמרי תרוייהו אין אומרים
כ״ו
ע״א הלל הגדול | אלא בנפש שבעה ובכרס מלאה איני
והא רב פפא איקלע לבי כנשתא דאבי גובר גזר
תעניתא וירדו להם גשמים קודם חצות ואמר להם
5 אמרו הלל הגדול והדר איזילו איכלו ואישתו שאני
בני מחוזא דשכיחא בהו שכרות:

הדרן עלך סדר תעניות אלו

CHAPTER IV

Mishnah 1. At three periods of the year the priests must raise their hands (in blessing the people) four times during the day—namely, during the morning, the Musaf, the Minḥah, and the Ne'ilah prayers:—on public fast days, on the fast days of the Ma'amadot,[371] and on the Day of Atonement. 2. This is the order of the Ma'amadot [It is said (Num., 28.2): "Command the children of Israel, and say unto them: My food which is presented unto Me for offering made by fire of a sweet savour unto me, shall ye observe to offer unto me in its due season." Now, how can the offering of a person be presented, if he does not stand by it? The Early Prophets[372] have therefore instituted twenty-four divisions. (Corresponding to each division there was present in Jerusalem a post of priests, Levites and Israelites.)[373] When the turn of a division came to go up to Jerusalem, the priests and Levites (as well as the lay representatives of the Israelites) of that

[371] For all details about the *Mishmarot* (divisions of priests and Levites) and *Ma'amadot* (lay-posts), see above, note 230.

[372] These are, according to the Talmud, below, p. 416, Samuel and David.

[373] The purpose of this addition within the larger addition is to emphasize that the lay Israelites also had their representatives in Jerusalem, which is the main thing in the explanation of the term Ma'amadot; see the Hebrew Notes.

פרק רביעי

מתניתין: בשלשה פרקים בשנה הכהנים נושאין

את כפיהן ארבע פעמים ביום בשחרית במוסף

ובמנחה ובנעילת שערים בתעניות ובמעמדות וביום

הכפורים אלו הן מעמדות לפי שנאמר צו את בני

5 ישראל ואמרת אלהם את קרבני לחמי לאשי ריח

ניחחי תשמרו להקריב לי במועדו היאך קרבנו של

אדם קרב והוא אינו עומד על גביו התקינו הנביאים

הראשונים עשרים וארבעה משמרות על כל משמר

ומשמר היה מעמד בירושלם של כהנים ושל לוים

10 ושל ישראל הגיע זמן המשמר לעלות כהניו ולויו

עולים לירושלם וישראל שבאותו המשמר מתכנסין

תורה אור	מסרת הש"ס והמדרשים
4 במדבר כ"ח ב'.	1 (בשלשה) יומא פ"ז ב'; ירושלמי
	ברכות ד' א'; תוספתא תענית ד'
	א'. 7 (עומד ע"ג) סוטה ח' א'; ספרי פנחס קמ"ב. 7 (הנביאים)
	ירושלמי פסחים ד' א'; תעניות ד' ב'; תוספתא שם ד' ב'. 10 (הגיע
	תוספתא שם ד' ג'.

division went up to Jerusalem, while the bulk[374] of the Israelites belonging to that division assembled in the synagogues of their respective towns and read the chapter on Creation (Gen., 1. 1–31; 2. 1–3)]:[375] 3. On the first day of the week they read Genesis, 1, verses 1–8; on the second, verses 6–13; on the third, verses 9-19; on the fourth, verses 14–23; on the fifth, verses 20–31; on the sixth, verses 24–31, and chapter 2, verses 1–3. A long portion was divided between two men, and a short one was read by one.[376] This procedure was adhered to only during the morning and Musaf prayers,[377] but in the afternoon prayer everybody recited (the whole text) for himself by heart in the manner one recites for himself the Shema'. On Fridays the assemblage in the synagogues for the afternoon prayer did not take place, because the time was

[374] That is, the Israelites who remained at home in the various country towns. Their services were patterned after those of their representatives in Jerusalem and were also called Ma'amadot. These services were the origin of the synagogal services as developed in later ages; comp. Elbogen, *Der Jüdische Gottesdienst*, Leipzig, 1913, pp. 237–240. The Ma'amadot as prescribed here in the Mishnah, though generally discontinued in practice, are, with some later accretions, still part of the complete orthodox Ritual Orders (סדורים); see Baer, עבודת ישראל, pp. 495ff.

[375] This passage is an addition *à propos* of the term Ma'amadot. It explains in an incidental manner its origin and meaning. The straight text of the Mishnah ran thus: This is the order of the Ma'amadot: On the first day

בעריהן וקוראין במעשה בראשית ביום הראשון

בראשית ויהי רקיע בשני יהי רקיע ויקוו המים

בשלישי יקוו המים ויהי מארת ברביעי יהי מארת

וישרצו המים בחמישי ישרצו המים ותוצא הארץ

5 בששי תוצא הארץ ויכלו השמים והארץ וכל צבאם

פרשה גדולה קורין אותה בשנים וקטנה ביחיד

בשחרית במוסף ובמנחה נכנסין וקורין על פיהם

כקורין את שמע ערב שבת במנחה לא היו נכנסין

מסרת הש״ס והמדרשים

1 (ביום הראשון) מגלה כ״ב א';   תוספתא שם ד' ד'.   7 (נכנסין)
ירושלמי מגלה ד' ב'.   6 (פרשה)   תוספתא שם.

---

of the week they read Genesis, etc.; see the Hebrew Notes.

376 See the explanation of the Talmud, below, p. 424.

377 This clause has reference only to the Ma'amadot
services held in the country towns, for, as we read later
on (see note 379), on days when a Musaf prayer was required, there were no Ma'amadot services in the Temple
of Jerusalem either in connection with the Shaḥarit or
Musaf or Minḥah prayers.

needed for preparations in honor of the Sabbath.
4. On days when Hallel is recited,[378] there
is no Ma'amad service in the morning (שחרית);[379]
on days when an additional (Musaf) offering
is brought,[380] there is no Ma'amad service
during the Minḥah prayer; on days when a
wood-offering is brought, there is no Ma'amad
service during the Ne'ilah (closing) prayer;
this is the opinion of R. 'Aḳiba. Ben 'Azzai
said to him: thus R. Joshua taught: On days
when an additional offering is brought, there
is no Ma'amad service during the Ne'ilah
prayer, but when a wood-offering is brought,
there is no Ma'amad service during the Minḥah
prayer. R. 'Aḳiba then accepted the version of
Ben 'Azzai.

5. There were nine days on which the priests
and the people used to bring their wood-offerings:
on the first of Nisan wood was donated by the
family of Arah of the tribe of Judah (Nehemiah,
7. 10); on the twentieth of Tammuz, by the
family of David from the tribe of Judah;[381]
on the fifth of Ab, by the family of Parosh from
the tribe of Judah (ib., 7. 8); on the seventh of Ab,
by the family of Jonadab, son of Rechab (Jeremiah,
35. 6); on the tenth thereof, by the family of
Senaah of the tribe of Benjamin (Nehemiah, 7.

[378] As on the Ḥanukkah days when there is a Hallel,
but not a Musaf service. This paragraph, again speaking
of offerings, can, of course, refer only to the services in
the Temple; see the preceding note.

[379] So as not to take up too much time. The same reason

מפני כבוד השבת כל יום שיש בו הלל אין בו מעמד

שחרית קרבן מוסף אין במנחה קרבן עצים אין

בנעילה דברי רבי עקיבא אמר לו בן עזאי כך היה

רבי יהושע שונה קרבן מוסף אין בנעילה קרבן

עצים אין במנחה חזר רבי עקיבא להיות שונה   5

כדברי בן עזאי זמן עצי הכהנים והעם תשעה באחד

בניסן בני ארח בן יהודה בעשרים בתמוז בני דוד

בן יהודה בחמשה באב בני פרעוש בן יהודה בשבעה

בו בני יונדב בן רכב בעשרה בו בני סנאה בן בנימן

---

applies also to the days of Musaf and wood-offerings;
for the latter see below.

[380] On New Moon, Sabbaths, and all holidays.

[381] No such family is listed either in Ezra 2 or in
Neh. 7. Hattush in Ezra, 8. 2, cannot possibly be
meant, as he is not mentioned by name, as are the others,
nor does his name occur in Neh. 7, among those who
offered wood, which is the main thing here. I assume
that דוד is an old scribal mistake for לוד, Neh., 7. 37;
see in detail the Hebrew Notes to fol. 28a, bottom; below,
n. 404.

38); on the fifteenth, by the family of Zattu of the tribe of Judah (*ib.*, 7. 13). With the last mentioned family wood was offered also by priests, Levites and all Israelites who were not sure of their tribe,[382] as also by those who deceived (the Roman officials) by a pestle and dry figs;[383] on the twentieth, by the family of Pahath-Moab of the tribe of Judah (*ib.*, 7. 11); on the twentieth of Elul, by the family of Adin of the tribe of Judah (*ib.*, 7. 20); on the first of Ṭebet, by the family of Parosh for the second time.

On the first of Ṭebet there were no Ma'amad services at all, because on that day Hallel was recited and an additional offering as well as a wood-offering were brought.

6. Five calamities befell our ancestors on the seventeenth of Tammuz and five on the ninth of Ab. On the seventeenth of Tammuz [fol. 26b] the tables of the law were broken,[384] the daily offering ceased, a breach was made in the walls of the city (of Jerusalem), Apostomos[385] burned the Torah and set up an idol in the Temple. On the ninth of Ab it was decreed that our ancestors should not enter the Holy Land, the first and the second Temples were destroyed, Bettar was taken and the City of Jerusalem was plowed over.

7. With the beginning of Ab we should limit our rejoicing. During the week in which the

---

[382] See Ezra, 2. 59ff.

[383] See the explanation below, p. 432.

[384] See Talmud, below, p. 440.

[385] See *J.E.*, *s. v.*, and below, p. 442.

בחמשה עשר בו בני זתוא בן יהודה ועמהם כהנים

ולוים וכל מי שטעה שבטו ובני גונבי עלי ובני קוצעי

קציעות בעשרים בו בני פחת מואב בן יהודה

בעשרים באלול בני עדין בן יהודה באחד בטבת

5 שבו בני פרעוש שניה באחד בטבת לא היה בו

מעמד שהיה בו הלל וקרבן מוסף וקרבן עצים

חמשה דברים ארעו את אבותינו בשבעה עשר

בתמוז וחמשה בתשעה באב בשבעה עשר בתמוז ׀

כ"ו נשתברו הלוחות ובטל התמיד והבקעה העיר ושרף
ע"ב

10 אפוסטומוס את התורה והעמיד צלם בהיכל בתשעה

באב נגזר על אבותינו שלא יכנסו לארץ וחרב הבית

בראשונה ובשניה ונלכדה ביתר ונחרשה העיר

משנכנס אב ממעטין בשמחה שבת שחל תשעה באב

מסרת הש"ס והמדרשים

7 (חמשה) פס"ר כ"ו. 9 (הלוחות)   תוספתא סוטה ו' י'. 11–12 (וחרב–
יומא ד' ב'. 9 (התמיד) ערכין   ונחרשה) ר"ה י"ח ב'. 13 (שבת)
י"ב א'. 9 (הבקעה) ר"ה י"ח ב';   לקמן כ"ט ב'; יבמות מ"ג א';
ירושלמי כא׳ ד' ט' (ס"ט ב'); יבמות ספ"ו.

ninth of Ab falls, one should not cut one's hair
or wash (one's clothes) but one may do so on
Thursday in honor of the coming Sabbath. On
the day before the ninth of Ab, one should not
partake of two courses,[386] nor eat meat or drink
wine; Rabban Simeon B. Gamaliel said, one
should merely modify (his usual way of living).
R. Judah made it obligatory to turn over the
couches,[387] but the other Sages did not agree
with him.

8. Said Rabban Simeon b. Gamaliel: The Israelites never had such joyous days as the fifteenth
of Ab and the Day of Atonement, for on those
days the sons of Jerusalem used to go out dressed
in white garments, which they borrowed from
one another in order not to cause shame to him
who had none of his own. All these garments
had to be immersed (before they were used).[388]
The daughters of Jerusalem too used to go out on
these days and dance in the vineyards, saying,
"Young man, lift up thine eyes, and consider
what thou wilt select for thyself (as a wife); do not
fix thine eyes upon beauty, but consider the family." And the young man replied (Cant. 3.11):
"Go forth, O ye daughters of Zion, and gaze upon

[386] See Isr. Lewy, *Vortrag über das Ritual des Pesach-
Abends*, Breslau, 1904, p. 13.

[387] As a sign of mourning; see the Talmud, below, p. 472;
Shulḥan 'Aruk, Yoreh De'ah, § 387.

[388] As some might be levitically unclean, for example
garments of a menstruating woman.

404

להיות בתוכה אסורין לספר ולכבס ובחמשי מותרין

מפני כבוד השבת ערב תשעה באב לא יאכל אדם

שני תבשילין לא יאכל בשר ולא ישתה יין רבן שמעון

בן גמליאל אומר ישנה רבי יהודה מחייב בכפית

5 המטה ולא הודו לו חכמים אמר רבן שמעון בן

גמליאל לא היו ימים טובים לישראל כחמשה עשר

באב וכיום הכפורים שבהן בני ירושלם יוצאין

בכלי לבן שאולין שלא לבייש את מי שאין לו וכל

הכלים טעונים טבילה ובנות ירושלם יוצאות וחלות

10 בכרמים וכך היו אומרות בחור שא נא עיניך וראה

מה אתה בורר לך אל תתן עיניך בנוי תן עיניך

במשפחה וכך הוא אומר צאינה וראינה בנות ציון

תורה אור	מסרת הש"ס והמדרשים
12 שה"ש ג' י"א.	1 (ובחמשי) לעיל י"ב ב', ט"ו ב',
	לקמן כ"ט ב'; יבמות מ"ג א'

וירושלמי כאן ב' י"ב (ס"ה ד') ד' ט', מו"ק ריש פ"ג; יבמות ספ"ו.
3 (ב' תבשילין) לקמן ל' א'; סנהדרין ע' א'; תוספתא תענית ד' י"א;
איכ"ר (באבער) ג' ט"ו. 3 (רשב"ג) ב"ב קכ"א א'; איכ"ר פתיחתא
ל"נ. 8 (לבייש) לקמן ל"א א'; פסחים פ"ב א'; כתובות נ"ד ב'.

King Solomon,[389] even upon the crown wherewith his mother hath crowned him in the day of his espousals, and in the day of the gladness of his heart."

"The day of his espousals" refers to the day on which the Torah was given, while "the day of the gladness of his heart" refers to the day on which the building of the Temple was completed. May the latter soon be rebuilt in our days![390]

Gemara: *At three periods of the year the priests must raise their hands*, etc. Is there a Musaf prayer on days of public fasts or on the days of the Ma'amadot? Answer. There is an omission in this text, it should read as follows: At three periods of the year the priests must raise their hands each time they pray, occasionally even four times daily, namely during the Shaharit, Musaf, Minhah and Ne'ilah prayers, and these are the three periods: On public fast days, on the days of the Ma'amadot, and on the Day of Atonement.[391] Said R. Nahman in the name of Rabbah b. 'Abuha, this is the opinion of R. Meir, but the Sages say, there is raising of hands only during the Shaharit and Musaf prayers, but

---

[389] When a young man accepted the proposal of the girl, he would quote to her this verse, which contains allusions to espousals. This entire paragraph of the Mishnah was heretofore misunderstood. For details see the Hebrew Notes.

[390] This clause, which gives a new turn to the verse from Canticles, has no connection with the preceding statement of Rabban Simeon b. Gamaliel. It is taken from *Seder 'Olam Rabbah*, ch. 15 and, as often at the end of tractates (see

במלך שלמה בעטרה שעטרה לו אמו ביום חתנתו
וביום שמחת לבו ביום חתנתו זה מתן תורה וביום
שמחת לבו זה בנין בית המקדש שיבנה במהרה
בימינו:

גמרא: בשלשה פרקים בשנה הכהנים נושאין
את כפיהן כו': תעניות ומעמדות מי אית בהו מוסף
חסורי מחסרא והכי קתני בשלשה פרקים בשנה
כהנים נושאין את כפיהן כל זמן שמתפללין ויש
מהן ארבעה פעמים ביום בשחרית במוסף במנחה
ובנעילה ואלו הן שלשה פרקים תעניות ומעמדות
ויום הכפורים אמר רב נחמן אמר רבה בר אבוה
זו דברי רבי מאיר אבל חכמים אומרים שחרית

מסרת הש"ס והמדרשים

1 (חתנתו) ס'ע פט'ו; ספרא שמיני
דמלואים; פסדר"כ ויהי ביום כלות
(באבער הערה פ'ו); פס'ר ויהי
ביום כלות (קרוב לסוף ושם
המאמר מקוטע ע' ר' מא'ש הערה
12 (חכמים) תוספתא תענית ד' א'.

ק'ז); שמ'ר נ'ב ה'; במ'ר ב' כ'ה,
י'ב ח': שהש"ר ספ'ג; איכ'ר
פתיחתא ל'ג; תנחומא (הנדפס)
אחר מות אות ו' (באבער אות ח').

notes 222, 440), is placed here in order to close the tractate
of the Mishnah with words of consolation (דברי נחמה).
The commentators, misunderstanding both paragraphs,
tried in vain to explain the difficulties; see the Hebrew
Notes.

391 Accordingly the words "during the... *Musaf*" of the
Mishnah do not refer to days of public fasts and Ma-
'amadot, but to days on which Musaf services are held.

not during the Minḥah and Ne'ilah prayers. Who
is meant by "the Sages"? R. Judah; for a
Baraita teaches: There is raising of hands in the
Shaḥarit, Musaf, Minḥah, and Ne'ilah. This
is the opinion of R. Meir; R. Judah said there is
raising of hands in the Shaḥarit and Musaf
prayers, but none in the Minḥah and Ne'ilah
prayers; R. Jose said there is raising of hands
in the Ne'ilah prayer, but not in the Minḥah
prayer. What is the underlying principle of
their diverging opinions? It is this: R. Meir
argues that since the priests are allowed to
raise their hands daily, during the Shaḥarit
and Musaf prayers, because drunkenness is not
common at that time of the day, they ought
to be allowed to do so on fast days even during the Minḥah and Ne'ilah prayers, since on
fast days drunkenness is out of the question;
R. Judah, however, is of the opinion that inasmuch as drunkenness during the time of the
Shaḥarit and Musaf prayers is not a common
occurrence even on ordinary days, it is not
necessary to prohibit the raising of hands during
these prayers on fast days either, but in the Minḥah and Ne'ilah prayers, during the time of
which drunkenness on ordinary days is a common
occurrence, it is necessary to prohibit the raising of hands during these prayers even on fast
days; R. Jose holds that in the service of
Minḥah, which is a prayer of every day, the raising of hands is to be forbidden even on fast days,
but in the service of Ne'ilah, which is not a matter of every day, the raising of hands need not
be forbidden.

ומוסף יש בהן נשיאות כפים מנחה ונעילה אין בהן

נשיאות כפים מאן חכמים רבי יהודה היא דתניא

שחרית ומוסף מנחה ונעילה כלן יש בהן נשיאות

כפים דברי רבי מאיר רבי יהודה אומר שחרית

5 ומוסף יש בהן נשיאות כפים מנחה ונעילה אין בהן

נשיאות כפים רבי יוסי אומר נעילה יש בה נשיאות

כפים מנחה אין בה נשיאות כפים במאי קמיפלגי

רבי מאיר סבר שחרית ומוסף דכל יומא טעמא מאי

פרסי כהני ידיהו משום דלא שכיחא בהו שכרות

10 מנחה ונעילה דהאידנא לא שכיחא בהו נמי שכרות

ורבי יהודה סבר שחרית ומוסף דכל יומא לא שכיחא

שכרות לא גזרינן מנחה ונעילה דכל יומא שכיחא

בהו שכרות גזרינן ורבי יוסי סבר מנחה דאיתה

בכל יומא גזרינן נעילה דליתה בכל יומא לא גזרינן:

מסרת הש"ס והמדרשים

2 (מאן חכמים) לעיל ו' א' (עיי"ש במסרה).

R. Judah said in the name of Rab, R. Meir's
view is *law;* R. Huna said, it is established
usage; R. Johanan said, the people *adopted* it as
a usage. [The opinion of him who says that
a view is *law*, carries with it that we must teach
it in the school sessions; if one says that a
view is established *usage*, it means that we do
not teach it in the school sessions, but, if asked,
decide accordingly; if one says that the people
have *adopted* a view as usage, it means that we
do not even decide according to it, but that
when someone has already acted in accordance
with it, we do not nullify his action.]³⁹² R.
Naḥman said, R. Jose's view is law and, indeed, R. Jose's view has been recognized as law.
Why then do the priests nowadays spread their
hands during the Minḥah service of public fasts?
Inasmuch as they do it close to sunset, it is as
if it were done during the Ne'ilah service.

It is at all events generally admitted that a
drunken priest is not allowed to raise his hands.
Whence is this view derived? Said R. Simeon
b. Pazzi in the name of R. Joshua b. Levi,
who reported it in the name of Bar Ḳappara,
Why is the portion dealing with the blessing
priest placed (in the Bible) immediately after
the portion dealing with the Nazir?³⁹³ In order to
convey the lesson that as the Nazir is forbidden to drink wine, so is the priest who
is to pronounce a blessing. An objection was
raised against this statement by 'Ahabah, son of

³⁹² The passage in brackets which interrupts the discussion is probably an insertion of the so-called Saboraic

אמר רב יהודה אמר רב הלכה כרבי מאיר
ורב הונא אמר מנהג כרבי מאיר ורבי יוחנן אמר
נהגו העם כרבי מאיר מאן דאמר הלכה דרשינן
לה בפרקא מאן דאמר מנהג מדרש לא דרשינן
אורויי מורינן ומאן דאמר נהגו אורויי נמי לא מורינן 5
ואי עבוד לא מהדרינן להו ורב נחמן אמר הלכה
כרבי יוסי והלכה כרבי יוסי ואלא האידנא מאי
טעמא פרסי כהני ידיהו במנחתא דתעניתא כיון
דסמוך לשקיעת החמה קא פרסי כתפלת נעילה
דמיא: 10

דכולי עלמא מיהת שכור אסור בנשיאות כפים
מנהני מילי אמר רבי שמעון בן פזי אמר רבי יהושע
בן לוי משום בר קפרא למה נסמכה פרשת כהן
מברך לפרשת נזיר לומר לך מה נזיר אסור ביין
אף כהן מברך אסור ביין מתקיף לה אהבה בריה 15

מסרת הש״ס והמדרשים

1-3 2-3 (הלכה מנהג נהגו) ערובין ד׳ א׳; ערובין ו׳ ה׳ ח׳ (דף כ׳ג
ס׳ב ב׳, ע׳ב א׳; ירושלמי תענית ע׳ג וע׳ד); מגלה ב׳ ג׳ (ע׳ד ד׳).
14 (נזיר) ירושלמי תענית ד׳ א׳.

period, of which there are many in the Talmud; comp.
Brüll, *Jahrbücher*, II (1876), pp. 41ff., 69, nn. 111, 112.
[393] Num. 6, 22ff.

R. Zera, or, as some say, by Joshua b. Gizora: If this deduction is correct, we ought also to say that as the Nazir is forbidden to eat the kernel (Num 6.4), so is the blessing priest! Said R. Isaac, Scripture says (Deut., 10.8): "To minister unto Him, and to bless in His name," which indicates that as the ministering priest is allowed to eat the kernel, so is the priest who is to pronounce a blessing [fol. 27a]. If you go by such analogy, then, just as a ministering priest must not have any blemish, so must a priest pronouncing the blessing be without blemish! No, in this respect the latter has been compared to a Nazir! But why do you choose your analogies so as to derive a lenient rule? You should rather make the analogies so that a rigorous view is obtained! Answer. The analogies are merely a suggestion of the Rabbis for the purpose of supporting their own view, hence any rule derived therefrom must be in the direction of leniency.

This is the order of the Ma'amadot. It is said: Command the children of Israel, etc. What does he mean to say? He means to say this: This is the order of the Ma'amadot; but why have the Ma'amadot been instituted? Because it is written: "Command the children of Israel, and say unto them: My food which is presented unto Me for offerings made by fire of a sweet savour unto Me, shall ye observe to offer unto Me in its due season." Now, how could the offering of a person be presented, if that person did not stand by it? The Early Prophets have therefore instituted twenty-four divisions.

דרבי זירא ואמרי לה יושוע בר גיזורא אי מה נזיר

אסור בחרצן אף כהן מברך אסור בחרצן אמר

רבי יצחק אמר קרא לשרתו ולברך בשמו מה

משרת מותר בחרצן אף כהן מברך מותר בחרצן **כ״י**
ע״א

5 אי מה משרת בעל מום לא אף כהן מברך בעל

מום לא הא איתקש לנזיר ומאי חזית דמקשת לקולא

אקיש לחומרא אסמכתא דרבנן היא ולקולא:

אלו הן מעמדות לפי שנאמר צו את בני ישראל

וכו': מאי קאמר הכי קאמר אלו הן מעמדות ומה

10 טעם תקנו מעמדות לפי שנאמר צו את בני ישראל

ואמרת אלהם את קרבני לחמי לאשי ריח ניחחי

תשמרו להקריב לי במועדו היאך קרבנו של אדם

קרב והוא אינו עומד על גביו התקינו נביאים

הראשונים עשרים וארבעה משמרות:

תורה אור
3 דברים י' ח'.   10 במדבר כ״ח ב'.

413

Twenty-four divisions[393a] *[corresponding to each division there was present in Jerusalem a post of Israelites] of priests, Levites, and Israelites. When the turn of a division came to go up to Jerusalem, the priests and Levites of that division went up to Jerusalem.*

The Rabbis have taught: Twenty-four divisions were in the land of Israel and twelve in Jericho (and twelve in Jericho? That would amount to more than twenty-four! Read "twelve *thereof* were in Jericho"). When the turn of a division arrived, half of the division would go up to Jerusalem, while the other half would go to Jericho, in order to supply from there water and food to their brethren in Jerusalem.

Said R. Judah in the name of Samuel: The priests, Levites, and Israelites were all indispensable for the offering up of the sacrifices. In a Baraita it was taught: R. Simeon b. Eleazar said: Priests, Levites, Israelites and musical instruments were indispensable for the sacrifice. What is the underlying principle of this difference of opinion? The one authority (Samuel) holds that the essential feature of the Temple music was singing, while the other authority holds that it was the playing of an instrument.

[393a] The words "Twenty-four divisions," to which the immediately following bracketed passage belongs, is not in the text, because the talmudic redactor of the Mishnah did not take that passage as an insertion, but as the beginning of an independent paragraph, with which he starts the quotation. Later copyists did not even notice that it is a separate quotation, taking it as a continuation

על כל משמר ומשמר היה מעמד בירושלם
של כהנים ושל לוים ושל ישראל הגיע זמן המשמר
לעלות כהניו ולוייו עולין לירושלם: תנו רבנן
עשרים וארבעה משמרות היו בארץ ישראל ושתים
עשרה ביריחו שתים עשרה ביריחו נפישו להו טובא
אלא אימא ושתים עשרה מהן ביריחו הגיע זמן
המשמר לעלות חצי המשמר עולה לירושלם וחצי
המשמר עולה ליריחו כדי שיספקו מים ומזון
לאחיהם:

אמר רב יהודה אמר שמואל כהנים ולוים וישראל
מעכבין את הקרבן במתניתא תנא רבי שמעון בן
אלעזר אומר כהנים ולוים וישראל וכלי שיר
מעכבין את הקרבן במאי קמיפלגי מר סבר עקר
שירה בפה ומר סבר עקר שירה בכלי:

מסרת הש"ס והמדרשים

3 (ת"ר) ירושלמי תענית ד' ב';   י' י"ב; פסחים ד' א'; תוספתא
פסחים ד' א'. 11 (במתניתא) ערכין   תענית ד' ג'. 14 (עקר שירה)
י"א א'; ירושלמי כאן ד' ב'; סוכה נ' ב', נ"א א'; ע"ז מ"ז א';
ערכין י"א א'.

of the preceding paragraph of the Talmud, which likewise
quotes the Mishnah, but ends with the words עשרים וארבעה
משמרות; see the Hebrew Notes and above, n. 373.

Said R. Ḥisda in the name of R. Ḥama b.
Gurya, who had it in the name of Rab: Moses
instituted for the Israelites eight divisions, four
from the descendants of Eleazar and four from
those of Ithamar; later, Samuel brought the divisions up to sixteen; finally, David brought them
up to twenty-four, as it is said (I Chron., 26. 31):
"In the fortieth year of the reign of David they
were sought for, and there were found among them
mighty men of valour at Jazer of Gilead." An
objection was raised from the following: Moses
instituted eight divisions for the Israelites, four
from the descendants of Eleazar and four from
those of Ithamar; later, David and Samuel (con-
jointly) brought them up to twenty-four, as it
is said (I Chron., 9. 22): "Whom David and
Samuel the seer did ordain in their set office!"
This passage is to be understood thus: From
the original institution of Samuel the Ramathite
the number was increased by David to twenty-
four. Another objection was raised from
the following: Moses instituted for the Israelites sixteen divisions, eight from the family
of Eleazar and eight from that of Ithamar,
but when the children of Eleazar became more
numerous than those of Ithamar they were
redivided into twenty-four, as it is said (*ibid.*,
24.4): "And there were more chief men found
of the sons of Eleazar than of the sons of Ithamar; and thus were they divided: of the
sons of Eleazar there were sixteen, heads
of fathers' houses; and of the sons of Ithamar,
according to their fathers' houses, eight"; further
it is said (*ibid.*, 24. 6): "One father's house

אמר רב חסדא אמר רב חמא בר גוריא אמר
רב משה תקן להם לישראל שמונה משמרות ארבעה
מאלעזר וארבעה מאיתמר בא שמואל והעמידן
על ששה עשר בא דוד והעמידן על עשרים וארבעה

5 שנאמר (בשנת הארבעים למלכות דוד נדרשו וימצא
בהם גבורי חיל ביעזיר גלעד מיתיבי משה תקן
להם לישראל שמונה משמרות ארבעה מאלעזר
וארבעה מאיתמר בא דוד ושמואל והעמידום על
עשרים וארבעה שנאמר) המה יסד דויד ושמואל

10 הראה באמונתם (הכי קאמר מיסודו של שמואל
הרמתי העמידום על עשרים וארבעה) מיתיבי
משה תקן להם לישראל ששה עשר משמרות שמונה
מאלעזר ושמונה מאיתמר וכשרבו בני אלעזר על
בני איתמר חלקום לעשרים וארבעה שנאמר וימצאו

15 בני אלעזר רבים לראשי הגברים מן בני איתמר
ויחלקום לבני אלעזר ראשים לבית אבות ששה עשר
ולבני איתמר לבית אבותם שמונה ואומר בית אב

תורה אור

5 דה"א כ"ו ל"א. 9 דה"א ט' כ"ב.
14 דה"א כ"ד ד'. 16 דה"א כ"ד ו'.

מסרת הש"ס והמדרשים

2 (משה תקן) ירושלמי כאן ד' ב';
תוספתא כאן ד' ב'. 10 (באמונתם)
ירושלמי כאן ד' ב'; סוכה ה' ח'.

being taken from Eleazar, and proportionately for Ithamar." Now why does this Baraita add "further it is said"? Because you might otherwise assume that just as the divisions of the sons of Eleazar increased in number (from four to sixteen), so also those of the sons of Ithamar increased (from four to eight), and that originally each had only four divisions. The Baraita therefore calls your attention to the verse: "One father's house being taken for Eleazar, and proportionately for Ithamar." This Baraita is thus a refutation of the view of R. Ḥisda! R. Ḥisda can answer your objection by saying that there are two different opinions of Tannaim on this matter, and that he agrees with that Tanna (who says that Moses instituted only eight divisions, four of each).

Our Rabbis have taught: Four divisions went up from the (Babylonian) Exile (to Palestine). They were: Jedaiah, Harim, Pashhur and Immer. The prophets of that generation then [fol. 27b] subdivided them into twenty-four. Signal-cards for the thus formed twenty-four divisions were then mixed together and put in an urn.[394] A member of the division of Jedaiah drew first a card which showed his division, then five additional cards, which likewise showed his division; that made six. The same was done by Harim, Pashhur and Immer, for the prophets that were among them had stipulated that even if the house of Jehojarib which, at the time of

---

[394] This was necessary in order to decide which family should be given the honor of serving first. Jedaiah (as

אחד אחז לאלעזר ואחז אחז לאיתמר מאי ואומר

וכי תימא כי היכי דנפישי בני אלעזר הכי נפישי

בני איתמר ומעיקרא ארבעה הוו תא שמע בית אב

אחד אחז לאלעזר ואחז אחז לאיתמר תיובתא דרב

5 חסדא אמר לך רב חסדא תנאי היא ואנא דאמרי

כי האי תנא:

תנו רבנן ארבעה משמרות עלו מן הגולה ואלו

הן ידעיה חרם פשחור ואמר עמדו נביאים שביניהם

כ"ז וחלקום לעשרים וארבעה בללום ונתנום בקלפי
ע"ב

10 בא ידעיה ונטל חלקו וחלק חבריו שש בא חרם

ונטל חלקו וחלק חבריו שש וכן פשחור וכן אמר

וכן התנו נביאים שביניהם שאפילו יהויריב ראש

מסכת הש"ס והמדרשים

7 (ת"ר) ערכין י"ב ב'; ירושלמי   (וע' במשנה ב"ק קי"י א' ובנמרא
כאן ד' ב'; תוספתא כאן ב' א'   שם קי"א א ובמ"ר ח' ז').

Rashi, 'Arakin, 12b, bottom, has it) drew six cards, all
of which happened to bear the name of his division, and
so Harim and the other two.

the First Temple, headed all the twenty-four divisions (I Chron., 24. 7), should happen to go up to Jerusalem,[395] Jedaiah should not be removed from his place as the first, but should form the head-division, while Jehojarib should take rank as his inferior.

The bulk of the Israelites belonging to that division assembled in the synagogues of their respective towns and read the Chapter on Creation. What is the basis for this provision? Said R. Jacob b. 'Aḥa in the name of R. 'Asi: Were it not for the Ma'amadot, heaven and earth would not exist, as it is said (Gen., 15. 8): "And he (Abraham) said, O Lord, whereby shall I know that I shall inherit it?" Abraham said to the Holy One, blessed be He: "Master of the world! Peradventure the Israelites will sin before Thee, and Thou wilt then do unto them as Thou hast done unto the generation of the Flood and the generation of the Dispersion!"[396] The Holy One replied: "No" (I will not do so unto them)! Whereupon Abraham said: "Master of the world! Whereby shall I know it?" The Holy One then said to him (*ibid.*, 15. 9): "Take me a heifer of three years old." Abraham again said: "Master of the world! This may well be done when the Temple is in existence, but what shall become of them when the Temple is not in

---

[395] Among the priestly families which returned with Ezra to Palestine (Ezra, 2. 36–39) that of Jehojarib, which headed the divisions in the first Temple (I Chr., 24.7), is not mentioned, and the assumption is that the family refused to return. It was therefore decided that if by

משמרות עולה לא ידחה ידעיה ממקומו אלא ידעיה
עקר ויהויריב טפל לו:

וישראל שבאותו המשמר מתכנסין בעריהן וקורין
במעשה בראשית: מנהני מלי אמר רב יעקב בר
אחא אמר רב אסי אלמלא מעמדות לא נתקיימו
שמים וארץ שנאמר ויאמר ה׳ אלהים במה אדע כי
אירשנה אמר אברהם לפני הקדוש ברוך הוא רבונו
של עולם שמא חס ושלום ישראל חוטאין לפניך
ואתה עושה להם כאנשי דור המבול וכאנשי דור
הפלגה אמר לו לאו אמר לפניו רבונו של עולם
במה אדע אמר לו קחה לי עגלה משלשת אמר
לפניו רבונו של עולם תינח בזמן שבית המקדש
קיים בזמן שאין בית המקדש קיים מה תהא עליהם

מסרת הש״ס והמדרשים   תורה אור

6 בראשית ט״ו ח׳. 11 בראשית   5 (מעמדות וכו׳) מגלה ל״א ב׳.
ט״ו מ׳.

change of mind the house Jehojarib should desire to
return, it should not receive the honor of being first.
This place was henceforth to be given to Jedaiah, who
in the first Temple was second (I Chr. *l. c.*); comp. *Tosafot*,
'Arakin, 12a, *s. v.* שאפילו.

[396] Gen. 11.

existence?" Said the Holy One: "I have already ordained for them the recitation of the order of sacrifices. Whenever they will recite it, I will account it unto them as if they offered up the sacrifices themselves and thus forgive them all their sins."

Our Rabbis have taught: Members of the division[397] prayed that the offering of their brethren should be favorably accepted, while those of the Ma'amad assembled in the synagogues and observed four fasts in the week. On Monday they fasted for the safety of those who were on the high sea; on Tuesday for those travelling in the desert; on Wednesday, that the croup should not spread among the children; on Thursday for pregnant and for nursing women, for the former, that they should not miscarry and for the latter, that they should succeed in raising their infants. On Friday they did not fast, in honor of the Sabbath and, of course, not on Sabbath.

Why did they not fast on Sunday? Said R.

[397] The commentators differ as to the meaning of משמר (division) in this passage. According to R. Gershom the Baraita refers to the priests of the division who pray for those of the sub-division (בית אב), which is actively engaged in the service one day of the week (note 230). But the words קרבן אחיהם (the offering of their brethren) do not favor this interpretation, as they seem to refer to the Israelites, who send the offerings, rather than to the priests of the sub-division, who merely act as their temporary agents. Rashi, indeed, takes משמר here in the sense of מעמד, the lay representatives, who are loosely

אמר לו כבר תקנתי להם סדר קרבנות שכל זמן
שקוראין בהן מעלה אני עליהם כאלו הקריבום
לפני ואני מוחל להם על כל עונותיהם:

תנו רבנן אנשי משמר מתפללין על קרבן אחיהם
שיתקבל ברצון ואנשי מעמד נכנסין לבית הכנסת
ויושבין ארבע תעניות בשבת בשני על יורדי הים
בשלישי על הולכי מדברות ברביעי על אסכרא
שלא תפול בתינוקות בחמשי על עוברות ומיניקות
עוברות שלא יפילו ומיניקות שיגדלו את בניהם
בערב שבת לא היו מתענין מפני כבוד השבת וכל
שכן בשבת עצמה באחד בשבת מאי טעמא לא אמר

מסרת הש"ס והמדרשים

4 (תנו רבנן) ירושלמי תענית ד'   תל"ט והלאה); מס' סופרים פי"ז.
ד': איכ"ר א' (פסוק על אלה   10 (בע"ש) ירושלמי שם ואיכ"ר
אני בוכיה, ע' באבער הערה   שם ומס' סופרים שם.

called משמר, because of their being attached to a priestly
division, and who pray that the offerings of their brethren
at home, whom they represent, may be accepted. This is also
the interpretation of Maimonides, הלכות כלי המקדש, VI, 2.
Elijah Gaon and others suggest reading in the first place
מעמד and in the second משמר, that is, the members of the
Ma'amad pray for the Israelites at home who are called
Mishmar, because they, like the priests and the Levites, were
divided into 24 Mishmarot. This is in keeping with the
Baraita above, fol. 22b, bottom (note 318). The MSS.,
however, do not bear out this reading.

423

Johanan, because of the Christians;[396] R. Samuel b. Naḥamani said, because Sunday is the third day after the creation of man;[399] Resh Laḳish said, because of the additional soul; for Resh Laḳish holds that an additional soul is given to man on Friday eve, which is taken away from him at the expiration of the Sabbath, as it is said (Ex., 31.17): "He ceased from work and rested"—alas, the soul is gone after the Sabbath is over.[400]

On the first day of the week they read Genesis, 1, verses 1–8. It was taught: The portion "In the beginning" (Gen., 1. 1–5) was divided between two readers, but the portion "Let there be a firmament" (*ibid.*, 6–8) was read by one. It is quite correct that "Let there be a firmament" should be recited by one, because it contains only three verses, but how could "In the beginning," which has only five verses, be divided into two? Was it not taught in a Mishnah that no one who is called up to read in the Torah should read less than three verses?[401] Rab answered this by

[398] Who might feel offended if the Jews made a fast day of their holiday.

[399] By a strange deduction from Gen., 34. 25, the third day after an operation or after birth was thought to be the most critical. As man was created on Friday, Sunday is not a proper day for fasting.

[400] The verb שבת, he ceased from work, is translated: He ceased keeping the Sabbath (because of its expiration), and וינפש, and rested, is divided into וי = woe! and נפש = soul, that is, woe! the soul is gone.

[401] As the law required that three men (a priest, a Levite and a lay Israelite) should be called up to read in the Torah,

רבי יוחנן מפני הנוצרים רבי שמואל בר נחמני אמר

מפני שהוא שלישי ליצירה ריש לקיׁש אמר מפני

נשמה יתרה דאמר ריש לקיש נשמה יתרה נתנת

בו באדם בערב שבת ובמוצאי שבת נטלת הימנו

5 שנאמר שבת וינפש כיון ששבת וי אבדה נפש:

ביום הראשון בראשית ויהי רקיע: תנא בראשית

בשנים יהי רקיע באחד בשלמא יהי רקיע באחד

תלתא פסוקי הוו אלא בראשית בשנים חמשה פסוקי

הוו ותנן הקורא בתורה לא יפחות משלשה פסוקים

תורה אור	מסרת הש״ס והמדרשים
5 שמות ל״א י״ז.	3 (נשמה יתרה) ביצה ט״ז א׳.
	6 (תנא וכו׳) מגלה כ״ב א׳.
	9 (ותנן) מגלה כ״ג ב׳ (וע׳ ירושלמי כאן ריש ה״נ).

---

and as each one had to read no less than three verses, the
first paragraph in Genesis containing only five verses
(called in the Mishnah "a long portion") was not long
enough for two persons. The third verse had therefore to
be read twice or divided into two halves. The same was
done with the portion Gen. 9-13.

declaring that the second reader goes back (repeats verse 3), while Samuel said that he divides
the third verse into two halves. Why does Rab
advise to go back instead of dividing? Because
he holds that we must not divide any verse that
has not been divided by Moses. Samuel, however, holds that we may divide. But did not
R. Ḥanina, the Bible teacher, say: I had much
difficulty with R. Ḥanina the Great, who did
not allow me to divide a verse in two, except
for little school children, because it was for ed-
ucational purposes? Answer: Samuel is of the
opinion that as division was allowed for children
by reason of necessity, it is allowed here also by
reason of necessity. But why does Samuel insist
upon division, instead of advising to go back?
Because of the apprehension that those who come
in or leave the synagogue (while the third verse
is being read) will misjudge the situation.⁴⁰² An
objection was raised from the following: A portion
containing six verses must be divided between
two readers, but if it contains only five verses,
it should all be read by one person. If, however,
the first reader reads only three, the second should
read the two remaining verses and an additional
verse from the immediately following portion.
Others, however, say that the second reader must
take three additional verses from the following
portion, because one should never begin a portion

⁴⁰² Those who come in while the second reader recites
verse 3 will think that the first reader recited only the first
two verses, and conclude that this is permissible. Those
again who leave while the first reader recites the third

הא איתמר עלה רב אמר דולג ושמואל אמר פוסק
רב אמר דולג מאי טעמא לא אמר פוסק קסבר כל
פסוקא דלא פסקיה משה אנן לא פסקינן ליה
ושמואל סבר פסקינן ליה והאמר רבי חנינא קרא
צער גדול היה לי אצל רבי חנינא הגדול ולא התיר
לי לפסוק פסוק אלא לתינוקות של בית רבן הואיל
ולהתלמד עשויין ושמואל התם טעמא מאי משום
דלא אפשר הכא נמי לא אפשר ושמאל אמר
פוסק מאי טעמא לא אמר דולג גזרה משום הנכנסין
וגזרה משום היוצאין מיתיבי פרשה של ששה פסוקין
קורין אותה בשנים ושל חמשה באחד קרא הראשון
שלשה השני קורא שנים מפרשה זו ואחד מפרשה
אחרת ויש אומרים שלשה לפי שאין מתחילין בפרשה

מסרת הש"ס והמדרשים

1 (דולג פוסק) בירושלמי כאן   ברכות י"ב ב'; מגלה כ"ב א'.
ה"ג ומגלה ד' ב' ה' חזר וחותך   4 (והאמר) מגלה כ"ב א'.
ואיפליגו בה אמוראים אחרים וע'   9 (הנכנסין) מס' סופרים ספי"י.
מס' סופרים פי"א ופכ"א. 3 (משה)   10 (מיתיבי) מגלה כ"ב א'; מס'
סופרים פי"א.

verse, will think that the second reader will recite only
the two remaining verses.

unless he reads at least three verses. Now
(according to Rab who advises to go back), this
Baraita, too, ought to teach that the second
reader should go back? Answer. This Baraita
offers an entirely different case, where the second
reader [fol. 28a] has the whole ensuing portion
at his disposal.

*This procedure was adhered to only during the
morning and Musaf prayers, but in the afternoon
prayer everybody recited (the whole text) for himself by heart, etc.* The question was asked:
How is this passage to be understood? Does it
mean to say that in the morning and Musaf
prayers the portion is read from the book (Scroll)
and in the afternoon by heart, as one reads the
Shema', or that in the morning prayer it is
read from the Scroll and in the Musaf and
afternoon prayers by heart, as one reads the
Shema'?[403] Come and hear the reply: It is
taught in a Baraita: During the morning and
Musaf prayers the people assemble in the synagogue and read from the Torah in the same way
as they do during the entire year, but during the
afternoon prayer one individual recites the
whole portion by heart. Said R. Jose: Is an
individual ever allowed to recite the Torah for
the congregation by heart? You must therefore
say that all the congregants read it individually
(for themselves) by heart, as one reads the *Shema'*.

*On days when Hallel was to be recited, there was
no Ma'amad, etc.* Why should there be such

---

[403] From the wording of the Mishnah: בשחרית ובמוסף
ובמנחה it is not clear whether the middle word goes with

פחות משלשה פסוקין אמאי נדלוג דלוגי שאני התם

ודאית ליה רווחא:

בשחרית ובמוסף ובמנחה קורין על פיהם כו':

איבעיא להו היכי קאמר בשחרית ובמוסף קורין

5 בספר ובמנחה קורין על פיהם כקורין את שמע

או דילמא בשחרית קורין בספר במוסף ובמנחה

קורין על פיהם כקורין את שמע תא שמע דתניא

בשחרית ובמוסף נכנסין לבית הכנסת וקורין כדרך

שקורין כל השנה כלה ובמנחה יחיד קורא על פה

10 אמר רבי יוסי וכי יחיד יכול לקרות על פה בצבור

אלא כלן קורין על פיהם כקורין את שמע:

מסרת הש"ס והמדרשים

7 (דתניא) תוספתא תענית ד' ד.

---

the preceding or the following word, hence the question
of the Talmud.

a distinction between the one (the day with a Musaf offering) and the other (the day with a wood offering)? Answer. The Musaf offering is a biblical ordinance and therefore requires no additional protection by the Rabbis (hence it is enough when it is made to supersede the Ma'amad during Minḥah service only), but the wood offering is a rabbinical enactment and therefore must have special protection (hence the wood offering is made to supersede both the Minḥah and the Ne'ilah services of the Ma'amad).

There were nine days on which the priests and the people used to bring their wood offerings. Our Rabbis have taught: Why was it necessary to set special days for the wood offerings of the priests and those particular families? Because it is reported that when the Babylonian exiles returned to Jerusalem, they found no wood in the chamber and the families here enumerated donated wood of their own, wherefore it was ordained by the prophets of their generation that even if the chamber was full of wood, these families should have the privilege of donating from their own, as it is said (Neh., 10. 35): "And we cast lots, the priests, the Levites, and the people for the wood-offering, to bring it into the house of our God, according to our fathers' houses, at times appointed, year by year, to burn upon the altar of the Lord our God, as it is written in the Law."

With the family of Zattu wood was offered also by priests, Levites, and all Israelites who were not sure of their tribe, as also by those who deceived (the Romans) *by a pestle and dry figs.* Our Rab-

כל יום שיש בו הלל אין בו מעמד כו': מה
הפרש בין זה לזה הללו דברי תורה ואין דברי
תורה צריכין חזוק והללו דברי סופרים ודברי
סופרים צריכין חזוק:

5   זמן עצי הכהנים והעם כו': תנו רבנן למה הוצרכו
זמן עצי הכהנים והעם לימנות אמרו כשעלו בני
הגולה לא מצאו עצים בלשכה ועמדו אלו והתנדבו
משלהם וכך התנו נביאים שביניהן שאפילו לשכה
מלאה עצים יהו אלו מתנדבין משלהן שנאמר

10 והגרלות הפלנו על קרבן העצים הכהנים הלוים
והעם להביא לבית אלהינו לבית אבתינו לעתים
מזמנים שנה בשנה לבער על מזבח ה' אלהינו ככתוב
בתורה:

ועמהן כהנים ולוים וכל מי שטעה שבטו ובני
15 גונבי עלי ובני קוצעי קציעות: תנו רבנן מה הן בני

תורה אור   מסרת הש"ס והמדרשים

10 נחמיה י' ל"ה.   2 (הללו ד"ת) לעיל י"ז א'; ר"ה
                          י"ט א'; יבמות ט' ה'; ירושלמי
תענית ב' י"ג; מגלה א' ו'; יבמות ט' ה'; כתובות י"א ז'; תוספתא תענית
ב' ו'.   5 (תנו רבנן וכו') ירושלמי תענית ד' ו'; מגלה א' ו'; שקלים ד'
א'; תוספתא תענית ד' ה'; מג"ת פ"ה.   15 (תנו רבנן וכו') ירושלמי
תענית ד' ז'; תוספתא תענית ד' ח'; מג"ת.

bis have taught: Who is meant by "those who deceived the Romans by a pestle and dry figs?" It is reported that once persecution was decreed by the wicked government (of Rome) upon the Israelites, forbidding them to bring their first fruit-offerings to Jerusalem and placing guards on the roads, as did Jeroboam the son of Nebat, to prevent the people from journeying as pilgrims to Jerusalem for the festivals. What did the sin-fearing men of that generation do? They took baskets containing first fruits, covered them with dry figs, put a pestle on their shoulders and proceeded. When they reached the guards and the latter asked them where they were going, they replied: With this pestle on our shoulders we are going to make two cakes of pressed figs in that mortar, yonder! As soon as they passed the guards they decorated the first fruits in the baskets and brought them to Jerusalem.

It was taught that the sons of Salmai of Netofah were also among the donors of wood. Who are meant by the sons of Salmai of Netofah? It was reported that at one time the wicked government decreed persecution over Israel, forbidding them to bring wood for the altar and placing guards on the roads, as did Jeroboam the son of Nebat, to prevent the people from going to Jerusalem for the festivals. What did the sin-fearing men of that generation do? They took pieces of wood, formed them into a sort of ladders, put them on their shoulders and proceeded. When they came to the guards and the latter asked them where they were going, they replied: We are going to fetch two doves from that

גונבי עלי ובני קוצעי קציעות אמרו פעם אחת גזרה
מלכות הרשעה שמד על ישראל שלא יביאו בכורים
לירושלם והושיבו פרדסיות על הדרכים כדרך
שהושיב ירבעם בן נבט שלא יעלו ישראל לרגל
5 מה עשו יראי חטא שבאותו הדור הביאו סלי
בכורים וחפום בקציעות ועלי על כתפיהן והלכו
להם כיון שהגיעו אצל פרדסיות אמרו להם להיכן
אתם הולכין אמרו להם לעשות שני עגולי דבלה
במכתשת שלפנינו בעלי שעל כתפינו כיון שעברו
10 מהן עטרום בסלים והביאום לירושלם:

תנא ובני סלמי הנטופתי מה הן בני סלמי הנטופתי
אמרו פעם אחת גזרה מלכות הרשעה שמד על
ישראל שלא יביאו עצים למערכה והושיבו פרדסיות
על הדרכים כדרך שהושיב ירבעם בן נבט שלא
15 יעלו ישראל לרגל מה עשו יראי חטא שבאותו הדור
הביאו עצים ועשאום כמין סולמות והניחום על
כתפיהם והלכו להם כיון שהגיעו אצל פרדסיות
אמרו להם להיכן אתם הולכין אמרו להם להביא

מסרת הש"ס והמדרשים

4 (שהושיב) לקמן ל' ב'; גטין פ"ח   ס"ע כ"ב; ירושלמי תענית ד'
א'; מו"ק כ"ח ב'; ב"ב קכ"א ב';   י"א; איכ"ר פתיחה ל"ב.

433

dove-cote yonder by means of the ladders on our shoulders. As soon as they passed the guards, they took the ladders apart and carried the wood thereof as an offering to Jerusalem. Of them and their like it is said (Prov., 10. 7): "The memory of the righteous shall be for a blessing," but of Jeroboam and his like it is said (*ibidem*): "But the name of the wicked shall rot."

On the twentieth, by the family of Pahath-Moab from the tribe of Judah. Our Rabbis have taught: The sons of Pahath-Moab of the tribe of Judah are identical with the sons of David of the tribe of Judah; this is the opinion of R. Meir, but R. Jose said they are identical with the sons of Joab, the son of Zerujah.[404]

On the twentieth of Elul, by the family of Adin of the tribe of Judah. Our Rabbis have taught: The sons of Adin of the tribe of Judah are identical with the sons of David of the tribe of Judah; this is the opinion of R. Judah; R. Jose said they are identical with the sons of Joab, the son of Zerujah.

On the first of Ṭebet by the children of Parosh for the second time. With whom does the Mishnah agree? It agrees neither with R. Meir, nor with R. Judah, nor with R. Jose! For if it agreed with R. Meir, it should read, "by the children of David of the tribe of Judah for the second time"; if it agreed with R. Judah, it should likewise read, "by the children of David of the tribe of Judah for the second time"; and if it agreed with

[404] The doubt about the identity of Pahath-Moab and Adin arose from the fact that the "sons of David" are

434

שני גוזלות משובך שלפנינו בסולמות שעל כתפינו
כיון שעברו מהן פרקום והביאום לירושלם ועליהם
ועל כיוצא בהם נאמר זכר צדיק לברכה ועל
ירבעם בן נבט וחבריו נאמר ושם רשעים ירקב:

בעשרים בו בני פחת מואב בן יהודה: תנו רבנן
בני פחת מואב בן יהודה הן הן בני דוד בן יהודה
דברי רבי מאיר רבי יוסי אומר בני יואב בן צרויה:

בעשרים באלול בני עדין בן יהודה: תנו רבנן
בני עדין בן יהודה הן הן בני דוד בן יהודה
דברי רבי יהודה רבי יוסי אומר בני יואב בן
צרויה:

באחד בטבת שבו בני פרעוש שניה: מני מתניתין
לא רבי מאיר ולא רבי יהודה ולא רבי יוסי אי
רבי מאיר לתני שבו בני דוד בן יהודה שניה
אי רבי יהודה לתני שבו בני דוד בן יהודה שניה

תורה אור
3 משלי י' ז'.

---

not mentioned in the lists of Ezra and Neḥemiah. But
as pointed out above, note 381, לוד must be read in the
Mishnah for דוד, which removes all difficulties; see the
Hebrew Notes and n. 381 above.

435

R. Jose, it should read: "by the children of
Joab and the son of Zerujah for the second
time." The Mishnah indeed agrees with R.
Jose, but there were two Tannaim with diverging opinions as to the view of R. Jose.[405]

*On the first of Ṭebet there were no Ma'amad ser-
vices,* etc. Said Mar Ḳashshisha, son of R. Ḥisda,
to R. 'Ashi [fol. 28b]: Why is it that the recital
of the Hallel (which took place in the Temple
during the morning prayer) eliminates the corresponding morning prayer of the Ma'amad,
while the Musaf prayer does not eliminate the
corresponding Musaf prayer of the Ma'amad?
"What!" replied R. 'Ashi, "is it possible that
the Musaf prayer which eliminates even a non-
corresponding service of the Ma'amad (that of
Minḥah) should not eliminate the corresponding
Musaf service of the Ma'amad?" Said Mar
Ḳashshisha: What I meant to say is this:
Let the Musaf prayer eliminate *only* a Ma'amad
service that corresponds to it (the Musaf
but not the Minḥah). R. Jose actually
agrees with this opinion of yours, replied
R. 'Ashi, for we find in a Baraita: R. Jose
said, on all days on which a Musaf service is held
a Ma'amad service is likewise held. Now, to
which Ma'amad service does he refer? To that of
Shaḥarit? This (the retention of the Ma'amad's
Shaḥarit service on days which have the Musaf
prayer) is admitted also by the first authority of

[405] The one (in our Mishnah) ascribing to him the identi-
fication of the family of Adin with that of David, the other
(in the Baraita), with that of Joab.

אי רבי יוסי לתני שבו בני יואב בי צרויה שניה

לעולם רבי יוסי היא ותרי תנאי אליבא דרבי

יוסי:

באחד בטבת לא היה בו מעמד כו׳: אמר ליה

5 מר קשישא בריה דרב חסדא לרב אשי ומאי שנא

הלל דדחי דידיה ומאי שנא מוסף דלא דחי דידיה

אמר ליה השתא דלאו דידיה דחי דידיה לא כל

שכן אמר ליה הכי קאמינא לך לא לדחי אלא

דידיה אמר ליה איכא רבי יוסי דקאי כוותך דתניא

10 רבי יוסי אומר כל יום שיש בו מוסף יש בו מעמד

מעמד דמאי אילימא דשחרית הא תנא קמא נמי

437

the Mishnah (R. 'Aḳiba)! Or does he refer to the Ma'amad service during the Musaf prayer? Does not the Musaf eliminate even its own Ma'amad service? Or does he refer to the Ma'-amad's Minḥah service? That service *is* eliminated by the wood offering! No other alternative, then, is possible than to say that he refers to the Ma'amad's Ne'ilah service, which proves that the Musaf eliminates only that Ma'amad service which is simultaneous (and hence conflicts) with it (namely the Ma'amad's Musaf), but none of the services which are not simultaneous with it (as those of Minḥah and Ne'ilah). It stands proved.

Why does the Mishnah not say also that on the first of Nisan there was no Ma'amad service, because on that day there was the recital of Hallel, a Musaf and a wood offering? Said Raba, this omission proves that the recital of Hallel on New Moon is not a biblical ordinance, for thus said R. Johanan in the name of R. Simeon b. Jehozadak: On eighteen days of the year the whole Hallel[406] is recited, namely, on the eight days of the Feast of Booths, the eight days of Ḥanukkah, the first day of Passover, and on Pentecost; in the Diaspora,[407] however, Hallel is recited on twenty-one days: nine days of the Feast of Booths, eight days of Ḥanukkah, the (first) two Days of Passover, and the two days of Pentecost.

---

[406] Which includes Psalms 115. 1–11, and 116. 1–11. The New Moon days are not included in these 18 and 21 days respectively, which proves that the practice of

הכי קאמר אלא דמוסף דידיה נמי לא דחי אלא

דמנחה קרבן עצים דחי אלא לאו דנעילה ושמע

מינה דידיה דחי דלאו דידיה לא דחי שמע מינה

ולתני נמי באחד בניסן לא היה בו מעמד שהיה בו

‎5 הלל וקרבן מוסף וקרבן עצים אמר רבא זאת

אומרת הלל דראש חדש לאו דאוריתא הוא דאמר

רבי יוחנן משום רבי שמעון בן יהוצדק שמונה עשר

יום בשנה יחיד גומר בהן את ההלל ואלו הן שמונת

ימי החג ושמונת ימי חנוכה ויום טוב הראשון של פסח

‎10 ויום טוב של עצרת ובגולה עשרים ואחד יום ואלו

הן תשעת ימי החג ושמונת ימי חנוכה ושני ימים

טובים של פסח ושני ימים טובים של עצרת:

מסרת הש״ס והמדרשים

‎4 (באחד בניסן) תוספתא תענית   ירושלמי סוכה ד' ה'; תוספתא
ד' ד'.   7 (י״ח יום) ערכין י' א';   סוכה ג' ב'; מס' סופרים כ' ט'.

reciting the Hallel on New Moon is a later innovation.
[407] Where a second day was added to each of the three festivals.

Rab once came to Babylonia and, noticing that the people were reciting the Hallel on New Moon, intended to interrupt them, but seeing that they skipped over some portions thereof[408] he concluded that they were following a custom of their ancestors. It was taught that individuals need not commence the recital of the Hallel on New Moon, but having commenced they may finish it.

Five calamities befell our ancestors on the seventeenth of Tammuz, etc. Whence is it known that on that day the tables of the Law were broken (by Moses)? It is stated in a Baraita: On the sixth of the month (of Siwan) the Ten Commandments were given to Israel; R. Jose said on the seventh thereof. He who says that it was on the sixth is of the opinion that the giving of the Commandments took place on the sixth, and the ascendance (of Moses to Mount Sinai) on the seventh; while he who says that it was on the seventh is of the opinion that both events took place on the seventh. Now, Scripture says (Exod., 24. 18): "And Moses was on the mount forty days and forty nights." Further it is written (*ibid.*, 32. 19): "And it came to pass, as soon as he came nigh unto the camp, that he saw the calf and the dancing; and Moses' anger waxed hot, and he cast the tables out of his hands and broke them beneath the mount."[409]

The daily offering ceased. This is a tradition.[410]

[408] Those mentioned in note 406.

[409] This proves that the breaking of the tablets took place on the 17th of Tammuz, forty days after the 7th of Siwan. [410] That is, there are no verses to prove it.

רב אקלע לבבל חזנהו דקא קרו הלילא בריש
ירחא סבר לאפסוקינהו כיון דחזא דקא מדלגי
דלוגי אמר שמע מנה מנהג אבותיהם בידיהם:

תנא יחיד לא יתחיל ואם התחיל גומר:

חמשה דברים ארעו את אבותינו בשבעה עשר
בתמוז כו': נשתברו הלוחות מנלן דתניא בששה
בחדש נתנו עשרת הדברות לישראל רבי יוסי אומר
בשבעה בו מאן דאמר בששה בששה נתנו ובשבעה
עלה מאן דאמר בשבעה בשבעה נתנו ובשבעה עלה
וכתיב ויהי משה בהר ארבעים יום וארבעים לילה
וכתיב ויהי כאשר קרב אל המחנה וירא את העגל
ומחלת ויחר אף משה וישלך מידיו את הלחת וישבר
אתם תחת ההר:

בטל התמיד: גמרא:

מסרת הש"ס והמדרשים	תורה אור
10 שמות כ'ד י'ח. 11 שמות ל'ב	6 (הלוחות) שבת פ'ו ב'; יומא ד'
ב'; ירושלמי כאן ד' ח'. 14 (בטל	י'ט.
התמיד) ערכין י'ב א'; ירושלמי ברכות ד' א'; תענית ד' ח'.

A breach was made in the walls of the city. Was that on the seventeenth of Tammuz? Is it not written (Jerem., 52. 6-7): "In the fourth month, in the ninth day of the month, the famine was sore in the city," and further on it is said (*ibid.*, 52. 7): "Then a breach was made in the city"? Said Raba, this is no difficulty, for one statement refers to the time of the First Temple, and the other to the time of the Second, as is stated in a Baraita: On the ninth day of the month a breach was made in the city during the time of the First Temple, but during the time of the Second Temple the breach was made on the seventeenth thereof.

Apostomos burned the Torah. This is a tradition.[410]

He set up an idol in the Temple. Whence is this known? It is written (Dan., 12. 11): "And from the time that the continual burnt-offering shall be taken away, and the detestable *thing* that causeth appalment set up." Was there only one (detestable thing)? Is it not written (*ibid.*, 9. 27): "And upon the wing of detestable *things?*" Said Raba, there were two, but one fell upon the other, breaking off its hand. On the idol the following inscription was later found [fol. 29a]: "Thou wert desirous to destroy His house, but I delivered thy hand to Him."[411]

On the ninth of Ab it was decreed that our ancestors should not enter the Land. Whence is

[411] The text of this passage shows many variants and the interpretations differ accordingly; see the Hebrew Notes.

הבקעה העיר בשבעה עשר בתמוז הוה

והכתיב בחדש הרביעי בתשעה לחדש ויחזק

הרעב בעיר וכתיב בתריה ותבקע העיר אמר

רבא לא קשיא כאן בראשונה כאן בשניה דתניא

5 בתשעה לחדש הבקעה העיר בראשונה ובשניה

בשבעה עשר בו:

שרף אפוסטומוס את התורה: גמרא:

העמיד צלם בהיכל: מנלן דכתיב ומעת

הוסר התמיד ולתת שקוץ שמם וחד הוה והכתיב

10 ועל כנף שקוצים משמם אמר רבא תרי הוו

ונפל חד אחבריה וקטעיה לידיה ואשתכח

^{כ״ט} דהוה כתיב עילויה ׀ אנת צבית לאחרובי ביתיה

^{ע״א} וידך אשלימת ליה:

בתשעה באב נגזר על אבותינו שלא יכנסו לארץ:

מסרת הש״ס והמדרשים	תורה אור
2 ירמיה נ׳ב ו׳. 3 ירמיה נ׳ב ז׳.	1 (הבקעה) ר׳ה י״ח ב׳; תוספתא
8 דניאל י״ב י״א. 10 דניאל ט׳ כ״ז.	סוטה ו׳ י׳; ירושלמי כאן ד׳ ח׳
	ס׳ע ל׳. 4 (דתניא) תוספתא כאן
ד׳ י׳ ס׳ע ל׳ (וע׳ ירושלמי כאן ד׳ ח׳). 8 (העמיד) ירושלמי כאן
ד׳ ח׳.

443

this known? It is written (Exod., 40. 17): "And it came to pass in the first month in the second year, on the first day of the month, that the Tabernacle was reared up;" and it is further written (Num., 10. 11): "And it came to pass in the second year in the second month on the twentieth day of the month, that the cloud was taken up from over the Tabernacle of the testimony." [It was also taught that in the first year Moses had prepared the Tabernacle, but reared it up in the second year and then sent spies.][412] It is further written (*ibid.*, 10. 33): "And they set forward from the mount of the Lord three days' journey," which R. Ḥama b. Ḥanina interpreted to mean that on that day they turned aside from the Lord. Further it is written (*ibid.*, 11. 4): "And the mixed multitude that was among them fell a lusting, and the children of Israel also wept on their part," etc. Further it is written (*ibid.*, 11. 20): "A whole month" (which brings it to the 22nd of Siwan). Further it is written (*ibid.*, 12.15): "And Miriam was shut up without the camp seven days" (which brings it to the 29th of Siwan). Further it is written (*ibid.*, 13. 2): "Send thou men," and it is stated in a Baraita that Moses sent the spies on the 29th of Siwan. Further it is written (*ibid.*, 13. 25): "And they returned from spying out the land at the end of forty days." ["Forty days?" It is only forty minus one! Said 'Abbayi,

---

[412] The passage in brackets has no bearing on the subject, and came in incidentally from the parallel passages of the Talmud noted in the מסורת הש״ס; see the Hebrew Notes. The quotation of the following verses with the

מנלן דכתיב ויהי בחדש הראשון בשנה השנית באחד
לחדש הוקם המשכן וכתיב ויהי בשנה השנית בחדש
השני בעשרים בחדש נעלה הענן מעל משכן העדת
ואמר מר שנה ראשונה עשה משה את המשכן שניה
הקים את המשכן ושלח מרגלים וכתיב ויסעו מהר
ה' דרך שלשת ימים ואמר רבי חמא בר חנינא אותו
היום סרו מאחרי ה' וכתיב והאספסף אשר בקרבו
התאוו תאוה וישבו ויבכו גם בני ישראל וגו' וכתיב
עד חדש ימים וכתיב ותסגר מרים מחוץ למחנה
שבעת ימים וכתיב שלח לך אנשים ותניא בעשרים
ותשעה בסיון שלח משה מרגלים וכתיב וישבו מתור
הארץ מקץ ארבעים יום ארבעים נכי חד הוו אמר

תורה אור   מסרת הש״ס והמדרשים

1 שמות מ' י״ז. 2 במדבר י' י״א.   4 (אמר מר) סנהדרין ס״ט ב';
5 במדבר י' ל״ג. 7 במדבר י״א   זבחים קי״ח ב'; ערכין י״ג א'.
ד'. 9 במדבר י״א כ'. 9 במדבר   6 (אותו היום) שבת קט״ז א'.
י״ב ט״ו. 10 במדבר י״ג ב'.
11 במדבר י״ג כ״ה.

---

interrupting comments, of which there are more in the
editions, purports to bring out the fact that the weeping
of the congregation (Num., 14. 1) took place on the ninth
of Ab, and that there and then the latter was fixed as the
national day of mourning, as stated by R. Johanan.

Tammuz of that year was made a full month,
as it is written (Lament., 1. 15): "He hath called
a solemn assembly[413] against me to crush my
young men."][414] Further it is written (Numb.,
14. 1): "And all the congregation lifted up their
voice, and cried; and the people wept that night,"
which verse was thus commented upon by Rabbah
in the name of R. Johanan: That day was the
ninth of Ab, the Holy One, blessed be He having
said to the Israelites: You wept without cause,
therefore I shall establish for you a weeping (on
that day) that will last throughout generations.

(*On the ninth of Ab*) *the first Temple was destroyed.* Whence is this known? It is written
(II Kings, 25. 8): "In the fifth month, on the
seventh day of the month, which was the nineteenth year of king Nebuchadnezzar, king of
Babylon, came Nebuzaradan the captain of the
guard, a servant of the king of Babylon, unto
Jerusalem." Further it is written (*ibid.*, 25. 9):
"And he burnt the house of the Lord," etc. Further it is written (Jerem., 52. 12): "In the fifth
month, in the tenth day of the month, which was
the nineteenth year of king Nebuchadrezzar,
king of Babylon, came Nebuzaradan the captain
of the guard, who stood before the king of Babylon,

---

[413] מועד, assembly, means also holiday, and as New Moon
is also a holiday, the word מועד is taken as an allusion to
the fact that in that year the month of Tammuz, which
is usually defective (29 days), was made full (30 days),
so that New Moon (מועד) of Ab was "called" out a
day later, in order to make the day of the congregation's
weeping fall on the ninth of Ab.

אביי תמה דההיא שתא מליוי מליוה דכתיב קרא
עלי מועד לשבר בחורי וכתיב ותשא כל העדה
ויתנו את קולם ויבכו העם בלילה ההוא ואמר
רבה אמר רבי יוחנן אותו היום תשעה באב היה
5 אמר להם הקדוש ברוך הוא אתם בכיתם בכיה
של חנם ואני אקבע לכם בכיה לדורות:

חרב הבית בראשונה: מנא לן דכתיב ובחדש
החמישי בשבעה לחדש היא שנת תשע עשרה שנה
למלך נבוכדנצר מלך בבל בא נבוזראדן רב
10 טבחים עבד מלך בבל בירושלם וכתיב וישרף את
בית ה' וגו' וכתיב ובחדש החמישי בעשור לחדש
היא שנת תשע עשרה שנה למלך נבוכדראצר מלך
בבל בא נבוזראדן רב טבחים עמד לפני מלך בבל

תורה אור	מסרת הש"ס והמדרשים

1 איכה א' ט"ו. 2 במדבר י"ד א'.   1 (תמוז) פסחים ע"ז א'; שבועות
7 מ"ב כ"ה ח—ט'. 11 ירמיה נ"ב י"ב.   י' א'.   4 (אותו היום) סוטה ל"ה
א'; סנהדרין ק"ד ב'; ירושלמי
כאן ד' ח' (דף ס"ח ע"ד); במ"ר ט"ז כ'; תנחומא שלח סימן כ"א
(בנדפס י"ב); תדא"ר פכ"ט.

[414] This passage is inserted by the Talmud in order
to straighten out at once the seeming discrepancies in the
dates; see note 412.

into Jerusalem." Further it is written (*ibid.*,52.13):
"And he burned the house of the Lord," etc. Now,
a Baraita, commenting upon these verses, reads:
"On the seventh" is impossible, because the
other passage has "on the tenth"; "on the tenth"
is impossible, because the other passage has "on
the seventh"; how is this to be understood? On
the seventh of the month the heathen entered
the Temple, eating and drinking therein and
breaking down its walls throughout the following eighth and ninth days until the (ninth) day
declined, as it is said (*ibid.*, 6. 4): "Woe unto
us! for the day declineth, for the shadows of
the evening are stretched out." Towards the
evening of that day they set it afire and toward
sunset of the tenth of the month it had burned
down. Therefore R. Johanan b. Zakkai said,
had I lived in that generation, I would have fixed
the tenth (as the day of mourning), for the greater part of the Temple was burnt on the tenth.
Why did the Sages of that time select the
ninth? Because they held that the beginning of the punishment is the main event.

(*On the ninth of Ab*) *the second Temple was
destroyed*. Whence is this known? It is taught
in a Baraita: R. Jose said, fortunate events are
assigned to a lucky day, but calamities are
assigned to an unlucky day. It was reported
that when the Temple was destroyed for the
first time it was on the ninth of Ab which happened to be on a Sunday, while the year was one
following immediately upon a sabbatical year;
further it was in the week in which the division
of priests from the house of Jehojarib was on

448

בירושלם וכתיב וישרף את בית ה' וגו' ותניא אי
אפשר לומר בשבעה שכבר נאמר בעשור ואי אפשר
לומר בעשור שכבר נאמר בשבעה הא כיצד בשבעה
בו נכנסו גוים להיכל ואכלו ושתו וקרקרו בו
שמיני ותשיעי עד שפנה היום שנאמר אוי לנו כי פנה
היום כי ינטו צללי ערב לעתותי הערב הציתו בו
את האור ונשרף עם שקיעת החמה בעשור לחדש
והיינו דאמר רבי יוחנן בן זכאי אלמלי הייתי באותו
הדור לא קבעתיו אלא בעשירי מפני שרובו של
היכל בו נשרף ורבנן אתחלתא דפורענותא עקר:
בשניה: מנלן דתניא רבי יוסי אומר מגלגלין זכות
ליום זכות וחובה ליום חובה אמרו כשחרב הבית
בראשונה אותו היום תשעה באב היה ומוצאי שבת
היה ומוצאי שביעית היתה ומשמרתו של יהויריב

תורה אור   מסרת הש"ס והמדרשים

1 ירמיה נ"ב י"ג.   5 ירמיה ו' ד'.   1 (ותניא) ס"ע פכ"ז; תוספתא
כאן ד' י'; ירושלמי כאן ד' ט';
מנלה א' ו'.   11 (דתניא) ס"ע ל'; שבת ל"ב א'; סנהדרין ח' א', ק"ב
א'; ב"ב ק"ט ב'; ערכין י"א ב', י"ב א'; ספרי בהעלותך ס"ח, פנחס
קל"ג; תוספתא כאן ד' ט'; יומא ה' י"ב; סנהדרין י"ד ז' ח'; ירושלמי
סנהדרין י' ב'; מכילתא דרשב"י 125; שמחות ח'.   12 (אמרו) ס"ע
ל'; ערכין י"א ב'; תוספתא כאן ד' ט'; ירושלמי כאן ד' ט'; מדרש
תהלים צ"ד.

duty; the Levites were standing on their plat-
form. [What song did they intone? They sang
the verse (Ps., 94. 23): "And He hath brought
upon them their own iniquity, and will cut them
off in their own evil;" but before they were able
to add the words: "The Lord our God will cut
them off," the heathen came in and subdued
them.] All this happened also in the second
Temple.

Bettar was taken. This is a tradition.

The City of Jerusalem was plowed over. This is
a tradition. We read in a Baraita: When
the wicked Tyrant (Titus Annius) Rufus plowed
the site of the Temple Hall, Rabban Gamaliel was
condemned to death. A certain general then appeared and, standing up in the school-house,
said, "The man with the nose[415] is wanted! the
man with the nose is wanted!" When Rabban
Gamaliel heard the call, he hid himself from the
Romans, but the general called on him secretly
and said to him: "If I save you will you bring
me to the future world?" "Yes!" replied R.
Gamaliel. "Swear it unto me!" and R.
Gamaliel swore it unto him. The Roman thereupon went up to the roof, threw himself down and
died. The decree against R. Gamaliel was then
annulled, because there was a custom that if a
decree was issued and one of those who signed
it died, the decree was annulled. A heavenly voice then came forth declaring that the general was sure to have a share in the life of the
world to come.

[415] See Kohut, *Aruch, s. v.* בעל and חטם. One of the

היתה והלוים עומדין על דוכנם ומה שירה היו
אומרים וישב עליהם את אונם וברעתם יצמיתם
ולא הספיקו לומר יצמיתם ה' אלהינו עד שבאו
גוים וכבשום וכן בשניה:

5   נלכדה ביתר: גמרא:

נחרשה העיר: גמרא:

תניא כשחרש טורנוסרופוס הרשע את האולם
נגזרה גזרה על רבן גמליאל להריגה בא אותו הגמון
ועמד בבית המדרש ואמר בעל החוטם מתבקש
10 בעל החוטם מתבקש שמע רבן גמליאל אזל טשא
מיניהו אזל לגביה בצנעא אמר ליה אי מצילנא
לך מיתית לי לעלמא דאתי אמר ליה אין אמר ליה
אשתבע לי אשתבע ליה סליק לאגרא נפל ומית
וגמירי דכי גזרי גזירתא ומית חד מיניהו מבטלי
15 לה לגזירתא יצתה בת קול ואמרה אותו הגמון מזומן
לחיי העולם הבא:

תורה אור   מסרת הש"ס והמדרשים

2 תהלים צ"ד כ"ג.   7 (תניא) ירושלמי כאן ד' סוף

ה"ח; איכ"ר א' י"ג (באבער העדה

שנ"ו).

manuscripts (see the Hebrew Notes) reads חותם, the man
of the *seal*. This suggests a new interpretation.

Our Rabbis have taught: When the first
Temple was destroyed, groups of young priests
assembled and, holding the keys of the Temple
court in their hands, went up to the roof of the
Temple and said: Master of the world! Since
we have not been considered worthy of being
Thy treasurers, we hand over the keys to
Thee. So saying, they threw the keys towards
heaven, and something like a hand appeared
and received the keys from them, whereupon
they threw themselves down into the fire
beneath. In allusion to them Isaiah laments
(Is., 22. 1–2): "The burden concerning the valley
of vision. What aileth thee now, that thou art
wholly gone up to the housetops, thou that art
full of uproar, a tumultuous city, a joyous town?
Thy slain are not slain with the sword, nor dead
in battle." And even the Holy One, blessed be
He, cried over them like a hen that clucks for
her chickens, for it is said (ib., 22. 5): "Kir[416]
shouting and crying at the mount."

*With the beginning of Ab we should limit our re-
joicing.* Said R. Judah the son of R. Samuel b.
Shilat in the name of Rab: Just as we reduce
the indulgence in amusements with the beginning of Ab, so we increase it with the beginning
of Adar [fol. 29b]. Said R. Papa, therefore
a Jew who has a lawsuit with a heathen in the
month of Ab, should try to avoid it, because his
luck is bad, but if he has a lawsuit in the month
of Adar, he should prosecute it, because in that
month his luck is good.

[416] Kir (קיר) is interpreted as κύριος, God.

תנו רבנן כשחרב הבית בראשונה נתקבצו כתות
כתות של פרחי כהנה ומפתחות העזרה בידיהם
ועלו לגגו של היכל ואמרו לפניו רבונו של עולם
הואיל ולא זכינו להיות גזברין נאמנים לפניך הרי
5 מפתחות מסורין לך וזרקום כלפי למעלה יצתה
כמין פסת יד וקבלתן מהם והם קפצו ונפלו לתוך
האור ועליהן קונן ישעיהו משא גיא חזיון מה לך
איפוא כי עלית כלך לגגות תשאות מלאה עיר
הומיה קריה עליזה חלליך לא חללי חרב ולא
10 מתי מלחמה ואף הקדוש ברוך הוא מקרקר עליהן
כתרנגולין שנאמר מקרקר קיר ושוע אל ההר:

משנכנס אב ממעטין בשמחה: אמר רב יהודה
בריה דרב שמואל בר שילת משמיה דרב כשם
שמשנכנס אב ממעטין בשמחה כך משנכנס אדר
15 מרבין בשמחה | אמר רב פפא הלכך האי בר ישראל
דאית ליה דינא בהדי גוי באב לשתמיט מיניה
דריע מזליה באדר ליזיל בהדיה דבריא מזליה:

תורה אור   מסרת הש"ס והמדרשים

7 ישעיה כ"ב א'. 11 ישעיה כ"ב ה'.   1 (ת"ר) שקלים ו' ג'; פס"ר כ"ו
(צד קל"א); ויק"ר י"ט ו' (ושם
ובירושלמי הוא מסופר על יכניה מלך יהודה); אדר"נ ספ"ד (ובנוסחא
ב הוא ספ"ז) תרגום שני אסתר א' ג' (ובשניהם מסופר על כה"ג).   15 (ר"פ
הלכך) לעיל ו' ב'; ברכות נ"ט ב', ס' ב'; שבת כ' א'; מגלה כ"א ב';
יבמות ע"ב א'; סוטה מ' א'; חולין מ"ו א', ס"ה א'.

"To give you a future and a hope" (Jerem.,
29. 11). Said R. Judah the son of R. Samuel
b. Shilat in the name of Rab, this verse alludes
to the palm-trees and linen garments.[417]

"See, the smell of my son is as the smell of a field
which the Lord hath blessed" (Gen., 27. 27).
Said R. Judah the son of R. Samuel b. Shilat
in the name of Rab: As the smell of a field of
apples.

*During the week in which the ninth of Ab falls
one should not cut one's hair or wash (one's clothes).*
Said R. Naḥman, this applies only to washing
for immediate wear, but it is allowed to wash the
clothes in order to lay them aside (for future wear).
R. Sheshet, however, said, even to wash and lay
aside is also forbidden. Said R. Sheshet, you
can derive it from the fact that (during the week
preceding the ninth of Ab) the fullers of the
house of Rab[418] were idle. R. Hamnuna raised
an objection from the following sentence of the
Mishnah: On Thursday it is allowed (to wash
clothes) in honor of the Sabbath. Now what
is the supposed purpose of the washing to which
the Mishnah here refers? Will you say that
it refers to washing for immediate wear? What
has washing for such purpose to do with the
honoring of the Sabbath? The Mishnah can thus
mean only washing for the purpose of putting
aside (for a later time), and yet the reason given
for its permission is that it is Thursday, when
the washing is done in honor of the next Sabbath,

[417] Jeremiah speaks there of the Jews in the Babylonian
exile. R. Judah (Rab) therefore asks, what future was

454

לתת לכם אחרית ותקוה אמר רב יהודה בריה
דרב שמואל בר שילת משמיה דרב אלו דקלים
וכלי פשתן:

ראה ריח בני כריח שדה אשר ברכו ה' אמר
רב יהודה בריה דרב שמואל בר שילת משמיה
דרב כריח שדה של תפוחים:

שבת שחל תשעה באב להיות בתוכה אסורין
לספר ולכבס אמר רב נחמן לא שנו אלא לכבס
וללבוש אבל לכבס ולהניח מותר ורב ששת אמר
אפילו לכבס ולהניח אסור אמר רב ששת תדע
דבטלי קצרי דבי רב מתיב רב המנונא ובחמשי
מותרין מפני כבוד השבת למאי אילימא לכבס
וללבוש מאי כבוד השבת איכא אלא לאו לכבס
ולהניח וטעמא דבחמשי מותרין מפני כבוד השבת

תורה אור   מסרת הש"ס והמדרשים

1 ירמיה כ"ט י"א.   4 בראשית כ"ז,   11 (קצרי) ירושלמי כאן ד' ט'.
כ"ז.   11 (ובחמשי) לעיל י"ב ב', ט"ו ב',
                                   כ"ו ב'; יבמות מ"ג א'; ירושלמי
                                   כאן ב' י"ב (ס"ה ד') ד' ט'; מו"ק ג' א'; יבמות ספ"ו.

there for Israel? and answers that the verse contains only
promises of material, not of spiritual or political, value.
This and the following interpretation were placed here
because they are, like the preceding one, given by the same
authority (R. Judah); comp. above, note 243.

[418] Or house of learning?

but in the preceding days of the week it would not be allowed! You may nevertheless say that the Mishnah refers to washing for immediate wear, but has in view one who possesses only one shirt,[419] which interpretation is in keeping with what was said by R. Asi in the name of R. Johanan, namely, that one who possesses only one shirt is allowed to wash it on the Half-festivals.[420]

R. Benjamin b. Jephet also said in the name of R. Eleazar that the prohibition of washing refers only to washing for immediate wear, but washing for the purpose of putting aside is allowed. An objection was again raised from the following Baraita: It is not allowed to wash before the ninth of Ab (within the same week) even when the intention is to put the clothes aside for use after the ninth of Ab; our (Babylonian) fine laundry work is under the same rule as their (Palestinian) plain washing; linen garments are not subject to the law forbidding laundering! This, indeed, is a refutation.

R. Isaac b. Jacob Bar-Giyore sent the following statement in the name of R. Johanan: Although it was said that linen garments are not subject to the law forbidding washing, it is nevertheless forbidden to put on washed linen garments during the week in which the ninth of Ab occurs. Said Rab, this prohibition applies only to the days preceding the ninth (within the same week), but on the days following,

---

[419] Who will have to wear it also on the coming Sabbath.

[420] Ordinarily this is forbidden; see *Moed Katan* 14a.

אבל בשאר יומי לא לעולם לכבס וללבוש ובמי
שאין לו אלא חלוק אחד וכי הא דאמר רב אסי
אמר רבי יוחנן מי שאין לו אלא חלוק אחד מותר
לכבסו בחולו של מועד:

5 איתמר נמי אמר רבי בנימן בר יפת אמר רבי
אלעזר לא שנו אלא לכבס וללבוש אבל לכבס
ולהניח מותר מיתיבי אסור לכבס לפני תשעה באב
ואפילו להניח לאחר תשעה באב וגהוץ שלנו
ככבוס שלהן וכלי פשתן אין בהן משום גהוץ
10 תיובתא:

שלח רב יצחק בר יעקב בר גיורי משמיה דרבי
יוחנן אף על פי שאמרו כלי פשתן אין בהם משום
גהוץ אסור ללבשן בשבת שחל תשעה באב להיות
בתוכה אמר רב לא שנו אלא לפניו אבל לאחריו

מסרת הש״ס והמדרשים

2 (רב אסי) מו״ק י״ד א׳, י״ח א׳; 　　כתובות י׳ ב׳. 　　14 (לאחריו)
חולין ק״ז ב׳. 8 (גיהוץ שלנו) 　　ירושלמי כאן ד׳ ט׳ (ושם הוא
פלוגתא דר״י ור״ל).

the wearing is permitted. Samuel, however,
said, it is forbidden even on the days following.
An objection was raised from this Baraita: During the week in which the ninth of Ab occurs, one
is not allowed to cut one's hair or to wash one's
clothes. What is the exact meaning of this law?
It is as follows: If the ninth happens to be on
Sunday, it is allowed to wash during all the following days of the week; if it be on Monday, Tuesday,
Wednesday, or Thursday, it is not allowed to
wash on any of the days (of the week) preceding it, while on the days following, it is
allowed; if the ninth happens to be on Friday,
it is allowed to wash on Thursday for the honor
of the Sabbath; if, however, one failed to wash on
Thursday, he may do so on Friday from Minḥah
time and onward, but prior to Minḥah time
it is forbidden. ['Abbayi, however, or, as some
say, R. 'Aḥa b. Jacob, deprecated this deed.][421] If
the ninth be on Monday or Thursday, three men
are called up to read the Torah, the last one of
whom reads also the Haftarah, but if it be on
Tuesday or Wednesday, one man reads both
the Torah and the Haftarah; R. Jose said,
always three men must read the Torah, the last
one of whom also reads the Haftarah. Now, is
not this Baraita (which teaches explicitly that
on the days following the ninth, washing is allowed) a refutation of Samuel? Samuel can

[421] This is an insertion in the body of the Baraita; see
above, notes 316, 412, 414. The expression rendered in
the text 'deprecated' means literally, 'cursed.'

מותר ושמואל אמר אפילו לאחריו נמי אסור מיתיבי

שבת שחל תשעה באב להיות בתוכה אסורין

לספר ולכבס כיצד חל להיות באחד בשבת מותר

לכבס כל השבת כולה חל להיות בשני או בשלישי

5 או ברביעי או בחמשי לפניו אסור לאחריו מותר

חל להיות בערב שבת מותר לכבס בחמשי

מפני כבוד השבת ואם לא כבס בחמשי מותר

לכבס בערב שבת מן המנחה ולמעלה לייט עלה

אביי ואיתימא רב אחא בר יעקב אהא חל להיות

10 בשני או בחמשי קורין שלשה ומפטיר אחד בשלישי

וברביעי קורא אחד ומפטיר אחד רבי יוסי אומר

לעולם קורין שלשה ומפטיר אחד תיובתא דשמואל

מסרת הש״ס והמדרשים

2 (שבת) לעיל כ״ו ב׳; יבמות מ״ג א׳, כ״ב א׳; פסחים ק״ד א׳; מו״ק א׳; ירושלמי כאן ד׳ ט׳; יבמות י״ב ב׳; קדושין ל״ג ב ‎, ע״א ב׳; ספ״ו. 8 (לייט) ברכות י״ג ב׳, ט״ו נדה י״ד א׳. 9 (חל להיות) מגלה כ״ב ב׳.

459

answer that the Tannaim differ regarding this
matter, for it is taught in a Baraita: If the ninth
of Ab or the eve of the ninth of Ab is on
Saturday, one may continue eating as much
as one wants and one may place on his table
a royal banquet like that of king Solomon in his
time; cutting the hair and washing clothes are
forbidden from the first of the month of Ab to
the day of the fast; this is the opinion of R. Meir;
R. Judah said, cutting the hair and washing are
forbidden during the entire month; Rabban
Simeon b. Gamaliel says, they are forbidden
only during the week in which the ninth occurs.
Another Baraita teaches: Mourning must be
observed from the first of the month to the day
of the fast; this is the opinion of R. Meir; R.
Judah says, it must be observed during the
entire month; Rabban Simeon b. Gamaliel says,
only during the week in which the ninth occurs.

Said R. Johanan: All of these three authorities
base their opinions on one and the same verse
(Hosea, 2.13): "I will cause all her mirth to
cease, her feasts, her new moons, and her
sabbaths, and all her appointed seasons."
The authority that says: "from the first of the
month to the day of the fast" [fol. 30a] derives
it from the word "ḥaggah" (her feast, which
sometimes designates new moon); he who says
"the entire month" derives it from "ḥodshah" (her
new moon, which means also the whole month),
while he who says: "only during the week in
which the ninth occurs," derives it from "shabbat-
tah" (her sabbath, which means also week).

אמר לך שמואל תנאי היא דתניא תשעה באב שחל

להיות בשבת וכן ערב תשעה באב שחל להיות

בשבת אוכל ושותה כל צרכו ומעלה על שלחנו

אפילו כסעודת שלמה בשעתו ואסור לספר ולכבס

5 מראש חדש ועד התענית דברי רבי מאיר רבי

יהודה אומר כל החדש כלו אסור רבן שמעון בן

גמליאל אומר אין אסור אלא אותה שבת בלבד

ותניא אידך ונוהג אבל מראש חדש ועד התענית

דברי רבי מאיר רבי יהודה אומר כל החדש כלו

10 אסור רבן שמעון בן גמליאל אומר אין אסור אלא

אותה שבת בלבד אמר רבי יוחנן ושלשתן מקרא

אחד דרשו והשבתי כל משושה חגה חדשה ושבתה

וכל מועדה מאן דאמר מראש חדש ועד התענית[1] ל"א
ע"א

מחגה מאן דאמר כל החדש כלו אסור מחדשה

15 ומאן דאמר אין אסור אלא אותה שבת בלבד

משבתה:

תורה אור	מסרת הש"ס והמדרשים
12 הושע ב' י"ג.	1 (דתניא) ערובין מ"א א'; תוספתא
	תענית ד' י"ג; ירושלמי כאן ד' י'.
	12 (והשבתי) ירושלמי כאן ד' ט'. 12 (חגה חדשה שבתה) ירושלמי כאן
	ד' ט'.

Said Raba, the law is in accordance with R. Meir; Raba further said, the law is in accordance with Rabban Simeon b. Gamaliel. Both these statements of Raba were made for the purpose of indicating a lenient view, and both were needed; for if he had said only the law is in accordance with R. Meir, one might have understood it to mean that the prohibition is in force from the very beginning of the month to the fast day (as is actually the opinion of R. Meir), therefore he adds that the law is in accordance with Rabban Simeon b. Gamaliel (who restricts it to the week of the ninth); if, on the other hand, he had said only the law is in accordance with Rabban Simeon b. Gamaliel, one might have understood him to mean that the prohibition extends even to the days following immediately upon the ninth (as is the opinion of Rabban Simeon), therefore he said also the law is in accordance with R. Meir (who denies this).

On the day before the ninth of Ab one should not partake of two courses, etc. Said R. Judah in the name of Rab, this provision applies only to the time after twelve o'clock noon, but not to the time prior to this hour. Some report that R. Judah said in the name of Rab: This provision applies only to the last meal before the fast, but if it is not the last meal before the fast, one may eat of two courses. Both these statements were made to indicate leniency and both are needed for the purpose, for had it been said only that the provision applies to the last

462

אמר רבא הלכה כרבי מאיר ואמר רבא הלכה

כרבן שמעון בן גמליאל ותרויהו לקולא וצריכא

דאי אשמעינן הלכה כרבי מאיר הוה אמינא אפילו

מראש חדש קא משמע לן הלכה כרבן שמעון בן

גמליאל ואי אשמעינן הלכה כרבן שמעון בן גמליאל

הוה אמינא אפילו לאחריו קא משמע לן הלכה

כרבי מאיר:

ערב תשעה באב לא יאכל אדם שני תבשילין

כו': אמר רב יהודה אמר רב לא שנו אלא משש

שעות ולמעלה אבל משש שעות ולמטה מותר ואמר

רב יהודה אמר רב לא שנו אלא בסעודה המפסיק

בה אבל בסעודה שאינו מפסיק בה מותר ותרויהו

לקולא וצריכא דאי אשמעינן בסעודה המפסיק בה

meal, one might have understood it to include a meal taken (as the last) in the morning, therefore we are told that it applies only to a meal taken after noon; if, on the other hand, it had been said only that the provision applies to a meal taken after noon, I might have understood it to include even a meal which is not the last, therefore we are informed that it applies only to the last meal before the fast.

There is one Baraita that agrees with the first statement, while another Baraita agrees with the second statement. The Baraita that agrees with the second statement reads: He who takes a meal on the eve of the ninth of Ab, may, if he expects to take another meal at a later hour, eat meat and drink wine, but if he does not expect to eat again, he is not allowed to do so. The Baraita that agrees with the first statement reads: On the eve of the ninth of Ab one should not eat of two courses, neither eat meat nor drink wine; Rabban Simeon b. Gamaliel says, he should change his usual mode of living. Said R. Judah: How is this change to be made? If he was used to eat of two courses, he should eat of only one; if he was used to dine in the company of ten people, he should now dine with five; and if he was used to drink wine out of ten successive glasses, he should now drink the same quantity in five glasses; the foregoing prohibitions apply only to meals taken in the afternoon, but not to the forenoon.

Another Baraita reads: On the eve of the ninth of Ab one should not eat of two courses, nor eat meat or drink wine; this is the opinion

הוה אמינא אפילו משש שעות ולמטה קא משמע לן
משש שעות ולמעלה ואי אשמעינן משש שעות
ולמעלה הוה אמינא אפילו בסעודה שאינו מפסיק
בה קא משמע לן בסעודה המפסיק בה:

5 תניא כלישנא קמא תניא כלישנא בתרא תניא
כלישנא בתרא הסועד ערב תשעה באב אם עתיד
לסעוד סעודה אחרת מותר לאכול בשר ולשתות
יין ואם לאו אסור לאכול בשר ולשתות יין תניא
כלישנא קמא ערב תשעה באב לא יאכל אדם שני
10 תבשילין לא יאכל בשר ולא ישתה יין רבן שמעון
בן גמליאל אומר ישנה אמר רבי יהודה כיצד משנה
אם היה רגיל לאכול שני תבשילין אוכל אחד היה
רגיל לסעוד בעשרה בני אדם סועד בחמשה היה
רגיל לשתות בעשרה כוסות שותה בחמשה במה
15 דברים אמורים משש שעות ולמעלה אבל משש
שעות ולמטה מותר:

תניא אידך ערב תשעה באב לא יאכל אדם שני
תבשילין לא יאכל בשר ולא ישתה יין דברי רבי

מסרת הש"ס והמדרשים

6 (ערב ת"ב) לעיל כ"ו ב'; סנהדרין ע' א'; איכ"ר (באבער) ג' ט"ז.

of R. Meir, but the other Sages said, he should make a change, while in the case of meat and wine he should reduce the quantity. How is he to reduce it? If he was used to eat a pound of meat, he should now eat only half a pound; if he was used to drink a *log* of wine, he should drink half a *log;* and if he was not used to meat or wine, he should not partake of them at all. R. Simeon b. Gamaliel said, if he was used to eat radishes or salted food after the meals, he may do so.

Our Rabbis have taught: One is not allowed to eat meat or to drink wine at any meal that is intended to be the last before the ninth of Ab; nor is it allowed to bathe after this meal. If it is not the last before the ninth of Ab, meat and wine are allowed, and one may still bathe after the meal. R. Ishmael b. R. Jose said in the name of his father, as long as one is allowed to eat (any kind of food), he is allowed also to bathe.

Our Rabbis have taught: All the laws that apply to a mourner apply also to the ninth of Ab; on that day eating, drinking, bathing, anointing, wearing shoes, and cohabitation are forbidden; it is also forbidden to read in the Pentateuch, the Prophets and the Hagiographa, or to study the Mishnah, Midrash, Talmud, Halakot and Haggadot;[422] one may read, however, parts of the Torah which he was not used

[422] Because such studies give pleasure; see below.

מאיר וחכמים אומרים ישנה בבשר וביין ימעט
כיצד ממעט אם היה רגיל לאכול לטרא בשר
אוכל חצי לטרא היה רגיל לשתות לוג יין שותה
חצי לוג ואם אינו רגיל כל עקר אסור רבן שמעון
5 בן גמליאל אומר אם היה רגיל לאכול אחר סעודתו
צנון או מליח הרשות בידו:

תנו רבנן כל שהוא משום תשעה באב אסור לאכול
בשר ואסור לשתות יין ואסור לרחוץ וכל שאינו
משום תשעה באב מותר לאכול בשר ומותר לשתות
10 יין ומותר לרחוץ רבי ישמעאל ברבי יוסי אומר
משום אביו כל שעה שמותר לאכול מותר לרחוץ:

תנו רבנן כל מצות הנוהגות באבל נוהגות בתשעה
באב אסור ברחיצה ובסיכה ובנעילת הסנדל
ובתשמיש המטה ואסור לקרות בתורה ובנביאים
15 ובכתובים ולשנות במשנה במדרש ובתלמוד
ובהלכות ובאגדות אבל קורא הוא במקום שאינו

מסרת הש״ס והמדרשים

2 (היה רגיל לאכול ליטרא) ירושלמי
כאן ד' י' (ושם קאי על ישנה וע'
ירושלמי סנהדרין י' ב' ופסדר״כ
שובה באבער הערה ע״ד ושהש״ר א'
פסוק שחורה אני). 7 (כל שהוא)
תוספתא כאן ד' י״א; איכ״ר ג' ו'.
12 (ת״ר) מו״ק כ״א א'; ירושלמי מו״ק
ג' ה' (דף פ״ב ע״ד); שמחות פ״ו.

14 (בתנ״ך) ירושלמי שבת ט״ז א';
ויק״ר ט״ו ד'; איכ״ר ד' כ'. 15
(ולשנות) לעיל ט״ז א'; ברכות כ״ב
א'; מו״ק ט״ו א', כ״א א'; תוספתא
ברכות ב' י״ג; ירושלמי מו״ק ג' ה'
(דף פ״ב ע״ד); שמחות פ״ו.
16 (שאינו רגיל) ירושלמי מו״ק ג'
ה' (דף פ״ב ע״ד).

to read before, and study parts of the Mishnah etc., which he was not used to study before;[423] one may read also the Book of Lamentations, Job, and the sad portions of Jeremiah; the children are not free from school; this is the opinion of R. Meir; R. Judah says, one is not allowed to read even parts of the Torah which he was not used to read before, nor to study parts of the Mishnah which he was not used to study before, but he may read the Lamentations, Job, and the sad portions of Jeremiah; and the children are free from school; the reason for the prohibition (of study) is that it is said (Ps., 19. 9): "The precepts of the Lord are right, rejoicing the heart."

One should not eat meat or drink wine. It was taught in a Baraita: But one may eat salted (pickled) meat and drink wine from his vat.[424] How long does pickled meat retain its original (natural) taste (so that it is prohibited on the eve of the ninth of Ab)? Said R. Ḥinena b. Kahana in the name of Samuel, as long as it is within the time set for the eating of the meat of a peace offering (*i. e.,* 60 hours).[425] How long is wine to be considered as coming fresh from the vat? As long as it is fermenting. It was taught in a Baraita: New wine that is still fermenting does not come under the law forbidding to drink liquids left uncovered.[426] How long does the fermentation last? Three days.

---

[423] Because it requires exertion.
[424] Because it does not taste good.
[425] See Mishnah *Zebaḥim,* V, 7.

רגיל לקרות ושונה במקום שאינו רגיל לשנות וקורא
בקנות ובאיוב ובדברים הרעים שבירמיה ותינוקות
של בית רבן אינן בטלין דברי רבי מאיר רבי יהודה
אומר אף אינו קורא במקום שאינו רגיל לקרות
5 ואינו שונה במקום שאינו רגיל לשנות אבל קורא
הוא בקנות ובאיוב ובדברים הרעים שבירמיה
ותינוקות של בית רבן בטלים בו משום שנאמר פקודי
ה' ישרים משמחי לב:

לא יאכל בשר ולא ישתה יין: תנא אבל אוכל
10 הוא בשר מליח ושותה יין מגתו בשר מליח עד
כמה אמר רב חיננא בר כהנא אמר שמואל כל זמן
שהוא כשלמים יין מגתו עד כמה כל זמן שהוא תוסס:
תניא יין תוסס אין בו משום גלוי וכמה תסיסתו
שלשה ימים:

מסרת הש"ס והמדרשים	תורה אור
2 (בקנות) ויק"ר ט"ו ד'; ירושלמי	7 תהלים י"ט ט'.
שבת ט"ז א'; איכ"ר ד' כ'. 9 (תנא)	

סנהדרין ע' א'. 13 (תניא יין) סנהדרין ע' א'; ע"ז ל' א'; ירושלמי תרומות
ח' ו' (ריש דף מ"ו); תוספתא תרומות ז' ט"ו.

---

[426] It was forbidden to drink wine, water, or milk from
a vessel that was left uncovered and unguarded, as a
snake might have drunk from it, depositing its poison; see
Mishnah, *Terumot*, VIII, 4.

Said R. Judah in the name of Rab: R. Judah
b. R. 'Il'ai had the following custom: On the eve
of the ninth of Ab he would order to be brought to
him dry bread with salt; then he would sit down
[fol. 30b] behind the oven,[427] eat the bread and
drink a pitcher of water and behave as if the
dead body of a near relative were lying before
him.

We read in a Mishnah (Pesaḥim, 54b):
Wherever it is customary to work on the ninth of
Ab, one may do so, but if it is the custom of the
place not to work, one must refrain from work;
scholars must abstain from work in whatever
place they may happen to be;   Rabban Simeon
b. Gamaliel said: Everybody should in this respect
always conduct himself as if he were a scholar.
We further read in a Baraita: Rabban Simeon
b. Gamaliel said, one should always conduct
himself as a scholar (and abstain from work), so
that he may be more conscious of his fast; Rabban Gamaliel said, he who eats and drinks on the
ninth of Ab, is as if he ate on the Day of Atonement; R. 'Aḳiba said, he who works on the
ninth of Ab will never see a sign of blessing
(success); the other Sages said, he who eats
and drinks on the ninth of Ab, will not live to
see the rejoicing of Jerusalem, for it is said (Is.,
66. 10): "Rejoice ye with Jerusalem, and be
glad with her, all ye that love her; rejoice for joy

---

[427] That is, in a humble, dejected place, literally, between
the oven for baking (תנור) and that for cooking (כירים).

אמר רב יהודה אמר רב כך היה מנהגו של רבי
יהודה ברבי אלעאי ערב תשעה באב מביאין לו פת
חרבה במלח ויושב│בין תנור לכירים ואוכלה
ושותה עליה קיתון של מים ודומה כמי שמתו מוטל
5 לפניו:

תנן התם מקום שנהגו לעשות מלאכה בתשעה
באב עושין מקום שנהגו שלא לעשות אין עושין
ובכל מקום תלמידי חכמים בטלים רבן שמעון בן
גמליאל אומר לעולם יעשה אדם עצמו כתלמיד
10 חכם ותניא רבן שמעון בן גמליאל אומר לעולם
יעשה אדם עצמו כתלמיד חכם כדי שיתענה רבן
גמליאל אומר כל האוכל ושותה בתשעה באב
כאלו אכל ושתה ביום הכפורים רבי עקיבא אומר
כל העושה מלאכה בתשעה באב אינו רואה סימן
15 ברכה לעולם וחכמים אומרים כל האוכל ושותה
בתשעה באב אינו רואה בשמחתה של ירושלם
שנאמר שמחו את ירושלם וגילו בה כל אהביה

תורה אור	מסרת הש״ס והמדרשים

17 ישעיה ס״ו י׳.

1 (ר״י בר׳ אלעאי) בירוש׳ כאן
ואיכ״ר ג׳ ו׳ מובא בשנוי לשון שרב
בעצמו נהג כך. 4 (שמתו) ירושלמי כאן ד׳ י׳. 6 (תנן) ברכות י״ז ב׳;
פסחים נ״ד א׳. 9 (תלמיד) לעיל י׳ ב׳; פסחים נ״ד ב׳; ירושלמי ברכות
ספ״ב; תוספתא תענית א׳ ז׳. 14 (מלאכה) ע׳ ירושלמי כאן א׳ ריש ה״ו.

with her, all ye that mourn for her"—that is to
say, all those who mourn for her will witness her
rejoicing, while those who do not mourn for her,
will not witness her rejoicing; moreover, of him
who eats meat and drinks wine on the ninth of
Ab, Scripture says (Ezek., 32.27): "And their
iniquities are upon their bones."

*R. Judah made it obligatory to overturn the couches,
but the other Sages did not agree with him.* It is
taught in a Baraita: The Sages said to R.
Judah: If your opinion be accepted, what shall
become of pregnant and nursing women? Said
R. Judah in reply to the other Sages: I am speaking only of those who can do it. The same
is taught also in the following Baraita: The
Sages accept R. Judah's opinion in the case
of people who can do it (overturn their couches),
while R. Judah accedes to the opinion of the Sages
in the case of those who can not do it. What then
is the difference between the two views? Said
'Abbayi, there is a difference with regard to other
couches in the house (upon which he does
not sleep), as is evident from this Baraita: One
should overturn not only the couch upon which he
sleeps, but also all the other couches in the
house. Said Raba, the law is in accordance
with the version given by the author of our
Mishnah, namely that the Sages did not accept
R. Judah's opinion at all.[428]

[428] That is, they do not require the overturning of couches,
even when it can be done.

שישו אתה משוש כל המתאבלים עליה כל המתאבל
על ירושלם זוכה ורואה בשמחתה וכל שאינו
מתאבל על ירושלם אינו זוכה לראות בשמחתה
וכל האוכל בשר ושותה יין בתשעה באב עליו
הכתוב אומר ותהי עונותם על עצמתם: 5

רבי יהודה מחייב בכפית המטה ולא הודו לו
חכמים: תניא אמרו לו לרבי יהודה לדבריך
עוברות ומיניקות מה תהא עליהן אמר להם אף אני
לא אמרתי אלא ביכול תניא נמי הכי מודים חכמים
לרבי יהודה ביכול ומודה רבי יהודה לחכמים 10
בשאינו יכול מאי ביניהו אמר אביי שאר מטות
איכא ביניהו כדתניא הכופה את מטתו לא מטתו
בלבד הוא כופה אלא כל המטות שיש לו בתוך
ביתו הוא כופה אמר רבא הלכתא כתנא דידן
דאמר ולא הודו לו חכמים כל עקר: 15

מסרת הש"ס והמדרשים	תורה אור

5 יחזקאל ל"ב כ"ז. 1 (המתאבל) תוספתא תענית ד'
י"ד; סוטה ט"ו ט"ו; פסדר"כ פסקא
אחריתא דשוש אשיש; פס"ר ספכ"ח ועי' ב"ב ס' ב' ומדרש תהלים קל"ז
ואיכה זוטא סי' כ"ח). 6 (ולא הודו) ע' ירושלמי כאן ד' סוף י'.
12 (כדתניא) מו"ק כ"ז א'; נדרים נ"ו א'; סנהדרין כ' א'.

Said Rabban Simeon b. Gamaliel, the Israelites never had such joyous holidays as the fifteenth of Ab and the Day of Atonement. This is quite right so far as the Day of Atonement is concerned, which is a day of pardon and forgiveness, a day on which the second Tables were given,[429] but why the fifteenth of Ab? Said R. Judah in the name of Samuel, the fifteenth of Ab is the day on which the (twelve) tribes were given permission to intermarry.[430] What was the Scriptural basis for this permission? The verse (Numb., 36.6): *"This* is the thing which the Lord hath commanded concerning the daughters of Zelophehad," etc., which means that 'this thing' (forbidding intermarriage) shall apply only to *this* generation (of Moses).

Rabbah b. Bar-Ḥanah said in the name of R. Johanan, the fifteenth of Ab is the day on which the tribe of Benjamin was permitted to enter the congregation of Israel (to marry the daughters of the other tribes), as it is said (Jud., 21. 1): "Now the men of Israel had sworn in Mizpah, saying: There shall not any of us give his daughter unto Benjamin to wife." How did they derive the permission? The phrase "any of *us*" was interpreted to imply: "but not of our descendants."

R. Dimi b. Joseph said in the name of R. Naḥman, the fifteenth of Ab is the day on which the last one of the generation that was doomed to die

---

[429] Deut., 10. It is figured out that this was on the Day of Atonement; see Rashi.

[430] Annulling the ancient law against it (Num., 36.7).

אמר רבן שמעון בן גמליאל לא היו ימים טובים

לישראל כחמשה עשר באב וכיום הכפורים:

בשלמא יום הכפורים יום סליחה ומחילה ויום

שנתנו בו לוחות האחרונות אלא חמשה עשר באב

5 מאי היא אמר רב יהודה אמר שמואל יום שהותרו

שבטים לבא זה בזה מאי דרוש זה הדבר אשר צוה

ה' לבנות צלפחד וגו' דבר זה לא יהא נוהג אלא

בדור זה:

רבה בר בר חנה אמר רבי יוחנן יום שהותר שבט

10 בנימן לבא בקהל שנאמר ואיש ישראל נשבע

במצפה לאמר איש ממנו לא יתן בתו לבנימן לאשה

מאי דרוש ממנו ולא מבנינו:

רב דימי בר יוסף אמר רב נחמן יום שכלו בו

תורה אור   מסרת הש"ס והמדרשים

6 במדבר ל"ו ו'.   10 שופטים כ"א   3 (בשלמא וכו') ב"ב קכ"א א';
א'.   ירושלמי כאן ד' י"א; איכ"ר פתיחה
ל"ג.   6 (שבטים) ב"ב וירושלמי
ואיכ"ר שם.   9 (שבט בנימן) ב"ב וירושלמי ואיכ"ר שם.

in the desert, died; for it was stated by some authority, God did not address Himself to Moses until the last one of that generation had died,[431] as it is said (Deut., 2. 16–17): "So it came to pass, when all the men of war were consumed and dead from among the people, that the Lord spoke unto me saying," that is to say: To me then came a message through speech.[432]

'Ulla said, it is the day on which Hosea (son of Elah) abolished the guards whom Jeroboam son of Nebat had stationed on the roads in order to prevent the Israelites from going up to Jerusalem for the festivals[433] [fol. 31a].

R. Matnah said, it is the day on which permission was given to bury those slain at Bettar,[434] which accords with what R. Matnah said elsewhere, that on the day on which the slain of Bettar were given over for burial, there was introduced in Jabneh (Jamnia) the benediction, "Who is good and beneficent,"[435] good, because the corpses had not become putrid, beneficent, because they were given over for burial.

---

[431] Comp. Rashbam to *Baba Batra*, 121b, top, who qualifies it as referring only to direct personal speech, to the exclusion of communications through the Urim and Tummim or through angels. Rashi quotes here this view anonymously and calls it erroneous (נמנום).

[432] Comp. Rashbam, *l. c.*

[433] This is based on II Kings, 17. 2, where it is said that Hosea did that which was evil in the sight of God, "yet not as the kings of Israel that were before him." Comp. *Giṭṭin* 88a; above, p. 432.

[434] During the Bar-Kokhba War; see the Mishnah.

מתי מדבר דאמר מר עד שלא כלו מתי מדבר לא
היה דבור עם משה שנאמר ויהי כאשר תמו כל
אנשי המלחמה וגו' וכתיב וידבר ה' אלי לאמר
אלי היה בדבור:

5 עולא אמר יום שבטל הושע בן אלה פרדסיות
שהושיב ירבעם בן נבט על הדרכים שלא יעלו
ישראל לרגל:

ורב מתנה אמר יום שנתנו הרוגי ביתר לקבורה
דאמר רב מתנה אותו היום שנתנו הרוגי ביתר
10 לקבורה תקנו ביבנה הטוב והמטיב הטוב שלא
הסריחו והמטיב שנתנו לקבורה:

מסרת הש״ס והמדרשים	תורה אור
	2 דברים ב' ט״ז–י״ז.

1 (מתי מדבר) ב״ב קכ״א א'
ובירושלמי ואיכ״ר שם מפורש
יותר וע' ר"ח ורש"י ותוספות ורשב"ם). 4 (בדבור) ב"ב קכ"א ב'; ספרא
ויקרא א' ספ"ב; מכלתא בא א'; ירושלמי תענית ג' ד'; שהש"ר
ב' י"ג אות ב'. 6 (שהושיב) לעיל כ"ח א'; גטין פ"ח א'; מ"ק כ"ח א';
ב"ב קכ"א ב'; ס"ע כ"ב; ירושלמי כאן ד' י"א; איכ"ר פתיחה ל"ג.
8 (הרוגי ביתר) ב"ב קכ"א ב'; איכ"ר פתיחה ל"ג. 10 (הטוב והמטיב)
ברכות מ"ח ב'; ב"ב קכ"א ב'; ירושלמי תענית ד' ח' (דף ס"ט ע"א);
ברכות א' סוף ה"ח, ז' ה"א; תנחומא מסעי ה' (בנדפס ו'); במ"ר כ"ג
ז'; איכ"ר ב' ב' (באבער צד 104).

[435] The fourth (added) benediction in the grace after
meals.

Both Rabbah and R. Joseph said, it is the day on which they ceased cutting wood (trees) for the altar, for we read in a Baraita: R. Eliezer the Great said, from the fifteenth of Ab and onward the power of the sun weakens and therefore they cut no more wood for the altar.[436]   Said R. Menashiya: And this day was called, "the day of Breaking the Axe."[437]   From that time on any one who increases his study of the Torah (because of the lengthened evenings), will lengthen his life, and he who does not increase his study, will be taken away.[438]   What does "taken away" mean?   R. Joseph taught: His mother will bury him.[439]

On those days the sons of Jerusalem used to go out dressed in white garments which they borrowed from one another, etc. Our Rabbis have taught: The daughter of a king borrowed from the daughter of the High Priest, the daughter of the High Priest from the daughter of the Segan,[439a] the daughter of the Segan[439a] from the daughter of the priest anointed as chaplain of the army, and the daughter of the anointed army chaplain from the daughter of the ordinary priest, and all the Israelites borrowed from one another, in order not to cause shame to him who had no garments of his own.

[436] The law forbade burning fresh, moist wood on the altar, because it produced too much smoke and also because it harbored wood-worms that made it unfit; see Mishnah, *Middot* II, 5. Between Nisan and the 15th of Ab, it was thought, the trees were dried by the strong rays of the sun.

רבה ורב יוסף דאמרי תרוייהו יום שהיו פוסקין
בו מלכרות עצים למערכה דתניא רבי אליעזר
הגדול אומר מחמשה עשר באב ואילך תשש כחה
של חמה ולא היו כורתין עצים למערכה לפי שאינן
יבשין אמר רב מנשיא וקרו ליה יום תבר מגל מכאן
ואילך דמוסיף יוסיף ודלא מוסיף יאסף מאי יאסף
תני רב יוסף תקבריה אמיה:

שבהן בני ירושלם וכו': תנו רבנן בת מלך שואלת
מבת כהן גדול בת כהן גדול שואלת מבת סגן בת
סגן שואלת מבת משוח מלחמה בת משוח מלחמה
שואלת מבת כהן הדיוט וכל ישרא ל שואלין זה מזה
כדי שלא לבייש את מי שאין לו:

מסרת הש"ס והמדרשים

2 (עצים) ב"ב קכ"א ב'; ירושלמי   6 (דלא מוסיף) אבות א' י"ג; ב"ב
כאן ד' י"א; איכ"ר פתיחה ל"ג.   ואיכ"ר שם. 7 (תקבריה) ב"ב שם.
5 (תבר מגל) ב"ב ואיכ"ר שם.   8 (ת"ר) ירושלמי סוף פרקין.

The 15th of Ab thus marked the beginning of a period of
more leisure and hence was proclaimed a holiday.

[437] As an instrument for which there was no immediate
use.

[438] Comp. Mishnah, *Abot*, 1.13.

[439] That is, he will die prematurely; see the Hebrew Notes.

[439a] See note 200 a.

479

All these garments had to be immersed. Said
R. Zerika in the name of R. Eleazar, this had to
be done even though the garments had been
folded up and lying in a chest.

*The daughters of Jerusalem used to go out...
and dance in the vineyards.* It was taught in a
Baraita that all single men used to betake
themselves to those places (to select wives).

Young man, etc. The beautiful ones among
them said: "Fix your eyes upon beauty, for
a woman is made only for beauty!" Those who
were of distinguished families said: "Give your
choice to family, for the purpose of woman is to
raise a family." The homely girls said, "Make
your purchase for the sake of Heaven, in
order that you may be adorned with wealth."

Said R. Helbo in the name of R. 'Ulla of
Bir, who said it in the name of R. Eleazar,
in the future the Holy One, blessed be He, will
arrange a chorus for the righteous in Paradise.
He will sit in the center and each of the righteous will be able to point to Him with his
finger, as it is said (Is., 25. 9): "And it shall
be said in that day: Lo, this is our God, for
whom we waited, that He might save us; this is
the Lord, for whom we waited, we will be glad
and rejoice in His salvation."[440]

---

[440] This homily of R. Helbo is given here in order to
close the tractate with words of cheer and consolation;
see above, notes 222, 390.

וכל הכלים טעונין טבילה: אמר רבי זריקא אמר
רבי אלעזר אפילו מקופלין ומונחין בקופסא:
ובנות ירושלם יוצאות וחלות בכרמים: תנא מי
שאין לו אשה נפנה לׄשם:

5 וכך היו אומרות בחור וכו': תנו רבנן יפפיות
שבהן אומרות תנו עיניכם ביפי שאין אשה אלא
ליפי מיוחסות שבהן אומרות תנו עיניכם במשפחה
שאין אשה אלא לבנים מכוערות שבהן אומרות קחו
מקחכם לשום שמים בשביל שתתעטרו בזהובים:

10 אמר רבי חלבו אמר עולא ביראה אמר רבי
אלעזר עתיד הקדוש ברוך הוא לעשות מחול
לצדיקים בגן עדן והוא יושב ביניהן וכל אחד ואחד
מראה עליו באצבעו שנאמר ואמר ביום ההוא הנה
אלהינו זה קוינו לו ויושיענו זה ה' קוינו לו נגילה
15 ונשמחה בישועתו:

הדרן עלך בשלשה פרקים וסליקא לה
מסכת תענית

מסרת הש"ס והמדרשים	תורה אור
2 (בקופסא) ירושלמי שם (והטעם	13 ישעיה כ"ה ט'.

שם שמתוך כך היא מׄשאילתן).
3 (תנא) איכ"ר שם. 5 (ת"ר) ירושלמי סוף פרקין ואיכ"ר שם. 7 (ליופי)
כתובות נ"ט ב'. 8 (לבנים) כתובות שם. 11 (מחול) ירושלמי מגלה ב'
ג' (ע"ג ב'); מו"ק ג' ז' (דף פ"ג ע"ב); ויק"ר י"א ט'; שהש"ר א' ג' סוף
אות ב'; ז' א' (פסוק אין זכרון); קה"ר א' י"א; מדרש תהלים ט"ח.

481

INDEX OF NAMES[1]

[1]Names of biblical characters have not been included.

INDEX OF NAMES

INDEX OF NAMES